IDEOLOGY AND POLITICS

By the same author

The Liberal Politics of John Locke (George Allen & Unwin)
The Marxist Conception of Ideology – A Critical Essay
(Cambridge University Press)

IDEOLOGY AND POLITICS

Martin Seliger

London George Allen & Unwin Ltd
Ruskin House Museum Street

First published in 1976

ISBN 0 04 320109 1 Hardback
0 04 320110 5 Paperback

Printed in Great Britain
in 11 point Baskerville type
by Willmer Brothers Limited, Birkenhead

To the memory of my parents
and
The future of my grandchildren
Neta, Adi and Amir

Preface

The subject-matter of this book is explained in the Introduction and can be gauged from the detailed table of contents. What perhaps needs dispelling at the outset is a misapprehension to which the diagrams and scales in Chapters VI and VII in particular might give rise. These are offered solely as visual illustrations in the main of the impact which strains and stresses arising in politically significant ideologies exercise upon them. Such visualization is of assistance to some people and for others complicates matters to the point of irritation, although even those prone to this reaction may here experience it only with regard to two over-crammed figures. These, as well as the other diagrams, may be disregarded, for they are only an explanatory device, and no substitute for explicit verbal argument.

The book has been long in the making and went through numerous drafts – and two final revisions. Eventually, the exploration of the implications and tenability of the ideas I had formed issued in two books, in the main because of the unforeseen necessity to re-examine in some detail the theory of ideology of Marx and Engels and their immediate successors, a re-examination* whose inclusion in the present study would have deprived it of its inner unity.† And while the two books are self-contained, the thematic connection involves some overlapping. However, this concerns almost exclusively the issues treated in Chapter V, most of which have been developed *in extenso* there and summarized in the other study; only in regard to a few issues is it the other way about.

In listing my acknowledgments of indebtedness, pride of place goes to the University of Manchester, which on the recommendation of its Department of Government elected me to a Simon Senior Fellowship for the academic year 1967–8, and extended it for a further term. During that period I lived at that comfortable haven for scholars,

* *The Marxist Conception of Ideology* —A Critical Essay (International Studies Series, Cambridge U.P.).

† Since the penultimate version, containing all parts, was completed in April 1973, and its revision bore only upon matters of form, not of substance, publications relevant to the subject of this study which have appeared since 1973 could be taken into account only in part.

Broomcroft Hall, where I did most of the reading and worked out the general structure and basic argument of the book. I enjoyed the lively atmosphere of the Department of Government and, most of all, continuous contact with and soon the warm friendship of Professor Samuel E. Finer, since then the Gladstone Professor of Government and Public Administration, Oxford. A rough outline of what I had in mind formed part of a paper presented at the annual meeting at Châtillon in July 1967 of the International Institute of Political Philosophy (and from that time dates my dialogue, progressing from opposed to more compatible standpoints, with Professor Giovanni Sartori), but it was in Professor Finer's staff-graduate seminar that the basic theses and framework elaborated in my 'Manchester manuscript' were first outlined and discussed. I also wish to thank Professor Ghita Ionescu and the late Max Gluckman for submitting that manuscript to careful scrutiny, and Professor Brian Chapman for the interest he has shown in my work. Outside Manchester I am indebted to Professor David D. Raphael, and for detailed comments and for the discussion of a more expanded version to Professors Bernard Crick and Leonard Schapiro. To the latter I owe an unrepayable debt for reading, and commenting on, the full penultimate version of this work. His comments, like those of some other friends and colleagues, were not the less valuable for being in part inspired by the conception of ideology which this study tries to demonstrate as untenable.

I wish to record my gratitude to the following scholars who between 1967 and 1971 provided me with the opportunity of addressing staff or graduate seminars: Professors Kurt Sontheimer (at that time, in Berlin), Klaus von Beyme (Heidelberg), Michael Oakeshott (London), W. J. M. Mackenzie (Glasgow), Carl J. Friedrich (Harvard), Stuart Hampshire (Princeton), Robert E. Lane (Yale), Aaron Wildavsky (Berkeley), and Herbert Schambeck (Linz). I also had personal talks with these scholars, as well as with another old friend, Maurice Cranston of the London School of Economics, with Robert A. Dahl and Joseph LaPalombara (Yale), and Reinhard Bendix (Berkeley). In 1971 I enjoyed the privilege of addressing the British Political Studies Conference with Professor Dorothy Emmet in the chair. In addition to the scholars named, I should like to thank the participants in all discussions, including those in a staff-graduate seminar in my department at the Hebrew University, for making me aware, through their comments and questions, of the need for further clarification or elaboration. A far from negligible contribution in this direction was made by the talented and dedicated graduate students who took part in my seminars on subjects related to various aspects of the present book.

I am indebted to Professor Alice H. Shalvi of our English Department for amending the English of some earlier chapters and to my friend and colleague Dr Brian Knei-Paz for assistance in this field at the penultimate stage. Thanks for the most incisive editorial help are due to two friends, my colleague, Dr David Ricci whose painstaking queries helped me to enhance the precision of this and the other book, and Dr Phyllis Gaba of the Department of English who refined the style of my final version and made helpful suggestions for compressing it.

Needless to say, none of the friends and colleagues mentioned shares in the responsibility for the views put forward in this book, or for any of its shortcomings.

I should like to record my indebtedness to Mrs Regina Alcalay who did most of the typing, coping with drafts at times hard to decipher, as well as to my assistants and research students, Mr Yigal Donyetz and Mr Gershon A. Seyman, who at various stages checked typescripts and were otherwise helpful. I also appreciate the assistance during one year of Mr Georg Heuberger. My thanks for unfailingly responding to repeated requests for funds to cover typing and editorial expenses go to the successive directors and members of the Research-Fund Committee of the Eliezer Kaplan School of Economics and Social Sciences.

I am grateful to the American Elsevier Publishing Company, Inc., New York, for having accepted an article ('Fundamental and Operative Ideology: The Two Dimensions of Political Argumentation', *Policy Sciences*, Vol. I, 3 [1970]) with the foreknowledge that the material contained in it (including the artwork of Figures 2, 3, 4, 5a–b and 6a–b) would be reproduced in revised form in this book (in Section 3b of Chapter III and Section 2 of Chapter VI). Chapter VII was read and discussed as a paper at the ISSC-IPSA seminar on 'Economic *v.* Cultural Models in the Comparative Study of Politics', held at the Rockefeller Centre in Bellagio, 12–16 June 1973.

Finally, despite a certain guilt about the fact that, while working on this study, I have too often been difficult to live with and remiss in family relations and friendships, I cannot in sincerity undertake that (albeit to a lesser degree) it will never happen again.

M.S.

Jerusalem, 30 April 1974

Contents

Introduction

I. PURPOSE AND PROCEDURE

It is generally agreed that ideologies contain unverified and unverifiable propositions. Differences of opinion do not pertain, however, only to the degree to which an ideological argument distorts or is unduly selective in its choice of facts. Opinions are also divided as to whether ideology is a mere reflection or rationalization of social conditions, whether it incorporates or derives from ideals, is exclusively linked to social action, or is a belief system or a dimension of one. As far as ideology in the context of concerted social and political action is concerned, opinions concerning the nature of ideology depend to a considerable degree on how one answers the question of whether or not the epithet 'ideological' is applicable to the set of beliefs professed by any political party or movement whatsoever. The importance of this question derives from its transcending the spheres of social and political relations. Despite the numerous studies which deal *inter alia* or directly with ideology in the varied fields of human activity, no generally accepted definition of the term exists.

One would have expected a sustained effort by philosophers, sociologists, anthropologists, poltical scientists and psychologists to establish a generally acceptable definition of ideology, rather than that they should proceed by way of stipulative definitions. After all, the theory of ideology is crucial for their disciplines, since it arose in conjunction with the Marxist theory of the derivation of human action and thought from socio-economic factors. Karl Mannheim, who produced the first and so far the last comprehensive elaboration of a theory of ideology,[1] could proceed as if no problem of a unitary definition of the concept existed. He accepted Marx and Engels's view that ideological thought was distorted thought but he also attempted to show how the attainment of knowledge was possible. A far-going consensus was not disturbed since meanwhile the separation of ideology from truth had been attenuated in varied degrees within the Marxist camp itself.

Afer Mannheim, the problem of definition arose in conjunction with the proliferation of studies of ideology within the humanities and social sciences. These deal with the causes of ideology in, and its effects on, the social and the personality system; its relation with the social sciences and intellectuals in general; its influence on mass publics through its manipulation by mass communication, political parties and various kinds of activists; and last but not least, the analysis of ideological systems, the great 'isms' and their fate, and so on. As Norman Birnbaum commented in his admirable 'Trend Report', 'the very diffuseness of the literature points to the continuing problem of an adequate definition of the notion of ideology'.[2] This deficiency obviously was connected with the discrepancy noted by Birnbaum, between empirical and theoretical developments in the treatment of ideology. In fact, the concept of ideology was severed from its philosophical base and 'discussions of it no longer entail epistemological dispute'.[3]

Some such dispute has been resumed without, however, a stringent relation to the structure and contents of known ideologies. Hence, even the few extended attempts to define the concept are in the main stipulative. Generally, the definitions thus defended can be divided into two categories. I propose to call one the restrictive conception, because it comprises the definitions which, like the original Marxian conception of ideology but on different grounds, confine the term to specific political belief systems. The other category comprises those conceptions which stipulate the applicability of the term 'ideology' to all political belief systems. I will call this category of definitions the inclusive conception. According to both conceptions, ideology, unlike philosophy and science, denotes sets of ideas not primarily conceived for cognitive purposes. What defines the inclusive use of 'ideology' in the context of social and political theory and science is that it covers sets of ideas by which men posit, explain and justify ends and means of organized social action, and specifically political action, irrespective of whether such action aims to preserve, amend, uproot or rebuild a given order. In the restrictive use of the term, 'ideology' is reserved for extremist belief systems and parties; or ideological factors are held to be present in some and absent from other belief systems; or at least, they are assumed to be more important in some than in others. The definition of the inclusive conception given above will be further expanded after I elaborate in Chapter III the structure and components of ideology on the basis of the critical survey and analysis of the uses of the restrictive conception and its reverberations presented in Chapters I and II.

To challenge the restrictive conception is not to raise a purely semantic or historical issue. No definition of concepts used in daily life is entirely arbitrary. Although, like other concepts, 'ideology' has for long been invested with a strange variety of meanings and has remained 'an egregiously loaded concept' even in social science,[4] 'ideology' has always denoted sets of attitudes and ways of behaviour which can be observed in the real world. In subsuming phenomena, a definition of ideology represents a distinctive intellectual perspective.[5] But language, as Stuart Hampshire has reminded us, 'is itself a kind of behaviour interwoven with other kinds'.[6] Hence, we can check the adequacy of the connotations of the term 'ideology' by referring to the articulated perspectives and the specific attitudes and kinds of behaviour with which the concept is associated. These criteria of correspondence merge with the criteria of coherence since, to be valid, the criteria used in singling out as ideological one category of political belief systems and attitudes must not be applicable to those excluded by definition from that category. In other words, both the phenomena classified as ideological and the consistency with which the criteria of classification are used, supply the grounds for deciding whether it is appropriate to call 'ideological' one kind of political belief system and not all kinds. Thus, in order to disclose the shortcomings of the restrictive conception and argue the case for the inclusive conception (which has not received even the kind of explanatory treatment undertaken on behalf of the contemporary restrictive conception) reference will be made, first of all, to the contents of the known political belief systems adopted and propagated by political parties and movements, but also to systems developed by social and political thinkers.

A definition of ideology that meets the requirements mentioned will be shown to entail the following propositions. Firstly, ideology is linked to politics no less than all politics are linked to ideology. Ideology requires politics as its mode of implementation while political decisions are always, at one stage or another, related to moral principles. These last are at the centre of the components that constitute the kind of more or less rational justification which needs to be called 'ideological'. Secondly, ideology can as little be divorced from factual knowledge as from tolerably rational justification and moral and other prescriptions. Thirdly, none of their constituent elements (like description, analysis, prescriptions, etc.) causes ideologies to be only opposed to or different from each other. In other words, no theory of ideology is adequate which does not take into account agreement or overlapping between ideologies, i.e. ideological pluralism. These three propositions are demonstrated in this study in conjunction with a treatment of the specific issues to which, like any theory of ideology, these propositions give rise. Fourthly, since ideology is action-oriented thought, i.e. thought conceived to guide political action and invoked to justify it, the way ideology functions in the political process, or is intended to function, must have a bearing on its nature. How something functions or is meant to function determines what it can be said to be. The elaborate inclusive definition arrived at in Chapter III, therefore, takes into account the fact that, just as ideologies are conceived to guide action, so also the exigencies attendant upon conceiving and implementing policies affect the structure and nature of ideologies and even of political philosophies.

It follows from what has been said that my main concern in this book is with ideologies as they are handled in the game of politics by the producers, technicians, manipulators and salesmen of the party ideology, not with the way they are held by the consumers; with the 'forensic', not with the 'latent' ideology.[7] The important issue of mass receptivity to ideological arguments enters my discussion only in so far as conclusions drawn from empirical findings in this field of research bear out, or are called in question by, my demonstration of the fact that the argumentation of party representatives proceeds normally on two intertwining but clearly discernible dimensions: one, the fundamental dimension, in which traditional principles are upheld, and another, the operative dimension, in which the actual policy decisions of a political party are defended. The nature of the interaction between the two dimensions will be demonstrated systematically in Part III and a theoretical framework for empirical analysis will be worked out. Its operational significance for the orientation of research is exemplified *inter alia* in the emendation of some current hypotheses and models concerning the relationship between ideology and the policy-orientation of parties. To outline systematically the patterns of interaction in political argumentation of ideology and the conception and execution of policies also means to show how the challenge of ideological change arises out of this interaction, how it is and can be met, and how it can be gauged, irrespective of whether it is admitted or remains unacknowledged as a result of either dogmatic intransigence (which may have eminently secular reasons) or the confusion of ideological convergence with de-ideologization.

Part III confirms, as a by-product, the case for the inclusive conception of ideology, inasmuch as it reveals that the patterns of interaction between the fundamental and operative dimensions of political argumentation are basically the same in all practised political belief systems. Since social and political philosophies are never quite aloof from matters of practical and topical significance, the awareness of two-dimensionality, apart from being the indicator of the changes in party ideology and a signpost of ideological reorientation, is also most helpful in the interpretation of political philosophies.[8]

All schemes, classifications and general conclusions offered in this study are buttressed, on the one hand, by ideological principles as they have been expounded and espoused by identifiable party leaderships and thinkers and, on the other, by concrete issues of policy. (In fact, the basic conceptual and classificatory foundations have been laid in two case studies of my own.[9]) The way is indicated for party leaderships, followers and political theorists to reassess political ideologies and embark on their renovation. By no means in isolation from this practical purpose, the way is indicated for case studies on a larger scale than the treatment of policy issues offered in this book amounts to. Such more extended studies might furnish the foundation for further refinements, emendations – or disproof. Whatever case studies in additon to those already completed or in progress[10] might indicate, I am fairly confident that I have demonstrated, on the grounds of logic and empirical evidence, that political argumentation proceeds on different levels and that politics is as little separable from ideology as the latter can be opposed without reservation to factual knowledge or considered either as inexorably determined by or opposed to tangible class conditions. Indeed, an unequivocally inclusive but clearly defined conception of ideology, as defended in this book, is justified in that it can be shown that politics cannot be reduced to argument over technicalities, but either proceed from or develop into argument over priorities, some of which are always of a moral texture, that is, ideologically determined. Because these two kinds of argument are inextricably interwoven in politics, as we know them, ideology cannot be consigned wholesale to the realm of distortion caused by moral fantasy and fanaticism – although without some unquantifiable portion of either of the two, it seems unlikely to sustain the aspiration for what most people would consider tolerably sound, even if uninspiring, government.

The object of this study is neither exegetical nor historical. What appears initially to be exegesis, and short- or long-range historical flashbacks, is subservient to the theory of ideology that is being advanced. The purpose of tracing in the first two chapters the emergence of the more important manifestations of the contemporary restrictive tendency, the intermediate positions and the attempts at reconsideration, is to show how prevarications, inconsistencies and insufficiently founded generalizations render the recently refashioned restrictive conception unacceptable, however throught-provoking its major expositions and however much I find myself in sympathy with the 'reformist' orientation of the proponents of the idea of the end of ideology, which presupposes the restrictive conception. Indeed there is no necessary correlation between one's notion of ideology and one's ideology.[11] The three short-range comparative flashbacks in Chapter II that conclude my critical survey of the manifestations of the restrictive tendency and the summary long-range backward glance that concludes this Introduction have the aim of showing that precedents have been unduly neglected. If the shortcomings of the Marxian theory of ideology had been taken into account, as well as its fate in Marxism after Marx, and if the comparability had been noted between the thesis of the end of ideology and some of Roberto Michels's views, between the attributes assigned to ideology as extremist political beliefs and the characteristics associated with charisma by Max Weber and with utopia by Mannheim in his fleeting opposition of utopia to ideology, then perhaps some overstated alternatives might have been avoided, or at least more deliberately attenuated. In the chapters whose object is to determine the structure and function common to all political belief systems, issue is taken likewise with the views of other scholars, so as to justify the replacement of any restrictive by the inclusive conception.

2. PREFIGURATION

Evidently, such a justification must first demonstrate the untenability of the first elaborate theory of ideology, that of Marx and Engels, since it is based on a restrictive and pejorative (truth-excluding) conception of ideology. I have devoted a separate study to this subject[12] for, while the Marxist conception of ideology has been widely commented upon, no complete critical study of it is available, at any rate none which approaches the subject by questioning its tenability on this basis. Given the perhaps not fortuitous coincidence of this *lacuna* with the lack of a systematic concern for establishing an adequate definition of ideology, it is not surprising that, despite the generally recognized impact of Marxist theory on the social sciences, no serious attention has been paid to the parallels and contrasts between the modern non-Marxist and the original Marxist conceptions of ideology, and of course not to the fact that the fundamental parallels have a bearing on the adequacy of any restrictive conception.

The non-Marxist conception reflects the centrality accorded in Marxism to the bond between politics and primarily material group interests. A case in point is the explanation of the until-quite-recently widely proclaimed end of ideology. The latter was assumed to be a concomitant of the advanced stage of economic development and its corresponding social consciousness. Yet although proponents of this idea, and many political scientists who oppose pragmatic to ideological politics, use 'ideology', like Marx and Engels, in a restricted and derogatory sense, modern theorists apply it, unlike Marx and Engels, to political belief systems which advocate radical structural change and, therefore, also to Marxism. In this respect, modern political theorists and scientists reverse the Marxian position according to which identification with the *status quo* attests ideological, that is illusory, consciousness. Nevertheless, these political theorists retain the juxtaposition in politics of ideological (*qua* illusory) to correct perception. Other political scientists oppose political behaviour conditioned by class interest to political behaviour motivated by ideological considerations, whereas for Marx and Engels, ideology is the reflection of class interest.

There exists, then, a fundamental parallelism which permeates the no less fundamental disparity between the two approaches: in the Marxist conception, the ideological superstructure of bourgeois society must do violence to facts and the bourgeoisie must do violence to the proletariat. According to the present-day non-Marxist restrictive conception, the latter represents reality-transcending orientation, i.e. it is concerned with the liquidation of the *status quo,* and for this reason ideology does violence to facts and justifies the use of violence against its opponents. Common to both conceptions is the attribution to ideology of distortion of facts and the justification of violence against the opponent. The essential difference is that in one case these attributes are associated with the aim of maintaining and in the other with the aim of subverting the *status quo*.

Indeed, as we shall see in Chapter II, the post-Marxian restrictive use of ideology for extremist doctrines can be traced back to Mannheim, in so far as such a use is an inversion of the meaning which Mannheim in the wake of Marx attached in one context only to ideology, in his unsuccessful attempt to distinguish the latter consistently from utopia. The characteristics here attributed to utopia serve to define ideology in the non-Marxian restrictive conception. Similarly, we can trace the present-day distinction between the ideological and the matter-of-fact approach back to Marx and Engels. Hence the importance of the fact that the two thinkers were unable to maintain consistently that the ideational and political superstructure represents 'false consciousness' (Engels's phrase) inasmuch as the superstructure is regarded as the conditioned reflex of the interplay between the forces of production and social relationships. The ideas that, since thought is false, because it is conditioned; that falseness is, above all, inherent in bourgeois thought; that, to the extent that all social thought is conditioned, it must be false while the division of labour lasts and that in any case 'false consciousness' does not greatly matter because ultimately the course of development is pre-determined by the development of the forces of production – all these ideas circumscribe what must be called the dogmatic position of Marx and Engels, which they never ceased to assert, although in all their writings they deviated from it.

If we discount the extreme poles between which Marx and Engels's notions about ideology oscillate in ill-adjusted swings, we can discern the elements of a tenable theory of ideology. Such a discounting of the extreme poles (e.g. that over and against proletarian class-thinking, all social thought, particularly bourgeois thought, is false) is invited by the fact that Marx and Engels themselves offended against the standpoints forming these poles and that they did so quite often out of scholarly consideration for factual evidence and in response to the political requirements of the cause their theories were meant to advance. The same considerations caused the immediate successors of Marx to move away from the dogmatic positions and thus to furnish at least indirect proof of their untenability.

Lenin adopted without much ado the inclusive conception of ideology. He rendered this use all the more unorthodox by allying with it the emphasis on purposeful political action-orientation over and against exclusive, or even primary, reliance on the socio-economic class struggle, invoking the authority of Kautsky for bringing into prominence 'the conscious element' and the corresponding attenuation of the deterministic element of Marxism. However, Lenin's voluntarism as well as his inclusive, and in this sense neutral, use of ideology agreed better with Bernstein's open critique of Marxist orthodoxy than with Kautsky's much more cautious reinterpretations. It is characteristic of the trend leading away from the dogmatic position that even Lukács in his faithful restatement of orthodox doctrine in the early twenties could not entirely evade the impact of Lenin's use of 'ideology' in a way the founders had never adopted, even in their own deviations from the dogmatic definition of the term.

Ideas which have been associated with ideology did not, of course, appear only after the term had come into use, nor were they afterwards advanced only in connection with it. The awareness of uncertain knowledge is expressed in Plato's distinction between *doxa* and *episteme,* whereas Locke's qualified epistemological scepticism was predicated on both the uncertainty of much of our knowledge and its sufficient exactness for human needs. Indeed, Locke's views served through Condillac's mediation as the starting-point of the new science of ideas known in the Napoleonic era as *l'idéologie.*

The assumption of the dependence of behaviour and ideas concerning political behaviour and organization on economic, psychologcial, environmental and political factors themselves has been advanced likewise in various forms since Plato. He believed that by political *fiat* and the education of a specifically endowed group of men and women, economic and institutional arrangements could be created which would ensure the proper political behaviour of the various groups of the population and the rational (efficient) ruling of the city. The underlying idea, which might be called the determinability of determination, was taken up by Harrington and remained a fundamental tenet of eighteenth-century political philosophy. It was Plato, too, who recognized that the usefulness of ideas for the guidance of the common run of men does not lie in their truthfulness. The idea of 'the noble lie' reverberates in Montesquieu's opinion that the efficacy of a false conception of honour is as great as the efficacy of its true conception for those who are capable of attaining it. This particular variation of 'false consciousness' perhaps found its most radical expression in that part of Pareto's theory of 'derivations' according to which their social utility is independent of their truth value.

The Marxian theory of ideology reflects, then, particular strands of a long tradition of thought. Yet no major thinker who contributed to that tradition adopted, like Marx and Engels and after them Pareto, the proposition that in existing society all social thought must be false because it is conditioned, while claiming exemption from this rule for his own system of social thought.

Considering the dogmatic association by Marx and Engels of ideology with falseness, illusion and deception (of self and others) and the kindred beliefs of latter-day scholars in the mutual exclusiveness of pragmatic and ideological politics, we must also not forget that we are faced with continuations of the stance in which the distinctiveness of ideological thought was conceived. The equation in politics of ideological with unrealistic or chimerical ideas occurred almost immediately after the word *idéologie* began its brief career in the realm of philosophy. Napoleon apparently confused two things that were rather tenuously related to each other:[13] the philosophical endeavour of the *idéologues* to explain the formation of *ideas* and their opposition to him on the grounds of their liberal *ideals*. The conceptual confusion and the loose derogatory connotation he gave the new word survived the Emperor. Obviously, he had political ideas and ideals of his own, and in deprecating those of his liberal opponents he proceeded from the simple-minded but widespread assumption that only one's own ideals are realizable and worth realizing. The same assumption is embedded in the system of a great thinker like Marx.

Between the unimaginative but effective twist Napoleon gave to the connotation of *idéologie* and Marx's theoretical elaborations of it (and both might have availed themselves of the negative evaluation of the new science of ideas by the theocrat de Bonald), those French historians of the Restoration who were the political heirs of the *idéologues* had in the light of the traumatic and exhilarating experiences of the Revolution and the Empire based their reinterpretation of French history on the causal interaction of ideas and social facts, attributing more or less equal weight to each.[14] Although Marx was familiar with their views of historical causation, so far they have never been assigned a place in the history of what ideology stands for. This is probably due to the fact that they neither accepted Napoleon's derogatory characterization of the *idéologues* nor used the word *idéologie* otherwise in their interpretation of events. Indeed, in the theory of causation underlying their interpretations they anticipated some post-Marxian notions which relate to the theory of ideology but which likewise were not put forth under that designation.

The attempts made after Marx in the Marxist camp itself to limit the assumption of the pervasiveness of 'false consciousness' and to divest 'ideology' of its restrictive sense were clearly a response to the exigencies of socialist politics as appraised by both revisionists and revolutionary Marxists. These exigencies demanded recognition of the importance of 'the conscious element' and attenuation of economic determinism. In this way the connection was re-established with the tradition of thought extending from Plato to the heirs of the *idéologues*. Nevertheless, none of the post-Marxian trends succeeded in eradicating the Napoleonic and Marxian legacy of styling ideological as distorted thought and of identifying it with only some categories of political belief systems. Just as the emergence, elaboration and overcoming of the original restrictive and pejorative conception of ideology were a corollary of political events and aims, so it is in conjunction with social and political developments and their evaluation that the new non-Marxist, if not essentially anti-Marxist, restrictive and derogatory conception of ideology gained wide currency.

Part One

THE SHORTCOMINGS OF THE RESTRICTIVE CONCEPTION

Adherents of all major political belief systems who denounce all but their own as ideologcial do not necessarily use 'ideology' consistently in the restrictive sense. By and large, communists now subscribe to the 'dual' conception of ideology, that is, while not shunning the use of 'ideology' for their own doctrine, they regard all other political doctrines as ideologies in the original Marxian sense of distortions of reality. Actually, the problems arising from Lenin's unacknowledged but obvious break with orthodoxy are still noticeable in the communist debate about the standing of communist theory itself in regard to ideology, science, philosophy and their relationships.[1] Similarly, in order to disqualify all other doctrines, Hitler proclaimed national socialism as anti-ideological, and in this sense as unideological, though this attitude seems not to have been maintained at all levels in his party.[2] The post-war tendency in the West to confine 'ideology' to belief systems of the extreme Left and Right was also a manifestation of political convictions. It was a concomitant of the latest theory, that of the end of ideology, whose major proponents did not disguise that what they claimed to be ending was that which they wished to be ending.

Of course, a mutual involvement of political convictions and scholarly concerns does not necessarily prejudge the validity of a theory, but lack of consistency and judgments not borne out by the facts they call to mind surely do. These are the major shortcomings which in the following chapters will be seen to characterize the elaborations of the *differentia specifica* of the restrictive conception of ideology. But one shortcoming underlies all others. Most adherents of the restrictive definition who equate ideology with doctrinaire extremism actually equate it with totalitarianism. They have failed to ask themselves the simple question: what advantage accrues from reserving for the analysis of the ideational foundations of totalitarianism the word 'ideology', which provides no verbal clue to the phenomenon at hand?

So far as I know, only Hannah Arendt has tried to align the literal meaning of 'ideology' with this new connotation.[3] However, she immediately invested her literal explanation – 'the logic of ideas' – with the presuppositions of her conception of ideology, namely, that 'the idea' in ideology is 'the idea by which the movement of history is explained as one consistent process'; 'that one idea is sufficient to explain everything in the development from the premise and that no experience can teach anything',[4] and 'that not before Hitler and Stalin were the great political potentialities of ideology discovered'.[5] None of this is indicated by the word 'ideology' but rather derives from the presupposition that ideologies are inherently totalitarian and that this is fully brought out by racism and communism. By contrast, 'totalitarianism' itself, or in conjunction with it 'communist dictatorship' or 'fascist dictatorship', does give a verbal clue to what is under discussion. Those who use ideology in the modern restricted sense also do not seem to be concerned that since the word gained currency in politics, it has never been employed to denote political extremism. Both Napoleon and Marx called liberals *idéologues*. For Napoleon, they were opinionated radicals for wishing to set constitutional bounds to his rule, but as a radical innovator the Emperor could well hold his own. For Marx, liberals held on to an order that was doomed.

Of course, Napoleon and Marx themselves changed the meaning of the word, which at first denoted simply the science of ideas. Moreover, the inclusive no less than the twentieth-century restrictive definition involves a change of meaning. The change of the connotations of a term is arguable if the differentiating qualities that are attributed to it are consistent with each other and with the phenomena, in this case the political doctrines and attitudes on which the term is predicated. In this regard, mainly on the basis of 'immanent criticism', Chapter I reviews the emergence and consummation of the restrictive tendency and part of Chapter II the drift in recent years towards reconsideration. In Chapters III and IV, the case for the inclusive definition is set out. First the central criterion of the restrictive conception is divested of its differentiating character, and then the components that form the structure common to all political belief systems are identified. Chapter IV exposes the falseness of the notions adduced to support the distinction between pragmatic and ideological politics, the distinction on which the modern restrictive conception rests.

Chapter I

VICISSITUDES AND VACILLATIONS

I. PRONOUNCED CONTRASTS AND UNACCOUNTED CONTIGUITIES

a. *The Emergence of the Pattern and its Background*

The emergence of the latter-day restrictive conception of ideology did not affect a considerable number of scholars.[1] Indeed many, if not most, students and practitioners of politics in the wake of the developments in the Marxist camp either explicitly subscribed to an inclusive definition or implicitly proceeded on its basis. In the 1920s we have the example of Julien Benda who, like many Western scholars today, analysed and was opposed to the excess of passion in politics. But for him, the true intellectual, the 'clerk', betrays his mission not just when he embraces extremism but 'when ... [he] descends to the market place' instead of remaining in the position of 'the officiants of abstract justice'; true intellectuals must forego 'passion for a worldly object'. Also, unlike later scholars who identified ideology with the extremism of the Left and Right, Benda allied ideology to whatever aims and positions incite political passions. Viewing all political passions as furnished with 'an apparatus of ideology', he explicitly included 'bourgeoisism' and insisted that 'all political ideologies claim to be founded on science'.[2]

In the 1940s, we find the term ideology indiscriminately applied to all political belief systems in dictionaries such as *Webster's New International Dictionary, The Dictionary of Sociology* and *White's Political Dictionary.* R. M. McIver's well-known textbook, *The Web of Government,* states that 'the term "ideology" has become current to mean any scheme of thinking characteristic of a group or class'.[3] During the fifties, the inclusive conception was exhibited in T. Parsons's magisterial *The Social System,*[4] in the pioneer study, *The Authoritarian Personality,* and in Karl Deutsch's seminal *Nationalism and Social Communication.*[5] *Democracy in a World of Tension,*[6] which was the first instalment of a UNESCO project to assess the effect of current political ideologies on conceptions of liberty, democracy, law and equality, treated the major rival belief systems as ideologies as a matter of course. A preliminary analysis of answers to questionnaires bearing on concepts related to democracy was to be followed by a real 'ideological analysis'. But its sequel,[7] did not, as the authors themselves explained, fulfil the original purpose of shedding light on both agreement and disagreement in the congitive, normative and volitional arguments of the major belief systems of East and West. The authors had also planned to investigate the extent to which verbal disagreement between rival ideologies reflected cognitive incompatibility.[8] Perhaps the failure to carry out this part of the project obscured the actual value and prevented the merited impact of the systematic survey and critique which Naess and his associates offered and in which they proceeded on the assumption that the term 'ideology' applied to all political belief systems. They also rejected the Marxian notion that objectivity and ideology were invariably incompatible.

These last two central points were not as much challenged, let alone disproved, as the opposite standpoints were espoused in conjunction with scholarly trends and in response to recent political experience. An attempt to isolate a 'pure' (Weberian) sociology of knowledge from a theory of ideology was made. Social determination was to be treated separately from ideology, which was to be relegated exclusively to the realm of falsification, and hence to psychology.[9] While in this conception the causal interpretation of the phenomenon 'ideology' became un-Marxian in that it was restricted to psychology, and the term 'ideology' was applied to all political belief systems, the most distinctly Marxian connotation of 'ideology' was preserved, i.e. that the ideas men espouse and try to force on others as true actually constitute a distortion of reality. While, in modern restrictive conceptions, ideology is seen as an instrument for conditioning men to obedience, indirectly and directly, distortion remains the prime cognitive characteristic of ideology.[10] Thus it was even suggested, though somewhat ambiguously, that ideology was not a doctrine or belief system but 'consists *only* of those parts or aspects of a system of social ideas which are distorted or unduly selective'.[11]

The tendency to set ideology apart not only from truth but from pragmatism and moderation, and hence to adopt the restrictive conception, was nourished by the ascendancy of American behavioural political science and British analytical philosophy. Phenomenology and existentialism, though not invariably requiring the restrictive definition, pointed in the same direction. The debunking attitude of American political science and British analytical philosophy towards grand speculation, focusing respectively on statistical methods and on language ('What do [the mythical] ordinary people mean when they say X, Y etc. ?'), fitted in well with the bitter aftertaste from the mounting tides of fascist aggressiveness that led to World War II and with the disillusionment with extreme leftist ideals in the name of which, too, horrifying excesses had been committed. The cold war probably reinforced the tendency to erect a fence between 'their' and 'our' belief systems, with ideologies that paraded as science and secured dominance by terror placed on one side, and largely consensual and pragmatic meliorism and purportedly value-free social science and philosophy on the other.

In 1947, the conservative aspect of the restrictive tendency found incisive expression in Michael Oakeshott's seminal essay 'Rationalism in Politics'. His 'Rationalist' is actually the ideologist, for he claims the superiority of 'technical knowledge' over 'practical knowledge' which exists 'only in use, is not reflective and (unlike technique) cannot be formulated in rules'.[12] All that can be set over and against traditional practices, any proposed remedy for a particular ill held to be universal in its application, and not necessarily the belief in one universal remedy for all political ills, attests the politics of rationalism, i.e. ideological politics. The confines of ideology, therefore, are widely drawn: from 'the notion of founding a society, whether of individuals or of States, upon a Declaration of the Rights of Man'; via ' "national" or racial self-determination when elevated into universal principles' or 'a self-consciously planned society'; to projects like 'a single tax' or 'the revival of Gaelic as the official language of Eire'.[13] Underlying these multiple manifestations of the politics of rationalism is a single principle that eventually served as the central criterion of the restrictive conception of ideology. This is the aim of changing suddenly and fundamentally one or more of the institutions of an existing order. On these grounds, in 1952 Jacob Talmon presented in his searching historical analysis, *The Origins of Totalitarian Democracy,* the forms of thought and action out of which the totalitarianism of the Left developed. In this and in a later work,[14] the notion emerges more specifically than in Oakeshott's essay that the doctrines of left and right-wing extremism form a category apart. Increasingly, the term 'ideology' was programmatically reserved for them.

It is probably not accidental that in 1944 Hannah Arendt distinguished only between the 'full fledged ideologies' of race-thinking and class-thinking, and other ideologies which, not being based on a single opinion, had failed to gain majority support;[15] having been 'essentially' defeated by race-thinking and class-thinking, other ideologies no longer qualified as 'full-fledged'. Nine years later, ideology as the guide to behaviour under terror, the novel form of government, was seen by her only to be predicated on statements about constant change.[16] Victorious racism and communism appear to have absorbed the totalitarian elements of all ideologies and as a result to have become the sole ideologies. For, if I read her correctly, she arrived at the view (or rather presupposed) that the nature of ideology is revealed only in its role in the apparatus of totalitarian domination. The elements of total explanation, imperviousness to tangible reality, its investment with a secret meaning and stringent self-generating logic, all attest that 'it is in the nature of ideological politics . . . that the real content of the ideology . . . is devoured by the logic with which the "idea" is carried out'.[17] Whatever one makes of the assumed annihilation of the logic of the idea by the logic of its realization, this much is clear: in the development of Hannah Arendt's conception of ideology, totalitarianism became the full manifestation of that which characterizes ideology *per se*. This view eventually gained currency as the logical corollary of the idea of the end of ideology. For if ideologies in the West are assumed to be on the way out, yet political beliefs or 'isms' are assumed to remain in force, then these latter must be considered unideological.

In 1955 Raymond Aron raised the question: 'Fin de l'âge idéologique?' and answered it in the affirmative.[18] He admitted that non-Marxist socialism and liberalism continued to inspire conviction and arouse controversy, but he claimed that it was becoming increasingly difficult, if not unreasonable, 'to transfigure such preferences into doctrines'. The contemporary dialogue 'does not assume the style of ideological debate because each of the opposed themes is no longer bound to a class or a party'. In line with over-stressing the class- and/or party-boundedness of themes in the past and the putative absence of such a connection in the present, Aron affirmed that the conditions for ideological debate had disappeared, in the West spontaneously and in the East through police oppression.[19] This stance prevailed at the World Congress on 'The Future of Freedom' held in the same year in Milan.[20] The Western participants generally saw a convergence and likeness between liberal and socialist thought, like the meeting during the previous thirty years of the practices of the extreme Right and Left.[21]

It seemed that the controversy between the political camps in the West was no longer about the direction, but about the realization, of change in different settings. In these circumstances social-democratic parties seemed to have replaced concern for structural change with competition over government personnel and policies. Hence the 'end of ideology', or at least far-going de-ideologization was the order of the day.[22] At the Congress, and afterwards, the assumption prevailed that, as in America long ago, so now in Great Britain, Germany and Scandinavia, millenarianism had been vanquished by reformism,[23] so that adherence in the West to extremism, especially left-wing, but in principle also right-wing, appeared as *the* ideological attitude.

It was characteristic both of the intellectual honesty and of the perceptiveness of those who made these assertions, and of the equivocation attendant upon them, that qualifications are already apparent in Raymond Aron's initial attitude. Although he stated that deep-reaching controversy had ceased in East and West alike, he set Great Britain and the United States apart from France as countries where political discussion had assumed a technical character because the compatibility of values had replaced their confrontation.[24] On these grounds he chided French intellectuals for their unwillingness to abandon the illusion that, unlike the liberal, socialist and conservative ideologies of the last century, Marxism had preserved its universal significance. For Aron, ideological debate had not ceased; he not only acknowledged that all the major belief systems of Europe had been ideologies, but he spoke of them also in their present state as ideologies, unlike some of his Anglo-Saxon colleagues. He thus contravened the restrictive use of 'ideology' and qualified further his affirmation of the end of the ideological age.

In connection with the generally made exception for the developing countries, Aron argued that the expansion of Western technology over the Earth was not accompanied by that of its institutions and the 'ideologies which glorified these institutions'. Appraising the appeal of Marxism outside the Western orbit, he denied that the free world possessed 'a uniform ideology comparable to Marxism-Leninism'.[25] Here, in accordance with French usage, Aron continued to use 'ideological' and 'ideology' also in the inclusive sense. On grounds which were not only semantically equivocal, he joined his American and other colleagues in considering such belief systems as ideological which possessed a great degree of uniformity and gave rise to violent controversy, as a result of their doctrinaire claim to universality and fanatical advocacy of radical change, or, as Shils epitomized, their 'obsessional visions and phantasies'.[26]

Although conceptual consistency did not increase with the spread of the idea of the end of ideology, its logical connection with the restricted conception is illustrated by the fact that, shortly before this version came into vogue, an attempt made to conceive the end of ideology on the basis of its inclusive conception involved self-contradiction. Feuer, who opposed free thought and action to ideology, defined its nature and function in mainly psychoanalytical terms. Ideology, the projections of wishfulfilments and interests through which largely the less engaging irrational drives find expression, attaches to fascist, Marxist, pluralistic and democratic party ideals. Yet 'liberal civilization', he summed up, 'begins when the age of ideology is over'.[27] Feuer's hope for an end of ideology led him to imply that only extremist political belief systems are ideologies.

If Suez and Hungary – 'the cock crow' which lifted 'the spell of impotence'[28] – saw the re-emergence in 1956–7 of ideological politics, this meant mainly the re-activation of the Marxist Left. In Hungary and Poland the criticism of both official Marxist and original Marxian theory and philosophy emerged into the open. Outside the Marxist camp, the 'thaw' afforded further support to the idea of the end of ideology. Conjointly the tendency to confine 'ideology' to the prevalence of doctrinal over practical concerns gained ground in the Anglo-Saxon countries, but less so in continental Europe, though in this respect, too, the Anglo-Saxon occupation-cum-re-education made a strong impact in Germany. Brunner, for example, aware of the difference between the continental and Anglo-Saxon stances, expressed the prevalent German view in arguing that since Napoleon it was intrinsic to the meaning of ideology to be opposed to the practicability of politics. The opposite view of Eduard Spranger, rooted intellectually in pre-war Germany, remained for some time a largely unheeded reminder.[29] Reinhard Bendix, who left Germany before the war and studied in the United States, also adhered to the inclusive definition in a study appearing in 1956. Characteristically, the American editor of the series in which the book appeared took exception to Bendix's use of ideology for both East and West.[30] In France, the inclusive use continued to predominate and was explicitly, though somewhat hesitantly, adopted by Aron, who had never dissociated himself entirely from that tradition.

During 1958 the Institut Belge de Science Politique held a series of lectures, reproduced in 1960 in a special volume of its quarterly *Res*

Publica under the title 'Les idéologies et leurs applications au XXe siècle'. All the contributors, among them W. Weidlé, J. J. Chevallier and M. Duverger, applied the term as a matter of course to all sets of political beliefs. Only a Belgian-born Marxist scholar living in England and a French right-wing senator echoed the identification of ideology with revolutionary beliefs. The Marxists found that the British Labour Party (not being revolutionary) rejected ideology.[31] The senator was ready to acknowledge that ideology was in part enlightening and as such 'a precious element of political thought', although generally sensibility and ideology were opposites and totalitarianism the consummation of ideology. Hence its disdain by the Man of the Right was his most salient trait.[32]

Raymond Aron's contribution, entitled 'L'idéologie – support nécessaire de l'action', confirms what the title indicates. Apparently somewhat shaken by the other participants' almost unanimous adherence to the inclusive use of the term, he was clearly ready to reconsider the exception to calling all doctrines 'ideologies'. When he appraised neo-liberalism and communism as representing different types of doctrines, those which were total and systematic and those which were less so,[33] he apparently did not mean to say that the latter were non-ideologies. He agreed that the justification of group interests – one of the three characteristics of 'doctrines dites idéologies' – was common to all parties and that on this score all parties invoked ideologies. He also admitted that the admixture of statements of fact and statements of values, of precepts for action and of analyses, which characterizes the ideological character of doctrines, is necessary in modern society in order to legitimize a political and social order, generally based on a conception of the good society.[34] However, just as he had made qualifying concessions in his previous affirmation of 'the end of the age of ideology', so in his admission of the function of ideologies in pluralist systems he did not shake free entirely of his previous distinctions, but sometimes still opposed 'preferences' and 'ideologies', implying that passion and dogmatism are the preserve of ideologies alone, which are thus viewed again as a particular category of belief systems.[35] However, his call to the West to make 'good use of ideologies '(*un bon usage des idéologies*), and his both resigned and cautionary conclusion that apparently 'one needs ideology, but not too much of it'[36] indicate a real change of position.

Yet what was probably understood by Aron himself as a change of attitude actually indicates the extent to which in the Anglo-Saxon association of ideology with extremism, and in the elaborations of the idea of the end of ideology, concepts were stretched beyond their literal meaning without entailing definitional revision.

b. *Elaboration*

The literal meaning of 'the end of ideology' could have been distinguished easily from the meaning of 'the end of the age of ideologies'. This was Aron's original formulation and, in view of his explicit qualifications, the second formulation could be taken to stand for the end of the predominance of ideological systems in politics, as distinct from the disappearance of ideological beliefs and their influence on politics, as the formula of 'the end of ideology' suggests. No such distinction between the two formulae was made at the time, though (together with the flaccidity of the restrictive definition) it was implicit in the attenuation of both formulae made almost from the inception of the idea of the exhaustion and the harmfulness of ideological systems. This assertion can be substantiated in connection with Shils's elaborations on Aron's initial position, which constitute the decisive programmatic contribution to the crystallization of the tendencies under examination.[37] In his exposition of 'the articles of faith of ideological politics' of which communism, fascism and McCarthyism are examples, Shils drew together and made explicit some widely, but not always conjointly, held views of ideological politics as a specific category of politics.

For Shils, the primary sign of ideological politics is its conduct according to 'a coherent, comprehensive set of beliefs' which override all other considerations.[38] Second comes the not less frequently used (though as little self-evident) mark of distinction of ideological politics: the attribution of 'supreme significance to one group or class', represented by a leader and a party. Only ideological politics exhibit, therefore, a 'dualistic' faith, in so far as the virtue of one's own group is set against the vice of another, and a 'friend–foe', or 'us–them', relationship ensues.[39] He stipulates further that ideological faith radiates into every sphere of life, allying this with the ideologue's belief that he possesses the truth concerning the ordering of life. In its turn this belief engenders 'a deep distrust of the traditional institutions',[40] a characteristic containing the central hallmark which in the modern restrictive and perjorative definition of ideology distinguishes the latter from all other political doctrines: the commitment to radical change. In Shils's terms, the extra-constitutionality of ideological politics is inherent in its essentially alienative character, expressing itself in revolutionism and withdrawal.[41] In the main, Shils presents here, in a generalized form, features of communist and fascist totalitarianism. This kind of generalizing explains why these widely accepted characterizations of ideology as a specific type of political belief systems are not incisive enough, for more than one *non sequitur* is involved in their application.

The 'friend–foe' and 'us–them' attitude applies to all political parties and their belief systems. Parties are distinguished by their ways of dealing with opponents, and not merely by the fact that they consider competitors as foes. Furthermore, nobody can demonstrate that traditional and, for that matter, pluralistic belief systems do not lay claim to possessing the truth about the ordering of life, since such a claim can be and has been used to sanction minimal no less than maximal intrusion of the public into the private sphere. The distrust of traditional institutions on principle is not incompatible with embracing the first version of the 'truth', the ordering of life by minimal public interference. Indeed, distrust of traditional institutions is part and parcel of the commitment to the liberal-democratic establishment embodied in its institutional arrangements. Criteria which Shils added ten years later also lack the distinguishing quality attributed to them. Surely, organization in 'a corporate collective form' to ensure discipline is essential for all political movements and parties whatever their 'ideological outlook'.[42] Moreover 'ideological outlook' is a self-contradictory phrase, for meanwhile Shils had distinguished between ideology and outlook in his additional differentiation between ideological and non-ideological perspectives as those of degree. He spoke of 'a high degree [in ideologies] of explicitness of formulation over a wide range of . . . objects . . . an authoritative and explicit promulgation'; relatively high systematization and integration 'around one or a few pre-eminent values'.[43] On this basis he distinguished between ideology on the one hand and 'outlook and creeds, systems and movements of thought and programmes' on the other.

Without explanation, outlooks are said to be 'pluralistic in their structure' and lacking almost all the distinctive properties of ideologies; creeds are asserted to be more like ideologies and movements of thought, and programmes still more so. It is likewise considered as self-evident that, like Buddhism, Protestantism (in Shils's earlier essay an integral part of the ideological tradition) 'bears only a loose relationship to conduct'. Hence Buddhism and Protestantism are 'outlooks', while Quakerism and Roman Catholicism 'aspire to a fuller influence', and are therefore 'creeds'; these 'have much less orthodoxy' and therefore 'cannot command the concerted intellectual power of ideologies'. Yet Catholic and Protestant orthodoxy surely bear comparison with Marxist orthodoxy, the Church Councils with the Comintern, and St

Thomas Aquinas or Calvin with Marx or Gentile in respect of intellectual power. One can easily agree that programmes are nearest to ideologies, not because a disintegrating ideology can become 'a programme of aggressive elements',[44] but because each party presents its ideology to the public in programmes that represent a compromise between concessions to circumstances and adherence to fundamental principles.

Together with changes of mind in regard to the exemplification of the ideological approach, like the evaluation of Protestantism, there also occurred a significant change in the characterization of the ideological orientation. In 'Ideology and Civility' Shils held that the Western tradition of ideological orientation 'regards authority as an agent of evil and as a compromise with evil'. As far as the penultimate page of this article he spoke only of the negative attitude to authority, and then attributed to the intellectual, the principal bearer of the ideological tradition, 'almost primordial terror of *and fascination by authority*'.[45] In 1968, we hear no more of the intellectual's 'terror of . . . authority', but only of his constant concern with it, reflected in 'thinking of nothing but politics'. For since, in ideologies, 'politics embraces everything else . . . , the evaluation of authority is the centre of the ideological outlook'.[46]

Shils's attempt to align Marxism with this view of authority falters on the terms of his correct interpretation of the Marxist position. If property relations are 'relationships of authority, supported by the power of the state', it clearly follows that political authority plays only a supporting role. What is more, he pairs his earlier *non sequitur* of deriving only totalist consequences from the claim to possess the truth about the ordering of life with another when he equates the paramount concern with political authority and the denial of autonomy to any other sphere. Clearly, only political authority effectively institutionalized, which also means strong authority, is able to guarantee the greatest possible degree of personal liberty and tolerance and hence of the autonomy of the spheres of art, religion, science and economics.

The principal terms according to which Shils opposes ideological politics to what in his earlier essay he calls 'civil politics' do not, then, possess the unequivocal differentiating quality that he claims for them. Definitional separatism is also not only impaired unwittingly, but qualified explicitly, even though perhaps more indirectly than directly. Shils advocates 'civil politics' which try to maintain and improve society by judging things on their own merits and respecting tradition.[47] Yet Shils is too honest and perspicacious to present 'civil politics' in the second half of the twentieth century as a clear-cut alternative to ideological politics. His belief in the possibility of the passing of 'the age of ideologies'[48] does not seem to require belief in the disappearance of ideological factors. The global schism and political trends in the old and new states militate anyway against 'civil politics', as do the traditions which have shaped the ideological orientation of intellectuals in the West and the new states and which cannot, and indeed should not, be entirely uprooted. Shils means the millenarianism of the Judaic-Christian cultures, which fostered religious enthusiasm and fused easily with all kinds of animosities and the corresponding visions of redemption, including those of modern revolutionary politics;[49] traditions peculiar to intellectuals, like scientism, bohemianism and romanticism, as well as the populism of the uneducated and humble allied with them in times of crisis:[50] all on their different and even contradictory grounds inclined people towards ideological politics.

According to Shils, it would be erroneous to believe that 'we can or should completely extirpate the ideological heritage'.[51] Although 'civil politics' involved neither heroism nor saintliness, and although no strong partisanship for values was essential to 'the good society', elements of the ideological orientation were valuable in their own right and 'worthy of conservation in any policy outlook' that justly claimed our respect. Even 'the call to a heroic existence, ... the belief in the earthly paradise and the realm of freedom, all have some validity in them'. No hard and fast distinction can be made, therefore, between 'ideological' and 'civil' politics, the less so since particularly the 'civil politician' – and preferably he alone – must at times cross the lines, move beyond legitimacy and practise both partisanship and its transcendence.[52] Since the fellow citizens of the 'civil politician' are incapable of responding to and sustaining a continuous relationship with 'the sacred' (a centre-piece of the ideological orientation) and ideals (which have their place in 'civil politics'), the politician must bear the brunt of the contact with both, because to disavow completely the affinity between ideology and civility would turn the latter into an ideology of pure power politics predominantly concerned with the maintenance of order.

Definitional separatism and the acknowledgment of common ground were both accentuated when Shils returned to the subject ten years after 'Ideology and Civility'. On the one hand, he continued to accord centrality to the attributes of ideologies pertaining to radicalism, concern with radical change and the totalist orientation.[53] On the other, ideological and non-ideological belief systems (the former 'civility') were now seen to belong to one family. Ideology 'is one variant of ... comprehensive patterns of cognitive and moral beliefs' and the others are outlooks, creeds, systems and movements of thought and programmes.[54] And, as we also have already noted, the differences between these and ideology are explicitly declared to be those of degree. In conformity with his introduction of one category of comprehensive patterns of beliefs, all criteria that distinguish ideology are qualified by the cogent observation that the elements shared by 'the ideological primary group' are never fully realized, being exposed to recurrent strains that give rise to divergencies in belief and attachment.[55]

Shils further narrowed the gap between political belief systems by stressing, in contrast to many of his like-minded colleagues, the affinity between 'progressive or traditionalistic, revolutionary or reactionary ... aggressive alientation',[56] i.e. between political belief attitudes (and systems) oriented towards transcending the *status quo* in opposed directions. Nevertheless he retained the view that ideologies were blueprints for total reconstruction also when he said that they focused on neglected aspects of the ongoing culture[57] and even stated that 'there are ... always marked substantive affinities between the moral and cognitive orientations of any particular ideology and those of the outlooks and creeds which prevail in the environing society and which affirm or accept the central institutional and value system'.[58] One reason for affinity would seem to be that in the process of the decomposition or dilution of ideologies under endogenous and exogenous pressures, some elements are absorbed in the prevailing outlooks or creeds, intensify and sharpen certain of their features, and often materialize in 'a programme of aggressive demands'.[59] On the other hand, the latter can emerge also from prevailing outlooks and creeds. The 'programmatic forms of ideological orientation', however, are 'quasi-ideological phenomena' because they concentrate on 'particular and segmented objects'.

While it may be doubted whether the abolition of slavery is a good example of segmentation, this evaluation is a good example of Shils's intention never to gainsay the specifity of ideology. True, he had attributed concentration on neglected aspects and hence segmentation also to full-blown ideologies; but he continued to distinguish them from 'quasi-ideological phenomena' by repeating that only ideologies demand the transformation of the whole society. He casually equates evaluative with ideological orientation, and shortly afterwards declares that 'no society can exist without a cognitive, moral and expressive culture'.[60] Yet this refers only to the persistence of outlooks, creeds, movements of thought and programmes, and Shils certainly did not mean to identify their persistence with 'the potentiality for ideology [which] seems to be a permanent part of the human condition'.

The intention to maintain the juxtaposition between the two categories of comprehensive sets of beliefs remains firm, despite the increase of conscious and unwitting allowances for their affinity and interpenetration. In 1958 Shils found that the 'civil politician' must 'share with his fellow citizens their membership in a single transpersonal entity'. In 1968, he ascribes only to adherents of ideologies the tendency to speak for 'a transcendent entity – a stratum, a society, a species, or an ideal value – which is broader than the particular body of believers',[61] as if there were any significant political movement or party which would and could speak otherwise, or as if he had not said this himself in 1958 and implied it in his *Encyclopedia* article.

The maintenance and even occasional over-emphasis of definitional separatism perhaps show best in the failure of one attempt, in retrospect, at bridge-building. Admitting the co-existence and the affinity of ideology and other forms of belief, Shils argued that we should aspire to 'the subsidence' rather than 'the end' of the ideological age, but his definitional separatism was expressed at the same time in his belief in 'the rising tide of civility', into which he hoped the intellectual will enter in order to 'bring the age of ideology to an end'.[62] Neither of these two contradictory conclusions bears out the claim made ten years later that, in the mid-fifties, the proponents of 'the end of ideology' wished 'to refer only to the situation existing at that time'. All he could have claimed is that he had not intended to say that, in and after a certain stage of development, 'ideologies could no longer occur'.[63] He could have argued that the belief in *the subsidence of ideology* and the belief in *the end of the age of ideology* are compatible, for most of the time he seemed to identify the age of ideologies with their predominance. In accordance with his view that 'the ideological heritage' should not be 'completely extirpated' and that the ideological orientation bent on the destruction of the existing order was coterminous with human society but entered the sphere of politics at a rather late stage,[64] Shils could have conceived ideology's playing again a subordinate role, to be handled perspicaciously by the civil politician and administered by him to the public in homoeopathic doses. Probably this is what the views held at the time by Aron, Shils, Lipset and Bell amount to *in fine*. It is certain, however, that all these men used 'the end of ideology' and 'the end of the ideological age' synonymously, and that they were not conscious that what they themselves said in contravention to its literal meaning rendered the first formula a misnomer. How else could Shils warn against the attempt to do away completely with ideology, thus in effect arguing against taking the idea of the end of ideology literally, and then speak in retrospect simply of the debate over 'the end of ideology', as he did previously in his comment on the Milan Conference? In 1968 he again used that formula although this time he associated with it even less of the literal meaning than he attributed in 1958 to 'the end of the ideological age'.[65]

Indeed the improvident use of the end-of-ideology formula led Shils to one of his most flagrant overstatements of the restrictive conception. At one point, he identified ideological with anti-political traditions, meaning not the withdrawal of ideologically oriented intellectuals from politics, as elsewhere in the same essay, but the disinclination of such intellectuals to espouse the cause of civil politics.[66] In the course of explaining the characteristics of 'ideological politics', Shils thus implied that civil politics alone is politics and hence that politics and ideology are mutually exclusive, as Crick later maintained. Yet ten years later, Shils spoke of the exclusive preoccupation of the ideologue with politics.[67] He similarly jeopardized his whole elaboration of the uniqueness of 'the ideological orientation'. Quite sensibly to my mind but not in line with his purpose of keeping civility and ideology distinct, he argued that it has not been the substantive values of ideological politics that have done so much damage, but rigidity, exclusiveness and extremity in the pursuit of particular values, and specifically the elevation of one – as such not 'wicked' – value above the rest.[68] This qualification leads to what I have tried to demonstrate, namely that the differentiating quality of what Shils calls 'the articles of faith of ideological politics' amounts only to differences in degree of political methods and attitudes in the pursuit of specific values. However, on Shils's definition, it is inherent in ideological politics to be guided by values that require the radical change of a given reality.

To Shils's conception of ideology applies what he has said on the ideological tradition, namely that traditions seldom die. Having once contributed his noteworthy share to the elaboration of a new version of a restrictive and on the whole pejorative conception of ideology, he held fast to it, although his changing qualifications and accentuations are a clear indication of its untenability.

c. *The Inconsistent Pattern and the Critique*

Whether the gap between qualifications and accentuations widened or narrowed, it was on a never quite consistent basis that the tendency to reserve the term 'ideology' for left- and right-wing extremism reached full bloom in the West at the beginning of the 1960s. It did so conjointly with the idea of the end of ideology, postulated as much as welcomed, but also bemoaned by radical thinkers. When Lipset mentions H. S. Hughes, B. Moore, H. Marcuse and H. Kenniston as left-wing subscribers to the end-of-ideology thesis he is right only in so far as they, too, stated and diagnosed the de-radicalization of politics. But, characteristically, Lipset fails to note the fact that the same men did not necessarily appraise the tendencies of de-radicalization as unideological nor see an end to ideology. As at least Marcuse said, 'the loss of . . . negative thinking . . . is the ideological counterpart' of the reconciliation of opposition in advanced industrial society, and the 'absorption of ideology into reality does not . . . signify the "end of ideology". On the contrary, in a specific sense advanced industrial culture is *more* ideological than its predecessor, inasmuch as today the ideology is in the process of production itself.'[69]

Lipset's oversight is not surprising if we consider his use of the term 'ideology'. In 1960 he said that 'the democratic class struggle will continue, but it will be a fight *without ideologies*', but a few lines later he spoke of British intellectuals who 'are troubled by the fact that the Labour Party is no longer *ideologically radical* . . .'[70] Thus he styled the less intense class struggle on one occasion as unideological, and then as no longer being fought with ideological radicalism. In his extensive treatment of the subject in 1964 he concluded that 'the decline of such total ideologies' – meaning integrated extremist *Weltanschauung* – 'does *not* mean the end of ideology', and that the political consensus of Western society reflects 'ideological agreement, which might be best described as "conservative socialism" [and which] has become *the* ideology of the major parties in the developed states of Europe and America'. It is characteristic of what at times looks like a terminological see-saw that, unlike in his treatment of the subject in *Political Man* and in his recent summing up, Lipset should throughout his delicately balanced and perceptive *Daedalus* article have explicitly, and particularly consistently, identified all political belief systems as ideologies, just as he used 'doctrine' as the synonym of 'ideology' for left, right and centre orientations. 'Clearly', he said in his conclusion, 'commitment to the politics of pragmatism, to the rules of the game of collective bargaining, to gradual change whether in the direction favoured by the left or the right, to opposition both to an all powerful central state and to *laissez-faire* constitutes the component parts of an ideology.'[71]

Thus, in regard to his *Daedalus* article of 1964, but by no means to the same extent in respect of *Political Man* (1960), Lipset was justified in pointing out in his recent *Encounter* article that what he, Bell and others had meant by the 'end' or the 'decline' of ideology was not 'the end of systems of integrated political concepts, of utopian thinking, of class conflict', but 'the passionate attachments' to revolutionary working-class doctrines and 'the consequent coherent counter-revolutionary doctrines'. Yet this distinction between non-extremist and extremist 'systems of integrated political concepts', which lies at the root of the distinction between ideological and non-ideological politics, leads Lipset again to self-contradiction when he concludes that 'ideology is not the common-sense term, meaning *any* kind of political thinking'.

Both those who have and those who have not been involved in the controversy about the end or decline of ideology therefore contravene the available textual evidence when they claim that views to the effect that ideologies had ended or were going to end had never been expressed by the 'decline writers'.[72] It is largely beside the point to stress that those mentioned, as well as other scholars (Tingsten, Himmelstrand, Kirchheimer, Hoogerwerf, Lane and others) have shown that in various countries political conflict had softened and ideological divisions had become blurred.[73] The point is rather that these scholars have used the notion of the end of ideology in its literal meaning and/or that they have been toying with it more or less ambiguously in so far as they have identified the tendency towards increasing ideological consensus with a continuous weakening in the economically advanced countries (or areas) of the impact of ideology on politics, and that this is just another way of affirming the existence and envisaging the growth of unideological politics and the eventual demise of ideology.[74] Indeed, only some years later, after Bell had turned to an inclusive conception, which Lipset continued to use as an alternate to, as well as together with, the restrictive conception, did Bell identify 'the end' of ideology with its 'abatement'.[75]

In his major contribution to the hypothesis of 'the end of ideology', in the book of that title, Bell remained semantically consistent in his restrictive use of 'ideology', but not more so than Shils, in respect of the substance of the argument. He underscored the identification of ideological with millenarian and apocalyptic thinking and strictured 'the compulsion' to commit intellect and feeling totally to the 'exhausted' ideologies of the nineteenth century, among which Marxism earned special mention. He argued that the revolt against ideology, however, was not directed against 'Marxism or any other radical creed' or against utopianism and its visions. 'The end of ideology' denoted the historical perspective of the permanent revolution for individual freedom, a revolution that admits of no 'final definition'.[76] Yet this is obviously just another way of rejecting Marxism, since Marxism offers precisely that 'final definition'. Any other politically significant radicalism is likewise excluded – yet only to the extent that it entails any suspension of the rules of the democratic game. Bell himself professed allegiance to a democratic socialism which seeks fundamental structural change in American economic life in demanding that 'the work place and not the market, must be the centre of determination of pace and tempo of work'.[77] Since at the same time he referred to Marx's appraisal of ideology as an illusion and declared (following Philip Rieff) that only an illusion can lead to 'the therapy of commitment', he must be supposing that the structural changes he endorses have ceased to be an illusion. But has Bell's adoption of democratic socialism also ceased to constitute a commitment? It obviously does not make sense to adhere to a socio-political belief and deny that this involves 'the therapy of commitment', even if one assumes that in the United States change and innovation, being built into the culture, have nothing illusory about them. Such change still requires, on Bell's own showing, 'relative standards of social virtue and political justice',[78] which surely constitute commitment as much as the embracing of 'abstract absolutes' does.

The self-defeating designation as unideological of the kind of commitments to which Bell and others subscribed was the consequence of their vision of the impending disappearance in the West of ideology *qua* radically transformative beliefs. The adequate definition of the phenomenon underlying this evaluation was proffered by a European who, in contrast to other critics of 'the ideology enders', had little quarrel with their political outlook. Only a year after the appearance of Bell's book, Meynaud employed the inclusive conception to re-define 'the end of ideology' as relative 'ideological appeasement'. In this connection he used the notion of 'ideological pluralism' to denote the overlapping of political belief systems. He also warned that there was no assurance that even 'ideological appeasement' would last, being attendant upon a shift rather than upon the disappearance of social conflict and ideological diversity. Nothing in Western societies suggested 'a complete reversal of the ideological array' which, for Meynaud, included all the political belief systems that competed in the political arena. He also raised the pertinent question of whether or not there had been previous occurrences of the phenomenon. Though difficult, only historical comparison could reveal whether slack or intensity was the norm for conflict over ideas.[79]

The debate over the end of ideology was a battle over doctrinal (ideological) issues, and analysis and taking sides were likely to influence each other. If mentioned at all, the qualifications made by the proponents of the idea were waved aside by its opponents as inconsistencies, as they often were. To consider the whole idea of the end of ideology as an ideology was no unreasonable objection, but it was also no excuse for ignoring the more or less inadvertent diminution on the part of the idea's advocates of the stipulated disparity between ideology and other belief systems. Neither side demonstrated the appositeness of its conception of ideology or the inadequacy of the other side's conception, and inconsistency in the use of the term was not the privilege of either.

C. Wright Mills, in his 'Letter to the New Left', appraised the anti-ideological standpoint of Bell, Lipset and others, as ideological, while saying that it resembled more a mood. He thereby came near to accepting the self-definition of the 'no-more-ideology school', and to contravening his inclusive definition whereby 'any political reflection that is of possible public significance is *ideological*'.[80] Mills was justified in opposing the necessarily fragmentary approach of piecemeal engineering to the constant structural critique of the Left; he certainly was not in charging the 'enders' with not recognizing what they themselves had stated to be the case, i.e. that ideology was still alive in the developing countries, and that, in both West and East, 'the end of ideological reflection' had taken effect.[81] Mills also unfairly saddled 'the enders' with the total abjuration of ideals.

Another critic, R. H. Haber, followed suit in 1962 and rejected the exclusion, by Shils and like-minded writers, of the reformist 'politics of civility' from their definition of ideology.[82] Haber, like Mills, defined ideology inclusively and spoke explicitly of '*status quo* ideology', but contradicted himself rather heavily on both scores. He acknowledged that the alleviation of mass discontent by government action had brought about 'the end of a revolutionary alternate', due also to 'red purges' in trade unions, unversities, etc. As a result, he argued, mass dissent was isolated from the Left and 'forced' to conform to 'a non-ideological mould'. This meant an end of (leftist) politics but not of (leftist) ideology.[83] Divorcing ideology from politics in this way, Haber offended against his own recognition of the inherent action-orientation of ideology, actually falling back upon Shils's distinction between revolutionary *qua* ideological and reformist *qua* non-ideological politics, and eventually opposing to each other the values of reformism and ideology.[84] On the same page he declared that there are 'two types of political thinking, ideological and reformist', and yet anticipated that an empirical study would show 'that the "end of ideology" [based on the reformist "politics of civility"] is a *status quo* ideological formulation . . .'[85]

Not all who opposed the idea of the end of ideology made false accusations against its proponents or became involved in inconsistencies over its corollary, the juxtaposition of ideology to other political beliefs. Aiken's position is of particular interest since in his discussion with Bell he opposed Bell's evaluations but not his restrictive conception. Aiken stated that as 'political discourse (as distinct from political science) on its most general formative level', ideology is directed beyond piecemeal reform towards principles and practices 'by which politically organized societies absolutely, or else in certain typical situations, *ought* to be governed'.[86] Not perceiving what Aiken's definition had in common with his own, Bell commented that Aiken's conception of ideology is barely distinguishable from a definition of political philosophy. Aiken did not object since he explicitly regarded ideology 'as the modern offspring and successor to political philosophy' and accordingly considered 'the more foundational doctrines of the nineteenth-century philosophers' as being 'also broadly ideological in character'.[87] For Aiken, if there is anything peculiar to ideology it is the appeal of its explanatory and arousing 'poetry'. Aiken's conception of ideology, like Bell's, is in accordance with the view of those American political scientists who, whether or not they accept the idea of the end of ideology, distinguish between democratic politics as a bargaining process and the search for compromise on one side and politics governed by morals and hence ideology on the other. Unlike Bell, Aiken, who declares himself to be neither a Marxist nor a Leninist, comes out for ideology and accords only a limited desirability to compromise.[88] Thus, while the restrictive conception is a necessary corollary of the idea and ideals of the end-of-ideology thesis, it is not invariably bound up with that thesis, and logic does not require it to be.

The critics of the idea of the end of ideology thus fall into three categories: those who, like Meynaud, sympathize with its political implications but reject both the prognosis of the end of ideology and its restrictive conception; those who, like Mills and Haber, are not in sympathy with the political implications and who also reject the prognosis and the restrictive conception, but fall back on the latter to varied degrees; and those who, like Aiken, accept the restrictive conception and on this basis defend ideology and reject the prognostication of its end. Indeed, as we shall see, there is a fourth category: those who either qualify or reject the prognostication, who accept the political implications of diminishing socio-political conflict over fundamentals in the West, and who adhere with varied degrees of consistency to either the restrictive or the inclusive conception – or vacillate between the two.

2. CONSUMMATION AND APPROXIMATION

a. *The Pitfalls of Pushing the Case to the Extreme*

In Britain at the beginning of the 1960s scholars who did not restrict the 'ideological impulse' to extremism were still notable exceptions.[89] One who seemed to adopt their position found it appropriate to distinguish between 'tacit' and 'creed-like' ideologies; he classified liberalism as a tacit ideology, 'the smallest ideology that actually can survive';[90] but in the main the movement was still further in the restrictive direction. Bernard Crick, admittedly under the influence of Hannah Arendt, carried the one-sided view of ideology to its extreme. He opposed ideology to politics *tout court*.

Not only is 'ideological thinking . . . an explicit challenge to political thinking', said Crick, but 'not all forms of government are political'. This view can be traced back to Franz Neumann, who had designated Nazi Germany as a 'non-state'.[91] Thus Crick identified totalitarian with ideological government and political with non-ideological government inasmuch as 'politics' distinguishes the form of government under which different interests are conciliated by being given a share in power.[92] In Crick's view, non-ideological politics are not, as other proponents of that notion often argue, severed from moral values. Politics are consonant 'at some level with some consistency' with principles and doctrines which have also some ethical significance for the search for 'particular and workable solutions to this perpetual and shifting problems of conciliation'.[93] Hence, for Crick, as for Shils, Bell and Lipset, non-ideological politics include change and invite and reflect generalizations about the nature of actual and possible societies based on pluralism, the safeguard of a reasonable amount of liberty and privacy.[94]

A sensible assumption underlies Crick's defiant battle-cry: 'politics is politics'. If the abyss between totalitarian and non-totalitarian government is such as to forbid our calling by the same name the ideas on which both rest, it is logical to extend the prohibition to the general activity which implements these ideas. Still, the merit of the semantic upheaval remains doubtful. Consistency requires it to encompass other concepts pertaining normally to social and political institutions and processes. If totalitarian government is non-political, a *Dictionary of Non-Politics* is in order. Consistency also demands that qualifications should entail modifications of the original propositions. This applies, for instance, to the qualification that 'some politics exists in most types of regimes'.[95]

When all is said, Crick squeezes out ideology by narrowing the meaning of both 'politics' and 'doctrines'. Doctrines guide political change, yet unlike ideology they do not foster 'utter', 'total', i.e. non-political, change.[96] Thus, like particular doctrines, particular forms of government – acceptable forms – are set apart from another category – objectionable forms – and for this purpose general terms like 'politics', 'ideologies' and 'political doctrines' are invested with particular meanings; an unusual usage, as Crick's 'Footnote' to his book indirectly confirms. Nevertheless, Crick says, for instance, that Robert McKenzie uses 'ideology' but 'plainly' means 'doctrine',[97] taking it for granted that for McKenzie it is as self-evident to exclude non-totalitarian doctrines from the confines of ideology as it is for Crick to exclude totalitarianism from the confines of doctrine. He likewise accuses Marx and Mannheim, and with the latter the sociology of knowledge, of having laid the ground for totalitarian implications of ideology,[98] although he actually uses the term in a sense entirely different from theirs.

Finally, Crick's semantic innovation is the less convincing since he himself is unable to abide by it. He speaks of 'totalitarian ideology',[99] which in his terms is a pleonasm, just as he speaks of 'different ideologies' which under totalitarian government are forbidden to co-exist and clash.[100] By these 'ideologies' he must mean non-totalitarian belief systems which he wishes to be called 'political doctrines', i.e. non-ideologies; and in ascribing ideological interests to the Labour Party[101] he does that for which he takes McKenzie to task.

If in this case, as in others, the logic of language reasserts itself against the intentions of those who use it, it merely reflects the logic which forbids conceptual distinctions that are borne out neither by the phenomena on which they are predicated nor by the criteria adduced for their justification. On these grounds, the systematic and formalized effort of Giovanni Sartori to circumscribe the sets of criteria that define the polarity of ideology and pragmatism also founders.

In an earlier essay, Sartori already held that ideology was the opposite of pragmatism, defining ideology rather loosely as 'a doctrinaire and somewhat unrealistic way of framing political issues'. In fact, he considered ideologization as a corollary of certain party systems. The existence of eight parties, let alone of twenty-six, could not be explained in pragmatic terms. However, it is not the degree of party-pluralism alone which accounts for ideologization. Parties are either pragmatic or ideological according to whether party systems exhibit simple or extreme (party-) pluralism, bipolar but not polarized, or multipolar but not polarized pluralism. Considering the varied degrees of party pluralism and polarization, Sartori seems to discount the fact that ideological divisiveness can be a cause as well as an effect. Indeed, Marxism is singled out merely as 'a formidable communication stopper' because the Italian Communist Party, for instance, produces by its organization, 'a culturally manipulated isolation' of given groups in given areas.[102] Sartori was justified, however, in concluding that 'the end of ideology' did not apply to multipolar politics, since there is no necessary connection in affluent societies between lessening ideological intensity and the existence of the ideological approach.[103]

In the essay which appeared three years later, Sartori abandoned the external organizational perspective and concentrated on 'structural elements bearing on *how* one believes'. According to them, the Western world in its widest sense can be divided into areas of 'rationalistic' and 'empirical' culture. The first is distinguished by '*rationalistic* processing-coding' of information (deduction prevails over testing, doctrine over practice, principles over precedence and ends over means, and some 'covering up' is involved). In the other culture, '*empirical* processing-coding' of information predominates (evidence prevails over deduction, practice over doctrine, precedent over principle and means over ends, and perceptions tend to become more direct).[104] Sartori assumes that in a rationalistic culture the majority will exhibit an ideological and, therefore, 'closed' mentality, 'just as an empirical [and, therefore, "open"] culture will breed ideological minorities'.[105]

The conclusions which follow, as well as the queries invited by his own scarce exemplifications, cast serious doubt on Sartori's whole scheme of distinction. To begin with, it would follow that the majority of those living under communist rule possess 'the ideological mentality' and that the 'hetero-constraining' belief system characteristic of this mentality secures what he calls the mobilization of 'populations and nations'.[106] Sartori himself would hardly discount the decisiveness here of the power structure of communist regimes or the combined use of force, beliefs and promises of communist movements engaged in revolutionary warfare. Conversely, England and America serve Sartori as the paradigms of the open, pragmatic and empirical culture, for he says that the ideologies of the third world stem from a rationalistic Western culture whose origin is neither Oxford nor London, let alone the United States.[107] The omission of Paris is certainly deliberate. Sartori therefore implies that France is an area of rationalistic culture, dominated by the ideological mentality. Since Marxism is the outstanding ideology, the question arises why this area, notwithstanding frequent crises of its parliamentary institutions, has never become Marxist or, indeed, fascist (except for a proto-fascist spell under Nazi occupation), as Russia, Germany, Italy, Portugal and other European countries as well as China have done without foreign intervention. (Hence I omit Spain.) On Sartori's terms, it follows that, unlike the UK and the USA, all these countries must be called areas of 'rationalistic' culture.

Actually, it is significant that he fails to mention fascism. Since I have it from him that he considers fascism, too, an ideology, he would have to agree that 'how Nazis believe' qualifies as 'rationalistic processing-coding'. If so, a rationalistic cultural matrix generates an ideology which is avowedly anti-rationalistic in content – 'the cult of blood and soil' – and requires those under its domination to relate information and principles according to an absolute authority, the *Führer* or *Duce*, however irrational its commands. Admittedly, what ideologists (or thinkers) say about their way of believing does not alone indicate to what extent their approach is empiricist or rationalist, but this does show in the ways ideologists and thinkers argue,[108] and in the case of ideologies, in what is done in their name also. Sartori's criteria of differentiation are as vulnerable here as in the respects already briefly indicated.[109]

Sartori himself attenuates the divide between the rationalistic-ideological and the empirical-pragmatic mentality. Compared with Marxism, 'the outstanding current example' of 'the typically ideological "isms" ', he contends, liberalism is 'the ideological apex attained by the empirical mind'.[110] We may presume that in Sartori's view this is not much of an apex. Even so, he clearly makes a dent in his divide here. His case suffers further from his reliance on the notions and criteria of other scholars who in effect use them in connection with a different conception of ideology. He appropriates, for example, Rokeach's distinction between the characteristics of the 'open' and the 'closed' mind which refer to the question 'how one relates to authority', but Rokeach does not ally 'a closed way of thinking', Sartori's 'rationalistic' *qua* 'ideological' mentality, with specific political and other beliefs. The 'closed' and the 'open' mind can go together 'with any ideology regardless of its contents'. Unlike Sartori, Rokeach makes no distinction between ideologies and other political belief systems, as follows from his view that 'openness' and 'closedness' can be displayed by right-wingers, conservatives, anti-communists and communists.[111] Similarly, Sartori refers to a work by Carl Friedrich where the latter ascribes action-orientation to ideologies. Yet Friedrich here designates by 'ideology' all political belief systems, whereas for Sartori only 'rationalistic' belief systems convert 'ideas into social levers'.[112] Such conversion entails '*a persuasive treatment* (not a logical treatment) of ideas leading to action-oriented ideals'. Ideals are no longer ideas and fall no more under 'the jurisdiction of logic and verification'.

In the first place, the implication that a persuasive treatment precludes a logical treatment of ideas is certainly untrue, unless by persuasion we mean the extortion of assent by terror. It also follows, and is likewise untenable, that in the areas of 'empirical culture' neither political democracy, nor liberal constitutionalism, nor the freedoms of expression, organization and bargaining, nor the welfare state and so on, are ideas that can be converted into social levers. All are action-oriented ideals requiring persuasive treatment. Sartori's own statements about the 'empirical culture' clearly refer to ways of believing and to beliefs propagated by persuasion and realized in specific ways of action. The implication to the contrary is also confuted by his cogent remarks elsewhere about democracy as the child of 'ideocracy' and about guarantist constitutionalism.[113] The intention of the overstatement that by virtue of their action-orientation ideologies are beyond the jurisdiction of both logic and verifiability appears to be that they are taken for granted – 'ideas that are no longer thought'. Here Sartori again refers to another scholar, Weidlé, who means, however, not simply 'thinking' but 're-thinking'. Moreover, Weidlé does not oppose ideology to other political creeds but distinguishes between 'totalitarian and partial ideologies'.[114] Clearly, the routinization of beliefs is no distinguishing mark between political belief systems. Sartori himself quotes from Dahl some of the different beliefs which dominate, i.e. are taken for granted, in the areas he considers as the seedbeds of the ideological and pragmatic mentality respectively. Only the preoccupation with construing contrasts that buttress his distinction between the two cultures could have caused such an astute practitioner of political theory to ignore the fact that the ideal of equality, for instance, though differently interpreted in both areas, has been constantly re-thought in them with reference to actual practice 'under the searchlight of consciousness'. To take political beliefs for granted does not in any post-tribal culture prevent their being re-thought and re-argued. They must be defended under the pressure of changing conditions and adapted to them; changes in their operationalization, i.e. interpretation and implementation, must be justified.

Thus, Sartori's attempt to establish a systematic differentiation between ideological and non-ideological political belief systems reveals the same basic weakness as the other attempts reviewed. They are all based on propositions that are untenable because they entail conclusions which contravene logic and the relevant evidence. Admitting from the outset that it is no *must* to 'oppose ideological to non-ideological politics',[115] Sartori does not demonstrate that one can do so. Even if not more were feasible than to regard a 'rationalistic' and 'empirical' configuration of cognitive elements as ideal-type opposites (and this, too, is not the case),[116] it would be necessary to clarify what the opposites have in common or how they intermingle in practice. The omission of such clarification is not justified by the 'a.c.p.' ('awaiting proof to the contrary') clause.[117] (While any scholarly argument is subject to that clause, it is illicit to invoke it as an excuse for indulging in largely assertive argument.) In any event, if the suggested *differences* between the two cognitive postures were demonstrable, one would still have to prove that they render the *equivalences* irrelevant. Since difference in some respect does not, of itself, invalidate equivalence in others, and vice versa, proof of one or the other – let alone mere assertion – is not enough.

Closer inspection reveals, then, the inconclusiveness of the criteria that served outstanding members of the profession in making a conceptual distinction that reflected the momentous concatenation of events during two world wars and two post-war periods. The totalitarian abominations committed before, during and after World War II and the eventual reassertion in the West of liberal democracy on a welfarist basis, induced these men to revert to the Marxian restrictive and pejorative use of the term 'ideology', yet to predicate it by way of inversion of its original meaning above all, on Marxism itself, though also on other beliefs in radical and violent change which give rise to sharp controversy and polarization. Theorists did not shun the need for qualifications; rather, they failed to appreciate their significance for the evaluation of the nature and role of ideology[118] as for the tenability of its restrictive conception. The tenacity of this failure can be gauged from the ambivalence that accompanied, in the Anglo-Saxon area, the more or less consistent admission of the existence of ideological elements in the pragmatic political culture and the more or less self-conscious attempts to come to terms with the inclusive conception of ideology. Insufficient awareness of the conceptual issue at stake goes so far that some scholars use the inclusive conception and attribute to it salient characteristics of the restrictive conception.

b. *Discordant Admixtures*

In the important collection of essays entitled *Political Opposition in Western Democracies*,[119] many of the contributors use, or implicitly abide by, the inclusive conception of ideology.[120] In contrast, the editor, Robert Dahl, follows the restrictive conception in assuming that the politics of the 'democratic Leviathan are committed to pragmatism and incremental change' and are, therefore, un-ideological and even anti-ideological.[121] Yet he also acknowledges the existence of a common and dominant traditional ideology which underlies the flexible give-and-take of American politics.[122] Dahl's use of terms such as 'common', 'dominant', 'traditional' and especially 'a single ideology' which is accepted by the electorate[123] appears to exclude the controversial in the platforms and policies of the contending parties from the sphere of ideology. But he also says that the electorate's acceptance of 'a single ideology' is the condition for avoiding '*long-lasting* ideological tensions'.[124] The statement is tautological, even though Dahl means a number of basic ideological elements which he confuses with a belief system by speaking of them as an ideology. Furthermore, if ideological elements are restricted to the common base of shared principles, no *ideological* tension at all ought to be envisaged so long as these principles remain common. Actually, then, only long-lasting ideological tensions, not all kinds, are excluded. Thus he speaks of shifts from one type of politics to another and says that in certain conflicts 'the style of American politics changes from pragmatic to "ideological" '.[125] Since he does not argue that the common ideological elements then become objects of controversy, he is led to allow for the occasional penetration of ideology into the pragmatic politics of 'the democratic Leviathan'.

Like some scholars who confront pragmatic and ideological politics and do so more rigidly on the programmatic level, Dahl speaks of a decrease in ideological tension in the economically more saturated and advanced countries, rather than of the end of ideology.[126] In fact, Kirchheimer in his influential essay 'Germany: The Vanishing Opposition', which first appeared in 1957, had admitted that even in the era of the de-ideologized catch-all party, 'goal differentiation may transcend the mere accumulation of personal, organizational, or social-status defence positions',[127] that is, may, ascend into the realm of ideology. Ten years later, Dahl explicitly refers to the prevalence, in Western democracies, of ideologies 'that *seem,* to some observers, less ideological', but denies that Americans are less ideological than Italians.[128] He thus resembles the scholars who use the inclusive definition of ideology but who are sometimes caught up again in the distinction between ideological and non-ideological politics.[129] The result is similar also when the opposite occurs, as in one of the latest variations of the distinction.

On the strength of instructive data about the views of British and Italian MPs, Putnam wishes to cast light on 'the changing relationship between ideology and political action in Western democracies'. He concludes, as others have done, that this relationship reflects the change rather than the end of ideology, a convergence of ideologies rather than de-ideologization.[130] In order to determine to what extent his respondents are ideological, Putnam employs Shils's main criterion for the restrictive definition, 'to conduct politics from the standpoint of a coherent, comprehensive set of beliefs'.[131] Not surprisingly, Putnam's data confirm that politicians of various political persuasions do thus pursue politics while others do not. Like Shils, Putnam offers no argument as to why the former must be called ideological. His only justification for his admittedly 'hypothetical "menu" of [fourteen] components' is that he had culled them out of the characteristics generally attributed to 'ideology', including, he says, many set down by Shils in 1958.[132]

Sartori's approach, however, though barely (and misleadingly) referred to, underlies Putnam's formulation of the characteristics of the three proposed different styles of political behaviour. He clearly echoes Sartori in saying that 'it is . . . not the *what,* but the *how* of political thought which makes it ideological'. The same applies to his shorthand definition of the ideological politician as 'one who focuses on general principles rather than specific details, who reasons deductively rather than inductively'.[133] But Putnam does not succeed any better than Sartori in keeping the 'how' apart from the 'what'. On the basis of his data, he concludes that 'ideologues as measured here *are* extremist and alienated from social and political institutions' but they '*are not* [as a group] ruthless, dogmatic, authoritarian, paranoid, intolerant, opposed to compromise and pluralism or hostile towards their opponents'.[134]

It is difficult to understand why what Putnam's ideologues are found not to be should not affect what he still finds them to be and *what* they believe. For how is it that readiness to compromise and acceptance of pluralism do not detract from (left and right wing) extremism and afford no indication of the content of beliefs? Indeed, Putnam's findings to the effect that characteristics often associated with ideologies in the restricted sense are not corroborated by the ways in which the individual actors of the elite public he has tested actually think about politics and policies;[135] they clearly speak against his uncritical retention of more than one *definiens* of the restrictive conception as the basis for distinguishing three political styles, and strengthen the objections to his distinction between 'Ideological Style', 'Traditionalism' and 'Partisanship',[136] objections which logic and common-sense observation invite anyway.

Putnam finds that Shils's equation of both progressive and traditionalist or revolutionary and reactionary beliefs with ideological beliefs[137] is borne out by his respondents, inasmuch as conservative MPs as well as communists show themselves to be more or less alienated from the *status quo*. The confirmation of the consonance is helpful, but it is only logical to expect it. It is not necessarily astounding that, as Putnam reports, 'the best example of [utopian] . . . thinking came from an Italian Rightist who unfolded for the amazement of his listeners an incredibly detailed plan for remodelling Italian society on corporativist lines'. After all, here is a traditional conservative (and fascist) comprehensive goal which in fairness should not be compared with the 'more typical, if less dramatic' and indeed 'pallid "utopia" ' of an Italian socialist designed to solve the problem of urban transport,[138] but with an Italian socialist's idea of a remodelled society.

At any rate, following Shils, Putnam designates the traditionalist as an ideologist, thus offending against his own distinction between 'ideological style' and 'traditionalism'. Furthermore, he designates 'reference to future utopia' as a characteristic of the 'ideological style' and 'reference to past utopia' as one of traditionalism. This is to refer to 'what' is believed and not to 'how' one believes, for faith in a future or a past utopia differs only in content. 'Stylistic' characteristics also include reference to an ideology and a tradition; that is, they refer not accidentally to 'what' one thinks in terms of established belief systems.

Putnam admits that correlation is low between the characteristics which he nevertheless makes 'go together' to form the three different styles.[139] He disregards the intermingling in belief attitudes as we know them of the characteristics of the three styles. Surely it is not extravagant to assume that people who think more or less coherently about politics – a political philosopher-ideologue or members of a committee composing party platforms – refer simultaneously to tradition, a past utopia and the historical context – the three characteristics of 'Traditionalism' – and in doing so proceed like a 'generalizer' – characteristic number one of the 'Ideological Style' – and a 'moralizer' who makes 'reference to group benefits' and '(negatively) ... to practicality' – the three characteristics of 'Partisanship' according to which one discusses 'issues in terms of blame and distributive justice'.[140] Might one not query why it is self-evident that 'not the ideologues but the traditionalists ... think in historical terms'? Is not the ideologue supposed to offer the key to the understanding of history – present, past and future? Moreover, generalizers who practise deduction, and who refer both to a named ideology and to a future utopia (the four characteristics of the 'Ideological Style'), often do all these things in historical terms, as Marx did. Reference to a past utopia, *vide Urkommunismus,* and the historical context (components of 'traditionalism') forms an organic part of the ideology not only of conservatives like the Tories but also of revolutionaries like Marx and many of his predecessors.

In sum, Putnam's findings help to clear the way for the inclusive conception by debunking some of the generalizations used to set ideologies apart from other sets of political beliefs. Yet while he himself perpetuates the restrictive tendency by the ill-founded typology of three political styles, he also uses the inclusive conception as a matter of course in regard to political doctrines, though this is not presented as, nor does it amount to, an instance of consistent adherence to the distinction between 'how' and 'what' one believes.

The inclusive use of ideology appears in connection with the definition of the ideological politician. The latter's prime concern with general principles and reliance on deduction, Putnam now argues, is found especially among those who hold beliefs attesting their alienation from the *status quo*. Thus Putnam explicitly relates to each other 'how' his elite groups think on politics, that is the 'style' of politics, and 'what' they think, i.e. the content of beliefs. And, quite casually, he speaks of all major 'isms' as ideologies or *Weltanschauungen*, or plainly implies that they are such.[141] Evidently he is unaware that the question arises that if all political 'isms' are ideologies, why are not all political styles ideological? In using the adjective 'ideological' differently from the noun 'ideology' and turning unreflectingly to the inclusive conception,

Putnam is led to imply that one can believe in, and act upon, an ideology both in an ideological and in a non-ideological way.

Since he holds that only those people who can be placed at one of the poles of the Left-Right continuum can be said to exhibit 'the ideological style',[142] it follows that the style of those situated in the centre qualifies as non-ideological. But since all 'isms' are called ideologies, the contents of the beliefs which determine one's place in the centre are also ideological. Accordingly, the ineluctable result of using 'ideological' in the restrictive and 'ideology' in the inclusive sense is that only the adherents of the more pointedly rightist and leftist ideologies can act in both an ideological and non-ideological style, while the adherents of ideologies situated more in the centre are practitioners only of a non-ideological style. Thus extremism is given up as the hallmark of a distinct category of political belief systems called ideologies but is retained for identifying a style of politics as ideological, while, as in Sartori's case, the segregation from each other of the criteria of style (how one believes) and of content (what one believes) is constantly impaired.

Putnam's contradictory use of 'ideological' in the restrictive sense for personal attitudes and 'ideology' in the inclusive sense for political belief systems tilts the balance still further in favour of the inclusive conception, since his empirical findings scarcely support the restrictive conception. Neither the extremism of the ideologues nor that of the ideologies is, on Putnam's showing, a hindrance to bargaining and compromise and to preferring the feasible to the desirable. As a result, dogmatism and partisan hostility are found to be unrelated to the 'Ideological Style Index'.[143] In the end we are left with moderate and extremist ideologues, just as we are left with moderate and extreme ideologies, it being understood that any kind of ideology may be espoused by any kind of ideologue. Unawareness of the mutual exclusiveness of the two conceptions of ideology also prevents this conclusion in Christoph's advance towards applying the term ideology to all politics.

Rather than inadvertently use the same word differently, Christoph explicitly proposed to use 'ideology' in a wider and a narrower meaning designated as *Weltanschauung* and 'attitude structure' respectively. It is in the second sense, more limited and diffuse than *Weltanschauung*, that, in Christoph's view, ideology plays an important role in British politics. 'Attitude structure', he says, is 'an ideology of pragmatism' serving as a foil 'to the ideology of total ends'. To support this perfectly sensible distinction, however, Christoph referred to Crick's conception of ideology,[144] unaware that in joining together ideology and pragmatism he connected what for Crick are 'the incompatibles', ideological and political thinking, and used 'ideology' where Crick, on principle, wished 'doctrine' to be employed. It is also doubtful whether Christoph was consistent in saying that the beliefs manifested in British politics do not add up to a *Weltanschauung,* if these beliefs 'embody values and principles of action connected to a larger view of man, society and state'.[145] For what is such a 'larger view' if not a '*Weltanschauung*'?

A rather striking example of the improvident conflation of the restrictive trend which Crick had pushed to the extreme and the inclusive definition of ideology is furnished by Preston King. He defines ideology as 'a coherent system of ideas of whatever kind involving some understanding of man and the world and which attempts to relate this understanding to a programme of political action, so that the understanding does not remain abstract . . .'. He likewise declares that any ideology, be it based on theology and/or science, can be revolutionary, conservative or reactionary.[146] But then the same author maintains that any such belief system can also be non-ideological, as political systems can be, and in this spirit the whole array of Shils's criteria, according to which only certain sets of ideas are turned into ideologies, is variously referred to.[147] King's notion of 'the ideological fallacy' also amounts to a distinction between ideological and non-ideological sets of ideas.[148] However, like others who make the distinction, he points to instances or possibilities of non-ideological beliefs and institutions according to most questionable terms.

He asserts that, like interest groups, governments need not have an ideology, but admits that the assertion rests on a necessarily arbitrary judgment of how coherent a system of political ideas is.[149] However, he later claims that, as a rule, a political system is non-ideological if it has no belief system or if several more or less equal ones compete.[150] Now there does not seem to be any reason, and King offers none, why such competition renders a system non-ideological, nor does (or can) he produce a convincing example of a political system without a (predominant) belief system.[151] If we need not treat a constitution as the embodiment of an ideology because it enjoins how to proceed and not what to do, then it is difficult to imagine an unideological constitution. Instructions of how to proceed are instructions for doing certain things and for not doing others. Likewise a constitution, we are told, need not be treated as an ideological system, although it can operate as such if it becomes the object of devotion and belief.[152] Not surprisingly, he offers no example of a constitution that does not embody beliefs and that can survive without evoking some devotion, at least in a free society. Monarchy, according to King, is not normally ideological, since it does not invoke a highly coherent world order and is just another name for hereditary one-man rule;[153] reasoning patently refuted by Plato's justification of one-man rule.

Plato's advocacy is firmly anchored in a coherent and systematic view of the world, as are the not less comprehensive and coherent justifications of monarchy formulated by a galaxy of thinkers ranging from, say, St Thomas Aquinas through Bodin, de Bonald, and de Maistre to Hegel and Stahl, including on a lower theoretical plane James I, the common lawyers and Filmer. Actually, it is natural that monarchy should so often have been defended in the context of a coherent world view, since kingship has prevailed longer than any other form of government. King himself remarks that the 'de Maistres' are always systematically superior to 'the Kropotkins and Bakunins'.[154] His contradictions are really inevitable if one considers that he both stipulates an inclusive definition of ideology and retains Oakeshott's opposition of non-ideological to ideological politics, with Crick's separation of ideology and politics.

A similarly indiscriminate reliance on conflicing criteria pervades Rejai's introductory chapter to the collection of essays that he edited, as well as the contribution he made with Mason and Beller. The authors define and use 'ideology' in the inclusive sense,[155] completely unaware that outstanding proponents of the hypothesis of the end or decline of ideology, as well as others, have defined ideology as a particular category of political belief systems. On this basis, they say that no 'decline writer' has denied the existence of a wide range of ideologies, such as liberalism and conservatism,[156] and draw indiscriminately on both 'restrictive' and 'inclusive' authors.[157]

Notwithstanding their own inclusive definition, they uphold the notion of unideological politics which, for no obvious reason, they consider to be manifest in the left and right extremist fringes, as well as in the reaction to it of the silent majority. Rejai also adopts the main restrictive criterion that it is more characteristic of 'the action and programme of ideology' to be directed 'toward the transformation of the existing society' rather than to its preservation.[158] He further undermines the consistency of his inclusive definition and use of ideology by accepting as part of his framework for the comparative analysis of ideologies the distinction between 'high-intensity and low-intensity belief systems'. The criterion of intensity is associated with the contents of belief systems, and as a result the verbally upheld inclusive conception is inadvertently adjusted to, if not transformed into, the restrictive conception. For the transition from a high-intensity belief system – evinced in its radically transformative content – to a low-intensity belief system – consisting of 'instrumental' systems of which liberal democracy and democratic socialism are cited as specimens – signifies not just the transition from one kind of ideology to another but the decline of ideology in general.[159]

Disregard of the *differentia specifica* of the restrictive conception, of course, does not alone account for an inconsistent adoption of the inclusive conception. Still, such a disregard mars one of the most recent (purely assertive) treatments of the concept of ideology that I have been able to consider. Mullins – with only one eventually forgotten reservation – posits and adheres to the inclusive conception. His objective is to explore 'the theoretical bases for conceptualizing ideology in a particular way', which he does by pointing out boundaries between ideology on the one hand and other cultural phenomena, including cultural forms related to ideology, on the other. In this way, it is assumed, the essential components of ideology can be pinpointed.[160] In this exploration, no issue is taken with, nor mention made of, the restrictive definition, while its main criterion, orientation towards change, is used to stipulate an inclusive definition. The ubiquity in Western thought since the French Revolution of the imagination and pursuit of 'qualitatively new social arrangements' also remains for Mullins the distinguishing mark of ideology, which incorporates this change-oriented 'type of "historical consciousness" characteristic of the modern age'.[161] As if nobody had ever voiced a view to the contrary, the conceptualization of this new consciousness and the role of ideology as 'an active agent of historical change' – *pace* Marx and Engels – is designated as characteristic of 'most variants of liberalism, socialism and fascism'[162] and of 'ideological conservatism'. However, since it is stipulated, likewise without demonstration, that in a traditional view, as distinct from 'ideological conservatism', no preoccupation with historical change arises,[163] it appears to be implied that a traditional perspective is an unideological perspective. This is a casual vestige of the restrictive conception, since it remains unconsidered in the inclusive definition of the concept with which Mullins concludes.

The inclusive conception, which I shall defend directly and indirectly in the various parts of this book, is not consistently maintained even when we witness either a determined effort to oppose the inclusive to the restrictive conception or the none-too-advertised or tacit exchange of the latter for the former. Scholars who do one of these things still tend to retain in one way or another the most salient *definiens* of ideology in the restrictive conception: the commitment to socio-political change.

Chapter II

REORIENTATION AND ANTICIPATIONS

I. RECONSIDERATION AND RESTRICTIVE REVERBERATIONS

Since North European scholars have demonstrated that, with the exception of one country (or specific areas of it),[1] political polarization has also decreased in their countries, and since to varying degrees they have appraised the tendency in terms of the decline, if not the impending end, of ideology, it is worth mentioning that the trend towards appraising the situation in these terms has not remained unopposed. As elsewhere, however, the nominal adoption of the inclusive definition has not necessarily obviated restrictive remnants altogether.

In a comparative study of the programmatic pronouncements of various categories of representatives of six European parties, the author Helenius attempts to refute what he regards as the implication of Michels's 'law of transgression' which he identifies with the idea of the decline of ideology.[2] The refutation is linked to a distinction between 'manifest' and 'latent' ideology, and Helenius concedes the possible absence of ideology in its 'manifest' form, normally expressed in the official party programmes. At the same time, he argues, ideology exists in its 'latent' form, by which he means highly articulated views which, though not officially adopted, agitate a party and eventually influence its policy.[3] Admittedly induced to make this distinction by the claims of politicians that their parties are unideological as well as by the theories of political scientists who accept such claims and who also assume that ideology is declining,[4] Helenius does not entirely reject either this assumption or the possibility of unideological party orientations when he concludes that there remain still 'a lot of differences [between the parties] which can be labelled as "ideological" '.[5]

Helenius's concessions to the restrictive conceptions are due to the absence of a consistently critical attitude towards the claim of the spokesmen of certain parties that their parties and policies were free from any ideological taint. If a British Conservative respondent insists that his party is guided by practice and a philosophical attitude in virtue of which the party rejects the socialist attitude towards property,[6] Helenius does not raise the question why the conservative 'philosophical' commitment to the defence of private ownership should not be judged as ideological as is the advocacy of its gradual socialization. Only occasionally does Helenius expose as semantic subterfuges claims to an unideological orientation. Thus he equates 'the decision of fundamental principles, adopted in 1962 by the German Christian-Democratic Union (CDU) and the British Conservative's reliance on Burke with 'manifest party ideology'.[7] However, a page later, we read: 'Labour have their Clause IV and the Conservatives have no programme at all.'[8] Helenius's distinction between 'manifest' and 'latent' ideology allows him to subscribe to the inclusive conception of ideology, and at the same time, in accordance with the restrictive conception, to agree to the possible absence of ideology from fundamental pronouncements on the nature and direction of a party's political orientation.

Parallel to the end-of-ideology debate, but not necessarily related to it, there emerged in the early 1960s a trend in America away from the restrictive and in the direction of the inclusive conception which, as has been pointed out already, many scholars had never stopped using. Thus Minar, for example, in his useful typology of ideologies,[9] generally still considered them the property of modern radical mass movements (in his category B 1).[10] Minar, however, also pointed to the way in which the restrictive had to give way to the inclusive definition. He observed that the connection between ideology and politics had still to be demonstrated, and he suggested that ideology would show up as 'a sort of background to politics' if more attention were paid to all the components constituting 'the chain between ideology and politics'.[11]

In a well-documented essay published in 1967, LaPalombara made a notable attempt to break free of the fetters of the restrictive conception. He lent impressive support to the view that ideology may or may not be dogmatic, utopian or attuned to the claimed rationality of science.[12] Nevertheless, although LaPalombara also admits that ideology serves the maintenance of an existing state of affairs, he accords to conservative movements 'strong ideological dimensions' only, that is, he does not equate their belief systems *in toto* with ideology. What is more, in a book which appeared in the same year as his article, he and Weiner accepted the distinction between ideological and pragmatic parties.[13] Although the self-contradiction is minimized because the LaPalombara–Weiner fourfold typology relates primarily to the rapidity with which parties move to implement change, the distinction between ideological and pragmatic politics is implied, as in the case of the threefold classification of Almond–Coleman, for whom 'multi-value-oriented' parties are pragmatic and 'absolute value-oriented' parties ideological, both being distinguished from particularist or traditional parties.[14] If, as LaPalombara cogently asserts in his article, an ideology may or may not be dogmatic and utopian, then it also may or may not be pragmatic, especially if pragmatic means merely to opt for slower instead of more rapid change. In any case, if 'non-utopian' and 'non-dogmatic', which are generally equated with 'pragmatic', can characterize an ideology, it is obviously illogical to contrast ideological and pragmatic parties.

The absence of a sustained awareness of the problem of conceptual precision is illustrated by the fact that Bell himself, in an essay published in 1965, retreated from the restrictive conception in an unduly incidental but nevertheless explicit manner. Only in his reply to critical comments did he refer in parenthesis to 'the habit of regarding [ideology] as most of us have in the past, as an attribute of groups seeking to change or overthrow a system'.[15] Moreover, this vein is not entirely abandoned. The review of the four historical uses of 'ideology' destined to lead to a working definition of 'the elusive term' is preceded by the opening statement that ideologies are 'prime agencies of movement' in a world committed to change, and often to violent change. Change-orientation, the major characteristic of ideology in the restrictive conception, is now generalized in so far as it is considered as the new mode of thought that distinguishes modern society.[16] But ideology is not just the expression of change-orientation characteristic of modern society. While all social movements '*to some extent* use ideas in an instrumental sense', which is one of the four historical uses of the term, ideologies are the 'prime agencies of movement' inasmuch as their instrumental use of ideas is fully manifest in 'revolutionary politics'. In it, 'ideology becomes completely instrumental, becomes in fact a way of life' as the Leninism of *What Is To Be Done?* shows best.[17] Although Bell now argues that one does not have to accept this use of the concept which, in his view, equates ideology with 'total belief',[18] it is this conception which remains for him, above all, associated with ideology, despite its apparently inclusive definition.

'More formally defined' ideology is 'an interpretative system of political ideas embodying and concretizing the more abstract values of a polity (or social movement) which, because of its claim to justification by some transcendent morality (for example history) demands a legitimacy for its belief system and a commitment to action in the effort to realize those beliefs.'[19]

The definition is based on a distinction between ideology and 'the established doctrine'. The latter presents the values formulated in documents such as the Declaration of the Rights of Man, the American Constitution and the Communist Party Programme. These represent the central value system in reference to which it becomes clear what it means to be a member of a given society, a Bolshevik or a Catholic.[20] Ideology turns these 'directions' into 'directives', i.e. it provides 'the sharper specifications of doctrine'.

The distinction between values and ideology is not, to my mind, well founded, since values *qua* directions are as much prescriptions for behaviour as directives *qua* ideology. Also, on Bell's own showing, the specifications of a doctrine such as communism do not necessarily amount to its clearer embodiment in concrete form but often to a dilution of its fundamental values or a deviation from them. More importantly in the present context, the definitionally unqualified inclusiveness of Bell's conception of ideology as the ideational instrument of rendering concrete any value system whatsoever is impaired, since the indiscriminate association of ideology with change-orientation is not upheld. Although ideology is declared to be the mode of thought of modern society, it is particularly in a society seeking 'consciously to shape social change' that ideology is the mechanism for the codification and concretization of doctrine. Hence the value system of the Soviet Union is 'one of "ideological activism" '.[21]

In resorting to the pleonasm 'ideological activism' (for on his own terms 'a commitment to action' is part of his definition of ideology), Bell predicates ideology, above all, on radical change and somewhat blurs his distinction between value system and ideology (and thus is not on safe ground in chiding Lichtheim for doing the same). What is more, in accord with his earlier juxtaposition of ideology and pragmatism, the phrase 'ideological activism' is introduced in order to pair it (as its opposite) with Parsons's characterization of the American value system as 'instrumental activism' in the sense of a pragmatic attitude. Accordingly Bell also considers that the mobilization of the population for war or economic development requires 'an official ideology' and that to the extent to which a society becomes pluralistic and diverse, ideology becomes more diffuse. Nevertheless, in the

American system (which in war or in times of economic reorganization apparently does not need 'an official ideology') 'some ideological base always remains'.[22]

Bell clearly advanced from the restrictive to the inclusive conception, although apparently unable to liberate himself entirely from his previously held identification of ideology with extremist belief systems in general and with Marxism in particular. Still, on these new grounds he could claim that the end of ideology signifies 'the abatement of the *dynamism* of a creed, and the reduction of ideology as a "weapon" against external and internal enemies. . .'.[23] Bell was as unjustified as Shils in claiming retrospectively that this is what he had meant earlier by the end of ideology. The claim, contravened by his substantive arguments proffered at the time,[24] attests what is as surprising as it is characteristic, namely that Bell disregarded the significance of the fact that meanwhile he had shifted his grounds of definition.

If such disregard was exhibited by one of the leading participants in the 'end of ideology' debate and if from the outset, as much as in retrospect, hardly any of the participants was precise and consistent about its meaning and that of ideology itself, it is perhaps not astonishing, but not for this reason excusable, that scholars not involved in the controversy should, as we have seen, take no note at all of the existence of conflicting conceptions of ideology.

Ambiguity or inconsistency are not inevitable, especially when scholars turn away more or less consciously from the restrictive conception. Yet even then one cannot be sure that a concession over one of its salient features will not be made at some point or in some particular context. In the first edition of *Totalitarian Dictatorship and Autocracy* (1956), Carl J. Friedrich and Z. K. Brzezinski had restricted ideology to belief systems which propose 'how to change and reform a society'.[25] By 1963, Friedrich had come to define ideology as applicable to all political belief systems.[26] Accordingly, in the 1965 edition of *Totalitarian Dictatorship and Autocracy* Friedrich added that ideology served also to defend a society.[27] However, this function still comes second after that of changing and reforming a society, at any rate in Friedrich's 'Ideology in Politics', published with Bell's 'Ideology and Soviet Politics' in the *Slavic Review*. Curiously enough, neither of the two scholars acknowledges the close similarity of their definitions. Apart from putting in brackets the function of ideology to preserve a body politic – after mentioning its concern with change and reform – Friedrich associated ideology, even more clearly and in a more generalizing manner than Bell, first of all with revolution and totalitarian parties. Ideologies 'are most visible and perhaps also most influential in periods of revolutionary upheaval' and, although ideology 'designates a complex of phenomena common to all parties', it is 'more especially characteristic of totalitarian parties'.[28] The politics of other parties exhibits 'the more limited kind of ideology'. This statement again implies consistent correspondence with Friedrich's general use of the inclusive conception, according to which revolutionary and totalitarian ideologies are not more ideological than others but represent different species of the same genus, i.e. different kinds of ideologies.

But there is something more important to be noted than another instance of the persisting resonance of the earlier exclusive identification of ideology with change-orientation, and that is that Friedrich and Brzezinski criticized in their first edition of *Totalitarian Dictatorship and Autocracy* the assumption of a sharp contrast between utopia and ideology. Since Mannheim had attempted such a distinction, its critique leads us to one of the intellectual antecedents of the two interlaced trends of thought so far reviewed. If the antecedents had been recognized as such, exaggerated assertions and distinctions which cannot withstand criticism anyway might have been avoided. To support this assertion, I propose to show first that the presuppositions of the proponents of the idea of the end of ideology amount to an elaboration and extension of conclusions reached by Roberto Michels concerning the pressures exerted on a party's ideals by its mundane aspirations and organizational dynamics. Then I shall show that prominent aspects of Shils's presentation of the restrictive conception of ideology, as well as some of his qualifications, run parallel to Max Weber's ideas about charisma and its transformation. The incompleteness of this parallelism is all the more instructive since Shils's own treatment of charisma will show it to be irreconcilable in decisive aspects with his assertions about ideology. Finally, I propose to demonstrate that the original Marxian conception of ideology, adopted by Mannheim in his inconclusive distinction between ideology and utopia, is an inverted model of the modern restrictive conception of ideology.

2. NEGLECTED PROTOTYPES

a. *Michels's Law of Transgression*

One of the conclusions Michels drew from his observation of the development of the German Social-Democratic Party was that the importance of party ideology was declining. This was the upshot of 'the law of transgression', which Michels conceived in conjunction with the much better known 'iron law of oligarchy'. Unlike the leading proponents of the idea of the end of ideology who predicated the phenomenon on specific conditions and recognized it in retrospect as time-bound,[29] Michels viewed the fate of ideology as an inevitable concomitant of democratic party politics:

> Party denotes division, seclusion; *pars,* not *totum.* However, other circumstances, [like] the power of numbers and the objective inherent in each party to become the state, entail the emergence of *a law of transgression.* According to this law the party pursues the immanent tendency not only to enlarge itself but to expand beyond its social clientele [*Bestand*] which is the base of its formation and demarcated by its fundamental programme.[30]

All parties transgress these bounds in the struggle for votes. The socialist parties, for example, eventually extend the notion of 'the working people' so far as to come near to including 'the upper ten thousand'.[31] Unlike Downs and other modern behavioural scholars,[32] Michels did not coolly and dispassionately remark that ideology plays a subsidiary role to vote-catching. With hardly concealed anger and irony, the idealist who eventually became so disappointed that he accepted a professorship from Mussolini, noted the ideological dilution attendant upon successful democratic domestication and hence bureaucratization of mass parties.

> With the growth of organization the fight about great principles becomes impossible. We observe that within the democratic parties of the present the great contrasts of opinion are decreasingly fought in a principled way and with the pure weapons of theory ... *Vertuschungspolitik* [the politics which blurs essentials] is the unavoidable result of a bureaucratically oriented organization and of an agitation whose prime objective is to win over the greatest possible number of new members and since ... each fight about ideas within one's own ranks is an unwelcome encumbrance of its [the party's] most important task, it is to be avoided as far as possible.

One notes that Michels does not suppose that ideological controversy can be altogether avoided. He speaks about its restriction within parties in the first place and about the disappearance of principled discussions '*from the surface*'.[33] True, he anticipated the modern identification in the West of political with 'pragmatic' orientation when he said that parties, especially in England and America, strive for the circulation of government with 'a clearly formulated but purely practical programme containing only demands for the immediate present'.[34] In this instance Michels, too, seems to have hastily abstracted from the ideological character of such demands, for he sometimes overstated the retreat from principled orientation. Thus he stated that in practice all parties eventually aim to conquer power through elections and 'for the rest leave everything as it was'. He also pointed out that the size of parties and their bureaucratization had caused 'energetic and daring tactics' to be disfavoured for fear of endangering the legal status of the party. He went so far as to assert that hatred was focused on the opponent less because of his *Weltanschauung* than because he was the competitor.

Still, the inevitable result which Michels predicted was the loss not of all ideological differentiation but of the ideological purity and essence of the party. Concluding that merely organization remained, and yet believing in the intrinsic ideological *raison d'être* of a political party and the class-bound ideological orientation of people, he spoke of the permeation of the party's ideology by elements alien to it and did not expect, let alone hope for, ideological dilution to be consummated. In fact, the priority accorded to the requirements of organization which everywhere took oligarchic-cum-monarchic form, did not exclude the intermittent counter-attacks of the trustees of ideology. Occasionally the 'oligarchs' turned against 'the concealed monarchy' (of a Marx) and the idealists turned against both – only to end up by forming a new oligarchy.[35] Indeed the existence of oligarchy even within a party attests the existence of the basis of ideological division.

Michels believed in the persistence of economically-based class contrasts which he considered the source of ideological divides between and within mass parties. He said that 'the party is no social, no economic unit. Its basis is the programme'; which is not to say that the programme is not class-bound, or that economic interests are irrelevant. On the contrary, Michels noted that only in theory are members of the bourgeoisie capable of adopting the programme that suits the interests of the proletarian class. In practice, only a few bourgeois can really 'declass' themselves. The condition for the identification of bourgeois members with the socialist parties is for their material interests to coincide with the material interests of the party organization. This is the lesser evil from the point of view of the socialist programme, for 'where the workers' party needs the help – and leadership – of capitalists who are economically independent of it' we are faced with an aggravation of the general divergence of interests between the mass of members and the leaders.[36] Since, according to Michels, the roots of ideological diversity lie in the unbridgeable divergence of material interests, which cut even through democratic mass parties, logically he could not, and actually he did not, assume that the dilution of party ideology leads to its dissolution.[37]

Nevertheless, Michels believed that the oligarchic character of parties did not prevent them from pursuing democratic or socialist policies. Such politics has an effect on the state, and will come to a halt only when the ruling classes succeed in drawing the extreme Left into the government. 'The socialists, therefore, could gain victory but not socialism which is lost at the moment of its adherents' victory.'[38] There is no contradiction here, for the thrust of Michels's debunking realism, not to say pessimism, extends first and foremost to party democracy. He was, above all, concerned with the elitism and 'the leader principle' of mass parties, and he made it clear that only from this point of view could the differences between socialist and communist final and intermediate goals be neglected. Consequently, it is all the same whether the masses or a party are led towards compromises in order to keep the organization going or whether the aim is achieved, as in the Bolshevik Revolution. Here, too, the decisive fact is that 'not a workers' democracy in the form of a party of millions has reached its goal, but an elite of resolute men in accordance with Blanqui's ideas'.[39] If it is a vain hope that even those democratically elected to office will not exercise the equivalent of aristocratic power over the electors, it does not follow that ideology has ceased to play any role in party politics. This is not contradicted by Michels's denunciation of the lack of fighting spirit among the leaders of democratic mass parties, their immobility in thought and action, or by his expression of doubt as to the truth of the explanation of party apologists that the undemocratic organization of power in the hands of a few party leaders was a means of saving energy for the future to liquidate the opponent when the opportunity offered itself.[40] This criticism carries with it two implications. First, democratic mass parties are subject to ideological stagnation and even erosion because, to attract supporters from strata beyond the social base of the parties, their leadership also practise ideological dissimulation to account for the ideological deviations deemed necessary to attain governmental power. Second, in attributing ideological dissimulation to party apologists, Michels acknowledged in fact that the revolutionary and other parties were not ready, or could not permit themselves, to gainsay their fundamental commitments and final goals, even if they eventually adapted to the role of constitutional opposition parties, as the German Social-Democratic Party had done prior to World War I.[41]

The manipulation of ideology in the pursuit of electoral success and the interests attendant upon holding party and/or government office, which for Michels were the causes of ideological dilution, impressed the end-of-ideology theorists as symptoms of the waning of the social and political reasons for sharp polarization over both ends and means. Far from being opposed to either democracy or socialism, Michels thought that the expectations of truly democratic government were disowned by all experience. Still, he believed that the democratic idea provided an ethical measuring rod by which the degree of oligarchy (which exists in every social order) can be determined in order to be subsequently reduced by genuine democratic movements and also by proletarian-revolutionary movements.[42] Whether or not Michels could have assumed or foreseen as a possibility that which the proponents of the end-of-ideology thesis stated to be a fact, namely that the means of solving the social problems of industrial society were finally at hand and that the West was blessed by a general political readiness to work for solutions,[43] he clearly did assume the persistence of sharply divided class perspectives that remained unaffected, if they were not exacerbated, by the combined effect of 'the law of transgression' and 'the iron law of oligarchy': the dilution of party ideologies. These views appear today less dated than the idea of the end of ideology. In any event, careful consideration of the implications of these two 'laws' might have had a sobering effect on the 'ideology-enders' precisely because Michels did not associate ideological dilution with the compatibility of values but with their betrayal – that is with ideological change – and, last not least, because he made his observations on the basis of equating the function of all political belief systems and the repercussions on them of their function.

b. *Weber's Conception of Charisma*

Another potential corrective of the idea of the end of ideology and its corollary, the restrictive conception of ideology, lay in the similarities between the attributes imputed in the 1950s to ideology and those Max Weber associated with charisma.

Shils included 'The Transformation of Charisma', Chapter X of Weber's *Wirtschaft und Gesellschaft,* in a short bibliography to his 1968 article 'Ideology'. The only connection between ideology and charisma he mentions is that charismatic persons create ideologies in times of crisis and thereby express the previously latent.[44] Neither the proponents nor the opponents of the equation of ideology with anti-*status quo* beliefs have noticed that this equation corresponds to the attribution by Weber of a pronounced revolutionary character to charisma. It is particularly intriguing that the parallelism which extends beyond this characteristic of charisma should have escaped Shils's notice, since in his attempt 'to analyse charismatic authority more systematically than Weber was able to do',[45] he suggested the working of an attenuated and dispersed charisma, just as in his defence of a pointedly restrictive conception of ideology he attenuated that conception in important respects. Yet while Shils is aware that his extension of Weber's ideas concerning the transformation of charisma goes far beyond Weber, he is totally unaware that the views he advances in this context also go far beyond the qualifications of his restrictive definition of ideology and indeed reach the point of contradicting its terms. To reveal the generally overlooked prototypical significance of the Weberian conception of charisma for the restrictive conception of ideology we must establish a twofold comparability: that the characteristics which Shils and like-minded theorists attribute to ideology and those which Weber attributes to 'genuine' charisma are comparable; and that the same applies to the qualifications of the restrictive conception, especially Shils's on the one hand, and Weber's view of the transformation of 'genuine' charisma on the other. Obviously, only on these grounds can we maintain that the irreconcilability of Shils's views of ideology with his own elaboration of Weber's notion of charisma attests that had the two parallelisms been noted, they might have provided a corrective of the restrictive conception. In the present study, the demonstration of parallels is not meant to be exhaustive. But the aspects highlighted for comparison are striking enough to warrant the assertion of the parallelism, as distinct from its exact delineation.

In contrast to Shils's failure to relate to each other his treatments of charisma and of ideology, the fact that Weber did not comment specifically on ideology in his treatment of charisma is in no way astonishing. For Weber, genuine charisma was anti-*status quo* and therefore opposed to the only restrictive conception of ideology current at his time, namely the Marxian conception, which confined ideology to pro-*status quo* beliefs. On the rare occasions that Weber mentioned 'ideology', he did so in accordance with the immediate post-Marxian trend, that is, in a neutral and inclusive sense.[46] The comparison between the modern restrictive conception of ideology and Weber's conception of charisma is also not impeded, because by charisma

Weber designated specific bodily and spiritual gifts which are 'transnatural ... in the sense of not being available to everybody'.[47] Their existence is attested by the success of persons in having such gifts attributed to them and in attracting dedicated followers. Clearly, whatever the attractive power of the leader, it cannot be separated from the appeal of his mission, even if the followers believe in what he says to them and do what he asks of them only because they believe in him. Perhaps it is too much to say that charisma provides 'the real opening through which ideas break into the multiplicity of spiritually and materially conditioned relations', though it is safe to postulate that under the revolutionary impact of charisma 'ideas turn into ideologies'.[48] In any event, we can relate charisma to revolutionary belief because, in Weber's usage, charismatic belief has both an address and a specific content.

The specific content of pure charisma consists in its 'eminently revolutionary character'[49] and hence in its 'message'. This characteristic is central to Weber's conception of charisma and also to the conception of ideology used by those who identify it with a set of extremist and subversive beliefs. In Shils's formulation, commitment to radical change in trans-epochal perspective is the ideological expression of 'aggressive alienation'. This is the motivation and aim Weber ascribes to most types of charismatic leader. Charisma revolutionizes 'from within' in transforming things and orders in the light of the ethical, artistic, political and other beliefs that the leader propagates.[50] The rise and activity of the leader occurs in response to 'physical, economic, ethical, religious, political distress [*Not*]', arousing enthusiasm in extraordinary situations for extraordinary undertakings. Generally, the charismatic personality embodies that which leads beyond everyday life [*Alltag*].[51] These aspects of genuine charisma reappear distinctly when Shils and others postulate that ideology arises in times of crisis, opposes the *status quo* (everyday life), and demands an extraordinary enterprise to be launched by or for a specific social entity in extraordinary (revolutionary) circumstances under the auspices of laws that lie more or less beyond human manipulation. Shils's notion that ideologies require complete subservience and the permeation of conduct by ideology corresponds to Weber's view of the original life-regulating charismatic authority, the acceptance of which is regarded as a duty by the followers and the leader.[52] The peculiarities of Shils's ideological 'primary group' and movements are also a replica of Weberian criteria, since Weber's charismatic leadership involves specific forms of organization adapted to the out-of-the ordinary character of the man and the mission. Initially, 'a specific kind of charismatic aristocracy' forms itself, and all rationally planned economic activity for profit's sake is held in contempt. Thus, charisma comes second after the family community (*Hausgemeinschaft*) as the historical bearer of the communism of consumption.[53]

Apart from the way (or 'why') of believing, the specific content and nature of what is believed constitute the charismatic. Only the latter, however, constitutes the ideological, whereas the former does not apply to ideology. Unlike charisma, the conception and acceptance of ideology are not normally dependent on the relationship between the personal quality of leaders and the belief in their supernatural powers. It is one thing to argue that charismatic leaders usually create an ideology and quite another to maintain, as Shils does, that ideologies are generally created by charismatic persons. Was Marx such a person, or Locke or Mill? (And, for that matter, what are the specific grounds for drawing the line between efficient and charismatic leadership, especially in the non-religious and 'rational-legal' context? How can we distinguish the effective leadership of a Harold Macmillan from the charismatic leadership of a Winston Churchill, and how do we know whether to speak of Harold Wilson's halcyon days in office as charismatic leadership, as distinct from the prosaic sequel of holding on to office and then only to party leadership – and yet leading his party back to power again?)[54]

Although some central characteristics of 'pure' charisma correspond to characteristics that Shils and other proponents of the restrictive conception attribute to ideology, a decisive difference is to be noted. Weber conceived the uniqueness of these characteristics without having to resort to qualifications which are not definitionally accounted for, as happened quite normally in the restrictive view of ideology. It is due to this difference that the parallels do not provide any support for the restrictive conception. Unlike its proponents, who identified ideological with revolutionary orientation, Weber took care to clarify that not only charisma but bureaucratization and economic change also revolutionize. The difference is that charisma revolutionizes 'from within', and the other two 'from without'.[55] Whatever the precise delineation between the two forms of revolutionizing, the important point is that from the outset Weber exercised discrimination in ascribing a revolutionary function to charisma. He did the same in respect of 'sacredness'.

In one context, Shils connected sacredness only with ideological *qua* anti-*status quo* belief systems and merely assumed the devolution of some ideological ingredients on other belief systems in the course of the disintegration of an ideology.[56] For Weber, however, genuine charisma 'turns all concepts of sacredness upside down', creates subjection to what is totally new and unique and, therefore, becomes itself 'divine' and 'sacred'. Charisma arrogates to itself the sacredness formerly inherent in existing institutions. Neither charisma nor tradition, 'the two incompatibles', rests on rational rules but on the belief in the sacredness of authority. Although the exterior forms of traditional and charismatic rule may thus be almost identical, 'the spirit' on which they thrive makes all the difference.[57] Similarities serve Weber to delineate the limits within which charismatic remains distinct from traditional sacredness and charismatic from bureaucratic revolutionizing of tradition. Sacredness attaches, then, to various types of rule in their own right and also devolves on incumbents of offices and institutions by virtue of their derivation from the pure charisma of their founders.

Charisma itself persists not merely as an institutional residue of the genuine article. The likelihood of genuine charisma materializing as an all-encompassing though transient type of rule is, according to Weber, strongest in a stage of development where religion still predominates. Afterwards, charisma recedes before the development of permanent rational-legal institutions. But even within their framework, genuine charisma remains possible. Although Weber distinguishes between confirming the charismatic ruler by acclamation and electing him democratically, he says that elections are not 'charisma-free' for they require 'the charisma of speech'.[58] Furthermore, the capitalist economy, like democratic politics, witnesses genuine charismatic leadership in, for example, the activity of stock exchange pirates and the really great financial and colonial exploiters. In modern politics and in modern economics, pure charisma functions in conflict and involvement with the *Betrieb,* the regular management of business or the party machine.[59]

In more than one respect, Shils ascribes to ideology in a 'civil' culture the same function which Weber connected with the continued reappearance of genuine charisma in the various spheres of non-charismatic political cultures: to challenge these cultures and drive them ahead. However, in Weber's analysis, the revolutionary function of genuine charisma in modern society is limited. Among other things, the removal of the opprobrium attaching to the acquisition of possessions for one's family and the rationalization of the techniques of life are part of the process in which the original revolutionary character of charisma is lost.[60] In the modern restrictive conception of ideology, revolutionary change remains the immutable core *definiens*, whatever other concessions are made. Nevertheless, even on this score, as well as in other respects, qualifications that definitionally remain unaccounted for reflect in substance Weber's views concerning the transformation of charisma and its persistence in non-charismatic types of rulership. Thus, the self-consistency of the restrictive conception is not enhanced any more by this parallelism than by the limits mentioned so far of the parallelism between the restrictive conception of ideology as maintained by Shils and others and Weber's views of genuine charisma. Rather Shils contradicts basic principles of his exposition of that conception when he enlarges on Weber's views of the transformed, viz. institutionalized, charisma.

In his article 'Ideology', Shils admits in the context of establishing links between ideology and other belief systems that a high integration of cultural elements indicative of 'the ideological state', or situation, is 'inherently marginal and unstable'.[61] This is to apply Weber's view that the inherent instability of charisma lies in its nature, so that the fervent wish to perpetuate charismatic rule manifests itself regularly in the attempt to institutionalize and reify charisma, turning it from a singular gift of grace into a perpetual possession.[62] When Shils on the one hand allies with the instability of a fully ideological condition the disintegration of ideologies and the absorption of some of their elements by other belief systems and on the other affirms the persistence of ideological elements in 'civil politics', especially through the intermediacy of the civil politician, he again applies Weberian notions concerning the transformation of charisma. Its essence is the separation of 'the thing' from the person and its natural connection with an office [*Amtscharisma*]. This development is a matter of establishing links with already existing, even long-established, conceptions used in the promotion of bureaucratization.[63] The tendency is most conspicuous in modern re-eruptions of charismatism which, as in the form of French Caesarism, eventually settle down to create institutional norms, as much as to restore old ones, thus causing 'the everyday power of tradition and the belief in its sanctity to regain the upper hand'.[64] In other words, Weber consistently adheres to the view that the sanctity of institutions is not by itself evidence even of transformed charisma. In 'Charisma, Status and Order', Shils proceeds from the opposite standpoint.

Eisenstadt says that Shils has made an important contribution towards bridging the gap between 'the charismatic as an extraordinary event or quality and as a constituent element of an orderly social life'.[65] But there seems to be little doubt that Shils's attenuation and dispersal of the Weberian charisma not only blurs the difference between pure and institutionalized charisma but also that between the latter and any awe-inspiring institution or personality. Shils remains on Weberian ground perhaps only as far as Weber did not identify the charismatic preponderantly with the pathological (or demonological).[66] Shils's all-encompassing ascriptions of charisma stand in flat contradition to the principal criteria of his restrictive conception of ideology. Evidently, to the extent that important characteristics of pure charisma correspond to similarly important ones attributed to ideology, the ascription of charisma in the process of its attenuation and dispersion to all kinds of institutional and value systems necessarily contravenes a restrictive conception of ideology as much as it is apt to empty the notion of charisma of its specificness. Shils does not consider that, for Weber, 'the spirit' of externally almost undistinguishable traditional and charismatic rule makes all the difference between the sacredness of these orders and hence between the sacredness all institutional and value systems eventually lay claim to and receive. Perhaps Shils is as right to imply the irrelevance of that distinction as he is in investing with charisma all effective rulers and institutions, the electorate and the nation,[67] but he is obviously all the more wrong in attaching the concern with sacredness and transcendence only to ideologies and in stamping them as comprehensive belief systems predicated on distinct institutional and value systems.

It remains a mystery how Shils could insist in his treatment of ideology that the concern with 'the sacred' is a distinctive characteristic of radically transformative sets of political and social ideas, while in his essay on charisma he allied 'the sacred' with the concern for order embodied, above all, in existing institutional and value systems which despite dissensus prevail at 'the centre' and are 'integrated with a transcendent moral order'.[68] When he dealt with charisma, it appears Shils simply forgot all about his conception of ideology and followed Weber in not relating sacredness or revolutionizing exclusively to genuine charismatic leadership and beliefs. In obvious contradiction to the way he contrasted, in his articles on ideology, belief systems sustaining an existing order and those demanding its subversion, Shils portrayed in his essay on charisma 'the charismatic propensity' (connected, like ideology, with 'the sacred') as a response both 'to great ordering power' and to 'order-destroying power'.[69] Shils's extended charisma explicitly pertains to comprehensive belief systems which are embodied in any given political system and link that earthly order to the transcendent order. The Justices of the United States Supreme Court provide one such link. They interpret individual articles of the Constitution in reference to 'general principles of rational justice and the common good' which are 'at the very centre of transcendent order'. The major religions are also preoccupied with such 'ordering patterns', and so are 'metaphysics, the philosophy of history, political and moral philosophy' and 'more secularly, the constitution and the legal system'. They all deal with the 'charismatic and transcendent order'.[70] This last, therefore, is conceived as the point of reference or fount of legitimation of both prevalent and envisaged institutions and their agents.

It hardly needs to be pointed out that 'ideology' is arbitrarily omitted from the array of intellectual and spiritual comprehensive belief systems which connect political activity with the 'charismatic and transcendent order', or that the unwarranted omission of 'ideology' cannot conceal the fact that, by considering as charismatic all (pretended or genuine) awe-inspiring and reverence-evoking authority Shils leaves little, if any, distinctiveness to the notion of 'genuine' charisma. He leaves no distinctiveness whatsoever to ideology in the restricted sense, since he ascribes to all institutional and value systems the most important characteristics reserved in his treatment of ideology for ideology alone, that is, for orientations alienated from the central and institutional value system. By both following and going beyond Weber in the matter of transformed charisma, Shils inadvertently damages beyond repair his restrictive conception of ideology, maintained in all his treatments dedicated to the subject 'ideology' – including the one which appeared three years after 'Charisma, Order and Status'.

At the end of his essay on charisma, Shils says that his 'concluding but not definitive observations' concerning the contest between 'the discerners and interpreters of the transcendent order, the agents of the earthly order, and the populace . . . about the ultimate locus of charisma' lead back to Weber's 'famous proposition about the revolutionary character of charisma'; an assertion defensible but not there justified. The fact that, in conformity with the Weberian conception, Shils recalls the linkage renders still less understandable his ignoring to what extent he uses in his conception of ideology Weber's terms of definition of pure charisma and in his qualifications of his conception of ideology avails himself of the Weberian criteria of the inevitable transformation and institutionalization of charisma. On the other hand, without allowing himself this oversight he could hardly have upheld a restrictive conception of ideology for which neither of the two parallelisms affords any support. Conversely, yet by the same token, this oversight enabled Shils to attenuate and generalize charisma to the extent of making it central to political organization *per se,* in terms irreconcilable with his conception of ideology.

These conclusions, for which I have provided the evidence in the preceding comparisons, circumscribe the prototypical significance of Weber's conception of charisma for the restrictive conception of ideology. While it is surprising that the eminent social theorist who treated both subjects ignored the connection between them, the terrain we have traversed so far, and some of that which still lies ahead, reveals that this is a peculiarity rather than an exception. Adherence to the restrictive conception seems to ensure that scholars steer clear of comparative analysis of either specific political belief systems or distinct socio-political processes, and it certainly does not seem to encourage them to take serious issue with the views of immediate predecessors, even if these views bear directly on the conceptual problem in hand. It should therefore come as no surprise that, although Mannheim in one context formulated a restrictive definition of ideology, the one thing we cannot justify by reference to him is the post-war tendency of calling only extremist belief systems 'ideologies'.

c. *Mannheim: the Inverted Paradigm*

When in 1950 Lasswell and Kaplan defined utopia as the political myth designed to *supplant,* and ideology as 'the political myth functioning to *preserve* the social structure', they were following Mannheim when almost no one else did.[71] But they did not trouble to take into account the difficulties besetting his distinction.

Generally, Mannheim treated all major political and social currents of the nineteenth and twentieth centuries – bureaucratic conservatism, conservative historicism, liberal-democratic bourgeois thought, socialist-communist and fascist theory – as ideologies. This he did *inter alia,* when he argued that in accordance with the social and political interests to which an ideology responds, it contains the truth about certain aspects of total reality.[72] In this context, Mannheim used ideology not only inclusively but also neutrally, i.e. not in a pejorative sense. Ideology represents 'the outlook associated with a given historical and social situation and the *Weltanschauung* and style of thought bound up with it'.[73] Mannheim insisted that the socialist-communist claim to be free of such a limited outlook and hence free of 'any ideological taint' was untenable. Like Bernstein before him,[74] Mannheim applied Marxist categories to Marxism itself. Mannheim accepted, however, Marx's claim that Marxism was not utopian socialism, because Marx 'refused to lay down an exhaustive set of objectives' for the future communist society and instead assumed that the future will be decided according to 'the dialectical relationship between theory and practice'. Mannheim believed that this 'dialectical' interaction even implied revising the theory in case of its failure in practice.[75]

Here, Marxism is for Mannheim an ideology and not a utopia, not because it affirms the *status quo*, but because it denies it and envisages its transcendence in the process of an on-going interaction between theory and reality. The assumption of such interaction requires us to understand reality in the twofold sense of the life-situation brought about by going beyond the *status quo* and the situation which had bred the tendency to transcend that situation. On these grounds Mannheim could impute to revolutionary communism, alongside fascism, and indeed to all political currents, not correspondence but constant reference to reality, which he held to distinguish ideological from utopian transcendence. This interpretation of Mannheim is apparently in conformity with his view that, in contrast to 'situationally congruous and adequate ideas' which belong to sociology, both ideologies and utopias are 'the two main categories of ideas which transcend the situation'.[76] However, this statement was made in a context in which Mannheim used 'ideological' and 'utopian' differently from his use of these terms in connection with the appraisal of Marxism that I have commented upon thus far. In fact we now come upon that part of Mannheim's work in which he used 'ideological' as he did not use it in most of the other parts of *Ideology and Utopia*.

In his attempt to distinguish in principle between ideology and utopia, Mannheim said that the utopian frame of mind was 'incongruous with the state of reality within which it occurs' inasmuch as it is not merely 'oriented toward objects which do not exist in the actual situation'. Those orientations only are utopian 'which, when they pass over into conduct, tend to shatter, either partially or wholly, the order of things prevailing at the time'.[77] Ideologies, too, may orient themselves 'to objects that are alien to reality and which transcend actual existence', yet in contrast to utopias, ideologies are 'nevertheless ... effective in the maintenance of the existing order of things'. Since Mannheim obviously had not meant to say of Marxism that it contributed to maintaining the existing order, the terms of his grossly overstated distinction between 'utopia' and 'ideology' contradicted his agreement with Marx's claim that his theory was non-utopian, though even after his shift of ground Mannheim still could regard Marxism as 'ideologically tainted' by virtue of its being historically and socially conditioned. The assumption here is that, although man's ideas transcend the existing order more frequently than they are 'immanent in his existence', transcendent ideas reflecting ' "ideological" states of mind' fall short of being utopian in so far as they are rendered 'socially impotent' and 'confined to a world beyond history and society, where they could not affect the *status quo*'. In this way, the reality-transcending elements of ideology are ' "organically" and harmoniously integrated into the world-view characteristic of the period' and they therefore do 'not offer revolutionary possibilities'. Although it does not follow logically or empirically (and is not upheld consistently by him), this means, according to Mannheim, that ideologies 'never succeed *de facto* in the realization of their projected [i.e. reality-transcending] contents'. Utopias, by contrast, 'are not ideologies in the measure and so far as they succeed . . . in transforming the existing historical reality'. Pushing this train of thought to its logical conclusion, Mannheim asserts that, the moment their aim is achieved, utopias 'become exclusively ideological'. On the other hand, if under certain conditions ideologies succeed in the realization of their 'projected contents' – though by his own definition this is opposed to their very nature – 'ideologies become utopias'.[78]

Just as success serves for Max Weber as evidence of the existence of charisma, success 'in transforming the historical reality' (or failure of containment of the reality-transcending elements of ideology) attests, according to Mannheim, that a belief system is a utopia. Yet, although it is similar to charisma in containing the seeds of its eventual transformation, utopia, according to Mannheim, turns into ideology the moment it proves its realizability. Thus we are presented, in effect, with a continuous Jekyll and Hyde transformation and re-transformation, though re-transformation of ideology into utopia, or rather the realization of its utopian elements, is not assured. The distinction between ideology and utopia hinges on what I take to be the imprint of the perplexing Marxian identification of 'real' not simply with a given situation but, above all, with what is supposed to indicate the nature of the changes of this situation. This is to identify 'real' ultimately with that which lies beyond the given reality.[79] The Marxian assumption of the predictability of what is realizable in the future is being used in un-Marxian fashion as the differentiating characteristic of utopia. On this basis, which is confused not only from the Marxist point of view, Mannheim temporarily buttressed the Marxian pejorative conception of ideology. In contrast to utopian ideas, he designated those ideas as ideologies which are unrealizable and which are for that reason 'distorted representations of a past or potential social order'. Unlike the 'real utopia', ideologies are 'illusory ideas adapted to the present order . . . to conceal reality'.[80]

Since realizability can be proved only by realization, it cannot serve as a criterion for identifying a political belief system except after the event, that is, when it has forfeited its chance to be called utopian. It is reasonable to assume that the utopian state of mind ceases to exist when its orientations appear to be realized. It is not less reasonable, however, to assume their previous existence as a style of thought and belief system. Mannheim clearly bestowed the adjective 'utopian' on sets of beliefs when their realizability was still a belief and not a fact. He therefore had to retrace his steps from his sharp-edged distinction. In the first place, he never denied the similarity of ideology to utopia. Having stressed that ideologies, too, are 'situationally transcendent ideas' and contain 'projected contents', he explained that utopias contain in effect '. . . the unfulfilled [i.e., as yet unrealized] tendencies which present the needs of each age' and therefore arise 'dialectically' out of the existing order.[81] The utopian mentality, too, 'hides certain aspects of reality', indeed 'everything which would shake its belief or paralyze its desire to change things'. Thus, Mannheim slowly but surely effaced the simplifying, oblique and basically Marxian antinomy that that which, as it were, 'must' be assumed to be realizable – utopia – can grow out of thinking which is 'incapable of correctly diagnosing an existing condition of society', while that which is adapted to the existing order – ideology – is illusory and by concealing reality 'thereby stabilizes it'. Mannheim also anticipated many of his critics, by himself admitting that it is extremely difficult 'to determine concretely . . . what in a given case is ideological and what utopian'. We will only know this, he admits, 'if we look into the past'.[82] Moreover, he reverted to the view that 'the utopian and ideological elements do not occur separately in the historical process'. Their coexistence and relatedness is admitted again after another overdrawn distinction.

Mannheim first argues that 'the dominant group' determines, in consequence of its affirmation of the existing order, 'what is to be regarded as utopian'. Since 'the ascendant group' opposes the existing order it determines 'what is to be regarded as ideological'. Yet he immediately retrenches and says that the utopias of ascendant groups are often heavily 'permeated with ideological elements'.[83] Since in modern times these utopias are the socialist-communist systems of thought, Mannheim supposes now that they exhibit a utopian character after having accepted previously Marx's self-defence against utopianism. Moreover, although Mannheim declared that the conservative mentality 'as such has no utopia', he was very well aware that the conservatives see an ideal in the order they defend. He could not keep that ideal separate from a utopia. Under the attack of the ascending classes, he said, conservatives are forced to engage in 'historical-philosophical reflection concerning themselves', and with the help of 'a body of ideologists who attach themselves to the conservatives' they create 'a counter-utopia'. This is done in response to the problems the ascending classes raise by their 'counter-ideologies' which are 'antagonistic' among themselves and oriented toward each other.[84]

The retreat from – or muddle around – the erstwhile neat distinction between utopia and ideology is almost complete. Mannheim goes back on himself to the point of admitting sensibly that utopias are not engendered with supreme disregard for existing conditions but are accompanied by, if not part of, the ideologies that oppose the ideologies defending the *status quo*. Conversely, the pressure brought to bear on the ideologies of the *status quo* causes them in their turn to put up a counter-utopia. One party counters another party's utopia by unmasking it as an ideology. The next and last step is the flat contradiction of the criterion Mannheim has proposed for distinguishing between utopia and ideology.

It hardly needs to be stressed that we can omit the 'counter' which Mannheim prefixed here to 'ideology' and 'utopia'. In defending or attacking anything, one is always poised to counter something. The important point is that when Mannheim himself substituted 'utopia' for 'counter-utopia' in respect of the conservatives, he should have said: 'The utopia in this case is, from the very beginning, embedded in existing reality' and 'has become completely congruous with concretely existing reality'.[85] With this characterization of the conservative utopia the argument has come full circle.

What had distinguished ideology from utopia – rootedness in the *status quo* – has become the distinguishing mark of a particular utopian mentality. Mannheim also designated here the rational liberal-humanitarian idea as a utopia which though 'often born of the chiliastic mentality', became the prime antagonist of chiliasm. The 'idea' of the rational liberal utopia, that is, liberalism normally labelled ideology, like all other 'isms', serves as 'a measuring rod' and not as a blueprint of reconstruction.[86] Nevertheless, the 'idea' is realized in 'gradual improvement' and, being realizable, falls under the category of utopia.[87] No wonder that, with the exception of fascism (presumably on account of the stress on 'the irrationality of the ... apotheosis of the deed' over and against programmes),[88] Mannheim presents us with as many utopian mentalities as ideological currents. The utopian element appears in each ideology whether under the attack from, or in the attack on, other political currents; it represents the goals which embody the guiding values of the belief system. In short, the utopian element characterizes ideology in its positive aspirational aspects.

Mannheim's distinction between utopia and ideology has sometimes been attacked, but only partly, if at all, has it been noticed that the more recent distinction between non-ideological and ideological politics has its forerunner in Mannheim's attempt to set apart a belief system predicated on the *status quo* from one that tends 'to burst the bounds of the existing order'.[89] A scholar who perceived that 'what Mannheim called utopias, these [end-of-ideology] writers call ideologies and label extremist', did not mention that, in the context of his distinction between the two, Mannheim, like Marx, restricted ideology to the affirmation of the *status quo*.[90] With Shils it is the other way about. The co-translator of *Ideology and Utopia* said that, in contra-distinction to utopia, Mannheim designated as ideology that which 'existed in the past but exists no longer'. Then Shils added what was actually a badly needed self-correction, i.e. that 'within the category of ideology he [Mannheim] included sets of beliefs which affirm the existing order'.[91] Shils did not mention that Mannheim generally included *all* political belief systems within the category of ideology; and, while Shils clearly stated that he did not follow Mannheim's terminology and classifications, he did not acknowledge the obvious, namely that he used 'ideology' as Mannheim used 'utopia'.

On the one hand, then, it escaped notice that to label only extremist transformative sets of beliefs as ideologies was to invert the meaning Mannheim attributed to the term when he tried to draw a clear distinction between ideology and utopia. On the other hand, Mannheim's inability to maintain the distinction and his quick reversion to the application of ideology to all political belief systems were also largely ignored. Awareness of the two points might have induced some critical self-questioning concerning the difficulty of classifying categories of political belief systems merely by dint of their attitude towards an existing order. The extravagance to which such an undertaking can lead is well reflected in Mannheim's addition of realizability to the traditional hallmarks of utopia, that is in his use of a Marxian residue for non-Marxian purposes. Here there was a lesson, precisely because it left no mark on Mannheim's treatment of the actual contents of the major political systems and of the relations and clashes between them. In this treatment he beat a quick retreat from the still-born venture of distinguishing between ideology and other political belief systems.

All this was lost upon those who repeated the attempt. They, as well as those who used the inclusive definition of ideology, did not seriously join battle over the definitional issue. It was symptomatic that Shils simply announced that he did not follow Mannheim's conception of ideology; he did not think it necessary to give any reason.

The praise of pragmatic over ideological politics, produced by a conjunction of political and academic trends, together with this distinction between categories of politics, would seem not to have been without political consequences. In part, the revolts of academic youth in the 1960s may have been a reaction against the vulgarized self-presentation of the 'system' as non-ideological in the sense of having little, if anything, to do with the realization of values but only with the adjustment of material interests. The moral devaluation of politics attendant upon its putative divorce from ideology probably helped to clear the way for the revaluation of old extremist and purposefully divisive ideologies. It is certainly an irony of fate, though quite understandable, that the crude elitism and disdain for normative political theory which accompanied much of behavioural research and teaching should have eventually driven militant students to turn for idealistic inspiration to varieties of traditional leftist radicalism rooted in the teachings of historical materialism.

Actually, there were opponents and a few proponents of the end-of-ideology thesis who discerned, or even foresaw, such a development, which they, of course, evaluated differently. Already in 1955, when the end of the age of ideologies was ushered in, Shils had warned that to reject ideology without examining 'how and in what measure grandiose visions and austere standards have their place' will 'only rehabilitate the need for ideology; it will creep in through the back door, or more particularly, through a rebellious younger generation'.[92] Five years later, Mills welcomed what had been the object of Shils's apprehensions and claimed that all over the world young intellectuals were getting fed up with the situation, thereby proving that they were the new historic agency of structural change.[93]

It is not the least characteristic fact among the variety of vicissitudes and vagaries I have been discussing that the political and academic confrontation of pragmatic and ideological politics should have proceeded without much heed being taken on any side of Shils's and, eventually, also Aron's insistence that each society needs a certain amount of vision or ideals – though not too much. The plea was repeated by Daniel Bell. Instead of ideology, the 'irretrievably fallen word', he urged, very much like Mannheim, that we should keep ideals and utopia alive.[94] He added that in broaching their realization, we combine passion with intelligence and with a sober assessment of the relation between means and ends. Bell's use of the terms 'ideology' and 'utopia' was typical of the unexplained inversion of meanings which had occurred. Ideology had become the epitome of millenarian extremism and utopia signified an idealism tamed by awareness of what the realization of ideals was to cost and whom it was going to benefit and whom to hurt. If it was characteristic that such pleas for the indispensable role of ideals in politics failed to leave much of a mark, it was also typical that an otherwise thoughtful critic tried to dispose of Bell's demand for social cost-benefit calculation by accusing him of failing to live up to his own rule 'to think in terms of degree' (which I think is precisely what Bell was doing) because the demand, if taken seriously, was of such a 'magnitude and complexity' as to 'paralyze thought'.[95] Thus, the confluence of post-war political and academic trends gave rise to a new overstated and under-demonstrated restrictive conception of ideology whose advocates almost totally neglected previous conceptions and what could be learned from them.

It is hoped that the critical survey proffered in the two preceding chapters bears witness to the need for a conception of ideology which permits us to relate ideology without contradictions to politics or, what is the same thing, to reassess the relationship between ideology and politics without doing violence to logic and facts. To elaborate the case of the inclusive definition for this purpose is, therefore, not merely a matter of setting the record straight but, above all, of defending, like Naess, a definition which, in accord with the objectives of scientific endeavour, is suitable for the ordering of data and the formulation of confirmable hypotheses.[96] And this is a matter of laying bare the structure which political belief systems, as we know them, have in common and the ways in which they are used.

Indeed, neither the fact that in the wake of the post-war *malaise* the new restrictive definition of ideology gained ascendancy, nor my remarks on the political consequences of the restrictive conception, should create the impression that anything specific which has happened during the last decade and a half makes the restriction of 'ideology' to extremist belief systems untenable. Rather, it was a mistake from the outset, as the title and subtitle of Daniel Bell's book already indicate, to confuse 'the exhaustion of political ideas' with 'the end of ideology' and to assume that a distinction between ideological and non-ideological politics was required to mark the difference between politics aiming at total change and politics defending piecemeal change of the *status quo*. This was mistaken precisely if we take as our cue the attitude toward change.

Part Two

THE CASE FOR THE INCLUSIVE CONCEPTION

Chapter III

BASIC LINKAGES

1. THE ATTITUDE TOWARDS CHANGE – A SITUATIONAL CRITERION

In the justification of the restrictive conception of ideology, the attitude towards change has been shown to figure as the most important mark of distinction between ideological and unideological politics. We may begin, therefore, by observing why this criterion is unsuitable for its purpose. The demonstration of this point provides sufficient ground for elaborating on the main general characteristics of all political *qua* ideological belief systems and for establishing the criterion according to which their structure must be conceived.

All political and social conflict centres around change and we cannot distinguish consistently between the effect of positive action and its omission,[1] nor between what it takes to avert change and what it takes to bring it about. Both opposition to change and commitment to gradualism may require means similar to those envisaged in radical and revolutionary politics, if for no other reason than to defeat the latter. We bear the same responsibility in either of these cases, and in each public justification is attempted. Inaction, too, may be used to achieve a definite purpose. Like positive action, it can serve to stultify other people and render them inactive. As Montesquieu explained, the right of the King of England to prevent legislation by withholding his consent gives him the same powers as the right to approve would give him: '. . . le droit d'approuver n'est autre chose qu'une déclaration qu'il ne fait point d'usage de sa faculté d'empêcher, et dérive de cette faculté'.[2] Furthermore, whether we want change or wish to prevent it, in either case beliefs are involved: belief in a world as it should and could be, and the resulting beliefs that guide action or motivate inaction. With each set of beliefs goes the use of all the paraphernalia of the game of politics. As that which guides and defends political action, ideology must therefore be defined so as to refer to political belief systems, whether they are revolutionary, reformist or conservative (traditionalist) in outlook.[3]

A special word about conservatism is in order here. Huntington has argued that, unlike liberalism, democracy, communism and fascism, but like radicalism, the word 'conservatism' does not convey how a society should be organized. Even though conservatism means 'the articulate, systematic, theoretical resistance to change', in different concrete cases, conservatism amounts to defending different political systems. For Huntington, then, Burke was a most consistent conservative when he defended the *status quo* in England, France and India, despite their different political systems.[4] Of course, it is also true that, as Huntington stresses, each ideology turns conservative once its defenders consider it sufficiently realized. It is not less true, however, that conservatism does not necessarily mean even the defence of an existing order. Both historical and contemporary data confirm that conservative politicians can be alienated from a given *status quo* and adopt a commitment to change a society in the image of its past.[5] Evidently, the difference between a conservative and a progressive commitment to change lies in the nature of the change which is sought, that is in the contents of ideals. And, in respect of their contents, conservative and radical ideals, notwithstanding their different complexions in different countries, reveal both in Europe and beyond some basic similarities in nature and development, especially since the French Revolution. Indeed, one needs only to specify the time and context in relation to which the words 'conservative' or 'radical' are used in order to know exactly what kind of society is being defended or which restorative or innovating change is envisaged. In each case valuations are involved which add up to faith in an ideal order that embodies the ways in which things ought to be done. So, contrary to Huntington's view, conservatism contains an 'ought' demand reflecting an 'ideational' and not merely a 'positional' belief. Hegel's political philosophy certainly proves that an 'ideational' theory can be satisfactorily used for the defence of established institutions. With Plato in mind one must also disagree with the statement that no conservative utopia has ever been described by a political philosopher.[6]

Still, the notion of 'positional' belief remains pertinent, not because it is an alternative to 'ideational' belief but inasmuch as it can be elaborated to show that no ideology should be classified by its contents alone as extremist, moderate or conservative – epithets which depend on the given situation. If at some point the neo-liberal establishment must become conservative in order to safeguard its values,[7] the same applies also to communist and fascist regimes. In the latter, liberalism represents a more extreme ideology than either communism or fascism since its realization would radically transform the communist and fascist *status quo*. On this score, too, falters the supposedly neat distinction of the adherents of the restrictive conception between Marxism and fascism on the one hand as typical radical belief systems and hence ideologies, and liberalism on the other hand as moderate and hence as non-ideological or less ideological than either of the others. All three do what an ideology does. They posit and justify a distinct conception of society and they lay down the ways and means to establish and maintain it through a specific political system. Any one of these three can take the place of any other as either a conservative or radical ideology. For the distance between the vision and reality is the measure of extremism and radicalism. In other words, and as commonly understood, extreme and radical ideas are those which affirm that which as yet does not exist, or exists at best only rudimentarily in a society, and oppose the maintenance of an existing order or those of its traits which denote its nature more than any others.

Judged by this criterion of radicalism, Marxism and fascism outdistance liberalism in the West. But the reverse is true by now in Eastern Europe and China, as it is in countries with relatively long-established fascist, proto-fascist and other *de facto* one-party systems. After two generations of communist rule in Russia – and after even a much shorter time in the rest of Eastern Europe – the pressure for change is in the direction of liberal aspirations. The conservative tendency is thus reflected there in the defence of revolutionary communism, just as it is reflected in the defence of fascism in Spain or of neo-liberalism in America. The possible revolutionary and extremist role of liberalism is further highlighted if one recalls that, with the exception of Czechoslovakia, no communist country has ever experienced a fully developed, stable, liberal democracy. This applies also to present-day fascist Spain, pre-war fascist Italy and Germany, and the illiberal one-party systems in the developing countries. In these countries, then, justification of liberal democracy over and against the authoritarian rein on freedom of political organization and expression represents the more radical ideology.

In some developing countries the goals of Marxism and liberalism are almost equally far removed from the situation obtaining today.[8] Liberalism is there even more radical than Marxism whether, as African leaders claim, the traditional basis of their societies is some form of communal ownership or whether, as anthropologists object, pre-colonial ownership of land by kinsmen coexisted with individual rights over that land.[9] In these conditions, the Marxist plea for the collective ownership of the means of production is nearer to reality than a liberal structure in which individualist-competitive norms are pervasive.[10] Marx and Engels would probably not have subscribed to the conclusion that in such cases liberalism qualifies as the more radical ideal than communism. They had at first agreed with Narodnik socialism that a direct passage from primitive, collective, communal property to the highest communist form of landed property was possible in Russia. Later, however, they thought that the avoidance of 'all the fatal vicissitudes of a capitalist regime' depended on a successful revolution in the West which would provide a model communist village agriculture that could be emulated in a backward country.[11]

Thus, without altering its salient content, each political belief system can be conservative, moderate or radical, according to whether it underlies the prevailing political culture, whether it is intended to change that culture, or to replace it by the one superseded by the existing political culture, or whether the belief system aspires to establishing a political culture which in its entirety is unprecedented in a given country or area.

My argument against a non-contextual appraisal of ideologies as extremist, moderate or conservative is in no way intended to deny the validity and usefulness of the Left-Right continuum for the ranking of political parties, nor their re-ranking in the wake of ideological change, as I shall show in Chapter VII.[12] My intention here has been merely to demonstrate that ideologies which in virtue of their contents can be placed at the extremes or the centre of the Left-Right divide, do not thereby necessarily qualify as extremist, moderate or conservative, but that these three characteristics merely circumscribe the degree of affirmation or negation of any *status quo,* and, therefore, serve on their part to classify ideologies on a continuum in a given situational context. And this continuum is not necessarily identical with the traditional Left-Right continuum. In regard to these two continua only 'conservative' causes a semantic difficulty, since it serves to designate position both in regard to change and in regard to the overall specific contents which the traditional Left-Right continuum reflects. Still, despite the fact that the same beliefs qualify as conservatism in one context and as extremism in another (and 'context' relates to different political cultures as well as to different situations in the same political culture), it does not follow that in any concrete case conservatism or radicalism are merely 'positional' as distinct from 'ideational' ideologies. It merely follows that, in different circumstances, the same or similar ideational right, left and centre positions can favour or oppose change, while politics in either of the two directions may require the same means, including revolutionary action. Depending on the nature of the existing order, either a classless (extreme leftist) or a pluralistic (centre, left- or right-of-centre) society may be the objective of a revolution or a counter-revolution, of the politics to defend or to attack the *status quo*.

The distinction between what is moderate or radical within a given political culture cannot be buttressed on, and reference to the situational context cannot, therefore, be evaded by, associating a certain mode of argumentation with a certain category of goals or intentions. It is simply wrong to postulate that the promotion of 'aggressive' (i.e. radical) intentions requires greater justification and rationalization than the support of 'benevolent' intentions.[13] Apart from the fact that quite often aggressive intentions are claimed to serve a benevolent purpose, it is far from self-evident that to ward off aggressive intentions requires less justification and rationalization than to promote them. Supposing that only benevolence towards a given order is meant, the success of the aggressive intentions of the Nazis in destroying the Weimar Republic would not seem to have been due to the greater justification and rationalization mustered by the Nazis, if we do not identify 'rationalizations' with Pareto's 'derivations', i.e. rationalizations of illogical behaviour. The victory of the Nazis might be attributed to a combination of causes among which insufficient political acumen and toughness on the part of both German and non-German democratic politicians (statesmen is not the right word here) were probably the most decisive. The assertion that the necessity of defending one's position (which is to offer justification and rationalization) arises more often at the extremes than in the centre, and that to be an extremist one must be more 'thoughtful',[14] is not supported by historical and other empirical observation. According to what sensible connotation of the word can we say that the attacks of Nazis and Communists on the Weimar Republic were more 'thoughtful' (and what evidence shows that they were more frequent?) than the defence put up by its supporters? If 'thoughtful' (like rationalization) is taken to mean also an intellectually impressive standard, then less extreme and highly subtle right-wing detractors of democracy and liberalism, like the distinguished historian Friedrich Meinecke, have certainly achieved a standard of 'thoughtfulness' which can hold its own against anything coming from the extreme right or left. Common-sense observation, unlikely to be refuted by statistical evidence, would also seem to indicate that latter-day extremist opposition to 'the system' does not surpass the frequency and 'thoughtfulness' of the defence available to it.

Actually, there does exist one similarity in the mode of political argumentation which I have already indicated at the beginning of Chapter I and which reflects at least one identical level of thoughtfulness – or lack of it. Adherents of Marxism, liberalism, conservatism and fascism tend to consider all these 'isms', except their own, as ideologies. The exemption which a considerable number of political scientists and theorists have come to demand for the pragmatic and liberal approach – and in England also for conservatism – was claimed for their respective systems by Marx as well as by Hitler. And this is in accord with the habit of intellectuals and scholars who apply the concept pejoratively to the approaches of colleagues with whom they disagree.[15]

2. GENERAL CRITERIA

a. *Coherence and Correspondence*

If ideology is involved in whatever attitude towards change guides action, it does not in principle matter whether the belief systems are those of tribal, developing or developed societies. As presuppositions and qualifications the following are demanded: first, the phenomenological frame of reference becomes unduly widened for purposes of classification and verification if each and every belief system is regarded as an ideology, rather than only those which directly guide organized social action or analyse it for the sake of guiding it.[16] Second, in political theory and political science, the main concern does not lie with the isolated ideological statement and its distinction from a statement of testable facts.[17] In political life, the interest of single statements derives from their being part of a system of beliefs. Third, the term 'system' may be applied, at one end of a continuum, to the beliefs of tribal societies and, in post-tribal societies, to the apparently loose contexts in which men place information and invest it with meaning,[18] and at the other end, to the set of beliefs of major opinion and/or party leaders.

Whether the ultimate point of reference of a party ideology is a philosopher-ideologue like Marx, or whether ideologies are buttressed in a much less coordinated way by the teachings of a number of political philosophers, or whether the ideologies take their cue from religious authority, as an action-oriented set of beliefs, ideologies form a belief 'system' in the sense that in a post-tribal culture those who create, mould and maintain a belief system do so with a view to presenting a more or less coherent, rationally defensible configuration of ideas.[19] Different standards of justification and rationalization do not distinguish from each other, as I have previously argued, extremist and moderate or aggressive and benevolent beliefs; but self-consciously rational justification constitutes as such a difference between cultures in which belief systems are merely practised and cultures in which these systems also have to be defended on more or less rational grounds against competitors from without or dissenters from within. Despite the absence of such a defence, a 'rationality of purpose' (Weber's *Zweckrationalität*) is inherent in merely practised beliefs, which form a 'system' to the extent that they contribute significantly to the cohesion of a social entity. Hence a belief system is present, even if it is not self-consciously appraised in terms of logical defensibility by those who live by it. The system of socially important beliefs that is merely practised, even if the believers are aware of its usefulness, and the leaders manipulate it to serve their interests (as in tribal societies),[20] stands in the same relation to ideology as religion to theology. Where there is religion and no theology, the belief system is made known in order to be practised; the practices are left unexplained beyond their immediate significance and purpose. Theology adds self-consciously rational argument to sustain the beliefs and rituals as a system. As a result, ground is provided for clashes between rationalist and religious commitment.

Here is a further point of propinquity between theology and ideology, since for both rationality has been a prop and a burden, just as both have been a threat to genuine rationalism. On the one hand, we see conflicts between the rationalist and the Protestant traditions,[21] despite the relative congeniality between them. Not for nothing did theocrats like de Maistre and de Bonald consider Protestantism as the progenitor of the rationalism which begat the Revolution. On the other hand, there are the frequent agreements between Catholicism and Bolshevism in the face of both evidence and reason on the problem of population growth.[22]

Evidently, the fact that a self-consciously rational though far from logically rigorous exposition characterizes post-tribal or, broadly speaking, 'post-traditional'[23] belief systems neither makes all doctrines rationalistic in their specific content nor pre-empts a distinction between more rationalistic and more empirical belief systems and ways of believing, or between both on the one hand and more emotional and mystical ones on the other. Indeed, in a culture where resort is taken to self-consciously rational justification of at least some beliefs, even belief systems which are anti-rationalistic in their orientation, like those of the French theocrats and German romanticists and Nazis, must be presented with at least a minimum of rational coherence in order to be intelligible. In this context, Novalis's plea for new hieroglyphs to express the truly and fully romantic creed attests strikingly the awareness of a connection, besides the distinction, between form and content. It attests the fact that to dispense with rational presentation altogether or to reduce it to its barest formal and secretive minimum confines communication to a limited and enchanted circle. However, in the sets of political ideas as they are shaped by political thinkers and subsequently handled by those responsible for the politics of an organized action-unit, particularly of parties or of groups within them, the political belief 'systems' summarized under names like democracy, socialism, liberalism, conservatism, fascism and combinations of some of their elements are consciously assimilated, propagated and shaped in order to pursue through concerted action certain social, economic and political aims. Ideologies serve political groups, just as political groups serve ideologies, and this interplay determines the character of the doctrine, as a 'system'. Thus, in national parties, in situational or positional contexts, as for instance in backbench groups, a belief 'system' fulfils an integrating function to the same extent as the group's activity gives these beliefs some coherence.[24] A set of propositions more or less consistently held by a group may, as in the case of the Labour backbenchers observed by the Keele group of scholars, represent the core of the otherwise more diffuse Left, and yet it may reflect at the same time a mitigated version of the universalistic body of socialist doctrine embodied in the party's statutes in general or expressed on its behalf in more or less representative expositions of party philosophers.

The connection of the components of such group beliefs in a reasonably logical fashion does not prevent the presence in the belief system of logically conflicting constituents or of 'detachable elements' that might as well form part of another system.[25] Indeed, these last two may often be a necessary part of the ideology.[26] Quite apart from the fact that even in their purest form ideologies exhibit ideological pluralism, that is, contain identical assessments of facts and some identical elements of belief and disbelief, the support of a wide range of interest groups and groups holding variously mixed aggregates of beliefs must be gained in order to ensure electoral success. Thus, from the outset, the formation of doctrines that go together with the formation of parties requires adjustments between the beliefs of constituent members or groups, as Marx himself had occasion to experience and to curse. Once party and doctrine are formed, the process of accommodation goes on in a never-ceasing process though not in an equal rhythm.

All ideologies are, then, neither paradigms of logical argumentation nor entirely illogical structures. They are 'systems', inasmuch as certain values, factual assessments and commitments to ends and means are deliberately fused in order to ensure that through concerted action certain forms of social organization will be defended, abolished, reconstructed or modified. Hence, in so far as politics implies the pursuit of policy – i.e. a somehow interconnected sequence of projects of action – there is no politics without ideology. This, I argue, must be so because there are no policies which are conceived and executed without some relation to ideals that embody moral judgments in favour of the justification, emendation or condemnation of a given order. Rational justifications touch at some point or other on such judgments. As the defence of any of the major 'isms' demonstrates, these justifications and judgments account for their 'boundedness',[27] as well as for their inner 'constraint' or 'functional interdependence',[28] or what simply might be called 'relative coherence'. Now, even a moderately rational explanation of any aspect of a political belief system, including moral justifications, requires reference to a minimum of generally known facts and verifiable statements about facts, for otherwise no ideological argument makes sense. Logical coherence between statements cannot be achieved with complete disregard of the correspondence between statements and facts.[29]

b. *The Conception of Structure*

Factual assessments and commitments of both a moral and technical-cum-prudential nature to ends and means joined together in any political argument, and particularly in the clusters of argument that form a political belief system, constitute what I suggest may be called their structure of formal content. In other words, the structure of a political belief system is conceived in regard to the kinds of statement – e.g. prescriptive and others – that are used in any political argument or belief system, whatever their specific content.

To the extent that this structure can be said to be the same in all political belief systems, however different their specific contents, a principal foundation is laid for the disproof of the restrictive conception of ideology and for proof of the inclusive conception. To abstract entirely from specific content in the conception of structure (but not in the justification of that conception) is all the more arguable since radical change, for instance, which in the definitions of a restrictive conception has served scholars as the major characteristic subsuming specific content, has been shown to be far from an unequivocal criterion of distinction. If, despite different specific contents, political belief systems can occupy each other's place in respect of the attitude towards change, that is if a political belief system retains its salient specific contents irrespective of whether in accordance with the situational context its overall orientation becomes moderately or radically conservative or transformative, it is not unreasonable to suggest that each political belief system exhibits an identical structure of formal content which underlies, and therefore must be borne out by, the specific contents advanced in any politically relevant belief system in any situation.

To proceed, like Sartori, from 'structural elements bearing on *how* one believes'[30] is no alternative to conceiving structure in terms of the kinds of statement that go into arguments put forward in political belief systems. In the first place, the answer to the question 'how one believes' does not provide any clue for discerning what is peculiar to two different categories of political doctrines, since their specific contents defy differentiation by Sartori's structural criteria.[31] What is more, quite apart from the fact that his two cognitive approaches, 'rationalistic' and 'empirical' processing-coding, involve the use of the same kinds of statement – description, analysis, moral and technical prescriptions (i.e. the same structure of formal content) – Sartori cannot confine himself to the question on which his two approaches and their structural elements are said to bear. He inadvertently treats the 'how one believes' as if it were determined by and subject to the same criteria as 'what' is believed. Rokeach, on whom Sartori professes to rely, really confines himself to the question 'How one relates to authority' and he therefore uses the question or criterion clearly and consistently in order to reveal 'similarities among *persons* in their orientation to authority even though they may adhere to different ones [i.e. authorities]'.[32] Sartori, however, associates 'openness' and 'closedness' with different categories of doctrines and in the process subsumes alike under 'ideological mentality' what pertains to personal belief systems and to doctrines. Thus not only are the structural elements which he relates in an undifferentiated manner to general doctrines and personal attitudes as much philosophical (or epistemological) as they are psychological,[33] but his use of 'ideological mentality' for both personality and cultural traits, and the explicit assumption of their confluence,[34] lead Sartori eventually to attribute, at least by implication, a specific mentality to 'isms'. The conflation hardly speaks in favour of Sartori's conception of the structure of belief systems.

However we look at mentality, it is obvious that there are quantitative and qualitative differences between the beliefs of an individual and of a group. Not all the beliefs entertained by individuals form part of the beliefs individuals embrace as members of a group. The beliefs of groups, includings the great 'isms', are in many, if not in most cases less comprehensive than the beliefs of individuals.[35] Conversely, not every element of a doctrine that unites members of a group necessarily finds a place among their personal beliefs. The sum total of the beliefs of an individual and the beliefs characteristic of his group, and particularly the ways in which individuals and groups behave and act consciously and unconsciously in accordance with certain beliefs and standards, may be said to reflect their respective mentality. Yet, when speaking of a group mentality, one is never far from using a figure of speech. There is at the very least this difference between the mentality of a group and that of an individual: the former exists only intermittently, that is only when individuals adopt certain attitudes and engage in certain actions as members of a group, which obviously no one does all the time, and which the majority of the supporters of a political party rarely do at any time.

For these and other psychological reasons, the mentalities of persons and of groups may be related to each other, but may not be treated as if they were identical. Moreover, whatever the mentalities of individuals and of groups have in common, and notwithstanding the varied degree to which personal belief systems and political belief systems may overlap, it remains a hypostatization to designate the doctrines adopted by a group as a mentality. To be created or adopted, a specific doctrine may – or may not – require specific mentality traits. Or, what is more likely, acculturation to an 'ism' may produce, like education in other fields, a certain outlook or even mentality traits. Yet only in regard to the individual personality system can one say that a certain mentality 'qualifies an ideological structure of belief in its difference from a pragmatic structure'.[36] Otherwise, one is saying that doctrines such as liberalism, populism or democratic socialism are characterized by, or quite simply possess, a mentality. This obviously does not make sense and hence is no proper foundation for conceiving the structure of political belief systems. In addition, Sartori's criteria of 'how one believes' anyway serve his attempt (and bear its imprint) to distinguish between two categories of doctrines, and therefore invite reference to 'what' is believed, i.e. to the content of doctrines. Not only does Sartori's approach to structure fail to be what it is said to be, but the distinction between rationalistic and empirical belief systems according to the structural criteria suggested by him is not substantiated by the specific content of belief systems,[37] as all structural characteristics attributed to them must be.

3. THE IDEOLOGICAL COMPOSITE

a. *The Components and their Configuration*

As the analysis of any sustained political argument and of any politically relevant belief system will show, they are composed of statements or propositions concerning description, analysis, moral prescriptions, technical prescriptions, implements and rejections. While reference to some of these structural components has been made already in the preceding discussion of what renders an ideology a relatively coherent belief 'system', it will be noted that these components do not include rational justification or even action-orientation, which in the last resort determine the nature of the ideological composite as a 'system'. The same is true of other modes in which the ideological composite is presented and activated. Systemic and general functional characteristics require the structure of formal content in that they are made possible by it, but they are not part of it. This point will become clear after we account for the various structural components in view of their interdependence within and relatedness to the ideological composite both as a whole and in its relation to other such composites. This perspective determines the sequence and contexts in which the components will be discussed.

If the ideological composite is conceived as a relatively coherent and never entirely non-factual and non-empirical configuration of thought and speech used for concerted social action, the notion that politics and ideology are inextricably tied to each other does not entail the conclusion that ideologically pure politics exists. From the outset, ideologies are asymmetric structures and some of their principles and assessments are advanced by more than one ideology.[38] In practical politics, too, principles and judgments prevail which are justifiable by more than one ideology. As a result, party politics do not become unideological or less ideological but more multi-ideological.

Overlapping of ideologies is inevitable on both the theoretical and the practical levels because belief in different values or different admixtures of values admits of the use of similar means. In fact, the management of any polity demands adherence to some identical principles of organization. That is why we find laws, taxes, the machinery of law enforcement and defence in all regimes and their equivalent in 'stateless societies'.[39] Or, irrespective of the diverging fundamental ideological principles on which an industrial economy is based, production by machines coincides in its management with bureaucratization on the basis of the local concentration of processes of production and working discipline.[40] It follows that, if ways and means of organization denote the implements of the ideological structure, as an action-oriented system of thought, some of these implements for coping with basic social needs are ideologically neutral, in so far as any ideology has to care for those needs and cannot do so in greatly diverse ways. The justification of such implements, therefore, is largely based on the relatively objective description and analysis of needs and circumstances.

However, many of the ubiquitous organizational means are neutral only in a purely formal sense. For instance, just as conservatism as such means resistance to change (or its abolition), law as such provides the ground for exercising sanctions. But only in respect of the socio-political nature of the regime which conservatives wish to maintain unchanged or to restore, and only by virtue of the content of the laws, do both conservatism and laws become specific and as a result expressive of a distinct ideological orientation, or at least conducive (though at times also counter-productive) to its maintenance. True, laws regulating traffic, weights, measures, etc. are ideologically neutral; but they may cease to be so when the question of their change arises. There are other laws and certain institutions – especially bureaucratic and military organizations[41] – which turn out greatly alike in different regimes or about which ideologies are less divided than they might pretend to be, if they pretend at all. But at some point such laws and the functioning of organization reflect the specific value-judgments of political belief systems, or compromises over them. This can be seen in legislation concerning education, inheritance, marriage and divorce as well as criminal offences. Legislation which most clearly reflects fundamental value-orientation is normally considered crucially important because it also bears on many of the other legislative acts, such as laws or constitutional provisions that either guarantee, abolish or limit property rights, personal liberties, the right of association, political pluralism, effective constitutional checks and balances, and so on.

Strictly speaking, politics can become entirely unideological only if they become completely incoherent. And if complete incoherence endures for any length of time in the politics of a party or the polity, neither is likely to subsist. Since such incoherence in party and/or national politics is extremely unlikely, politics will remain ideological. This will be so whether or not agreement exists that we live in the best of all possible worlds or as to what such a world should and could be like. In either case, coherence and with it its ideological character accrue to politics from the generally observable fact that patterns of decision about policies are the result of ends-means calculations in terms both of norms of justice, the public good and so forth, and of norms of expediency, prudence and efficiency. In ideologies, both kinds of 'ought'[42] tend to take on the form of prescriptions. The latter kind, here briefly called technical prescriptions, are more or less directly derived from facts, i.e. from their descriptive and classificatory as well as from their analytical and causal perception and presentation. Moral norms and prescriptions are also predicated on the description and analysis of facts, but they present a value judgment on them which may run counter to and prevail over the technical norms. It should be noted that the avoidance of the naturalistic fallacy of deriving values from facts does not presuppose that judgments of value and statements of facts are unrelated to each other. Moral norms and prescriptions are conditioned by the factual world inasmuch as they are 'provoked' by it and intended to contribute towards its ordering, serving to stigmatize, repress, recommend and protect given forms of behaviour, i.e. social facts. These also provide the testing ground for the effectiveness, usefulness and appositeness of moral norms and prescriptions. Even without subscribing to moral relativism, it does not follow that, because what is maintained to be morally correct is not necessarily so in virtue of its being effective and useful, what is moral needs to be opposed to effectiveness and usefulness. If that were the case, morality might never have gained much currency among men.

To neutralize the ideological elements in the scholar's interpretation of politics and thereby clear the way for the production of responsible ideology, one must distinguish tested and testable empirical claims from claims that are neither. To spot them and where possible to replace them by tested propositions is certainly an important assignment. Untested or untestable empirical claims do not alone protect 'the higher level commitments' of their supporters in problematical situations.[43] No doubt tested and testable empirical claims also play such a protective role, a protection needed not only in problematical situations. The extent to which a situation is unproblematical, i.e. relatively stable, is obviously a function of the extent to which the dominant 'higher level commitments' are well protected. Likewise, it is by no means self-evident that political programmes of action are more necessary in times of crisis[44] than in ensuring the stability of settled political orders. The trite and certainly verifiable truth is that within the life-span of any government problematical situations will determine the core of its activities, and that settled conditions will give way to unsettled conditions as the result of drifting along.

Ideology is present wherever policy-making is present, and policy-making is the attempt to solve problems – or sidetrack them. However embarrassing the 'higher level commitments' may become to the policy-makers, empirical claims (whether or not they have been tested and are testable or not) do not have the sole function of protecting promulgated commitments. Empirical claims derived from accurate description and unbiased analysis of situations play a role in the conception of commitments in the first place, and serve also as the criteria for the ways and means of implementing commitments and adapting them to the requirements of the moment – or as excuses for shortcomings and compromises in this respect. The debate over which decisions can be justified by what kind of principles and evidence, and how to mobilize support for various standpoints, is the essence of politics. Where politics are publicly competitive, such debate and the decisions finally adopted are the essence of the 'democratic translation of the class struggle',[45] that is, of 'politics' in Bernard Crick's sense (considered, though, as one form of ideological politics). Yet where the class struggle in its 'higher' form excludes 'antagonistic' debate in public, the willingness to seek and reach open or secret compromises and to impose decisions, however arrived at, is also defended by the party in power by invoking, on the one hand, the moral norms and organizational implements prescribed by the ideology and, on the other, the technical norms which rest primarily on the description and analysis of the given situation and its possibilities.

The components of ideology discussed so far require one further addition to complete the make-up or structure of the formal content of ideologies. Essential fundamentals of one ideology are contested by the proponents of other ideologies, so that Rokeach has suggested making specific allowance for disbeliefs in belief systems.[46] He calls them in effect belief-disbelief systems. In a sense 'disbelief' is covered by belief, since belief includes what one thinks to be both true and false. But it is not only Rokeach's research objectives that amply justify the usefulness of dealing with disbeliefs as a category apart. What in belief systems is positively affirmed does not necessarily reflect (or evoke) stronger convictions, nor is it always better founded on logic and fact, than what it negates in other ideologies. In the personality system, rejections might be more important than acceptance; they might be the reason for accepting certain standpoints or attitudes. In the ideologies espoused by political parties and movements, the hues and emphases of certain principles of belief, or even some basic principles themselves, might be determined by the rejection of other principles, e.g. social democratic constitutionalism by the rejection of communist dictatorship, or the division of powers by the rejection of the divine right of kings. In the comparative analysis of party ideologies, disbeliefs or rejections of principles and valuations are certainly not less important for assessing what ideologies have in common than are affirmations of principles and valuations. It is, after all, of eminently practical significance that communism and fascism share, for instance, the rejection of liberal individualism and parliamentary democracy.

We are now in a position to summarize and present in a kind of 'facet' the interacting components of an ideology.

D (description)
A (analysis)
Pm (moral prescriptions)[47]
Pt (technical prescriptions)
I (implements, i.e. the ways and means of implementation)
R (rejections)[48]

The order in which the components are listed suggests that one first notices and describes phenomena, then analyses them and finally decides according to moral norms and in view of the technical possibilities what to do about them and what not to do. In real life things are, of course, much more complex; indeed, they are too complex to be formally determined.[49] Analysis and description, no less than the choice between technical possibilities, may be prejudged by moral commitments. Yet, whether or not moral commitment has such a 'falsifying' influence (since it is not necessarily cut off from factual analysis and description), it must be accorded a good measure of centrality. To illustrate this centrality, and to indicate that the order in which one proceeds from one component or group of components to another varies, we may arrange the components in a circle round the element of moral prescription (Figure 1).

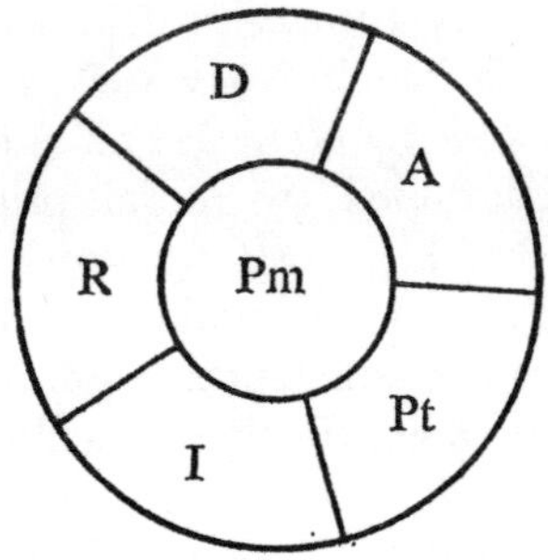

Figure 1

It will be noted that the components of this configuration are strictly confined to what I have defined, at the beginning of this section, as formal content. They do not include, therefore, rational presentation and justification or logical coherence, which are the main overall characteristics that distinguish ideology from merely practised belief systems. Action-orientation and emotive appeal have likewise been excluded since, like logical coherence, they do not constitute but presuppose the components of formal content. In other words, because they are action-oriented, ideologies have this structure of formal content, and because ideologies have this structure they can be more or less coherent action-oriented belief systems and invested in varying degrees with emotive appeal. Nor have 'factual statements' been listed as a component because they are assumed to form the subject-matter, and hence to be 'represented' by description and analysis. While the latter are not necessarily untarnished by value judgments, no component is by definition precluded from being related to statements of fact.

Thus the forms in which the configuration of formal content, as it were, permits itself to be used are rooted in its components, just as the forms of their activation determine their nature.[50] All components require for their presentation regard for logical coherence and facts, but rejections, for instance, and, above all, moral prescriptions, lend themselves more readily to emotive appeal than others. True, cognition and affect can vary independently in respect of mass phenomena,[51] and indeed generally in individual and social action. Still, emotive appeal and interpretation could not come to the fore in political debate as much as they do if such debate turned only on descriptive, analytical and technically prescriptive arguments. Although analyses and descriptions, not to mention implements and technical prescriptions, can be presented in wildly emotive terms, there is a limit to the extent to which one can wax enthusiastic over them for their own sake, let alone arouse public enthusiasm on their behalf. Conversely, while rational interpretation and regard for facts are by no means an impediment to the parts of political argument determined by moral principles, rejections and implements, these do furnish the better grounds of emotive appeals and judgments. There is, then, no hard and fast division here. All I wish to argue is that, like systemic coherence, cognitive approaches and the more or less affective or non-affective appeals and interpretations do have a basis in the various components of the structure of formal content, while the latter is the matrix or basic frame of reference for all the characteristics of the ideological composite.

We must now consider how deviations from and consequently tensions between the components of specific content affect the structure of formal content.

b. *The Bifurcation of Ideological Argumentation*

When ideology is made to fulfil its function, to guide concerted action, it is relied upon to devise and/or justify specific practical measures and to pronounce on the topical issues of day-to-day politics. In the process, both the purity and the centrality of prescriptions based on the commitment to essentially moral principles and goals are likely to become endangered by the requirements of political action. This is why political argumentation bifurcates.

All political belief systems, from political philosophy down to party ideology, contain from the outset practical considerations reflecting a preoccupation with specific secular ends-means calculations for the justification and/or attainment of immediate objectives. In such short-range calculations of a party holding power or engaging in active contest about it, the need for a more or less frank restatement of immediate goals inevitably arises. Repeating a platitude as old as politics, Lenin declared that to rule out compromise in principle is 'childishness';[52] it is, indeed, an impossibility for any political leader and movement.

In shaping specific policies in deference to prevailing circumstances, no party has ever been able to avoid committing itself to some lines of action which are irreconcilable with, or at least doubtfully related to, the basic principles and goals of its ideology. A conflict therefore ensues not simply between ideology and action but within ideology itself. Out of the interdependence between thought and action, action-oriented thought arises; and out of the permanence of the interaction, a tension evolves within action-oriented thought itself. Disinterested observers easily perceive this dissonance, and both the opponents and the die-hards of an ideology are likely to denounce a reality that its official spokesmen have eventually to acknowledge but will always try to minimize, namely that it is often impossible to invoke central principles of the 'authorized' version of the party's ideology, expounded over the years, to account for policies that are carried out or proposed. Ostrogorski's view that each party is like a Church has remained true in the sense that every party maintains a tradition of fidelity to certain principles. It is not less evident that, in accordance with overall national interests, the preservation of commitments in changing circumstances has not prevented conservatives from turning from protectionism to free trade; and socialist parties have not refrained from defending national sovereignty and protectionism while continuing to sing the 'International' and to proclaim worldwide fraternity.[53] Commitment to socialism did not prevent Lassalle from entertaining the vision of German soldiers and workers holding Eastern Europe and standing on the shores of the Bosphorus, nor did such commitment prevent the Webbs from accepting imperialism.[54]

Thus, ideology applied in action inevitably bifurcates into two dimensions of argumentation: that of fundamental principles, which determine the final goals and the grand vistas in which they will be realized, and which are set above the second dimension, that of the principles which actually underlie policies and are invoked to justify them. This second dimension of argumentation I have proposed calling operative ideology. In each, all the components of ideological thought are activated, yet with different emphases. Description, analysis, moral and technical prescription, implementation and rejection combine in any ideological argument, but the combination takes one of two particular forms that together constitute two interacting dimensions of argumentation. As against the continued assertion of principle in the dimension of fundamentals, there develops a line of argument whose purpose is to devise and justify the policies executed or recommended by a party, whether or not they deviate from the fundamentals. In the justification of policy in the operative dimension, description and analysis exert greater influence through the enhanced consideration paid to the norms of expediency, prudence and efficiency, i.e. to technical prescriptions, which share in, or even replace, the centrality accorded to moral prescriptions in fundamental ideology.

In accordance with the circular arrangement of components used earlier we can illustrate, with exaggerated neatness, the difference between the two dimensions in Figure 2.

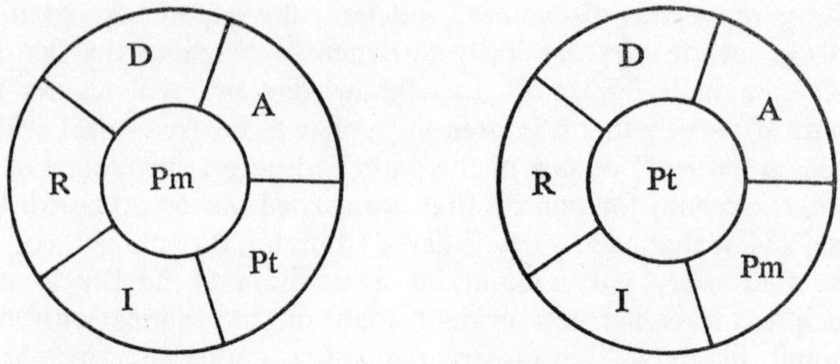

a
Fundamental dimension

b
Operative dimension

Explanation of abbreviations: D=Description, A=Analysis, Pm=Moral prescriptions, Pt=Technical prescriptions, I=Implements, R=Rejections.

Figure 2

The examination and illustration of the bifurcation of all political belief systems, the ways in which their dimensions interact and the significance of all these processes form the subject-matter of Chapters VI and VII. Here I merely wish to justify the necessity of including the phenomenon of bifurcation in the detailed definition of ideology. Even at this stage it must be made plain that the proposition of bifurcation does not simply refer to what is often called ideological double-talk, if not double-dealing. I do not deny the existence of either. But I do hold that they are only possible, and not necessary, concomitants of the inescapable bifurcation of the belief system professed by any political party. Two-dimensional argumentation does not necessarily mean double-talk, because deviation from fundamental principles or their modification is sometimes publicly acknowledged or sincerely believed to be temporary. Moreover, changes in the realization of principles may attest rather their continued pursuance by different methods, than deviation. At any rate, in any of these cases, including intentionally misleading double-talk, the relatedness of policies to basic principles is argued. This linkage is missed if, for instance, we follow Lindblom in viewing 'synoptic problem solving' and 'disjointed incrementalism' as mutually exclusive.

According to the first model of policy analysis, decision-making proceeds in accordance with what I call the fundamental dimension. This can be explained in Lindblom's terms as follows. The decision-maker offers a consistent ordering of value-related objectives in order to ensure that the choice of a solution is in conformity with these objectives. He proceeds by way of a comprehensive survey of the means suitable for the implementation of these values, examines the probable consequences, and decides on policies designed to realize the maximum of these values by which he declares himself to be guided.[55] Unlike Lindblom, I do not think that the model is entirely impractical or fully replaced by the strategy of 'disjointed incrementalism'.[56] I readily admit that 'operative ideology' quite often explains and justifies, or even covers up 'disjointed incrementalism'; but the latter is not, as I shall show later, unrelated to the fundamental principles used in attempts at 'synoptic problem-solving'. Policies which Lindblom himself adduces as examples of incrementalism show that it is by no means as 'disjointed' as he would have us believe.[57]

Just as the models which Lindblom regards as mutually exclusive assume their complementary significance in the framework of bifurcation and interaction between the two principal dimensions of action-oriented socio-political thought, so do Sartori's criteria, 'bearing on *how* one believes', reveal their real differentiating properties within that same framework. The criteria of '*rationalistic* processing-coding' (where deduction prevails over evidence, doctrine over practice, principle over precedent and ends over means, and where perceptions tend to be indirect)[58] are generally more characteristic of argumentation in terms of the fundamental than of the operative dimension. Conversely, '*empirical* processing-coding' (where evidence prevails over deduction, practice over doctrine, precedent over principle and means over ends, and where perceptions tend to be more direct) is more characteristic of the operative than of the fundamental dimension of ideological argumentation, regardless of which political belief system we consider. The divide in real life between the two kinds of processing-coding is not absolute, nor is their fusion with the two dimensions of ideological argumentation complete. Just as *all* the components of ideological argumentation are the same in the fundamental and in the operative dimensions while *some* have a different impact in each dimension, so *some* 'rationalistic' and *some* 'empirical' cognitive elements can be found to determine argument in *each* of the two dimensions. Like the components of formal content, the elements of the two sets of cognitive approaches clash and combine with one another, while some dominate more in one dimension than in the other.[59]

There is some obvious co-ordination between the constant shifts of emphasis: between the components of formal content and the not less constant shifts between 'rationalistic' and 'empiricist' cognitive postures. The postures Sartori identifies with rationalistic processing-coding are more conducive to conceiving and expressing (in either the fundamental and operative dimension) moral prescriptions, implements and rejections than description, analysis and technical prescriptions, which are more naturally conceived and conveyed through the cognitive postures associated with empirical processing-coding.

It remains to be added that the relative prevalence of '*empirical* processing-coding' in the operative dimension and the corresponding relative prominence of analysis, description and technical prescription do not necessarily entail a reduction in emotive persuasion. Policy-makers sometimes decide to make concessions over some fundamental principles on the grounds of empirical inductionism (which I take to be a no less rational form of drawing conclusions than rationalistic deductionism), but do not wish to gainsay the validity of the principles in question. In such a case, either highly emotive or soberly rational language might be used to account for the deviation; it all depends on the personality of the leaders and quite a number of other variables conveniently subsumed under 'prevailing internal and external conditions'.

c. *Meta-ideological Principles and the Ideological Composite*

Since political ideologies are derived from social and political philosophies, or seek support in them, the question arises, why should we not identify the dimension of fundamentals with political philosophy? Basically, political philosophies possess the same structure of formal content as ideologies.[60] The two-dimensionality of ideological argumentation can also be found in them when, as always happens at some point or other, the political philosopher's attitude becomes directly action-oriented. Nevertheless, political philosophy should be judged to occupy a dimension altogether above ideology, a dimension which does not lack connection and similarity with ideology but which cannot replace the fundamental dimension without ceasing to be philosophy. Once again the divide is fluid – but a divide it is.

As Barry says, there are 'ultimate considerations' referring to justice and freedom which are so 'ultimate' that they cannot be associated with anybody in particular or with any policy; yet we can deal with them not abstractly but in the manner in which they 'weigh with people'.[61] Now, the manner in which 'ultimate considerations' weigh with people must be presumed to express itself in the attitude of people towards principles that have a direct bearing on politics and can be ascribed to identifiable persons and groups. Such principles of immediate political relevance are, in Barry's terms, either 'ends of a medium level of abstraction' – e.g. the maintenance of private enterprise – or 'medium-range considerations', which refer to problems like economic growth, inflation and so forth.[62] What I call fundamental ideology may thus contain 'ultimate considerations', but it consists in the main of 'ends of a medium level of abstraction', which generally follow from 'ultimate considerations' after it has been specified how the latter should 'weigh with people' in terms of specific basic orientations in politics. For I include in the dimension of fundamentals both general principles and their broad organizational-institutional specifications.

The maintenance of private property is a broad specification of the general principle, or fundamental, of individual liberty. The fundamental and the specification belong as much to political philosophy as to ideology. Yet the specification represents ideology in philosophy more than the converse, particularly if the specifications are conceived and adopted in order to guide political action and organization directly and immediately. Then they are linked to, or turned into, what Barry calls 'medium-range considerations' and I call the operative dimension of ideology. Barry's elevation of 'ultimate considerations' over 'ends of medium-level abstraction' and of these over 'medium-range considerations' helps, thus, to illustrate the distinctions and relationships among what are here called meta-ideological principles (or philosophical meta-fundamentals), fundamentals, and operative ideology. If Barry's demarcation of 'ultimate' from other considerations in effect circumscribes the domains of political philosophy and ideology respectively, one reason is that his 'ultimate considerations' represent to some extent a reformulation in terms of analytical philosophy of Jaspers's conception of *Weltanschauung*.

As Jaspers has said, 'when we speak of *Weltanschauung*, we mean ideas, what is ultimate and total in man, subjectively as experience, power and conviction as well as objectively as the tangibly formed world'. *Weltanschauung* is more than universal contemplation because it comprises impulses that affect human totality and emanate from it.[63] *Weltanschauung* has not improperly been allied with ideology, as is implied when it is defined as the reflective view of life according to which an individual behaves.[64] While the world view of ideology is primarily a framework for beliefs and insights that have immediate relevance for social and political action, these beliefs are related to *Weltanschauung*, or 'ultimate considerations', in so far as they touch also upon man's self-comprehension, his place in the world and his share in shaping it. Metaphysics, aesthetics, language, religion and the *Weltanschauung* which refers to them are not treated for their own sakes in an ideology to the same extent that they are in philosophy.

Ideology is 'an abstraction that is less abstract than the abstractions contained within it'.[65] If ideology too lays claim to ultimate norms and insights, it does so for the purpose of particularizing universal ideals for concerted action.

This view of the relationship between ideology and theorizing on a higher level is implicit in Touchard's summary (and terminologically not too felicitous) distinction between political doctrines and ideas. He defines a 'political doctrine' as 'a complete system of thought which rests on a theoretical analysis of the political datum (*fait politique*)'. Over and against doctrines which evidently stand for political philosophy and/or theory, *idées politiques* are placed in the more diversified and wider context of historical effectiveness. Like a pyramid, they contain the 'floors' of doctrine, *praxis* (in the Marxist sense), vulgarization, symbols and collective images (*représentations collectives*).[66] In view of what Touchard says about the transformation of doctrines into political ideas, their functions and forms, it does not come as a surprise that he uses the term 'ideology' two pages later as a synonym for 'political idea'.

The distinction and relationship indicated so far between philosophy and ideology gain in explicitness in Jenkins's attempt to establish a neutral but substantive concept of justice. If we posit, Jenkins argues, that justice means the creation through law of an order permitting cultivation of personality, authority, responsibility and continuity, we may consider the ideal of justice to be objectively grounded, universally relevant, and comparable to the conceptual models which scientists use to synthesize findings and direct research efforts extending into the future.[67] The ideal is action-oriented and thus necessarily related to politics, but not directly. Ideology is the intermediary required to apply the universally valid ideal to specific nations, times and places. In the process, the ideal becomes the subject of honest differences of opinion.[68] Eventually, the great ideologies claim universal applicability for their particularization of the ideal. To put it in my terms, ideologists (and not a few political theorists and scientists) confuse, if they do not deny, the difference between the spheres of philosophical and scientific meta-fundamentals and the domain of ideological fundamentals. Rendered in natural law terminology, which I have already been using and to which not only propositions of analytical philosophy are adaptable, ideologists (and some theorists) either confuse positive and natural law,[69] or claim, like Plato and Marx, to have derived the best or the only correct particularization of immutable laws of reason or history.

To insist on the distinction between meta-ideological and ideological principles is not to deny that they interact; they readily do so like the dimensions of ideology. Universally formulated insights and beliefs accepted as valid within the context of what Kuhn calls 'shared paradigms'[70] are appropriated by the ideologist. Ideals which resemble scientific models are significantly de-universalized not only by becoming embodied in the political and legal factors of a concrete order and its institutions, but even earlier, when they are adopted by a political movement fighting for their realization. We cannot assume that, once under way, this process has no repercussions on the vision, as distinct from substantive criteria of judgment, and that it can be preserved unimpaired for long in the realm of meta-ideological standards.[71] Therefore we cannot postulate with Germino an absolute distinction between 'authentic' political theory (traditional political philosophy) and ideology.[72] The difference between political philosophy and ideology stems from the fact that political philosophies, both revitalized traditional and analytical, do not serve political action directly, at any rate not nearly to the same degree as do ideologies. Their greater detachment from immediate involvement in political action provides the lever for the degree of autonomy and objectivity which can be attained by both normative political philosophy and empirical political theory. This difference of degree cannot be measured precisely; nevertheless it is demonstrably real, as a comparison even of *Kapital* and the *Manifesto* will corroborate. Ideology, as it were, transposes social and political philosophy into the key appropriate for political action and the mobilization of elite and mass support. But political philosophy no less than empirical theory can preserve its vitality only by constructing and reconstructing in the light of experience analytical and normative reality-transcending models. For political philosophy to fulfil the function of a meta-ideological discipline that not only criticizes concepts and beliefs[73] but serves as a fount of ideological fundamentals, it needs to proceed by way of a modified natural law theory which in reliance on and critique of empirical research and theory becomes increasingly refined in the formulation of norms, while at the same time it renounces the claim to their immutability.

The transposition of political philosophy into ideology is more often than not performed by party ideologues-cum-leaders, like the authors of *The Federalist*, a Kautsky or a Lenin, or by mere ideologues like Paine, Cobden and Plekhanov. At times, however, social political philosophers pursue both tasks to varying degrees, *vide* Plato, Aristotle, Locke, Mill and Marx. To some extent this is almost unavoidable in political philosophies, since hardly any political philosopher of note has refrained from formulating general propositions concerning political life with a view to the more mundane and particular exigencies of the day, or from directly taking issue with them at some stage or other of his argument. In these cases, the entanglement between fundamental and operative ideology intrudes into political philosophy. Locke's recommendation to rely on executive prerogative for the reform of the franchise led him to engage in a complicated and by no means logical attempt to reconcile this recommendation with the fundamental principles of his theory of consent.[74] Interpreters of Marx have been exercised not only over his interpretation of the 18th *Brumaire* of Louis Bonaparte and his attitude towards the Paris Commune – while it lasted, and later. Similar questioning of Marx's adherence to his fundamental principles has also arisen in view of his tactical considerations concerning organizations, like the First International, in which he himself took a leading part.[75] Indeed, difficulties of the Marxian theory of ideology itself and its post-Marxian development can be explained best in the light of the tension between adherence to fundamental principles and concessions over them in the operative dimension.[76]

If they are not purely utopian, and hopelessly dogmatic, political philosophies reveal occasional awareness of the need for temporary or permanent deviation from their envisaged organizational embodiment. At times, they indicate also that such proposed embodiment can be improved upon. If this leads to explicit reformulation and modification, or if room is left for such changes in the light of future experience, we witness one aspect of the 'openness' which Germino attributes to all 'authentic' political philosophies. Actually that openness graces only a very few of them, nor can one deny, except by discounting them as ideologies, that there are ideologies which are 'open' in this sense and leave room for the reconsideration of fundamentals. It is no accident that the most influential founding-father of modern liberalism, Locke, despite his defence of executive prerogative, pointed out that parliamentary control would be more effective if the chief executive were excluded from participation in the legislative. He indicated clearly how the division of powers he advocated in the *Second Treatise* might have to be changed if the executive should abuse its parliamentary prerogative.[77]

It appears warranted, then, to stipulate that in philosophy and scientific theory an ideal or model can be retained or reconstructed to serve as the foundation of intellectual and moral appeals against the excess and shortcomings of ideology. To be carried out, the appeal must be espoused and transposed by ideology so as to meet the requirements of action; a process more spiral than circular. It is certainly not a *circulus vitiosus,* but rather a foundation of the critique of ideology. Obviously, this foundation provided by political philosophy in general, and not merely by its narrowly limited analytical brand, cannot be effectively utilized as long as ideological argumentation itself is taken to be undifferentiated. First we must discern the distinct dimension in which policies are devised and defended, and relate it to that dimension of ideology in which the principles of the recommended order, its institutions and their purposes are laid out, and only then can we evaluate and judge an ideology in a politically relevant way in the light of philosophical ideals and scientific models which can lay some claim to a more disinterested and objective status than either of the two dimensions of ideology.

d. *The Elaborate Definition*

We are now in a position to expand the initial inclusive definition of ideology. What can now be spelled out in greater detail are, firstly the logically and empirically defensible characteristics of the ideological composite which have been and continue to be associated with the concept. In the course of our discussion those criteria of distinction have been disqualified which have proved self-defeating after being related to the content of political belief systems. Allegedly distinguishing properties have not been conceded to be such if they could be shown to apply fully or largely in the same or in different cultural contexts to all political belief systems. Secondly, and on the other hand, a specific notion of structure has been offered which can be said to be shared by all political belief systems. Furthermore, the impact made on the structure of political belief systems by their function in the political process has been demonstrated. The elaboration of the configuration or facet of the structure of formal content (Figure 1) and the repercussions of function on that structure (Figure 2) epitomize the central additions through which the more or less commonly used and the more or less formalized characteristics can be tested and shown to assume their proper significance.

In order to advance on these grounds an elaborate definition of ideology, I propose to use as a foundation the definition which Naess and his associates have offered as the result of their exhaustive classification and highly perceptive critique of the uses of the term up to the beginning of the 1950s.[78] A few exceptions, however, must be taken to their evaluation of some defining properties of ideology.

The inclusive definition developed by Naess and his associates can be summarized as follows. Ideology is a group of direct or indirect value-sentences or appeal sentences accepted by a group; these sentences, which coexist with factual statements that may even outweigh them, can be arranged and interpreted as a doctrine which is not necessarily self-consistent.[79] These terms of definition are cogent enough, but they are too confined to the structure of formal content.

First, among the characteristics of the ideological composite, action-orientation seems to be underrated. The authors find that ideology falls more under the key-term 'patterns of ideas' than under the key-term 'patterns of attitudes', and that a distinction must be drawn between static and dynamic key-terms.[80] This distinction and the closer association of ideology with ideational key-terms are problematic in so far as they tend to obscure the fact that action-orientation is no less important in the inception of ideologies than in their propagation or their translation into policies. The beliefs of a group indeed comprise, among other things, mere intentions and preferences of a moral and political nature. But this is no reason to restrict the significance of action-orientation as a criterion of ideology.[81] Here, as in Sartori's conception of the ideological 'mentality',[82] the difference between the nature and function of belief systems of persons and of groups appears to be disregarded, perhaps unintentionally. Unlike the moral and political intentions of individuals, those that are expressed on behalf of an organized group normally require some involvement in the political process, and in any event acquire their significance only in relation to action.

Second, the neutrality of a definition of ideology is not adversely affected if it is closely related to the *definiens* of either sincere or insincere evaluation, nor is neutrality endangered because a judgment regarding such evaluation would place us on the plane of theories about ideologies.[83] A definition of ideology places us on this plane anyway. Theories about ideologies can reflect both philosophical and political trends, as, for instance, the Marxian theory of ideology and the end-of-ideology debate. Theories about ideologies do not forfeit the claim to be ideology-free by checking and pronouncing upon the sincerity or insincerity of ideological evaluations, just as they are not biased because they distinguish between factual and non-factual statements in ideologies or because they reveal contradictions in them.

In all these instances, aspects of what has been acclaimed since Marx as the most characteristic trait of ideologies, namely falsification, is the object of critical examination. Hence Naess and his associates are not on safe ground in singling out the issue of sincerity as being more likely to affect adversely the neutrality of a definition of ideology than the kindred issue of objectivity. They not only quite cogently maintain that ideology and objectivity do not necessarily exclude each other,[84] but they also explicitly include in their definition the *definiens* of the admixture and, therefore, the distinction of objectivity and non-objectivity. The judgment of the sincerity or insincerity of ideological evaluations does not invite more bias, nor is it so much more difficult to perform, than the appraisal of the factuality of ideological statements. The sincerity of statements can be judged by comparing the actions which logically ought to follow from these statements with the actions which are actually contemplated and/or carried out. There is some difficulty in distinguishing insincerity from inconsistency. Yet, if intentions and preferences continue to be loudly proclaimed while opportunities for their realization are not seized, the question of insincerity clearly arises and can be objectively answered. Since action is in this and in other respects the decisive ground of verification, the suggestion of Naess and his associates not to relate the definition of ideology too closely to what contributes to its 'falsifying' effects tallies with their reservation over giving its due to action-orientation and, therefore, to the function of ideology in politics. The interdependence of thought and action, of 'patterns of ideas' and 'patterns of attitudes', also requires us to supplement Naess's definition by including both the two-dimensionality of ideological argumentation and the relationship between political philosophy and ideology.

Having now discussed the aspects which, in my view, pertain to the structure and function of ideology, I propose the following detailed definition of ideology.

> An ideology is a group of beliefs and disbeliefs (rejections) expressed in value sentences, appeal sentences and explanatory statements. These sentences refer to moral and technical norms and are related to descriptive and analytical statements of fact with which they are arranged and together interpreted as a doctrine bearing the imprint of the centrality of morally founded prescriptions. A doctrine, which is to say an ideology, presents a not entirely self-consistent, not fully verified and verifiable, but not merely distorted body of views. These views relate in the main to forms of human relationships and socio-political organization as they should and could be and refer from this

perspective to the existing order and vice versa. Ideologies share with others some morally and factually based views and thus attest ideological pluralism without thereby losing their distinctiveness.

An ideology is a belief system *by virtue of being designed to serve on a relatively permanent basis a group of people to justify in reliance on moral norms and a modicum of factual evidence and self-consciously rational coherence the legitimacy of the implements and technical prescriptions which are to ensure concerted action for the preservation, reform, destruction or reconstruction of a given order.*

According to this core-definition of ideology, politics is inseparable from ideology since all political action is in the last resort directed towards one of these objectives.

Ideology shares with political philosophy the structure of formal content and in most cases it depends for its fundamental principles on the specific content of political philosophies. As joined together in an ideology, fundamental principles assume a less disinterested and less objective complexion than their philosophical models. This difference is due to the immediate action-orientation of ideology. The function of ideology affects the structure of the ideological argument inasmuch as at least temporary compromises over principles are demanded by the mere involvement in political action and by the objective to mobilize as much support as possible (or desirable) for a programme of action.[85] Compromises cause ideology to bifurcate into the purer, and hence more dogmatic, fundamental dimension of argumentation and the more diluted, and hence more pragmatic, operative dimension. In the latter, morally based prescriptions are often attenuated, or have their central place momentarily occupied by technical prescriptions. The tension between the two dimensions gives rise to the question of the sincerity of the valuations which are advanced, whereas out of the interaction between the two dimensions, which normally signifies an increase of ideological pluralism, arises the challenge of ideological change.

Some central aspects of this definition of the inclusive conception of ideology need further attention. They will receive it in the remainder of this book in the appropriate contexts. To begin with, we must substantiate beyond doubt the sameness of the structure of all political belief systems by demonstrating further the falsity of considering ideological and pragmatic politics as alternatives. This juxtaposition rests on the assumption that, unlike ideological politics, pragmatic politics is largely detached from, it not in the main opposed to, the moral justification of political objectives. If, therefore, pragmatic politics do not constitute an unideological category of politics, it must be shown that concern with compromises over conflicting interests does in no way cut the umbilical cord between the focal moral component and the components which can be summarized as the more factual.

Secondly, the demonstration of the inseparability in politics of interests and morals, supplemented in Chapter IV by the disproof of related criteria for the distinction between pragmatic and ideological politics, leads us in Chapter V on the one hand to examine the behavioural separation of ideology from class interests and on the other to compare interest-based and other beliefs. Both subjects invite reference to the dogmatic core of Marx and Engels's theory of ideology, namely the stipulation that in virtue of its being conditioned by socio-economic relations, the consciousness of men is 'false consciousness'. Although the present-day distinction between pragmatic and ideological politics is un-Marxian in decisive respects, it reflects much more the Marxian emphasis on the contrast between ideology and factual, or objective, knowledge than Mannheim's demonstration of the links between the two. It therefore seems appropriate to elaborate in this context what I have asserted in the previous stages of my argument (and stipulated as part of my detailed definition of ideology) about the necessary relatedness of ideological argumentation to facts. In this way arises the issue of the very possibility of assuming the achievement of factual and objective scientific insights – a possibility which is logically precluded by a major strand of Marxian argumentation.[86] To show grounds for the assumption to the contrary, as well as to demonstrate that commitment and objectivity are not necessarily mutually exclusive and that the function of ideologies limits their distortion of reality, is to reveal the basis of agreement between them and, therefore, the existence of ideological pluralism. Indications of its nature and extent will serve us to round off the discussion of the interconnected issues of the limits of distortion and of the class- and time-boundedness of ideologies.

Chapter IV

PRAGMATISM versus IDEOLOGY

I. INTERESTS AND MORAL PRINCIPLES

a. *Untenable Confrontations*

American party politics in particular are often defined as pragmatic and unideological because they are held to reflect nothing but the contest for reaching compromises over mainly material interests.[1] The rejection on these grounds of the designation 'ideological' for the American parties is in keeping with the use of 'ideology' by Napoleon, as reported by Sir Walter Scott. He said that the French ridiculed the spirit of resistance in Germany to Napoleon's yoke by giving it 'the name of Ideology; by which nick-name the French ruler used to distinguish every species of theory, which resting in no respect upon the practical basis of self-interest, could, he thought, prevail with none save hot-brained and crazed enthusiasts'.[2] The evaluation in this vein of American politics as the prototype of unideological politics invites a number of reminders.

The obviously ethical foundations of the norms of the American Constitution make it impossible to deny the ideological character of the founder-era. The American founding fathers certainly do not confirm that 'the take-off point of a pragmatic elite' is likely to be a less 'fixed' position than that of an 'ideological elite'.[3] The fundamental principles of the American Constitution and 'the self-evident truths' and 'inalienable rights' of the Declaration of Independence represent principles of liberal doctrine that are no less 'fixed' than the principles of Marxist doctrine.[4] The founder-era may be assessed as one of ideological confusion, if, like Hartz, one holds that instead of basing their argumentation upon what was unique in the American situation – the absence of an authentic feudal tradition – the men of the *Federalist* and their opponents fought each other in the ideological idiom of the French Revolution.[5]

But, to some extent, such 'confusion' is a rather general characteristic. Each political belief system lays claim to universally applicable insights and norms; these are more or less openly 'borrowed' from country to country – *vide* the march of Lockean principles in the Anglo-French-American context. Similarly placed and similarly oriented parties in different countries acknowledge and utilize such identities. American politics have not lost their ideological character since the War of Independence or the Civil War, or for that matter since Calhoun enunciated the postulate of 'the concurrent majority', the morally grounded plea for safeguarding each minority interest, and thus furnished the philosophical foundation of the pressure group system,[6] the paradigm of supposedly unideological American politics. Evidently, the two wars were fought for principles[7] that were not only intimately connected with, and conducive to, the vital interests of socio-economic groups alone but which touched on the existence of the nation as a whole. The same was true of the policies of the 'New Deal', the 'Fair Deal', the 'Good Society', the 'Great Society', the 'New Frontier', and the policies opposed to them. Each of these policies purported to be for the good of all and in accord with the 'American Way of Life' – which means in accord with a particular hierarchy of values, however loosely defined. Even if this way of life derived from purely pragmatic criteria, as is sometimes argued, it would still be ideological inasmuch as it remains founded on values. After all, there exists a specific philosophy and value-system of pragmatism. Like utilitarianism, it is not an alternative to morals but represents, or gives rise to, a specific system of ethics. Not only have the great pragmatists insisted that ideals have consequences, but Dewey's teachings of the continuum of means and ends certainly deserve to be evaluated as an important contribution to moral philosophy.[8]

The relationship between means and ends cannot be so construed as to corroborate a distinction between pragmatic and ideological orientations in terms of Sartori's 'empiricist' and 'rationalistic' cognitive elements. His attempt in this direction is immediately invalidated by the fact that any of the major political belief systems and the policies related to them reflect at one stage or another both his 'rationalistic' and his 'empiricist' elements. For example, is the defence of private property less indicative of the rationalistic prevalence of doctrine over practice than is the defence of the socialization of the means of production and distribution? Do the deviations from each of the two principles in the areas of open = pragmatic and closed = ideological cultures demonstrate the 'empiricist' prevalence of practice over doctrine in the first but not in the second instance? Or, take Locke's insistence on 'natural rights' prevalent in the liberal 'area of empiricism'. Locke derived these rights from reason and grounded them at the same time on historical precedent. Put in Sartori's terms, Locke proceeded by way of *'rationalistic* processing-coding', though by no means to the exclusion of the criteria of *'empirical* processing-coding'.[9] He accorded primacy to principle over precedent when he said 'at best an argument from what has been, to what should of right be, has no great force'.[10] It is often ignored that he hastened to proclaim victory over his paternalist opponents on the two fronts of reason and history: '. . . reason being plain on our side, that men are naturally free [i.e. by the law of nature which is the law of reason and of God], and the examples of history showing that the governments of the world, that were begun in peace . . . were made by the consent of the people'.[11] The unity of theory and practice, or (to use Sartori's terms, and treating Marxists somewhat discourteously) the wish to have it both the 'rationalistic' (ideological) and the 'empiricist' (pragmatic) way, is precisely what both Sartori's ideologist and his pragmatist are actually claiming and doing, although on Sartori's showing they should not. However, it is difficult to prove that behaving pragmatically is incompatible with behaving as a rationalist. It is, after all, a rationalistic calculation to oppose the imposition on reality of principles which one judges to be inimical and alien to that reality and, therefore, unlikely to withstand the test of application. It is neither more nor less rationalistic to turn against precedent and opt, like the American founding fathers and those of Soviet Russia, for a construct of government and/or society which was unprecedented and widely believed to be impractical: a republic beyond the size of a city state, a socialist society beyond the size of a sect.

To oppose empiricism and rationalism in the manner Sartori does is to be out of tune with a whole tradition of thought which is traceable in Bacon, Hobbes, Locke and Hume and to which Merton's term 'empirico-rationalism' applies.[12] The combination is found not only in classical and latter-day liberalism but also in Marxism, which, according to Sartori, is the 'rationalistic' apex of ideology. Much as Marx's theory might be found wanting in what it wished to be, 'the true positive science', it was in fact that kind of science, among other things. The verdict that 'the sentence "experience proves" proves nothing to an ideologically-minded actor'[13] is strikingly refuted by a massive block of Lenin's doctrines and corresponding programmes of action on the one hand, and, from the time of the Bolshevik takeover until his death, by the turns of policy and the accompanying doctrinal reassessments on the other. Certainly he was exaggerating when he said that 'practical experience ... is more important than all the theoretical discussion in the world',[14] but he acted often enough on this precept.

Thus, the 'rationalistic' prevalence of principle over precedent, which is characteristic of anti-traditionalism, can also reflect the 'pragmatic' prevalence of testing and evidence over deductive argument. And since they are combinable (as in Locke), the two can also be found combined with varied emphases in the traditional argument of a Filmer or a de Bonald, whom Mme de Staël appositely dubbed 'Le philosophe de l'anti-philosophie'. Indeed, if, in accordance with Rokeach's terms of reference, the criterion of differentiation between modes of believing is how information is related to information about its source, that is, to an authority, people can be supposed to yield to an absolute authority on the grounds of Sartori's five characteristics of '*rationalistic* processing-coding', but they may also yield on irrational grounds or on the basis of pragmatic considerations, i.e. according to the characteristics of '*empirical* processing-coding'. The prevalence of the latter is never complete since evidence in politics hardly ever points one way. A decision is called for as to which evidence shall prevail over which deduction, which practice is to be continued or discontinued in the face of a given doctrine, which precedent shall be adduced in order to override which principles, and which means should prevail over which ends. Even if purely 'empirical' decisions on these points were possible, to make them does not *eo ipso* place us in a pragmatic and open political culture. Such decisions can be made according to given preferences by an absolute authority like the philosopher-king, the Politburo or the Scientists of a 'Brave New World'. In Sartori's terms, this would mean that in each of these cases a society is being managed in a cognitively 'open' and 'empirical' manner, and information being judged to the same degree on its own merits. Nevertheless, Sartori cannot say that such a society belongs to the cultural area of empiricism, since he considers Great Britain and the United States, that is, liberal democracies, to be its prototypes.

The criteria of rationalistic and empirical processing-coding thus do not support a distinction between pragmatism and ideology as substantively different political belief systems and cultures. Not only are the two kinds of processing-coding interwoven in all political belief systems, but even if the relative prevalence of one of them could be presumed, it would not assume a differentiating significance unless it were related to the specific content of the belief system. Unless we know whether or not mass publics are free to accept or reject the judgment of evidence, or for that matter the deduction of goals, by one or more elite publics, we cannot tell whether or not an 'empirical' culture is 'open' and a 'rationalistic' culture 'closed'.

In point of fact, it is still most sensible and least confusing in the classification of political doctrines and systems to use 'open' and 'closed', in conformity with Popper's distinction between the 'open' and the 'closed' society, or, as an obvious elaboration, between 'open' and 'closed' ideologies.[15] With reference to specific content a continuum can be conceived which ranges from 'open' societies and their belief systems to 'closed' societies and theirs. Those are closed which, when dominating a political culture, are invoked (however contradictorily) to prevent non-members of the dominating elite from choosing the authorities on whom they rely for information and from assessing as they think fit the information supplied. Whether or not it dominates a political culture, a belief system is open if it advocates such freedom of choice. On this basis one can reformulate the distinction between pragmatic and other belief systems and say that an ideology which is open is on the whole more pragmatic, in so far as a pragmatic attitude on the part of both rulers and ruled, that is, an attitude evinced in weighing the immediate bearing upon human interests of principles and goals, is more easily reconcilable with the ideologies of the open society than with those of the closed society.

Although openness can thus be related to 'pragmatic', the latter is not for this reason invariably opposed to 'dogmatic'. Not only can openness as such be defended as dogmatically as closedness, but since there is hardly ever consensus on all or most decisions bearing on more and less immediate interests, different 'pragmatic' ends-means calculations or purely matter-of-fact judgments on the merits of a case may be upheld against each other dogmatically or not, in a manner which is less or more conducive to give-and-take practicalities. We may use 'pragmatic' also in this latter sense, as is customary, because *in sensu stricto* pragmatism pertains, above all, to a specific and morally defensible manner of ends-means relationship whose criterion is human interest and which at any given moment admits, besides a definable hard core, of a considerable variety of contents. 'Dogmatic' and 'pragmatic', therefore, are suited to denote how intensely or obdurately any belief is adhered to. This criterion suggests another continuum on which an open or a closed belief system can be placed. The continuum stretches from 'dogmatic', i.e. from obstinate adherence to the fundamental goals and principles, via their toning-down and amendment, to their abandonment. The opposite pole to 'dogmatic' is thus not 'pragmatic' but what one might call 'unprincipled'. It is between the 'dogmatic' pole and the end of the 'pragmatic' segment that any influential political belief system constantly moves, only rarely reaching that end of the continuum which represents the stage of giving up a belief altogether. Sartori's elements of rationalistic and empirical processing-coding help to denote the 'dogmatic' pole and the 'pragmatic' segment of the continuum respectively. They indicate cognitive elements involved in the oscillation of any ideology between a more dogmatic and a more pragmatic stance – and vice versa, a movement which may eventually result in ideological change.[16] But as we have just seen again, the two sets of cognitive elements are not conducive to setting pragmatism over and against ideology.

Indeed, in so far as pragmatism is supposed to underlie 'a political culture of participation',[17] like that of the United States and the United Kingdom, such a culture must by this very definition be said to rest on ideological orientation and discrimination. Almond and Verba, for instance, state that a 'political culture' means 'patterns of orientation towards political objects'. Since, according to these scholars, a 'civic culture' is that of an 'open polity' (*vide* Popper's 'open society'), the orientation towards political objects is obviously circumscribed by the values of liberal democracy.[18]

The typology of political cultures advanced by Almond and Verba is thus, in my view, a most valuable documentation of a typology of ideological attitudes. The paradigms of their 'civic culture', like those of Sartori's 'empiricist' culture, embody in their institutions elements of specific value systems and hence a specific configuration of ideological elements. This holds true even if the hallmark of such systems is reductively circumscribed as 'open bargaining' and considered to be opposed to the ideological style of politics, as Almond, together with Powell, argues in another work. There the authors place 'the ideological political culture' on 'the continuum from traditional to secularized political culture'. This is intended to distinguish the latter from the ideological political culture, since in their view the ideological style of politics presupposes the absence of 'open, bargaining attitudes' and the presence of 'rigid and closed . . . rules of conduct' which never permit 'accommodative interaction [bargaining] . . . beyond those rigid rules'.[19] This view is shared also by American scholars who do not assume that the politics of their country are entirely unideological.

b. *Self-defeating Concessions*

American theorists and researchers often admit that ideology is involved in party politics, but stress its incoherence and the lack of linkage between issue preferences and party preferences. On the part of the parties themselves, only the requirements of electoral strategy would seem to prevent ambiguity from becoming absolute.[20] Still, Riker, who subscribes to this view, allies his concessions to Lord Bryce's 'empty-bottle-theory' (all bottles [parties] are filled with the same blend of diluted whisky, i.e., ideology),[21] with the conclusion that on the national level the voter is presented with – and capable of making – rational choices between candidates on the grounds of the policy issues that divide the parties. The greater the issues the sharper is the division and the more pronounced the ideological foundation of the issues.[22] To the extent that this interaction of variables bears on the greater stability of majorities, the integrative function of ideological commitments seems to be best fulfilled by outstanding presidents as the intermediaries.[23] It is in any case rather widely accepted by mass publics that deep-seated ideological cleavages exist between the two major American parties. McClosky and others have found that, on some key issues, most Democratic and Republican followers, who otherwise are often nearer to each other than to their leaders, perceive the differences between the two parties in accordance with the image of the Democratic Party as the more progressive and radical and the Republican Party as the more moderate and conservative party.[24]

In such evaluations of empirical findings, the distinction between ideological and non-ideological politics is implicit in so far as the ideological character of specific issues only is acknowledged; they are held to be different from the normally prevailing pragmatic issues attendant upon the pursuit of immediate material group interests. The earlier conclusions of Campbell and his associates in *The American Voter* to the effect that party differentiation by the great majority of voters does not heavily depend on ideological considerations are assumed to be reaffirmed by the finding that the rank and file of supporters of the two parties are closer to each other than their leaders are, and consequently are judged to be less united by party beliefs than their leaders.[25] The point is not that these researches take ideology into account, even though strong loyalty to a party was not found to have much to do with ideology or policy.[26] Such findings (whether or not dependent on time-bound conditions and liable to change)[27] prove nothing against the basically ideological character of party policies. Whether or not these, and party loyalty, are held to be determined by ideology depends, first of all, on the researchers' and theorists' judgment as to which issues and which attitudes are ideological. Indeed, it is admitted that, despite the diversity in the nature, extent and coherence of the ideological commitments of the party leadership on one side and the mass of followers and voters on the other, 'the [American] parties develop integrated and stable political tendencies' which do not exclude 'deviations' reflecting the composite character – regional and otherwise complex – of these parties. This conclusion, however, is based on the supposition that certain issues evoke 'old-fashioned economic considerations' and that, 'when ideology and interests are *both* at work, partisanship is likely to be intensified'.[28] The presupposition is that questions of material interests, even though viewed in the light of 'stable political tendencies', can be detached from ideology.

In other instances, the distinction between ideological and non-ideological issues is also, or solely, based on whether or not the issues are controversial. Stokes uses Kurt Lewin's term of 'valence issues' for non-controversial issues, like corruption and depression, which, as he says, are not 'position [i.e. ideological] issues' since no party advocates either corruption or depression. Actually, these issues are non-controversial only to a very limited degree and not so much because, as Stokes himself admits, 'valence issues' can be easily turned into 'position issues',[29] but because the question in political debate is not indeed whether a political party advocates corruption or depression, but whether a party can be held responsible for having let them develop, how each party proposes to deal with them and to what extent it can be trusted to make good its word. How a party proposes to cope with issues like corruption, depression and, for that matter, with bread-and-butter issues of any significance – and how it actually deals with them in the event – reflects at the very least the different moral hues of its overall socio-economic orientation, that is to say, of its socio-economic ideology. These are the hues and accents which, as empirical researchers show, even the wider public associates quite consistently with basic orientations of the competing political parties in America, though only on a few key issues and to varied degrees.[30] And to these orientations empirical researchers accord a place among the determinants of 'habitual party affiliation', or party loyalty on the part of voters.[31] Yet by virtue of the distinction between interests and ideology researchers often do not appraise basic issue orientations of the parties as ideological.

Thus, in accord with the theorists' ambivalence, discussed in

Chapter II, some empirical researchers are prone to consider the involvement of ideology in American politics as suspended either by lack of controversy over an issue or by virtue of its arbitrary appraisal. In such studies ideological involvement is seen as weakened also by incoherence in the orientation of the party membership in different echelons – and within each echelon. What is more, neither incoherence of orientation nor any other putative indicators of weak or absent ideological involvement are regarded as dysfunctional, on the assumption that the party is less an ideological than an action structure.[32] As I have argued, incoherence, within certain limits, does not disqualify a belief system from being ideological and there is no contrast, but a definitional link, between action-orientation and ideology. Apart from the factors mentioned hitherto as being held to influence the ideological character of issues and policies, further influence is attributed to fluctuations in the salience of issues, to the diffuseness or concentration of policies in relation to each other, and to whether the times are those of crisis and electoral re-alignments or of prosperity and consensus.[33] In other words, whatever concessions are made to the role of ideology in American politics, for the most part theorists and researchers consider ideological politics opposed to pragmatism, epitomized in 'open bargaining'. However, can we really say that the restriction of bargaining by 'rigid and closed . . . rules of conduct' is as such the preserve of the political style prevalent in political cultures exemplified by communism and clericalism?[34] The negative answer can be demonstrated best in connection with the views of Dahl.

Dahl seems to leave behind the equation of controversial with ideological politics when he argues against the inference that, because ideological consensus is greater among Americans than among Italians, Americans are less ideological than Italians.[35] He also states that, owing to political activists, 'democratic, liberal and conservative ideological perspectives do have a significant effect on American political life'.[36] However, even his recognition of the ideological character of the basic consensus, that is, of ideology which, in Partridge's formulation, 'lies below the level of general political controversy',[37] does not induce Dahl to accept, like Partridge, the unexceptionally ideological character of politics. All the same, this conclusion follows logically from Dahl's own elaborate version of this assumption, as well as from Almond and Powell's characterization of an ideological culture.

According to Dahl, the saliency of 'fixed' elements in a belief system renders the style of politics ideological, because as a result conflict over principles is inevitable. Conversely, as in the Almond–Powell position, the style of politics is pragmatic if 'flexible' elements are salient. Yet, according to Dahl, politics can also be pragmatic if the fixed elements are salient but shared and the differences over decisions involve only flexible elements.[38] Thus, consensus which does not testify against the existence of ideological orientations (*vide* the comparison between Italians and Americans) remains nevertheless opposed to the ideological style of politics. But this juxtaposition is false precisely on the assumption that there exists consensus on fixed elements. Therefore, my first objection to Dahl's distinction between pragmatic and ideological style is that, when fixed elements are shared and the controversy involves only flexible elements, their flexibility is in fact determined by the fixed elements – 'the rigid rules', in the words of Almond and Powell which, as Dahl explains elsewhere, are embodied in 'the common ideology' or in 'the ideology of democracy', which in America consists of the commitments to 'popular government and constitutionalism ... an ideology favourable to private property'.[39] It is this 'common ideology' which keeps bargaining and compromise within the bounds of fixed constitutional rights and rules and thus elevates them to the rank of fixed principles. Ultimately, the commonly shared ideological principles ensure the pragmatic flexibility of all those involved in any kind of controversy, except a controversy on the right of controversy itself, because they permit the enforcement of flexibility. The decisions involving flexible elements are pragmatic by courtesy of fixed ideological elements.

All settlements of controversies by reference to the common fixed elements would be ideologically determined or simply ideological even if we were to subscribe, like Dahl, to the view that the absence of conflict over 'principles' attests the presence of pragmatic = unideological politics. The absence of conflict over 'principles' is by no means guaranteed by the willingness to reach compromise within the bounds of the common fixed elements. The ideological fundamentals which form the consensual basis of American politics may be taken to circumscribe also the 'long-run goals', which, for Dahl, may control the 'short-run goals'.[40] Neither such control nor the reference to the fixed elements of 'the common ideology' in daily political controversy excludes sharp divisions of opinion over the interpretation and implementation of commonly accepted 'fixed' elements in particular cases.

My second objection, therefore, is that conflict over 'principles' may exist also where the principles themselves, or rather the broad principles, as distinct from their specification and application, are non-controversial. It is only natural to expect that such 'fixed' principles become ambiguous, controversial and contradictory in the process of being invoked in order to justify, according to 'rigid' rules of conduct, diverse bargaining positions. Or, to use my terminology : as the result of the rebound on fundamental principles of their modification for the sake of their implementation in various circumstances, conflict arises among the principles of fundamental ideology as well as in their relation with principles of operative ideology, since attempts at application of principles often reveal their ambiguities and eventually the need for their re-specification.

Conflict over the explication and application of shared principles is certainly not characterized by the saliency of flexible elements. We may take as instances the attitudes and doctrinal elements involved in the debate over the Taft-Hartley Act, medicare, segregation and parochial schools, or the more recent and heated controversy about America's foreign policy, especially towards Vietnam. Dahl himself admits that Americans have often disagreed about the theoretical and practical meaning of their common 'ideology of democracy'. The cleavage patterns have been overlaid by outward consensus; the traditional ideology, viz., the 'fixed elements', is 'a patchwork of ambiguities and potential contradictions' which permit and encourage conflict.[41] So he eventually uses 'ideologies' for the liberal and conservative interpretation of 'the common ideology'.[42] Dahl also states that, in addition to domestic communism and international affairs (which for the most part are linked issues), economic policy and organization at home in general cause American politics to change from pragmatic to ideological.[43] One is tempted to ask : What remains for pragmatic politics, quite apart from the fact that any issue debated and settled with reference to the common elements of the ideology can also be said not to represent the pragmatic style of politics? The only possible answer is that nothing remains. Dahl's own concessions over the ideologization of issues make it extremely difficult to maintain the image of a 'democratic Leviathan' whose commitment to 'pragmatism and incrementalism'[44] derogates from its ideological character.

The crucial point in the admission of the coexistence of pragmatism and ideology in American politics is that the readiness to abide by the same basic fixed ideological elements guarantees *inter alia* open, flexible and pragmatic bargaining without excluding sharp conflict over the interpretation and application of the shared fundamental principles in particular circumstances. In any liberal-democratic system flexibility – a criterion one can take on trust even without assuming that it can be exactly scaled for all circumstances – is not merely the result of counsels of prudence and/or of the congeniality of the negotiating teams. To the extent that the issues are important, the necessity to manoeuvre and keep even sharp conflict within constitutionally defined limits derives from the common fundamental ideological principles on which the 'rigid and closed . . . rules of conduct' are based. And these form 'the rules of the game', whether the relations between political or other powerholders are concerned or the relations between them and their clienteles. To say that the British 'behave like ideologists in regard to rules and like pragmatists in regard to policies'[45] is therefore, to inflate a distinction into the separation of what is inseparable. It is as if one were to accept, like Bell, a connection between ethics and politics for the purpose of setting limits, i.e. for establishing the rules of the game, while rejecting the connection in order to determine political objectives.[46] On the grounds of neither logic nor experience can one separate dedication to the ethics of the rules of the game from dedication to the ethics of what the game is about. The rules are at once a formal expression and a guarantee of a style of life, and as such reflect principles of the ethos prevalent in a society. They serve various and conflicting contents at different times or even simultaneously, but not all and any contents. Adherence to the principles that rule the British and American game of politics precludes the excesses of communist and fascist policies.

In Britain, nationalization of steel may be followed by denationalization and later the industry may be re-nationalized. Total nationalization is no topical issue because so far majority consent to it is unachievable by the rules of the game. In America, pressure groups are able to stultify the endeavour to reduce violence through restrictions on the purchase of firearms, but they cannot prevent the adoption of policies of slum-clearance and of measures leading towards increased racial equality. Similarly, the principles underlying the British and American rules of the game preclude the adoption of policies aimed at the eventual extermination of a minority either directly (e.g. the Jews under Nazi rule) or indirectly (e.g. Stalin's policy towards Kulaks), just as the aims of communism and fascism preclude the adherence to pluralistic rules, which fascism opposes on principle, and communism on a putatively temporary basis as a prelude to the eventual redundancy of politics altogether. (So far, the greatest disservice communism has rendered to democracy and socialism is to have cast doubt on the possible coexistence of predominantly socialist contents and democratic forms of politics.)

The foregoing considerations show that no conflict is needed between parties and people of different fixed principles for a style of politics to become ideological. A 'style of politics' is indeed distinguished by fixed elements necessarily related with some consistency to certain value judgments. These elements render any political style ideological, since in the last resort policies are related to them, as is the case with any cluster of simple 'questions of fact, instrumental matters' that are somehow interconnected. Hence, whether composites of fixed elements are freely adhered to by competing groups or imposed by force on the whole nation, the style of politics remains ideological. Even if only compromises over mainly material interests were the core of the pluralistically organized game of politics, it would not follow that what prevails is 'a pragmatic non-ideological sense of compromise'.[47] It is not only rash to assume that clashes over material interests are by their nature less harsh and bitter than clashes over 'principles': the very juxtaposition of such interests and principles is false. Principles pertain to values and to material interests. No important fight over interest has been led and no aggregation, integration or compromise between interests has ever been achieved, for any length of time, without the eventual invoking of moral norms held to be generally applicable.[48] In political argument we always find the mutual involvement of 'want-regarding' and 'ideal-regarding' principles; and, in relation to either material or ideal interests and aspirations, 'self-regarding' considerations are always in the end justified by 'other-regarding' considerations.[49]

For once, Montesquieu was perhaps a trifle too cynical when he said that 'chacun va au bien commun, croyant aller à ses intérêts particuliers'.[50] For people do not always pursue only their own interests, or always refrain from acting consciously against their interest for some ulterior motives such as those associated with the 'public good'.[51] The adaptation of individuals to some common interest in accordance with given moral norms occurs even in a gang of criminals, whether it is persecuted by the agencies of government or dominates the state.

However repugnant the justification of interests by morals may become, especially in totalitarian regimes, the universal ascertainability of this linkage is also proof of the validity of the inclusive conception because it is denied in the restrictive conception; so it serves as the touchstone of what is to be considered 'ideological' according to both conceptions. The demonstration according to an agreed criterion of the ubiquity of the justification of interest by morals furnishes, then, the firm foundation of the inseparability of all politics and ideology.

The conclusion of their unexceptionable relatedness is also borne out on attitudinal grounds, i.e. by the intensity of commitment revealed towards the various political parties, as well as in respect of the ability of all major political belief systems to inspire intense commitment.

2. ATTITUDES AND BELIEFS

a. *Intensity and Content of Commitment*

In the study of personality and groups it is reasonable to assume that most ideologically-minded will be found among people who possess the greatest capacity for commitment. Obviously, it is a different matter to suggest a straightforward connection between the number of stalwarts and fellow-travellers and the nature of belief systems, and generally between these and the personality structure. The interesting hypotheses of *The Authoritarian Personality,*[52] about the correlations between the psychological make-up of groups of persons and their political inclinations, have turned out less unequivocal than was assumed at the time of their publication. Extremity of standpoint and intensity of commitment and partisanship may feed on each other and draw on the same psychological forces.[53] Yet strong partisan hostility is not an inevitable concomitant of adherence to extremist belief systems, just as intense commitment and partisanship are not restricted to issues espoused by extremist parties or to members of disaffected minority parties or minority groups. In America, a positive or negative stand on racial integration or the extension of medicare may divide communists and non-communists as much as Democrats and Republicans from each other and set up divisions within each group. The major consideration is that there is no reason to assume that a commitment to liberal, or generally moderate, or even conservative ideals must be weaker and less rationalized than the commitment to communist and fascist ideals or to any set of ideas that qualify in given circumstances as 'extremist', in being radically transformative.[54]

Stalwarts and fellow-travellers are to be found in both extremist and moderate parties. So long as the classical model of communist parties in non-communist countries was followed, or the Communist Party was outlawed, the almost exclusive recruitment of active militants was party policy. This model has long since been abandoned by the French and Italian Communist Parties. In America, 'every practitioner of politics knows the ideologue in party activity, the militant who fervently holds definite political views . . .'.[55] The empirical studies we have referred to show that there are hierarchical and intra-echelon variations among members and followers concerning the cohesion of the contents of party ideology and the attitudes towards it.

There is one obvious reason why embracing a political belief system associated with a particular party does not necessarily attest greater intensity of commitment than opting for another. Even if loyalty to a party is not as universally comparable to the identification with a religious group as Ostrogorski believed,[56] the trite truth is that just as a religion demands exclusive commitment to its faith, so normally does every party claim exclusive commitment to its aims and candidates. Partisanship in such liberal-democratic societies as the USA and the UK is also a corollary of the fact that 'the image of the active participating citizen is most often the normative ideal',[57] at least as far as pre-university public education is concerned. Equally dedicated stalwarts and militants pose a problem in every party in the West inasmuch as their convictions may cease to be an asset and become a liability when the top leadership has to modify its distinctive ideological fundamentals for electoral purposes.[58]

Experience also shows that 'the concerned citizen' can be incited against deviance from the fixed common ideological elements of the system to the point of active support for political witch-hunting. Nobody has as yet confuted the assumption underlying John Stuart Mill's *On Liberty* that intense dogmatism distinguishes both radical reformers and obdurate conformists. 'The concerned citizen' has had occasion to show that he can be as uncompromisingly dedicated to the politics of compromise – even to a particular version of it – as 'the true believer' is to his creed.[59] In the long run, which occasionally becomes rather short, the partisans of liberal democracy have been as ready to defend their principles and rules of government, and prepared to go in some respects as far in that defence as their opponents from the radical Right and Left. The built-in aspiration of communism to total victory over the liberal order is countered in putatively unideological America by the (near-) total denial to communists of an organized political existence. The denial is mutual and one kind of extremism is met by another kind that is not dissimilar.

On these grounds, dogmatism is associable not only with any belief or disbelief in the personality system, but also with the belief system propagated by any party or school of thought.[60] To be sure, one can be dogmatic without being passionate about it, but passionate activism normally presupposes dogmatic commitment. Intense partisanship and fanaticism as such attest no more than total commitment to any cause. Neither the passion aroused in some people by a belief system and which, at times, is required of the faithful, nor their more or less constant readiness for sharp conflict should be taken as characteristics distinguishing particular political belief systems. Passionate conflict over the fundamental and operative beliefs that guide policies is almost daily in evidence – and for obvious reasons much more in polities based on the elements common to 'open' ideologies than in 'closed' polities. By Western standards some of the latter embody extremist ideologies, while others do so only as far as authoritarianism on behalf of and/or in the name of one party is concerned. The readiness for sharp conflict and the capacity for passion and fanaticism tangibly underlie, and sooner rather than later express themselves overtly in political systems in which they can be kept (if necessary by force) within bounds freely endorsed and re-endorsed by the vast majority.

If we include among liberals all those who abide by the freely competitive multi-party system – whether, at one end of the continuum, a premium is put on 'private initiative', or at the other, on as near a socialist society as the majority of the electorate is ready to accept – we find that the majority of liberals react to totalitarianism with total rejection. Those near the right extreme of the Left-Right continuum might react less violently to authoritarianism of the Right and those nearer the left extreme less violently to totalitarianism of the Left. If, as we may presume, the hard core of the above-mentioned varieties of liberals is today the majority in the West and assumes towards authoritarians and totalitarians an 'either/or' stance, then they are doing, in a quite specific and very restricted sense, the same as the authoritarians and totalitarians. Both consider each other's ideology as mutually exclusive. While this is one more reason against classifying liberalism as a non-ideology, or a not fully fledged one, it is no reason to postulate that this 'either/or' stance on the part of liberals endangers the distinctiveness of liberal values.[61]

Liberalism and totalitarianism are comparable because, in the world as we know it, no influential political belief system can subsist without evoking in a number of people intense commitment and dogmatic fidelity to its basic principles. Inevitably, such dedication entails intolerance towards the principles and actions of the opponents. For this reason, liberalism and totalitarianism do not cease to be decisively different in this particular respect. It is over and against the religious and secular totalitarian dogma of the intolerance of tolerance that the liberal dogma of tolerance requires intolerance of intolerance and justifies, on the basis of eventually genuine majority support, intolerance towards those who would impose intolerance through enforced majority support. If the claim of exclusive commitment to basic principles does not affect the distinctiveness of liberalism, and if its distinctiveness does not render it less of an ideology than others, this is so partly because there is nothing missing in liberalism that, in comparison with other 'isms', would render it in any case inferior as the object of intense commitment.

Thoroughgoing explanation of human and political activity affords one of the grounds of intense commitment, and it is often – and quite wrongly – maintained that liberalism offers less in this direction than other political belief systems, or that, in contradistinction to them, it leaves such explanations to positive science.[62] Whether or not, as Williams thinks, an 'ism' (in his view liberalism) might for this reason be better suited to survival, there is no reason to attribute to liberal theory a low explanatory value in the first place and then evaluate it with Sartori as 'a poor competitor, ideologically speaking' of the fully 'rationalistic' (ideological) 'isms' which, as it were, reach 'a higher level of explicitness and especially of abstraction' and culminate in a more comprehensive *Weltanschauung*.[63] Neither scholar, nor any of those who advance similar views, has ever gone to the trouble of demonstrating such assertions. Judging from my study of Locke's political theory, as well as from acquaintance with the teachings of other liberal thinkers, and the examination elsewhere of aspects of Marxian and Marxist theory, I venture to assert that the body of liberal theory can stand comparison with the body of Marxist theory according to the criteria by which liberalism is so often assigned an inferior status. For example, take the criterion of comprehensiveness, in both the substantive and qualitative meaning. Liberal thinkers have touched on as many subjects, if not more, as the founders of Marxism, let alone fascism, and with at least as much coherence.[64] The thinkers whose teachings have contributed to the formation and development of liberalism have offered, as self-assuredly as others, quite definite notions for the understanding of the complexities of the human condition and for making it as satisfactory as possible. Mill, for instance, competently covered in his writings more fields of knowledge than Marx and much of what he said is still of interest beyond the immediate purposes of liberal theory and ideology.

The impression of diffuseness which surrounds both democratic and liberal theory stems from the fact that various thinkers in their individual ways have developed the belief systems eventually subsumed under the name of liberal and democratic theory. The writings of these theorists, unlike those of Marx and his heirs, have never been elevated to the rank of scriptures. Yet even Marxian canonization has not been stable, and, where disagreement may be voiced, Marxists have not reached agreement on the interpretation of either Marx's or post-Marxian Marxism. Where Marxism is declared to be in the process of implementation, an 'authorized version' is imposed from time to time by force and by threat of excommunication. The developments of liberalism by various thinkers have been conducive to its extension in various directions which seem not to be more numerous or less diverse than the various official versions of communism and the freely developed versions of Marxism in the West and of democratic socialism. In none of these instances have ideological developments affected all basic fundamentals.

Another fallacy implicit in judging liberalism to exercise a weaker appeal and evoke weaker convictions than Marxism appears to be the entirely unfounded assumption embraced by anti- or at least non-Marxist scholars that the dogmatic causal reductionism of Marxism (vexing even for Marxists) attests a higher level of abstraction than causal pluralism. Moreover, whether in this context 'abstraction' is used in a derogatory or a complimentary sense, it is at best a moot point whether the reductionism of a monistic-based hierarchic causal explanation still possesses that much advantage over pluralistic causality which it might once have had by dint of its propinquity to the monotheistic explanation of the world.

A further fallacy is the equation of the comprehensiveness of a political theory and belief system with the extent to which its norms affect the various aspects of the life of individuals. The quality of life is as deeply affected by a normative system encompassing directly many spheres of the life of the individual as by a normative system which guarantees as much non-interference in these spheres as possible. Moreover, to consider, like Williams, the explanation in liberal theory of human and political activity as at best not very thoroughgoing may be debatable in respect of human activity in general, but certainly not in respect of political activity. Liberal philosophers from Locke to Mill, Hobhouse and Croce, as well as their successors in contemporary political theory (R. Aron, C. J. Friedrich, B. de Jouvenel and others), were not parsimonious with analyses of the political process and practical proposals for the improvement of governmental organization. What they have proffered is much more explicit, detailed and clear than anything to be found in Marx for whom, after all, the explanation of political activity lay in principle outside politics. As a result, Marxism certainly has not proved helpful for the conduct of socialist politics, as Marx's reformist and revolutionary successors found out even while Marx and Engels were still alive.

It is, then, out of place to evaluate according to the criteria commonly adduced for the purpose, the explanatory value of liberalism as weak, when compared with Marxism-Leninism-Maoism, let alone fascism, whose intellectual poverty and incoherence are notorious in most of its versions. Likewise, there are no valid logical or empirical reasons for denying that democratic liberal belief systems can inspire intense commitment. The foundation of such commitment is provided by the demonstrable reference to central values in all political belief systems. Both fascist and communist condemnation of bourgeois morality in society and politics has its counterpart in the unashamedly moral rejection of the two totalitarian systems by reform-minded liberal democrats and democratic socialists. Therefore, the identification of liberalism or reformist socialism with non-moral, and hence non-ideological pragmatism must needs reveal itself as both unsound and paradoxical.

In the course of exposing extremist transformationism and fanatical commitment as dangerous and *dépassé*, Bell makes the self-defeating attempt to detach liberalism from morality in its most decisive aspect. This is logical in so far as, according to my terms of the unitary structure of political belief systems, any such system could qualify as non-ideological only if the moral component were expendable. Bell states that 'the historic contribution of liberalism was to separate law from morality'.[65] This is why the 'pragmatic give-and-take' could emerge and the tendency be curbed to convert concrete into ideological issues. The liberal intellectual and democratic socialist who, as we have seen, warned against excommunicating ideals from politics[66] hails the separation of legality from morality and thus inadvertently subscribes to that which has been condemned as ominous in legal positivism and which has manifested itself both in fascism and in the communist administration of 'socialist justice'. Bell did not in fact find it easy to face the implication of his divorce of liberal law from morality. When challenged on the point in a debate, he argued that he had meant not 'morals' but 'moralizing', an ideological 'distortion of the moral code', and pointed to Locke and Kant to show that 'pragmatic discourse' searching for a reasoned consensus is not without principle. But, as the passage quoted in this paragraph and others in the same context demonstrate, Bell clearly criticized the various equations of ideology and morality and opposed morals – not moralizing – to pragmatic discourse.[67] In his assertion of the liberal separation of law from morality and its immediate context, he ignored the mutual involvement of ethical form and content, of interests and morals, of procedural and substantive issues; above all, he did not realize that to praise liberal legality because it is untainted by morals cut the ground from under the liberal rejection of both fascist and communist practice. It seems to be fairly obvious that Bell would not have laid himself open to these charges, and particularly not to that of making historically untenable assertions, if it had not been required by the basic (and false) programmatical juxtaposition of 'pragmatic' (liberal) and 'ideological' (extremist, chiliastic, etc.) politics.

In his book, Bell recognized often enough the change in liberal American society, from interest-group argumentation to moralist (not 'moralizing') *qua* ideological argumentation, and he himself adopted moral-ideological criteria in his advocacy of fundamental changes in the structure of the American economy.[68] That he insisted on tests which should guide the introduction of such changes is, in my view, all for the best, but it does not dissolve the association of his guiding principles with morals. The confusion of the issue in his own standpoint is matched by the patent misapprehension as to the separation in liberal thought in general between legality and morality.

Locke, the most prominent and most influential founding-father of modern liberalism, whose teachings are well reflected in the American Constitution, neither confounded legality and morality nor dissolved the bond between them. The Law of Nature was the moral code with which man-made law ought to comply, although it often fails to do so. This explains why men possess the right of revolt. They may rely on the moral law to resist either the perversion by rules of good laws or the imposition of iniquitous laws.[69] 'Thus the law of nature stands as an eternal rule to all men, legislators as others. The rules that they make for other men's actions must, as well as their own and other men's actions, be conformable to the law of nature, i.e. to the will of God, . . . and . . . no human sanction can be good, or valid against it.'[70]

This connection between legality and morality was modified by Kant but not dissolved, as Bell maintains. Kant did not expect a progress of morality, only of legality; but he expected the 'moral politician' to amend faults in the constitution of the state in the light of the law of nature, even if this had to be done by sacrificing egotistic interests.[71] Although both utilitarian and idealistic liberalism after Locke dispensed more and more with the idea of a law of nature, the essence of this idea was retained. The liberal, like any other, adjustment and adjudication of interests cannot be divorced from the rationalization of moral standards in the light of which the adequacy of positive laws and established customs is judged. Neither J. S. Mill's humane utilitarianism nor Green's idealism, inspired by Kant and Hegel, are separable from the moral imperative of human perfectibility and dignity.[72]

The interplay of interests and moral norms in social life can be suitably summed up in the formulations of J. S. Mill, who was uninfluenced by Marxism (through which the understanding of the issues in hand became at once pungent and beclouded), while at the same time his conclusions anticipate Marx's assumptions about the sociopolitical basis of the normative framework of a society. As Mill put it, 'wherever there is an ascendant class, a large portion of the morality of the country emanates from its class interests, and its feelings of class superiority'.[73] But where 'a class formerly ascendant, has lost its ascendancy, or where its ascendancy is unpopular, the prevailing moral sentiments frequently bear the impress of an impatient dislike of superiority'. Mill thus accounts for the moral 'superstructure' in terms of clashes of interests and social aspirations, without denying that 'among so many baser influences, the general and obvious interests of society' have had a large share 'in the direction of the moral sentiments'. Not unlike Montesquieu, Mill enjoins us to make allowances 'in the establishment of moralities' for 'sympathies and antipathies which had little or nothing to do with the interests of society' and which have made themselves felt 'with quite as great force'. Whether or not we set particular and general interests further apart from each other and accord a more absolute standing to moral norms than Mill at times did, the mutual involvement of interests and morals is the essence of political debate, because it consists in the last resort in the attempt to justify interests by moral principles.

b. *Confines of Ascription*

In view of Mill's words and the discussion ahead of us on Marxist and modern non-Marxist notions about the class relatedness of beliefs, it seems appropriate at this point to clarify briefly the senses in which we can speak of the interests and systems of values, and hence of the ideologies, of a social entity or even an epoch.

From the discussion so far it should be clear that I do not imply that developed societies are held together by consensus to one inclusive system of values,[74] nor that we can speak of the ideology of an epoch or of a class. There is no 'total' ideology in the sense in which Mannheim also used the notion of 'the total conception of ideology', in its 'general formulation', i.e. as the total structure of the mind of an epoch although, in the main, the 'particular' and the 'total' conceptions of ideology were for Mannheim part of a general typology of ideological thought designed to reveal the nature of such thought and to indicate thereby the possibilities, or stages, of attaining truth.

In dividing the 'total' into the 'special' and 'general' formulations of the total conception of ideology, Mannheim assigned to the 'special formulation of the total conception' the function of exposing as socially determined the 'total' conception of our opponents alone. In this way the notion of the 'total' ideology of a class is implied directly not merely in the additive sense, i.e. as the sum total of the various opinions of the persons belonging to a class of people, nor as the elements common to the ideological outlooks to be found among the majority of the members of a social class or in an epoch. What is meant is a structure, not an assemblage of beliefs. The intention is the same in respect of 'the general form of the total conception of ideology', which includes not only the views of our opponents but our own as well and is said to provide us with the views of an age, if not 'of the whole historical process'. In order to establish the possibility of increasingly objective perception, Mannheim moved from belief systems providing the basis of action for organized groups, e.g. 'the intellectual armament of a party', to assuming the structured sum total of the beliefs of an age which the intellectually courageous analyst is able to perceive.[75] In speaking of the ideology – as distinct from the idoelogies – of an age or a class, Mannheim must be charged, like Marx, with confusing the categories proper for classifying people as a group in order to analyse what they have in common (or not), and the categories proper for action units. The first kind of category always applies where the second applies but not vice versa. This distinction must be maintained unequivocally in order to avoid widespread semantic confusion leading to reifications. It needs to be kept in mind that, as Max Weber said, a class 'is not itself a community' and 'group action (*Gemeinschaftshandeln*) arising from a common class situation is by no means a universal phenomenon'.[76]

Neither an epoch nor a class is an action unit. The workers of a nation or of the world, and for that matter the intellectuals, musicians or old-age pensioners of a nation or of the world, are a class in a purely classificatory sense, that is, when subsumed under a class-heading by an investigator or observer. Unless any of these groups forms one organization, we use 'group' and 'class' purely as classificatory categories and must in no way imply the applicability of the additional categories appropriate to action units.[77] Similarly, we may identify and classify the common interests of these classes of people quite objectively, but it does not follow that the interests so defined will induce all or most of the members of these classes of people to evaluate their pursuit and protection alike, let alone to act conjointly to promote them. It is immediately evident that it is illicit to apply indiscriminately the classificatory categories and those that in addition qualify action units. Nobody can deny that things have happened within an epoch and within and to a class. Anybody can see that nothing has ever been done by a whole class (not to mention an epoch) because no class has ever been organized and acted like an army, a party or the American Medical Association. In fact, Marx himself more than once acknowledged that to conceive of a class as an action unit, as he did, required the presence of organization, but he also contradicted himself on the point.[78] More often than not, Marx disregarded the fact that even the 'pure' classes, the bourgeoisie and the proletariat, had never been united in, or even spear-headed by, a single political organization.

Unlike a class, a nation-cum-state is in important respects an action unit, since in specific matters it is made to act like any organized group. Prominent and unique among such actions are the maintenance and continuous adaptation to changing conditions of the legal framework and the efficient maintenance of its rules, within which the interplay and accommodation of interests take place. In these actions – and this is the main point of what might otherwise seem a digression – the 'state' is not guided by the 'total' ideology in the sense of an inclusive system of values enforced upon and/or more or less freely endorsed by the nation or the most numerous class. The operationalization of the principles which a ruling party or coalition has seen fit, or been able, to follow in political practice is effected in the acts of government and creates the profile of the 'state' as an action unit. Given operative principles presuppose a configuration of values, and at the same time mould this configuration in sudden convulsions or piecemeal, by change, deletion and addition, as reflected in the changing body of laws, constitutional provisions and procedures, and extra-legal social conventions and public opinion(s). Such a configuration of norms presents the totality of prevalent norms, the normative infra-structure, but not the sum total of the normative and cognitive positions to be found in an age, nation or class. An aggregative totality includes also the dissensual norms of opposition groups which consider these norms to be incompatible with the prevalent value system, as well as those of opposition groups seeking a place for their dissensual norms within the prevalent normative infra-structure.

Whether or not these facts permit us still to attribute a structure to this ideological totality, the latter ceases to be an ideology, if we abide by the criterion that the function of ideology is to guide concerted action of a distinct social group or group of groups in the battle over interests, a battle both over moral and over technical norms.

To sum up, the reference to 'higher' values is ineradicable from any system of political beliefs, however low our opinion of some such values and their tangible contents in general may be. Their presence in political belief systems, together with the other elements of the formal structure of content, requires us to classify all political belief systems as political ideologies in so far as the belief system can be said to guide identifiable group action. Since in the real world political argumentation and action testify against the disjunction of interests from morals, and political belief systems, as we know them, testify against the way in which different cultural matrices and sets of cognitive elements have been assumed to confront each other, we cannot on these grounds set pragmatic politics apart from ideological politics. Nor can we do so by reference to the relative intensity of commitment incited and required by parties on behalf of the basic beliefs they propagate. This is not to deny that there are differences in the degree and prevalence of both fanaticism and extremism among party ideologies and party politics within a given political culture or between various cultures. It is simply to assert that, in principle, we cannot associate fanaticism and extremism with one kind of political belief system only. Nor can we distinguish between such systems according to the substantive and qualitative criteria (comprehensiveness, degree of abstraction, explicitness, explanatory level, etc.) that have been used for the purpose.

I trust I have disposed of the main false alternatives that have lately been relied upon to drive a wedge between ideology and politics, and having demonstrated the identical structure (with some reference to the function) of all political belief systems, I hope to have made out a case for the proposition that all politics are ideological. To say this is to accept a Marxian conclusion but it as little entails acceptance of Marx's dogmatic definition of ideology as illusory consciousness as of the definition of the modern political scientists, theorists and philosophers who distinguish between ideological and non-ideological politics. Indeed, they retain Marx's juxtaposition of ideology and factuality when they identify an ideological with an opinionated and prejudicial approach and oppose to it the pragmatic matter-of-fact approach. Hence in continuation of the discussion of the inevitable interaction between moral norms and interests, I propose to show that in so far as behavioural theory exhibits a Marxist stance in its distinction between ideological and factual orientation, it is likely to include the un-Marxist divorce of class-oriented from ideological beliefs. The demonstration that such a distinction is untenable, like the one between interest-based and other beliefs, supplements the discussion in Chapter IV of the relationship between interests and morals and brings us to the concluding part of the direct argument against a non-inclusive conception of ideology, particularly in so far as its most conspicuous Marxist residue, its truth-excluding aspect, is concerned. Our demonstration involves, therefore, an examination of the degree to which commitment and objectivity exclude each other and of the phenomenon of ideological pluralism. Not only does the latter reveal the limitation of disagreement between, and distortion of, reality by ideologies, but it also testifies against the class- and epoch-boundedness of ideological principles, goals and methods, the other major legacy of Marxist to non-Marxist theory.

Chapter V

CLASS INTERESTS, IDEOLOGY AND REALITY

I. BELIEFS AND INTEREST-ORIENTATION

a. *The Behavioural Separation of Class Consciousness from Ideology*

There are modern political scientists and sociologists who proceed from a basically Marxian premise,[1] in so far as, like Marxists, they consider it as rational that political orientation be determined by socio-economic interests. In accordance with their opposition of pragmatism to ideology and their disregard if not outright denial of the linkage between interests and morals, they contrast, in un-Marxist fashion, political behaviour motivated by material interests with political behaviour motivated by ideology.

According to Alford, voting in conformity with one's class position, that is class loyalty and class consciousness, is the foundation of party loyalty and of the politics of compromise in English-speaking countries. Alford contrasts ideological voting with class-voting, because he says that religious loyalties are 'ideological and value-laden' and, therefore, cut across and press counter to class loyalties.[2] So do other loyalties which in Alford's view do not reflect clear-cut class loyalties, such as voting for the British Liberal Party.[3] Dahl, too, contrasts ideological with socio-economic motivation in this way.[4] The same distinction is implicit in the assumption that partisanship is intensified as a result of the conjoint influence of ideology and economic interests.[5]

The distinction, if not opposition, of ideology and interest current among American and other behavioural political scientists, is the logical corollary of opposing ideological style or attitude to that of bargaining and compromise over mainly material interests. Not only does this use of the term 'ideological' carry with it the connotation of 'unrealistic' attached to it first by Napoleon[6] and then by Marx, but it does so in a specific sense that Mannheim adopted from Marx. When Mannheim designated as 'merely ideological' the resonance of the ideas of the French Revolution in Germany during the first half of the nineteenth century, he meant, like Marx in relation to Kant's political ideas, that the socio-economic conditions (*Realfaktoren*) for such ideas were at that time still lacking in Germany.[7] In this essentially self-contradictory extension by Marx of the direct class- and situation-boundedness of ideology, he conceded what for many modern behaviourists is a rule, namely that ideological attitudes can be adopted which neither tally with nor derive immediately from tangible class interests. Indeed, modern behavioural theories are at one with Marx in opposing ideological and factual orientation. Both share the assumption that the socio-economic interests of a class constitute the objective referent of social and political orientation with which ideology is at variance. In the behavioural conception, however, ideology is dislodged in principle from material interests, and political postures based on interests are contrasted with those based on ideology, which is neither dialectically nor otherwise conditioned by such interests. According to that approach, an example of the disjunction between class/party loyalty and ideology rather than of a clash of ideological motivations would be a class-conscious but strongly Protestant working man who normally voted Democratic but did not cast his vote in favour of the Catholic J. F. Kennedy. Or an equally class-conscious Catholic capitalist who normally voted Republican might be supposed to switch his vote to J. F. Kennedy for the same reason – the candidate's Catholicism. Indeed, in the Catholic vote for Kennedy religious almost entirely overrode class loyalty.[8]

The detachment of ideology from the socio-economic base occurs not only in the behavioural approach we have been discussing. The dissociation of ideology from economic determination which in Marx's work represents a deviation from his main theses, reappears in official communism, where it is presented as being in harmony with orthodox premises. The dissociation is taken to have occurred with the socialization of the means of production and distribution in the post-capitalist classless but not stratumless society.[9] The suspension of the conditioning effect of the relations of production is assumed to reflect itself in society's increased insight. Since some stratification still persists, ideology continues to exist in post-capitalist society both as the officially legitimate set of true beliefs and insights and as the greatly reduced residue of 'false consciousness'.

In Mannheim's view, the chances of an adequate total perspective grow to the extent that the factual insights embedded in class-based ideologies can be synthesized from the higher vantage point of the intelligentsia. The synthesis remains ideology in so far as it bears on political action. Such a bearing Mannheim certainly had in mind, and it is, as I argue throughout this book, the decisive characteristic of ideological thought. Intellectuals are capable of achieving a synthesis of partial truths by virtue of their specific social position which does not involve them directly in the economic process. For a small stratum education is in effect the substitute for the economic class-forming factor.[10] (Hence no 'Mannheim paradox'.)

The behavioural dissociation of ideology from the determining power of economic interests is also an exception, but it occurs on a much larger scale and is seen to prevail in the day-to-day life of politics, indicating an increase in unpredictability, not of rationality, as assumed in official communism and by Mannheim. The collection of data and the construction of explanatory hypotheses proceed from the premise that for people engaged in similar occupations it is more rational to reveal a similar political orientation (as witnessed in voting) than to behave ideologically, which is to deviate from the rational norm of class-determined or class-oriented political behaviour.

Despite the important differences between the views of both Marx and Mannheim and the behavioural approach in which ideological are opposed to prevalent interest-based norms of political behaviour, the Marxian dogmatic assertion of the 'falseness' of ideology is reflected in this behavioural approach. For any link is removed and the cleavage accentuated between a matter-of-fact attitude and ideology. To reject such an evaluation as unfounded is not, of course, to hold that 'ideological' can be entirely dissociated from 'unreal'. Also, the behavioural replacement of the Marxist *derivation* of all political beliefs from material interest by the insistence on the possible *confrontation* of interest-based and other beliefs is a corrective of the Marxist position. Yet to the behavioural approach mentioned, and to the juxtaposition of morals and interest generally, can be applied Bernstein's criticism of historical materialism to the effect that political postures presumed to be subservient to objective class interests incorporate moral judgment.[11] In other words, interest-based beliefs are the same as all the other political beliefs, since the conception and propagation of any political belief requires at one stage or another resort to ethical norms for the public justification of a socially important satisfaction and integration of demands.[12] On this fact founders, *inter alia,* the assumption of a non-ideological give-and-take politics, as I have shown in some detail in Chapter IV.

Evidently, any set of political principles, arising generally from political demands and attitudes and devised for their direction, has something unreal about it in the sense, both of 'meta-factual' and 'unrealized'. To decide on action for the gratification of specific interests is to set objectives necessarily connected with moral (meta-factual) justifications; to embark on action means more often than not that the envisaged outcome is, for some time at least, in abeyance (unrealized). In these two regards, as in others, there is no difference between the political pursuit of material class interests, and policies which have nothing to do with them. Moral judgments and uncertainty about the consequences of decisions are involved whether the aim is to restore or reduce a given differential of wages; to discriminate against, or in favour of, one kind, or all kinds, of religious education; to outlaw or legalize homosexual and lesbian relationships; or to defend or subvert the pluralist or the communist societies.

b. *Interest-based and other Beliefs*

In the behavioural approach we have been discussing it is, thus, assumed correctly that not all beliefs are determined by class interest and that, even if it corresponds to one's class position, a political attitude is a matter of choice. On these scores, as distinct from the failure to recognize that all political beliefs are ideological, the behavioural approach is really a corrective of Marxist theory. After all, just as the Benthamist axiom that everybody is the best judge of his own interests is an over-simplification, so there is something patently absurd about that strand of the Marxist theory of ideology which implies that, in the pursuit of the specific interests inherent in their social position, people necessarily misjudge the important facts of life.[13] No doubt, judgments are liable to be blinded by interests, but by no means in every instance. This is confirmed by the histories of successful individuals, such as self-made millionaires, manual workers, shop stewards and what not, on the one hand, and by big business and organized labour, as they have so far fared, on the other.

The adequate awareness of interests and of their promotion would not render choices predictable, even were there only one course of action open to satisfy given interests of the group to which a person belongs. He could still for perfectly rational reasons choose to support another course, depending, for instance, on whether he wished to support the interests of his present class or of that to which he aspired, or wanted his children to belong to. ('Anticipatory socialization' is the term for this motivation far from recently discovered.) It is likewise a rational attitude to embrace for reasons of justice the cause of the less privileged (Marx, Engels and latter-day middle-class student revolutionaries), and not merely for personal advantages people from the less privileged classes will side with the more privileged (Burke)[14] or support moderate reform (a considerable part of the students in recent student unrest). Finally, what is indisputably best for one's class is frequently the subject of argument. Hence any of the aforementioned decisions about supporting certain class interests which may or may not correspond to the correct assessment of how the interests of one's class are best served may be rationally and/or morally defensible. Interest orientation and class position are, then, open-ended referents, in the main not because more than one rational course of action can be derived from them, but chiefly because class loyalty is as little precluded from being a matter of rational choice as are all other socio-political beliefs.

While studies of voting behaviour and public opinion show that class membership is not the exclusive determinant of political behaviour, they also confirm that class-based solidarities still form a particularly strong belief element. Yet nationalism and regionalism, are at times hardly less important, and for many, religious allegiance still outbids class loyalty. Religion which is likely to clash with class loyalty also combines with it or with nationalism and regionalism.

However great its strength, class loyalty has never united the working classes, who, broadly defined, still form the largest section of advanced industrial societies. Even if the majority does exhibit such class identification, it is not necessarily expressed in votes. In England, the Labour Party, with no serious competition from another working-class party, cannot rely any more than the Conservatives upon more than one-third of the electorate, two-thirds of which can be classified as working-class. The vote Labour receives from the middle classes seldom exceeds 20 per cent, while working-class votes not cast for Labour rarely fall below 40 per cent. At most elections about half of the Conservatives' total electoral support comes from one-third of the working-class vote.[15]

Whether class membership and ideological commitment are more stringently or loosely related, depends of course on the political culture and the issues at stake. As the data of the Michigan Survey Research Center show, in 1956 the percentage in America of the sample favouring greater governmental activity in connection with unemployment, education, housing and the like was the largest in all occupational categories; it moved from 40 per cent among professionals to 68 per cent among unskilled workers.[16] These and other data show the limitation, as well as the existence, of the correlation between occupation (or class) and political opinions. John Stuart Mill anticipated the results of quantitative research in general terms when he said that 'though the persuasions and convictions of average men are in a much greater degree determined by their personal position than by reason, no little power is exercised over them by the persuasions and convictions of those whose personal position is different, and by the united authority of the instructed.'[17]

The far from negligible asymmetry between class membership and ideological commitment, and its corollary, the similarity between class-based and other beliefs, were no novelty for Marxists, such as Kautsky, Bernstein and Lenin, in so far as they stressed that political working-class consciousness has to be brought to the workers 'from without', i.e. it must be taught and cultivated – whatever the differences between the kinds of teaching the three ideologists had in mind.[18] This applies, of course, not just to the proletariat or to specific circumstances. Experience everywhere confirms that the masses, as well as elite publics, are being instructed in class consciousness as they are instructed in other beliefs, and as formerly they were especially in religion. Philosophers, priests and political leaders always realized, and needed no technicallly refined opinion surveys to tell them, that indoctrination and propaganda are required for any organization to gain and retain followers.[19]

Beliefs which Marxists and non-Marxists assume to be appropriate to a given class position, as the latter explicitly declare and the former cannot help admitting, are not universally adopted by those who are in that position. It has also been shown that, like all other beliefs, class-based beliefs are tied to values and must be taught to be accepted. Hence there is as little foundation for setting class-based beliefs apart from ideological beliefs as there is for considering all political beliefs as class-bound. Now, if for these reasons it also needs to be acknowledged that whatever men are told and taught for the purpose of committing them to certain political attitudes and actions is ideological, it does not follow that this purpose renders ideological thought entirely or even overwhelmingly prejudiced and incorrect.

2. COMMITMENT AND OBJECTIVE FINDINGS

a. *Science and Ideology*

On account of the role of valuational elements in their action-orientation, ideologies often contain biased and false assertions. Frequently, future events belie past ideological predictions and promises, and competition with political rivals invites the stretching of points as well as outright deception. But philosophical and scientific propositions, too, have proved to be false[20], and simplification is not peculiar to ideology but is generally attendant upon the exercise of rationality.[21] Indeed, a statement does not become ideological merely because it is false or because judgments of value parade as statements of fact,[22] but because simplification and the transgression-cum-manipulation of available knowledge serve to make out a case for the kind of action and aims that are recommended. For this purpose a problem is likely to be posed in the light of the solution one has in mind in the first place.[23] What ensues is a more complete picture of reality, of its potentialities and shortcomings, than can be verified. Yet just as not all that is false is ideological, so not all that is placed within an ideological context is false, non-factual, slanted or mendacious.

Of course, nothing could be correct in ideologies if science and philosophy were unable to gain correct insights about the character of the natural and social world. Notwithstanding the claims of Marxist or non-Marxist historist relativism and relationism, the far-reaching changes over the centuries in culture and class structure have not swept away the belief that some knowledge at least is testable and that this is made possible by some constancy in the relationship between the external world and our impression of it. Further, since some things are still believed to be true despite the passage of time, what has once been recognized as true may as well remain so.[24]

Awareness of the uncertainty and derivative character of knowledge has always spurred men to circumscribe the sources and limits of certain knowledge. The fundamental problem faced by the theory of ideology was already posed in the Greek distinction between *doxa* and *episteme*.[25] For mass consumption, Plato had put 'the noble lie' – the premeditated distortion of historical truth to make the best state acceptable to the majority – at the disposal of the philosopher who knows and, given the chance, will realize the truth. Bacon's theory of idols placed the source of error firmly within the social context. Locke's critical epistemology was not only claimed as godfather by the *idéologues* but, like much else in his thought, denoted the level-headed limitations of scepticism. Although very little knowledge is certain, he argued, knowledge of 'the grounds and degrees of belief, opinion and assent' that men can achieve is sufficient for their needs.[26] Within the assumptions about objectivity and correctness, limited in this way, science, philosophy and ideology are not totally incompatible with one another.

If a set socio-political aim and its normative foundation were to cast their shadow over all the rest of the ideological discourse and, as a result, its factual and logical contents were to become inextricably enmeshed in distortion, even modern behavioural political science would be hard put to it to substantiate the claim to any unbiased insight. Many empirical researchers and theorists wish to promote understanding and thus the maintenance and improvement of democratic systems and their supporting sub-systems. If such a commitment does not preclude correct insights, there is no reason to deny them to political philosophies and ideologies.[27]

It is certainly not easy to determine 'where ideology leaves off and [social] science begins',[29] since the latter is very often ideological in both its roots and its consequences. This does not, however, entail that the objectivity of the findings of social science cannot be kept from being prejudged by the ideologically determined objectives of an inquiry, the partial testing of hypotheses and the selective use of evidence.[29] The unadulterated significance of the findings of social science is hardly less important for those who believe that 'the special application of science in social affairs represents our commitment to the rational improvement of our society'[30] than for those who pursue social science for its own sake. In the long run at least, radical no less than gradual meliorism will not benefit from findings adapted to preconceived ideas. It is a concern of science and of ideology to find out, for instance, whether, and if so to what extent, the temporary forfeiture of existing advantages will ensure the availability of the means for an eventually fairer, and for the deprived minorities in any case greater, allocation of benefits. Science can best serve ideology if the willingness of the purveyors of ideology to adapt ends to means does not lag too far behind their readiness to adapt means to ends. Science can provide the means and know-how for the realization of goals inspired by strong passions and by little regard for human life and dignity in the here and now.[31] By the same token, science can reveal the nature of the means and the cost (in terms, above all, of human suffering and dignity) of achieving goals; it can then supply the basis for what has been aptly called 'responsible ideology'.[32]

Since science can be harnessed to commitment, as well as helping to judge it, more might be lost than gained by accepting social science as 'the ultimate ideology'.[33] It would no longer be science if it suggested only one set of ways of improving society, as an ideology does, instead of examining suggested programmes of improvement or exploring alternative projects, detailing in either case social costs in both the short run and the long run. Which project society should adopt involves decisions about priorities. Social science can clarify, but it cannot determine, the criteria of such decisions, let alone make them without endangering both its standing as a science and that modicum of self-determination that Western-type democratic institutions permit today to all men and women.

Even if precise prediction should become possible, conceptions and theories would still be needed to justify and influence choices between the alternatives indicated by the computers. Given that every social concept has, or can be invested with, 'an ideological force', or that 'the ideological relevance of social science is inherent in its very existence as social fact',[34] even the most objective concepts and conceptions can be geared to conflicting preferences and used to supply rational excuses for irrational commitments. Hence it is all the more important that such preferential concepts, or rather conceptions, should be critically approached, and this is possible only so long as there is a confrontation between ideology on the one hand and science and philosophy on the other. Only the possibility of such a confrontation can ensure that concepts and theories, such as those concerning elites, which are put forth in the name of either social science or ideology but actually feed upon both, will be constantly re-evaluated in order to achieve more adequate and truer assessments of facts than those we have,[35] and in order to decide what can be done about them. In other words, social science as 'the ultimate ideology' needs a science and a philosophy of social science to keep alive their critical function, and this brings the wheel full circle. It does not follow that, if ideology cannot become 'ultimate' even by being wedded to science, ideology and science can have nothing in common.

It cannot be proved that no ideological statement can ever be valid or that a doctrine forfeits its claim to objectivity because it contains judgments of value.[36] A considerable number of ideological statements referring to factual (and other) contents can be tested, and predictions are verified or falsified by events. For example, the kinds of institution permitted in a society and the way in which they function prove or disprove claims made about the ideological principles which that society is said to realize. For such a test of broad principles the generally-known features of a regime furnish sufficient evidence. So do the nature and results of specific policies in regard both to general principles and to their specification in the dimension of fundamental ideology. The degree to which equality of opportunity, as affirmed in Liberal-democratic ideology, is realized, or realizable, and the claims made in Marxism for the social effects of the socialization of the means of production and distribution, can be tested by reference to the clearly perceptible realities of the liberal-democratic and communist establishments respectively. For ideological controversy in these matters pertains less to the acknowledgment of the observable facts than to their significance. It is worth recalling, however, that not all statements concerning causal concatenation can as yet be conclusively tested; thus ideological propositions are not necessarily proved or disproved according to whether the predictions based upon them come true or not. That no communist revolution has occurred according to the general rule Marx laid down, does not by itself prove that his analysis of capitalist society was incorrect; as has been pointed out quite often, his predictions may well have had the effect of self-denying prophecies.

Ideologies are indeed neither first-order valuations nor first-order statements of facts,[37] except perhaps when the ideology is embedded in the work of a major thinker. Yet even as maintained by a party, not only does ideology borrow and incorporate but it also provides the impetus for the elaboration of scientific and philosophical insights. In all probability there is truth in Althusser's words that 'a new science detaches itself from the background of earlier ideological formations'. One can also say of ideology in general what Kolakowski says of Marxist ideology, namely that it grew out of science by way of its alienation from it, and although no ideology can 'forego the scientific façade . . . this façade on its part is subject to alienation from ideology'.[38] The perpetual tension between the rational values of scientific thought and ideology is thus reflected in the at once destructive and fertilizing influence of the latter on the former.[39] Generally enforced ideological principles in particular may be the undoing of whole branches of science (the Lysenko affair, Stalinist linguistics, etc.), just as the action-orientation of ideology, its inevitable efforts at rational self-presentation and justification of its moral foundations and aspirations, provides a challenge and impetus for the philosophical reassertion or reassessment of values, as well as for the scientific exploration of new socio-economic techniques and forms of organization.

As to the facts which are either part of an ideological argument or confute or confirm it as part of a scientific argument, those are meant which qualify normally as historical facts.[40] This leaves us with the difficulty to which Marx and orthodox Marxism gave a dogmatically tainted expression after Kant had faced it in his conception of the transcendental categories of apperception. I mean the difficulty 'of seizing the given as it is given', since 'facts . . . must themselves be given propositional form before theory can come to grips with them'.[41] This applies as much at the level of ordinary political discourse as at that of theory. Still, even bearing in mind the additional caveat that statements of fact are not as sharply distinguishable from judgments of value as their verbal juxtaposition seems to imply, ideological discourse can be said to relate to facts even in generalizing statements to the effect that 'capitalism in the West has changed in some respects and is no longer the enemy of the common man'. The first part of the statement is an incontrovertible fact, whereas the second part is an inference open to dispute, depending on the criteria of judgment. The statement is patently different from the following one: 'Capitalism is only one of the plots hatched by World Jewry to dominate the Aryan race (or to undermine the communist revolution)'. Enough in both statements can be falsified and verified to stamp the first as an inference from facts and the second as a smear in which facts are distorted and distortions are arbitrarily related to each other. This does not mean that fascist ideology, even Hitler's (or Stalin's) speeches, only distorts facts. No political belief system of any importance can be shown to consist wholly of unverifiable statements, conscious or unconscious lies and deceptions.

b. *The Experiential Barrier to Distortion*[42]

Although not any set of descriptive concepts and factual appraisals is equally compatible with any set of values,[43] ideologues cannot succeed by eschewing testable facts altogether. To be effective, ideas must be fitted to 'the culture of a target audience'.[44] While the adaptation serves the purpose of making the audience adopt beliefs and attitudes which it might not have adopted otherwise, this objective can be achieved only if the ideas put before an audience correspond with a minimal number of attested and attestable facts. Many people at least know where the shoe pinches and more often than not they are inclined to impart this awareness to others, to say nothing of laying the blame at the door of others again, which is, after all, an essential feature of the game of politics. Then there are the competing mass media and 'middlemen' who, notwithstanding Marcuse's half-truths,[45] are engaged among other things in mutual 'unmasking', thus helping the common run of men to know something about what is going on. Complete distortion, and hence the refutability of all its statements, would be the undoing of any ideology. As Lane puts it, 'total incongruence between ideology and experience extinguishes a social movement'.[46] Since philosophy was born, dogmas have been defended and attacked not just on the grounds of *credo quia absurdum est* (which itself attests a rearguard action against empiricist rational argument), but through reference to facts and rational inferences from them. Neither critical nor justificatory inferences can be ruled out in the choice of, much less in the discussion between, competing moral, religious, political or philosophical creeds.[47] The necessarily supplementary relationship between action and perception speaks immediately against the entirely arbitrary handling of tested and testable evidence in ideologies and in any kind of action-oriented belief system. On this basis members of mass publics, too, not only apprehend facts but relate them to one another, and judge their own actions and the words and actions of others.

Individuals and groups experience the rebound of their encounter with things and persons outside themselves. In such encounters their expectations may be proved wrong or right according to the standards they share with other people. Without such sharing society would be impossible, since actors and spectators could not proceed, as normally they do, on the assumption that it is possible to assess correctly, at least in the short run, a considerable number of causes and consequences of social actions. The account we give of our experiences and more especially of our motivations may be faulty. 'The principles which men profess on any controverted subject are usually a very incomplete exponent of the opinions they really hold.'[48] John Stuart Mill's observation is borne out by the fact, stressed by Riker, that nearly 80 per cent of American voters think of themselves as supporters of one of the major parties, and in many districts vote accordingly, while they tell the pollsters that they normally choose the man rather than the party.[49] Language itself may help to create a dissonance between comparable spheres of thought and action,[50] and so may the wish of respondents to say what they feel is expected of good citizens. Moreover, the ability to put into words what we are doing or experiencing is not the same as is required for knowing, deciding and doing.[51] The judgment of a person must be said to be correct if he achieves by his actions what he had intended, even if the account he gives of his actions does not make sense. If he fails in his endeavour, his inability to explain what he has learned is no proof that he has learned nothing. His further action will prove what his previous action or, for that matter, the actions performed by other people, has taught him.

The difference between the ability to act consistently and the ability to account for action consistently has been assumed not to count in the assessment of the degreees of coherence or 'constraint' between the idea-elements which inform outlook and political attitudes.[52] Even so, it is only too easy to go wrong and attribute too much coherence to the better-educated and not enough to the less-educated when it comes to the evaluation of their articulate judgment of general principles of public policy. Indeed, in a particular instance Converse is wrong in evaluating the answers elicited from a working man as an 'extreme case' of incoherence. There is no contradiction between his respondent's strong feeling against the rich and his styling himself a 'strong socialist' on the one hand, and on the other agreeing to let private enterprise handle electric power and housing,[53] if such an arrangement offers advantages to the workers. As I shall explain in Chapter VIII on another issue, the respondent is also innocent of ideological illogicality with respect to the 'American standard socialist doctrine'.

Here it is sufficient to add that in countries where socialism means more than business-like trade unionism, social democratic parties also have revealed increased flexibility or unsteadiness over government ownership and interference. Converse's working man was incoherent by the standards of the fundamentals of nineteenth-century European socialism; but not, as we shall see in Chapter VIII, by American standards, nor by those prevailing in the operative ideology of European Labour parties.

There is, therefore, a basis for arguing that even what enters the undistorted field of vision of mass publics through the filter of their immediate concern with their narrow interests (however modestly assessed) must be added to the competition of elites as a factor which requires the purveyors of ideology to base it upon a modicum of verified and verifiable statements. This is precisely what political philosophers and mere ideologists alike have always been doing. It is one reason why different political philosophies and ideologies share propositions about facts, and even about values. This phenomenon might be called propositional pluralism, of which ethical and ideological pluralism are specific variants.

3. LIMITS OF DISAGREEMENT

The existence of ideological pluralism severely restricts the validity of both the general historist notion about the time-boundedness of moral standards and the Marxist version of that notion: the dependence of the whole ideational and political superstructure on a given state of production and social relations.[54] Ideological pluralism also reinforces the case I have been trying to make out against equating ideological predominantly with truth-distorting argumentation and thus with being unexceptionally at variance with science and philosophy. This case is strengthened by the demonstration of agreements between ideologies, since agreement is a necessary though not, of course, a sufficient condition of the correctness of views.

The sharing of ideas between contemporaneous ideologies is evinced in the fact that ideologies of the Right, Centre and Left are not divided, for instance, over what brought the market economy about, its mechanism and its general social consequences, although they hold different opinions concerning the degree to which the market economy can ensure optimal production and/or a morally defensible distribution of benefits. Taxation is meant by all to have redistributive effects, but the extent of redistribution is a matter of dispute. Perpetual disagreements on these and other matters concerning the just order of priorities do not justify the assertion that the notion of 'false consciousness' struck root because 'the various standpoints' were not only inadequate but incompatible.[55] Marx, Guizot, Tocqueville, Spencer and Mill did not betray the slightest doubt about the adequacy of their respective standpoints, nor did their analyses of bourgeois society lack points of agreement.

Marx himself paid homage to British governmental commissions and inspectors for their courageous reports, and to the classical economists for their pertinent insights.[56] Although he was self-contradictory on the point, in the final analysis Marx apparently wanted to argue that bourgeois 'false consciousness' distorted the interpretation rather than the immediate apprehension of facts. He also did not deny that in his causal interpretations and evaluations of phenomena he built on foundations laid by bourgeois thinkers. He even charged bourgeois historians and politicians with having introduced the evaluation of history in terms of class war.[57] Contrary to his assertions on principle, Marx conceded in all contexts that fundamental evaluations and causal interpretations also transcend time and class.

The centrality in the ideological composite of ethical norms embodied in moral prescriptions, and their effect on all other components, constitute the distinctiveness of the ideology. But ideological pluralism also extends to this component, and to what it determines. Socialism opposes capitalism, yet an anti-capitalist strain and a highly critical attitude towards the values of industrial civilization characterize both nineteenth-century conservatism and socialism and twentieth-century fascism. Conservatism and Marxism elevate collective entities over individuals and assume as given, or preach as imperative, trans-subjective determination of individual will.[58] Liberalism has been attacked by the Right and Left, but feudalism, liberalism and Marxism are at one in denouncing etatism with varying degrees of fervour and consistency. In the name, and for the purposes, of both liberal and Leninist politics, social determination was severely qualified. Mill rejected the view that it is beyond the power of politicians and philosophers to direct 'the forces . . . on which the greater phenomena depend'. He cited various instances to show 'how far mere physical and economic power' is from being the only determinant of 'social power'. These views are matched by Lenin's belief in the 'inspired ideologist' who is able to obviate that which 'is determined by the interaction of the material elements and the material environment . . .'.[59] In Chinese communism, we find an official ' "populist" hostility to formal state administration',[60] which reflects at least the semantics of the pluralists' demands, whereas the situation in Yugoslavia led Lukić to expect the participation and mobilization in a fully communist society of 'free individuals, politically active' to be like the 'non-ideological' activity of American pressure groups.[61] A communist scholar accepts here as non-ideological one of the main characteristics of the prototype of advanced capitalist polities in order to claim that this characteristic can be a hallmark of the fully communist society.

Of course, similar organizational forms or their substitutes can be assimilated to different political systems without effacing the distinctive character of these systems and their predominant ideology.[62] A striking example is the Soviet aspiration in the early twenties to achieve 'communist Americanism'.[63] However, in industrial organization the similarities may reach a degree liable to impair severely the distinctiveness of fundamental principles and goals that the ideology of a system claims to realize. Indeed, too obstrusive facts forced Soviet ideologists long ago to admit that in the stage of socialist relations of production classlessness had not as yet been achieved. The polemic between communists and non-communists on this score, however, obscures the simple fact that 'to each according to his merit' is actually a liberal principle and it cannot be expected to have entirely different social effects in conditions of near-total nationalization and in a mixed economy. The few instances cited of contemporaneous ideological pluralism reinforce the conclusion that whatever the specific effect of the social condition of people is supposed to have on their attitudes and ideas, within a fairly developed society social position neither assures nor prevents consensus on matters of fact and their interpretation or on valuations.

Ideological pluralism is not a recent phenomenon; it is apparently coterminous with the emergence of political conflict and competition. Nor, as my examples have already intimated, is it confined to the relationship between the belief systems of one and the same epoch and country; it also exists at one and the same time between such belief systems and those of other epochs. For, in their responses to challenges of their time, belief systems attest that some specific problems of human relationship are basically perennial and have evoked similar aspirations for their complete or partial solutions – and similar kinds of controversies about them. This applies, above all, to the so far most persistent and central problem of social relations, the cleft between the poor and the rich. In point of fact, Marx (and Kautsky) admitted the persistence in time of ethical norms and beliefs about truths, that is of epoch-transcending ethical and ideological pluralism. His failure to cope with the phenomenon in conformity with the principles of 'historical materialism'[64] lends additional weight to the conclusion that the persistence in time of social problems and of thoughts about their solution, like the transcendence of class perspectives in the perception and causal interpretation of phenomena, affords evidence of the relative independence from, and impact on, specific economic and social condition, of feelings and ideas about social relations.

The role played in the management (or mismanagement) of men's social and political arrangements by ideas and feelings in their own right is evinced not only in the perenniality of problems and the reactions to them, but also in what relates divergent opinions to their time and culture. In other words, if despite changes in social and technological conditions, the time-transcending nature of social problems and the possibilities envisaged for their solution testify to the permanence and influence of thoughts and feelings, these can also be presumed to leave their imprint on, or to underlie, the specific complexion and complexity generally assumed by problems and solutions of social organization or beliefs in particular times and circumstances, because a common denominator transcends class divides and other cleavages. For example, the divergent assumptions and conclusions of socialist and liberal claims have rested on a common basis, particularly since the end of the eighteenth century: secular rationalism. This permitted, among other things, reliance on the same criteria of refutability and substantiation of arguments. Similarly, the Hebrew prophets, the critics of society and the priests, the defenders of the Establishment, invoked in their clashes, as the same authority, divine revelation. Reason and religion were simultaneously relied upon when notable shifts between them divided the two great traditions prevailing between 1500 and 1700, i.e. the Christian-inspired metaphysics of order and Baconian empiricism.[65] Liberalism and democracy as well as various gradations of autocracy have been defended on the basis of rationalist deductionism or empiricism, of a rational or irrational commitment to the lessons of history and/or to transcendent values and authorities.

Indeed, the moral foundations of prescriptions which play a central role in political philosophies as well as in secular and religious ideologies, provide considerable ground for ideological pluralism, in both its era-bound and era-transcending dimensions. Neither ends nor means follow straightforwardly from the underlying ethical and generally metaphysical premises of a belief system.[66] Affirming utilitarian norms over and against absolute norms, Hobbes opposed traditional absolutists, with whom, however, he shared the traditional Christian scepticism about human nature (though, like Machiavelli, in an essentially secularized form) and the insistence on the necessity of authoritarian government. Conversely, Aristotle accepted the premises of Plato's conception of ethics but rejected Plato's idea of the best state. Thus, conflicting moral and political maxims have often been derived from identical theological and metaphysical premises, just as similar moral and political maxims have been based upon divergent metaphysical premises.

Considering the trans-epochal comparability of both contents of conceptions and categories of judgment, the re-emergence in secular ideologies of religious motives and objectives deserves to be recalled, like the disparagement of earthly goods and the corresponding craving for and promise of the redemption of Man. Marx transformed rather than replaced conceptions and categories which occupied a central place in the Judeo-Christian tradition, including their eschatology.[67] His vague and indeterminate intimations of the classless and stateless society amount in fine to a secularized version of St Augustine's City of God, conceived by way of pushing to a naive extreme the liberal principles of individual liberty, freely-willed association and minimal state coercion.

Of course, such ramified ideational genealogies and parallels are incomplete and more often than not dissimilarities carry more weight than similarities. Also, there is no denying ideological change, or generally the overall distinctiveness of ideologies and other belief systems. Yet the fact of analogy does not admit of any doubt either, even though politically and otherwise its importance does not match its conspicuousness. Indeed, agreement on this point itself is very likely. People can be supposed to accept that in important aspects Marxist and non-Marxist socialism, or developed communist and developed neo-capitalist and welfarist societies, resemble each other. Nevertheless, in both instances, much greater importance will probably be attached to the remaining differences, whether the matter is judged from a communist, anti-communist or neutral standpoint. Yet the scales might tilt again in favour of similarity if we considered, for instance, that religious and different secular belief systems can arouse the same kind of fanaticism. The relationship between similarity and dissimilarity might again be differently evaluated in respect of the fact that fundamental questions of human existence, and of what we can know about it, have their origin in pre-theological magical thought. These questions have retained their importance in speculative and mythical theology, and philosophy has never liberated itself from this inheritance. Consequently, presuppositions concerning the demonstrability of statements and the methods of argumentation also fall within the range of the analogous. The dialectical method and the unity of theory and practice,[68] as well as alienation in conjunction with the knowability of truth, originated in religious thought.[69] There are Marxist philosophers who are far from denying such analogies.[70]

The main reasons why we find identical or similar concepts and conceptions in belief systems of one time and country and of various times and countries may be summed up as follows. Firstly, in political theories and ideologies ends and means are not unequivocally determined by the ethical norms to which they are related, and in itself the ends-means relationship is far from being a conclusive criterion of differentiation between ideologies. In politics different ends often require similar means, while some basic ends are necessarily shared by all known political systems. Secondly, together with specific epoch-bound problems, similar problems of social existence demand attention, and the assessment of their nature is not nearly as controversial as differences of opinion about their solution might suggest. Thirdly, since patterns of solutions and their criticism endure, political belief systems enlarge upon, and in the process transform, previously held and differently based ideals, in accordance with similar evaluation of given conditions. While in the course of such development belief systems of the same and different times therefore continue to share affirmations, agreement would seem to reveal itself particularly in what is rejected.

The phenomenon of ideological pluralism has been noted in the history of ideas, social beliefs and movements.[71] But the term has been rarely used[72] and not much attention has been paid to the significance of ideological pluralism for the validity of assumptions concerning the relationship between thought (especially ideological thought) and other existential factors. This significance of ideological pluralism can be summed up by enlarging briefly on two intertwined conclusions implicit in my previous remarks.

Firstly, ideological pluralism does not permit us to postulate that the contents and categories of thought are exclusively determined by a specific class structure and the specific conditions of an epoch. Secondly, to whatever degree political doctrines are so determined, they are not for this reason rendered entirely unlike one another. Ideological pluralism therefore weakens the assertion that by virtue of such determination thought is necessarily distorted. Agreement at least between persons competent to judge the merit of a case, does not disprove falsity, but it is a necessary condition of correctness.

In addition to agreements between ideologies, the fact that members of different classes adhere to the same ideology and support the same political party provides further evidence against the contention that ideology is inexorably tied to class or other interest orientation, or to one's personality structure (except in pathological cases). It is not an altogether rare occurrence that people with different social backgrounds and interests, as well as different personality structures, do agree with one another in political as in other matters. If this were not so, the existence of societies as we know them would be inexplicable.

It is by now a commonplace that the notion of the determination of ideas by social circumstances can serve only as the ground for formulating more precise hypotheses for historical and sociological research. Methodologically, propositional and ideological pluralism demand the demarcation of two configurations of thought and belief in order to establish with some exactness the degree to which thought and beliefs can be related to class and epoch. The one is the configuration attributable to most members of a society in a given epoch, and the other that which is unique to the majority of the members of various (two or more) classes of people. Even if broadly verified, such two-fold ascription of configurations of thought, beliefs and attitudes is as yet no proof that all common beliefs are directly determined by the general characteristics of the period and indirectly by its specific socio-economic structure and that the latter accounts directly for all different beliefs. At least some beliefs and attitudes may be 'inherited' and retained despite, or in re-established harmony with, incisive changes in the socio-economic structure and in the fortunes of a particular class.

Among the more prosperous workers in Great Britain persists a working-class outlook, or at least self-identification with the working classes. In addition to distinct habits of dress and speech which tend to perpetuate the feeling of status distinction,[73] its political significance is certainly fostered by the fact that the Labour Party has officially remained socialist. This again seems to be the result of the growth of militant trade unionism in developed industrial societies (as may be noted also where large communist parties exist, as in France and Italy). That militancy seems to be attendant upon the combined growth of affluence and expectations in the better-off strata of the working classes and the corresponding consciousness of 'relative deprivation', that is of the reaction to the continuation, if not growth, of disparity of incomes and status. On these grounds trade-unionism in developed industrial countries seems to provide the fuel for working-class radicalism, which is perhaps socialist more in some of its arguments than in its overall aspirations.

If, then, class membership and specific economic conditions are important but not sole factors in the formation of ideological postures, these appear to be determined also by the thoughts and feelings with which class membership and economic conditions are directly evaluated or weighed over and against other factors, such as religious or ethnic allegiances. The role of beliefs and disbeliefs in their own right as co-determinants of varying importance of political orientations and attitudes which must be inferred from the existence of ideological pluralism, is confirmed by data about the political behaviour of elites and mass publics. Both kinds of evidence indicate clearly that only in responding to the challenges of a given situation (which is unique in some respects but not in all) are political philosophies and the less systematic belief systems of any time conditioned by that situation. More precisely, ideologies are determined by both material and spiritual factors in so far as they respond to them through their different presuppositions. Hence, what can lay claim to validity (or probability) is not the assumption of a hierarchical order of causal factors within a monocausal framework, but the notion of a flexible, competitive and pluralistic configuration of causal determinants.

Ideologies are thus limited by specific material conditions because they reflect certain attitudes towards them, but limited they are to the same degree, if not more, by prevalent beliefs and disbeliefs. It is hardly open to dispute that existing beliefs and disbeliefs are not only affected by party ideologies but eventually affect them and/or the ways adopted or proposed for their implementation. This rebound plays a decisive part in the actual functioning of ideologies, a subject to which we now turn our attention.

Part Three

IDEOLOGIES IN ACTION

It has been said that philosophical systems are variations on a few 'unit-ideas'.[1] It can also be argued that the stuff of politics generally consists of a limited number of ingredients which can, however, be combined in very numerous forms. Four elements can make up 24 combinations, six, 720, and so forth. In virtue of the distinctiveness of each combination of similar and dissimilar elements, ideological pluralism as such does not preclude the relative consistency, much less the mutual exclusiveness, of ideological systems. We may nevertheless agree with Carl Friedrich and call ideologies 'programmatic congeries of ideas',[2] without implying that the asymmetry of belief systems cannot be diminished.

Not surprisingly, the pressures for diminishing asymmetry are the corollary of the pressure which enhances and brings into the open the inherent asymmetry of ideologies. In vindicating their *raison d'être,* ideologies are pushed further along the road of ideological pluralism than the configuration of their fundamental principles necessarily entails. In fulfilling their function of guiding political action, all political belief systems become subject to strains and stresses that endanger their (in any case relative) consistency, since, inevitably, circumstances arise in which political parties must compromise over basic principles. Hence, in dealing with change in all the spheres of public life, in attempting to furnish the guide-lines and justification for either effecting or averting change, party ideologies are confronted with the challenge of changing themselves. Two-dimensional argumentation reflects this process; it is the indicator of ideological change as well as the means of dissimulating it, and operates in a manner which is well known in practice but largely unexplicated in terms of systematic theory.

The very disinclination of the parties' leadership and ideologists to acknowledge the real extent of change could be expected to provoke interest in revealing the nature and mechanisms of ideological change. The same cannot be said about the devaluation of the ideological factor in empirical political science and the talk of theorists about 'the end of ideology' or 'de-ideologization'. If one assumes that ideology plays a subordinate role or is on the way out, the question of how ideologies change becomes largely irrelevant. However, as a closer look at political argumentation demonstrates, its division into two dimensions is universal, and reflects before long changes of content and direction in the ideology of a party. Two-dimensional argumentation in politics reveals the pressures for change as well as the initial stage of facing the challenge of change; it does not automatically, or necessarily, lead to change. However, two-dimensionality as such can be shown to pertain to all political belief systems. Although this is incidental to their purpose, the following chapters will, therefore, provide indirect support for the applicability of the term 'ideology' to all political belief systems. For if they 'behave' in the same way, why should they not bear the same name?

Chapter VI

FUNDAMENTAL AND OPERATIVE IDEOLOGY

In Chapter III, I have explained in general terms why two interacting dimensions or strands can be observed in all ideological argumentation. I have also stressed that, to whatever degree policies conform with fundamental principles, 'operative ideology' denotes the argumentation in favour of the policies actually adopted by a party. It is 'ideology' because it devises, explains and justifies action. It is 'operative' inasmuch as it is predicated on what is actually done or recommended for immediate action. Moreover, the explanations and justifications offered in operative ideology contain all the structural components of fundamental ideology. Operative deviates from or corresponds with fundamental ideology according to whether or not the specific contents (and the emphases of structural components) in one dimension are congruent with those found in the other.

There is no need to take issue here with the fairly numerous classifications of ideology that have elaborated upon or have been substituted for that of Mannheim, except in so far as the term 'operative ideology' or a similar one is used, and to the extent that views approximate or imply a two-dimensional conception. The critical discussion of these views and uses will assist clarification of what precisely is involved in the notion of the bifurcation of ideological argumentation.

I. ANTECEDENTS AND THE DIFFERENCE

Attempts at systematic discernment and analysis of dimensions of ideological argumentation are few, but by virtue of its very nature, some such discernment is implicit in at least some treatments of ideology. Much, of course, depends upon whether an ideology is dealt with it as if it were all of a piece, or as an asymmetric and fluctuating construct drawing heavily on other belief systems in its composition and application. Binder, for instance, complains about a lack of concern with ultimate value, inasmuch as the complete picture of ideological motivation evades us if we treat nationalism in developing countries as an epiphenomenon. Nationalism there is of the essence of the ideological complex, if for no other reason than that 'programmatic ideologies' which attract theoretical interest are in reality attached almost exclusively to nationalism.[1] There can be little doubt about the validity of the argument. Yet, as I shall intimate in the Epilogue, it is precisely the binding force of nationalism which highlights the existence of two-dimensional ideological argumentation and even makes it desirable. To anticipate, it is the recognition by leaders of the primacy of immediate national goals that makes possible the coexistence of consensus in the operative dimensions of 'programmatic ideologies' that conflict sharply in respect of their fundamentals.

A condition of discerning two-dimensionality is the awareness that 'tension and conflict over fundamental questions of moral and political philosophy' reverberate in the struggle for power and that in its course, to take one example, 'the ideal of hierarchy' has in Britain undergone many adaptations 'during its long history as an operative ideal'.[2] Scholars who point to lip-service – or rhetoric – as being apt at times to mislead about 'the operative ideal', do not, however, therefore assume a possible disparity in the developments of ideals and operative ideals, even though the assumption all the while is that a belief system often intersects or overlaps with others, even to the extent of appropriating planks from their platforms.

a. *Semantic and Substantive Intimations*

As with 'operative ideal', the use of the term 'operative ideology', or something similar, is in itself no indication of a two-dimensional approach. Thus, in one instance an observer says that 'operative ideology' refers to the 'vision' of the ultimate condition of society which actually guides totalitarian government. Here the vision is appraised in its totality as laid down and interpreted in the light of whatever practical steps are taken by a leader like Hitler or Stalin. Similarly, 'operative beliefs' are regarded as denoting, for instance, the particular versions of a religion practised by different social groups.[3] 'Operative ideology' is also used more specifically as opposed to beliefs 'which are most susceptible to change'. In this usage, a principle becomes 'operative' when, after some objective appraisal of the situation, it is adopted for political action and can be related to some element in the 'written', that is, the traditionally upheld, ideological system.[4] In these three cases 'operative ideology' is seen only as the application of principles, and no significant conflict between operative and fundamental principles is taken into account.

Likewise, in the case of American politics, 'operating beliefs' are regarded by theorists as reflecting those beliefs which find expression in official party statements and are tested 'in the market place or in the competition of the legislative struggle'.[5] Here one studies the different degrees of cohesion, comprehensiveness and dogmatism revealed by followers and leaders towards the beliefs associated officially with the parties. In the same vein, a comment on British politics opposes 'the official ideology' of the Labour Party to 'the operative ideology of its supporters at the grass roots'.[6] Thus, in connection with Western-type democracies, the assumption is often implicit that 'operating', 'operative' and 'official' beliefs reflect more or less authentic specifications of broad fundamental principles of party ideology, understood and/or adopted by leaders and followers to varying degrees. But there is no explicit assumption here about two-dimensionality within the 'official' ideology, as it is evinced in the tension between traditional principles and policies designed to realize those principles, as well as in the conflict between the traditional principles of a party and those underlying policies actually pursued.

I do not wish by any means to argue that tension or incongruence between principles officially professed and policies actually carried out or recommended, or the reasons for their occurrences have escaped notice. Nothing could be less true. What I suggest is that these phenomena can be more profitably discussed and analysed with the help of the proposed conceptual framework of ideological two-dimensionality. Indeed, many treatments of official party ideologies do make explicit, though in different terms, the phenomenon that I call two-dimensional argumentation. For instance, Scalapino emphasizes the rebound of policies upon long-standing ideological commitments, and also that policies, apart from mirroring change, cause inconsistencies between basic and practical commitments, just as inconsistency in this respect influences standpoints. He explains the positive response of Japanese intellectuals to Marxism not only by a traditional predisposition to abstraction, but also by the fact that these intellectuals are not encumbered in their doctrinaire imperturbability *vis-à-vis* the realities of the new Japan by the responsibilities or chances of wielding power. Their fidelity to fundamentals, I would say, is not disturbed by the requirements of practical politics reflected in operative ideology.

On the other hand, Scalapino stresses that 'a gap between commitment and practice' also reflects itself – though in reverse – in the new

Japanese conservatism. Its proponents do not defend intellectually concepts and practices which are legacies of the past, although, notwithstanding the official commitment to liberal democracy and the welfare state, their influence is still felt.[7] Conversely, yet by the same token, Harris styles 'the forward ends' of the British Conservative Party that counter radical demands and 'seem to differ from what exists' as 'inoperative, passive [and] marginal'. Even 'the "traces" of the past' in the main only 'colour the party's rhetoric'.[8] On my terms, when Japanese conservatives dissemble adherence to fundamentals that have become disreputable, or British Conservatives pretend adherence to fundamentals that remain inoperative, they are actually engaged in the intellectual activity of covering up discrepancies between the fundamental and operative dimensions, just as Japanese radical intellectuals do when they profess a faith in fundamentals without regard for what is done or what is possible.

Lowi also describes the practice of dissimulating change, and in doing so, in effect, implies the notion of two-dimensional argumentation. Although he neither uses that term nor appraises the phenomenon denoted by it precisely as I do, he applies 'operative ideology' to the principles which the American elite in practice follows more than any other body of doctrine.[9] He calls '*ersatz* public philosophy' the one serving to explain problems which arise in relation to deviations from 'the public philosophy'. 'Operative ideology' in this usage would seem to refer in the main, if not solely, to the 'ersatz' which veils the deviations of 'public policy' from the professed 'public philosophy'. As I conceive it, 'operative ideology' clearly applies also where there is no deviation, although the problem of two-dimensionality arises only when deviation occurs, as it is bound to do. However, Lowi takes into account another aspect attendant upon the relationship between what I call the operative and fundamental dimensions: the two ways of re-adapting the dimensions to each other. He suggests the elaboration of a new public philosophy consonant with actual public policy – that is, a change in the dimension of fundamentals and hence a change of the ideology. Alternatively, one might discredit the existing practice of 'incorporated pluralism' and make it amenable to political control[10] – that is, change policy and hence operative ideology in the light of the original intention of the fundamentals.

The normative involvement we witness here does not impugn Lowi's assessment of the phenomenon, since his analysis of it and its consequences are unchallengeable on factual grounds. The grounds of Bay's demand that behavioural scientists should desist from pretending to evade normative issues, while they re-admit them unchecked through the backdoor, are similarly verifiable. The adequacy of Bay's distinction between 'politics' and 'pseudopolitics' is not, therefore, necessarily affected by his deprecation of the latter. He conceives of 'politics' in terms not dissimilar to Crick's 'politics', but does not tie his plea for 'politics' to the condemnation of ideology and to its distinction from both 'politics' and 'doctrine'. 'Politics', according to Bay, is the activity of improving the satisfaction of needs according to 'some universalistic scheme of priorities, implicit or explicit'. The priorities are norms of choice determined by political ideals.[11] Pseudopolitics is the activity which is entirely subservient to private or private-interest advantage and utterly devoid of any 'articulate or disinterested conception of what would be just or fair to other groups'. Since Bay does not deny that, in the real world, 'politics' and 'pseudopolitics' intermingle to varied degrees,[12] his 'politics' implies the optimal correspondence between what in my terms are the operative and fundamental dimensions.

To the extent that it is more explicit than implicit, Bay's 'universalistic scheme of priorities' equals the fundamental dimension. While this dimension may represent the positive ideal-type pole of a continuum, and only in this sense are fundamentals an abstraction, operative ideology does not represent the negative pole of the continuum, but Bay's 'pseudopolitics' ultimately does so, and therefore is an abstraction. Unlike operative ideology, which may correspond to fundamental ideology, Bay's admixture of 'politics' with pseudopolitics' still leaves the latter as a deviation from the former, and if the two were to coincide, there would simply be no more 'pseudopolitics'. The latter represents, therefore, the negative ideal-type pole of the continuum and hence an abstraction, in so far as by itself 'pseudopolitics' is in fact the illusory anti-fundamental – not so much of 'value-free' politics as of politics absolutely divorced from an interest that is in any sense public. As such it has no counterpart in the real world of political argumentation and action, as Bay himself concedes, and it cannot therefore be considered the equivalent of 'operative ideology', which, in my terms, comprises the arguments used in the defence of policies actually executed or recommended. Irrespective of whether the policies thus defended may implement some fundamentals while deviating from others, 'operative ideology', unlike Bay's 'pseudopolitics', is never an antipode to 'politics', in Bay's sense, since it always contains reference at some point or other to morally based fundamentals – even when politicians betray the ideals they profess.

As I have shown in Part I, it is one thing to reject as untenable the juxtaposition of pragmatic and ideological politics, and another to identify the operative dimension of political discourse more with 'pragmatic' considerations than the fundamental dimension.[13] Indeed, the distinction between pragmatic and ideological politics is vertical, being one between kinds of political belief systems (and since it cannot be upheld, it casts a veil over the similarity of the relationship between all politics and all political belief systems). The distinction between a more and a less pragmatic dimension of political *qua* ideological argumentation is horizontal, being one between two dimensions of argumentation discernible particularly in the use of each political belief system by political parties and movements that are in power or have a chance of winning or sharing it. Thus, Huntington's classification of ideologies as 'inherent' or 'positional' – i.e. principled or adaptive[14] – would reflect the characteristics of the fundamental and operative dimensions respectively, if instead of a vertical distinction between ideologies he had in mind a horizontal distinction between dimensions within all ideological argumentation.

Such a distinction is again not the aim of Christoph's suggestion of using 'two distinct moulds' of the concept 'ideology', *Weltanschauung* and 'attitude structure'. This presupposition enables him to argue that present-day British politics is not 'profoundly un-ideological',[15] although the 'attitude structure', which pervades British politics, represents a less comprehensive and less tightly-woven belief structure than ideologies in the sense of *Weltanschauung* (of which Christianity and classical Marxism are the paradigms). Christoph thus conceives a vertical divide between less and more ideological ideologies, a divide both unwarranted by the rather close parallelism of his own terms of definition of both 'moulds',[16] and unfortunate (from my point of view) because 'attitude structure' could correspond to 'operative ideology'. Just as the latter is composed of the same components as fundamental ideology, so 'attitude structure' contains all the components of *Weltanschauung,* only in a lower key, as it were. Moreover, the interaction of the two dimensions is implicit in Christoph's analysis. On the one hand, he singles out four consensual elements, representing the major principles on which parties in Western-type democracies have moved close to one another. Evidently this is to say that the parties have agreed on principles in deference to prevailing public opinion, and such agreement is apparent first in the operative dimension, in the justification of policies which parties actually carry out or subscribe to, whether or not the principles of these policies had been an accepted part of their ideologies. On the other hand, Christoph's marking 'ideological' elements which still cause cleavages, i.e. those emanating from 'somewhat different conceptions of human nature, society and the state',[17] clearly reflects awareness of the continuing impact of the dimension of ideological fundamentals. Indeed, Christoph identifies what is one of the causes of bifurcation into two dimensions and what is also the substance of the continuous tension between the horizontally divided and interacting dimensions. For he comments that the ideological disputes in each of the British parties turn on 'preserving the party's doctrinal purity and historic values'.

While Christoph's awareness of the decisive cause and important implications of the bifurcation of ideologies does not emanate from an (in any sense) direct perception of the phenomenon, King obscures it by inconclusive terminological distinctions which are connected with what he regards as ideological or not. Indeed, it seems that his vacillation between a unitary inclusive conception and vertical divisions between ideological and non- or less ideological belief systems prevents the perception of ideological bifurcation. Thus in their very different substance and consistency the views of both Christoph and King represent at once an incomplete advance towards the inclusive conception of ideology (discussed in Chapters I and II) and the perception of two-dimensionality. Furthermore, while his retreats from the inclusive conception are less striking than those of Christoph and especially King, Helenius's quite clearly horizontal distinction between 'manifest' and 'latent' ideology has a very limited analytical value, by virtue of its rather extraneous and formal descriptive character.[18] In point of fact, if no systematic analytical framework exists concerning the universally recognized phenomenon of diputes in all regimes within and/or between political parties about their traditional doctrinal values and about the extent to which the policies of a party conform with the principles it continues to profess, sharpened awareness of the phenomenon and the rudiments of its conceptualization have mainly been a by-product of the attempts to realize Marxism, the philosophy-cum-ideology which produced the first theory of ideology.

b. *The Marxist Matrix*

The conspicuousness of two-dimensional argumentation and, most importantly, the awareness of the problems it raises, in Marxist parties are a corollary of the rather spectacular gap between Marxist teachings and the political fate of Marxist movements. The writings of Marx and Engels already show inconsistencies stemming from the failure to reconcile adherence to theoretical fundamentals with concessions to the requirements of their operationalization in party politics. Almost from the outset Marxists were bedevilled by the erosion of their dogmas by the political opportunities to alleviate the plight of the working classes within the capitalist system. As Bernstein recorded, Marx in his *Critique of the Gotha Programme,* went so far in his fight against these tendencies as to oppose the proposal to limit the working hours of children because this would prevent the dissolution of the old form of the family. Marx and Engels lost the doctrinal battle. The party paid no heed to this and other points of the *Critique* by 'the old men', and even revolutionary parties fought for measures which counteracted the need for revolution.[19]

Then came the universally undemocratic imposition and maintenance of communism(s). The explanation of actual policies in the light of the fundamental principles and goals of the movement quickly became a matter of gravest official concern and engendered authoritative formulae that presented breath-taking changes of policy as continuities, extensions, or revivals of original principles. Thus the seizure of power by communists has aggravated the problem which plagued and divided social-democratic Marxists when there arose the questions of entering the parliamentary arena, and of what to achieve in it.

Lenin and Leninists admitted that in their fight for communism they made use of the contemptible features of past and present regimes. This constitutes that part of Leninism which has been called 'the operational code', analysed by Leites in psychoanalytical terms.[20] The code is 'dialectically' related to the fundamentals, which means that its manipulative and Machiavellian elements are often opposed not only to the principles and goals that the code is said to serve but also to the vistas envisaged in the dimension of fundamentals for the realization of the final goals. But such Machiavellianism may also be used in fidelity to fundamental principles. A good example is Lenin's rejection of parliamentary democracy. He ruled that if one cannot destroy parliamentarism, one must work within its framework in order to prepare 'ideologically, politically and technically . . . for the dispersal of parliament by the Soviets'.[21] Although the exegetical manoeuvres that provide doctrinal cover for the 'operational code' have become particularly blatant in communist regimes, some students of communism are aware that *au fond* the exegetical problem is universal. One Sovietologist thus applies to Soviet ideology a general distinction in terms of modern analytical philosophy between 'grand and petty ideology', the first presenting unverifiable beliefs and the second verifiable but unverified beliefs.[22]

Since, either directly or indirectly, political beliefs (even some pertaining to 'grand' ideology or basic fundamentals) can be verified or falsified in actual policies, their feedback is not lost upon the leadership, communist or not. The top leadership usually first judges the feedback *in camera* and then explains it to the public in terms of the immediately motivating beliefs and aims. Simultaneously or soon after, this explanation is related to the traditional goals and principles of the party.[23] The parallel with the West is, of course, incomplete because of the official monopoly of interpretation and manipulation under communist rule. But these, and the exceptionally jarring dichotomy between 'the original doctrine and the twists of application',[24] attest neither that only communism (and fascism) are ideologies, nor that two-dimensional argumentation is an adjunct of totalitarian politics alone.[25] Rather, the huge distance between communist vision and realities goes a long way to explain why, despite their later formalistic monotony, the official attempts to cope with the conflict give an outsize picture of a universal occurrence.

In rather tenuous connection with the subtleties of the original doctrine of the dialectical relationship between 'theory and praxis', communist official explanations in fact still rely on the old down-to-earth social-democratic pairing of *Minimalprogramm* and *Maximalprogramm*, *Gegenwartsarbeit* (activity in the here and now) and fidelity to the *Endziel* (final goal).[26] In the use of these terms there is reflected the direct awareness of a distinction between essential and lasting principles on one side and contingent and transient commitments on the other.[27] Still adapting to his purposes the doctrinal development current in the German Social-Democratic Party, and in reliance on Engels's view that 'our doctrine . . . is not a dogma but a guide to action', Lenin distinguished between 'general fundamental aims, which do not change with turns of history so long as the fundamental relations between classes do not change' and 'the aims of direct and immediate action [which] have changed very markedly during this period [the previous six years]'.[28] Combining adherence to fundamentals with a thoroughly pragmatic attitude towards possibilities of abiding by them in actual fact, Lenin laid it down that after the proletarian state owns all the means of production, the only task which remains in the wake of the New Economic Policy (NEP) is 'to organize the population into cooperative societies' constituting 'a complete revolution . . . through a whole period of cultural development', which requires 'little philosophizing and as few acrobatics as possible'.[29] Here, as in the original social-democratic awareness of what amounts to ideological two-dimensionality, it is characteristic that whether the contrast between theory and practice is realistically assessed or played down, the ultimate correctness of the fundamental assertion of the theory is not called in question, though this, let alone the denigration of 'philosophizing', is not a rule without exception.[30]

Given the direct awareness in Marxist ideology of two-dimensional argumentation, it is not surprising to find that in the analysis of communist affairs Western scholars often elaborate upon communist self-interpretation. Thus Schurmann, an outstanding expert on communist China, has followed Mao Tse-Tung's distinction between thought and theory in distinguishing 'pure' and 'practical' ideology. I wish to discuss these terms to conclude the justification in principle of the proposed conception and conceptualization of ideological bifurcation, and then to proceed to the analysis of the interaction between the fundamental and operative dimensions.

Schurmann's treatment of 'pure' and 'practical' ideology reflects mainly the Chinese communist case and its self-presentation, although he also draws illuminating parallels between Chinese, Soviet and Western attitudes. Yet, particularly within this justifiable thematic limitation, the use of 'practical', although an improvement on the use of a pejorative adjective like 'petty', has a serious drawback, since it is at variance with the Marxist meaning of *Praxis*. In connection with a Marxist system, *Praxis* precludes any relationship between theory and practice other than 'dialectical' juxtaposition, which means mutual involvement and inseparability. The practice creates both reality and the correspondence between essence and reality.[31] Or, put otherwise: *Praxis* means 'a tool for changing the course of history and a criterion for historical evaluation'.[32] The specific Marxian connotation of the concept is not reflected in the identification on the one hand of a 'pure' component – 'ideas that give the individual a unified and conscious world-view' – and on the other of a 'practical' component – 'ideas to give the individual rational instruments for action'.[33] Moreover, quite independently of the claims of Marxian theory, 'practical' ideas as defined here are an essential part of the 'pure' component of any ideology. Ideology would not qualify as action-oriented thought if it did not refer to forms of action and organization which are immediately derived from basic principles and final goals, and in fact serve as their specifications on the plane of fundamentals. To that dimension, therefore, belong principles like class war and parliamentary supremacy, the dictatorship of the proletariat, and the division of powers, i.e. the prescription of 'rational instruments for action'.

Schurmann himself cannot avoid placing the 'pure' and the 'practical' components on the same plane (and leaving room for another plane) when he speaks of the possibility of 'a gap between ideology and organization'.[34] No major piece of organization remains for long without ideological cover, even if it could come into existence without it in the first place. Since neither the organizational principles followed by a party nor their justification are always compatible with the practical and theoretical principles of the 'authorized' version of the party's ideology, we have to distinguish two dimensions in each of which 'pure' and 'practical' aspects intermingle. They do so in the operative dimension in the kind of thinking which guides actions that make it questionable whether the underlying principles are those that (according to the fundamental principles) should have guided them. Whether the answer is affirmative or negative, the question of whether or not the action or posture of a party tallies with its ideology attests two-dimensionality. The question imposes itself inevitably when we compare the fundamental principles professed by one of the parties in or near power and the policies it has endorsed and rejected over a period of time, as well as when we compare the policies of the various parties.

2. CORRESPONDENCE AND DEVIATION: PARADIGMS

The nationalization of transport and steel is in accord with the fundamental principles of the British Labour Party, although other measures taken by Labour governments have a less exclusive claim to such an evaluation. By the same token, the de-nationalization of steel by the Conservative government and the increase of charges for medicines provided by the National Health Service are in conformity with the basic principles of the Conservative Party. Yet the absence of any intention to reduce drastically the present scale of the Health Service amounts to the legitimation of a serious breach in the socio-economic liberalism which the British Conservative Party has absorbed into its ideology. The discrepancy between fundamental and operative ideology becomes apparent also when parties continue to emphasize the uniqueness of their fundamental principles while their leaders, relatively secure in their authority, enter coalitions that require compromises with parties committed to opposed ideologies. Thus, in the *combinazzioni* of Italian post-War politics, the parties remain separated by their claims to represent different classes and ideologies, even though their mutual intolerance on this count is in contrast to the programmes of action they endorse as coalition partners.[35]

In the communist orbit, the vicissitudes of 'communization' in China – so excellently analysed by Schurmann – reveal no more than temporary retreats from the pursuit of fundamental principles; the same holds for Stalin's attitude towards collectivization, although in this case one may doubt how much – or for how long – respect for doctrinal commitment had anything to do with his attitude. Still, Stalin could claim that the sacrifice of the lives of millions was subordinate to the achievement of the final goals of communism. Similarly the almost immediate turning of 'the dictatorship of the proletariat' against the protests and opposition of the proletariat as well; the reversal by Lenin, within months, of the principles set out in *State and Revolution;* his latter-day NEP policies;[36] the methods and policies under Stalin and after his death; the introduction in China of NEP-type policies in 1961[37] – all these present both drastic, and, in many respects, persistent deviations from erstwhile pursued principles which for the most part still enjoy official sanction. On cardinal issues the relationship between means and ends had become tenuous, if not outright contradictory. It seems unwarranted, however, to claim that in communist politics means are always derived from ends,[38] except if one takes ends to signify those which are the immediate objective of whatever measure is taken, and accepts that whatever measure is taken by communist governments *eo ipso* conforms with the fundamentals of communism. This is in no way to deny that communist, or any other, *Realpolitik* depends on ideological preconceptions.[39] The question is: what kinds of ideological preconception? – i.e. to what degree, if at all, are specific policies derivable from the fundamental principles of the ideology which those engaged in *Realpolitik* claim to serve? If 'short-run goals' are not derivable from professed 'long-run goals' (and are therefore ideologically 'impure', but not unideological), 'long-run goals' do not fulfil the function they were meant to fulfil, namely to be 'dominant' or 'controlling'.[40] In this case, to revert to my terminology, principles of the fundamental dimension are not matched by the principles of the operative dimension. Such divergence testifies at least to temporarily increasing ideological pluralism or to actual ideological change.

a. *Schematic Exemplification*

Since the two dimensions of ideological argumentation are not uniformly related and operative ideology is not in all points (or even necessarily in most points) at variance with the ideology of fundamentals, the constellation normally prevailing is illustrated in the scheme of Figure 3.[41]

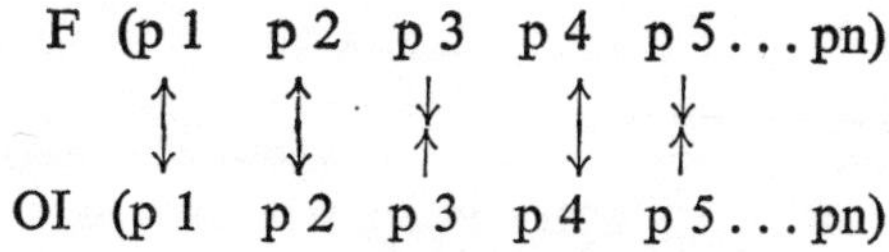

Figure 3

Explanation of symbols and signs: F = dimension of fundamentals; OI = dimension of operative ideology; p l, p 2 etc. = principles in both dimensions, such as the sanctity or abolition of the private ownership of the means of production and distribution and the principles of action and organization related to them; ↕ = correspondence between the principles of the two dimensions; ⤈ = conflict between them. The number of instances in which there is correspondence or conflict between the dimensions is immaterial in the present figure.

Principles are related not only to their counterparts in the other dimension but also to one another in the same dimension. The relationship, however, is both vertical and horizontal. In the ideal case, correspondence, or maximal 'constraint' (in the sense of full-fledged congruence between the interdependent components) would be, therefore, both vertical and horizontal, as illustrated in Figure 4. Here, the principles in the dimension of fundamentals are assumed to correspond with one another as well as with the principles underlying actual policies, and these principles – i.e. of operative ideology – are also supposed to be in harmony with one another.

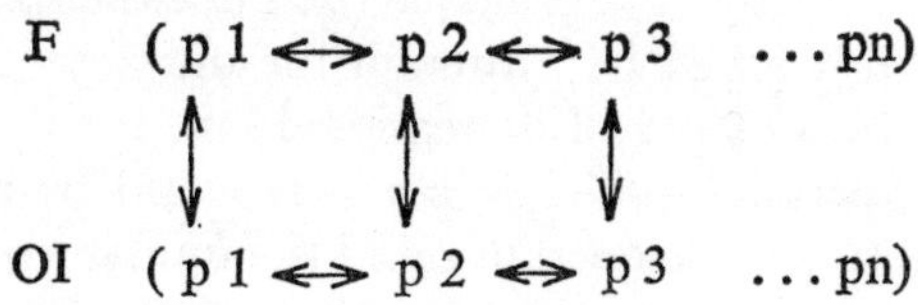

Figure 4

Explanation of additional sign: ↔ = correspondence between principles in the same dimension. (See Figure 3 for explanation of other symbols.)

Divergences between the principles in both the vertical and horizontal directions are unavoidable in the ideology of any party holding power or having a chance of doing so. The necessity of devising operational decisions reveals, often for the first time, a conflict between a fundamental principle and its counterpart in the other dimension and among principles in the same dimension, when the relationship among

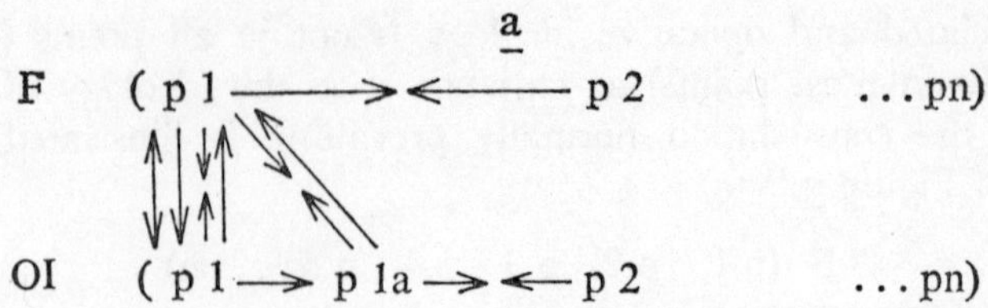

Explanation of additional signs: ↑ ↓ ↖ ↗ = direction of influence of principles in one dimension on those in another; → or ← = direction of change; ↗ ↙ = conflict between a principle and its changed counterpart in the other dimension or with a different principle in the other dimension. The order in which signs follow one another (↑ ⇅ ↓) indicates what is ass umed to happen first, second, and so on.

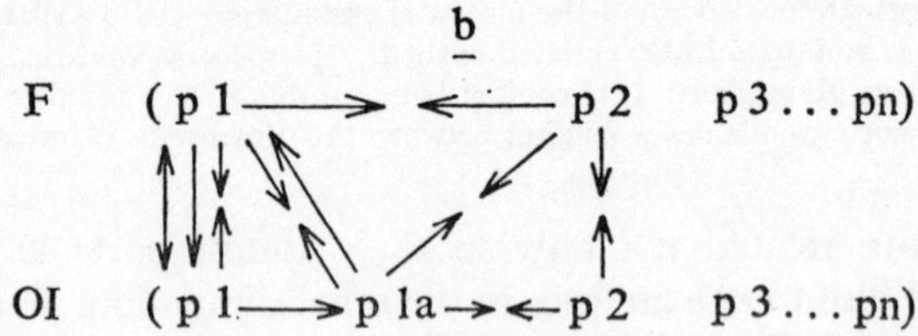

Figure 5

the principles in both the vertical and horizontal directions had originally been assumed to be supplementary. This process and its repercussions are indicated in Figure 5a.

Figure 5a illustrates the following sequence: the original assumption of harmony between the fundamental and the correspondingly devised operative principle (↕); the allied assumption that the fundamental would determine the operative principle (↓). But either p 1 on F and OI show themselves to conflict (⇅) through the unforeseen results of the attempted realization of p 1 of dimension F, or, for varied reasons of expediency, the operative principle p 1 is replaced by p 1a (→). This creates conflict between the operative and the fundamental level (↘↖); and if p 1 on F – the fundamental principle – is influenced by (↖) its incompatibility with its corresponding operative principle (p 1 on OI), or by the change of this operative principle (p 1 changes into p 1a on OI), as is assumed in Fig. 5a, the relation between the two fundamental principles (p 1 and p 2 on level F) may also change from correspondence to conflict (→←). It is also reasonable to assume that the incompatibility of the two p 1s (the fundamental and the originally corresponding operative principle), or the change of the operative principle p 1 into p 1a leads to incongruence between the changed and another operative principle (p 1a and p 2 on OI). This, as well as the possibility of a clash between the changed operative and another fundamental principle (between p 1a on OI and p 2 on F), may result in disturbing the correspondence between another pair of fundamental and operative principles (p 2 on dimensions F and OI). Figure 5a thus assumes the form of Figure 5b. The possibility is left open that the process which has begun and run its course in the first pair of principles, including its spread to the second, may run its course there, too, and spread from the second to the third pair of principles and so on. Such a spread is not inevitable, however, and an indefinite progression on that line would indicate the total change or disintegration of an ideology.

It follows, then, that principles collide with their counterparts in the other dimension as well as with one another in the same dimension when a fundamental principle is considered unrealizable and a policy is adopted which contradicts the fundamental principle. Or the all-round collision may occur because the attempts to implement the principle result in unforeseen consequences that work against the principle. The collisions among the principles in each dimension, and those of one dimension with their counterparts in the other, closely resemble cases of 'cognitive dissonance', to use Festinger's term.

I am not concerned here with the psychological problems which bifurcation of political argumentation poses for the policy-makers and consumers. It would also lead me too far afield to explore the possible relatedness of bifurcation to Freud's distinction in *Totem und Tabu* between primary and secondary processes in the analysis of dreams.[42] I wish merely to refer to the theory of 'cognitive dissonance' in order to add to the explanation of the phenomenon of ideological bifurcation, and in due course also to point out a few differences between cognitive dissonance in the personality system and in political parties. According to Festinger, cognitive dissonance refers to inconsistencies not only between single cognitive elements but also between clusters of cognitive elements. Dissonance occurs, then, when action is taken which is insufficiently justified by the knowledge people have of their situation.[43] Adapted to the collisions of principles in and between the dimensions of ideological argumentation, dissonance occurs when political action is taken or proposed whose justification is not readily reconcilable with the knowledge that those who devise, execute or recommend policies possess of ideological fundamentals or available resources (material and predispositional). Policy-makers may know that, in a given situation, policies that they initiate as a result of their dogmatic adherence to certain fundamentals demand a price that will adversely affect the wellbeing of many people and will eventually also offend against other fundamental principles of the ideology which the policy-makers profess to believe in. Dissonance also occurs when, in deference to immediate exigencies, policy-makers embark on a course of action which they know to be opposed to the fundamental principles of the ideology of their party.

b. *General Examples*

We may now supplement the brief introductory examples and illustrate the main stages of the foregoing schematic exposition with some more detailed examples. For the purpose in hand it is most instructive perhaps to begin with a case where the specification and implementation of the same principles are involved.

Not only do the principles of equality and liberty, for instance, cohabit in one ideology, but liberal democracy, like communsim and democratic socialism, subscribes to both ideals. All three ideologies are even justified in claiming 'non-egalitarian classlessness' as their present operative ideal, the more so since Ossowski's term is predicated on the long tradition of 'the co-presence of the ideal of equality with hierarchical tendencies', stretching from the Periclean to the Marxian ideal and to present-day predominating American culture and the official self-interpretation of communist societies.[44] In all these conceptions men are equal and free, though not necessarily in the same respects. Generally 'classlessness' prevails or is stipulated in some ways of life while inequality is accepted in others.

In the dimension of fundamentals, communism requires the abolition of the private ownership of the means of production and distribution as the instrumentality (the 'implement' of the ideological composite) for the realization of liberty and equality. In accord with the teachings in this dimension, when power is seized the abolition is usually immediately translated into operative ideology. Although it is likewise founded on this doctrine that distribution 'to each according to his needs' is not the immediate aim, a far more equal distribution of goods than that obtaining in the capitalist world was to be operative in the transitional stage of 'to each according to his merits'. However, after it had been restricted, inequality in the distribution of goods began to redevelop apace. Ideas which had previously served to condemn the effects of industry – the division of labour, highly differentiated rewards, the degrading cash-nexus: in short, with the exception of private ownership of the means of production and distribution, all that which had been claimed to cause and increase alienation – became part of the operative ideology of management in Soviet Russia.[45] These developments went hand in hand with the restriction of political and civil liberties attendant upon the increasingly dictatorial character of rule by the leaders, who carried with them the majority of the Politburo, the Presidium and the Central Committee and commanded the support of army and secret police.

In the language of our schematization, a specification of a fundamental principle – p 1 (fairly equal wages) – has proved impractical, and p 1 of operative ideology[46] is being replaced by p 1a (growing wage-differential). The rift between operative and fundamental ideology has repercussions on other fundamental specifications of the principle of equality as well as on those of the principle of liberty; or the cleavage caused by different incomes and status positions is a corollary of other deviations from these two principles, such as the replacing of democratic self-management in factories, farms and other branches of economic and public life by authoritarian centralism. Figures 5a and 5b illustrate such a concatenation. They can be used to demonstrate schematically that the restriction of political and civil liberties is a concomitant of the policy of rendering nationalized production effective by retreats from the introduction of equality and, above all, of keeping in power the party which sees itself entitled to rule for the professed pursuit of the final goals of communism.

The process which Figures 5a and 5b illustrate schematically can also be exemplified with regard to liberal-democratic ideology. Here, too, liberty and equality are fundamental principles, but differently specified. A fundamental specification of liberty is the freedom of individual competition. It is paired with the Aristotelian specification of equality in the (unegalitarian) sense of 'distributive justice', and hence coloured in the economic and political aspects respectively by what Aristotle understood as oligarchic and democratic justice.[47] With the political emancipation of the working classes, a specification of the fundamental of equality is realized in universal suffrage. This has contributed to the adoption of welfare policies by liberal and conservative parties. The increase of state interference, due also to economic development *per se*, means that principles of operative ideology in the spirit of *laissez-faire* have been counter-balanced, and in some respects replaced, by those which restrict free individual competition. As in the Soviet system, a discrepancy between operative and fundamental ideology reveals itself, although its tendency in liberal democracies is in the opposite direction. But here, too, the deviation hangs together as cause or effect with other deviations from specifications of the principles of liberty and equality. Not only do monopolistic trends hide behind the principles of liberty and restrict free competition in its name, but in the development of the Welfare State, governments spend an increasing amount of personal incomes for the good of the taxpayer. This opens up prospects which disturb even socialists: that too little should be left of the freedom of individuals to spend according to legitimate personal preferences.[48] Thus, one kind of operative principles subservient to the fundamental of liberty – largely unhampered individual competition and free enterprise – has proved impractical as a result of the realization of specifications of both the principles of liberty and equality in the form of universal suffrage on the one hand and of the freedom of organization on the part of business and labour on the other. Policies of another kind, those of welfare statism, realize the fundamental of equality but also tend to restrict liberty, even more than egalitarians would have it. These processes, like those chosen from the Soviet reality, can be expressed in the abstract-formal language of the schemes of Figures 5a and 5b. This would also hold true if we were to analyse for instance, the position of Southern Negroes in terms of correspondence to and deviance from constitutional specifications of the principles of liberty and equality[49] and compare the application of these principles – in two schematic boxes – to white and coloured Americans.

Underlying the kind of specific reasons for correspondence and deviations in the instances mentioned is the fact that deviations from fundamentals are a universal phenomenon: political aims need modification in any event. In politics, as in the case of the individual, evaluation changes with experience, the more so as decisions are never made on the basis of complete information, but rather follow the 'strategy of disjointed incrementalism'.[50] It is in the nature of ideological thought, as of all other, not only that it should run ahead of facts but also that it should lag behind them. In either case ideological principles might be found wanting as the compass of action. Thus whether conservative, moderate or radical, to retain a modicum of coherence ideologies require change by way of re-adapting their components and dimensions to one another.

c. *Directions of Adaptation*

The adaptation of ideologies to changing conditions, falsely evaluated facts, or unforeseen consequences of the realization of principles may take two main directions: the re-adaptation of operative principles to the original specifications of fundamental principles, or the adaptation of specifications to what is actually being done or to the possible alternatives. It is also sometimes possible to safeguard the original tendency of fundamentals by putting greater emphasis on other specifications of fundamentals and by strengthening their operative counterparts so as to contravene the deviation from one, or one set of, fundamentals.

Re-adaptation of operative to fundamental principles suggests itself when, to recapitulate the process shown in Fig 5a, the principle originally devised for implementing the specification of a fundamental principle

$$\begin{array}{c} F\ (p\ 1) \\ \updownarrow\ \downarrow \\ OI\ (p\ 1) \end{array}$$

shows itself, for whatever reason, derogatory to the purpose, or entails consequences that cause it to conflict with the fundamental principle

$$\begin{array}{lccccr} F\ (p & 1 & & & &) \\ & \downarrow\ \updownarrow & & \searrow & \nwarrow & \\ OI\ (p & 1 & \rightarrow & p & 1a). & \end{array}$$

For example, taxation and interest-group organization in America were meant to increase fluidity between the classes and to fortify personal independence and the autonomy of voluntary associations. But the results have turned out contrary to these original intentions. Taxes have become 'a bastion against . . . fluidity' and all interest groups have become conservative in outlook.[51] As Lowi further points out, entrepreneurial and labour interest groups have gained privileged positions in so far as, in some instances, the executive has delegated functions to such groups and so decreased state intervention. At the same time, however, these functions have been removed from congressional control, since the accountability of the executive for the devolved functions has ceased to be direct. Either a reversal of policy can obviate the unintended consequences (Figure 6a, p. 195) and/or other specifications of fundamental principles might be activated with greater vigour in order to achieve the same result (Figure 6b).

Indeed, even if the same principles are accepted in the socio-economic and the political sphere, their operationalization may turn out to have different consequences in each sphere, and the difference may be attenuated by reference to the same principle. Broadly speaking, maximal freedom of individual activity is a liberal fundamental in politics and economics. The response to pressures for curbing excesses of private initiative in economic relations has become increasingly positive in liberal democracies, especially since the democratization of liberalism. In fact, from the outset individual liberty had a more equitable effect in the political than in the economic sphere. Political institutions, therefore, provided both the model (and stimulus) for changing specifications of the fundamental of individual liberty in its bearing on economic relations. Thus mechanisms were legitimated and channels opened up through which the freedom of the many could be defended against encroachments attendant upon the concentration of socio-economic power which accrued to the few in accordance with the principle of individual freedom of action.[52] Likewise, the undesired effects of 'incorporated pluralism', of pluralism, that is, which has turned against the principles of voluntary association as a safeguard of individual freedom, can be offset by strengthening existing constitutional controls which have been bypassed, thus reanimating the practical significance of voluntary membership in professional and business associations, and reinforcing the still viable and desirable objectives of pluralism.[53]

The aim of attuning the socio-economic and the political sphere to each other can also be achieved by applying different fundamentals in each sphere. The principle of socio-economic inequality may be equally reflected in both the fundamental and operative dimensions; and so may that of political equality. In their respective spheres inequality and equality can operate so as to be mutually supplementary and to increase both socio-economic and political liberty, either of the few, as in pre-democratic liberalism, or of the many in a liberal welfare democracy. Different principles in each sphere have also been supplementary – or rather compensatory – under royal absolutism and fascism. Political centralism and authoritarianism in royal absolutism were by no means fully, and if at all then only indirectly, reflected in the sphere of economic organization. The two main ways of re-establishing greater coherence by securing a fundamental principle against falsification on the operative level are illustrated side by side in the schemes of Figures 6a and 6b.

The second main direction for restoring re-approximation to the ideal-type configuration (Figure 4, p. 187) is to accept the implication of deviations of actual policies from the traditional fundamentals, and refashion the latter. It would mean retaining the change of principles (from p 1 to p 1a) in operative ideology and accordingly changing the corresponding principle p 1 to p 1a) in the dimension of fundamentals.

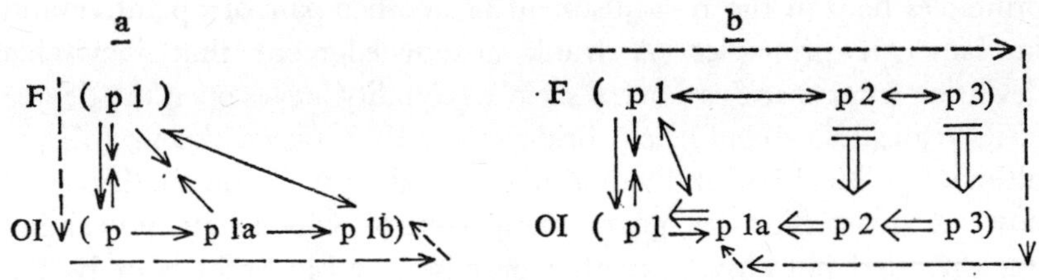

Explanation of additional signs: p̿ = heightened emphasis of p; ⇓⇐ = strengthened influence; ↖↘ = correspondence between a principle and its changed counterpart, or a different principle, in the other dimension; ↓⇢ ↖ or ↖⇠ ↓ = sequence of process.

Figure 6

The nationalization of the means of production and distribution having been shown as conducive to guaranteeing neither the equality of rewards nor individual liberty and genuine political participation, a re-examination of this specification of equality and its corollaries on the level of fundamentals could be undertaken. Or, the principle of unlimited individual or group competition having been an illusion all the time, and the principle of the welfare state being accepted all round, a re-formulation of the nature and extent of the principle of competition as a specification of the principle of liberty suggests itself. As both examples indicate, change of one specification usually entails change of others, but not in an indefinite progression. For instance, a socialist can abjure the ideal of a classless society and total nationalization yet still consider himself a socialist because he supports economic equality in terms of a less class-differentiated society more than would a liberal or a conservative. Moreover, he is still a socialist because he is ready to ponder not only nationalization, but also forms of collective ownership, whenever any such form can be expected to alleviate strains and stresses in the social fabric and in the individuals concerned without creating strains and stresses in other areas of society by increased economic cost.

The restoration of coherence in the two main directions may, of course, take place at one and the same time. In some aspects operative ideals can be re-adapted to fundamental ideology, and in conjunction with this the lessons of operative ideology can lead to the change of specifications of fundamentals. In this process, which is normally one of a limited chain-reaction, it may also happen that deviant operative principles help in the re-adjustment of another pair of operative and fundamental principles. A frank acknowledgment that inevitable deviation from specifications of socialist equality leaves open the degree of its realizability could help bridge the gulf between the promise of ultimate political and individual liberty and its denial in the here and now. A reassertion of government control which, by restraining 'incorporated pluralism', whether practised by big business or by big unions, may enlarge the domain of individual freedom surely invites a revision of the professed negative evaluation of government interference. In both instances, the deviation from one principle helps to strengthen correspondence between specifications of another fundamental principle and their counterparts on the operative level.[54]

There are also situations in which the need for adaptation is overriden in the name of change. As in the case of the Japanese new conservatism,[55] some fundamental principles of the past, are simply no longer acknowledged in official party pronouncements though their impact is still observable:

F (—)
OI ((p 1)).

To go by what governments leave to individual judgment, the principle of paternalism is hardly less activated in present-day politics in East and West than it was in the days of Filmer or Louis XIV. In the liberal welfare democracies, governmental paternalism tends to be much less personalized than in communist systems. But in neither case is the paternalistic spade called by its name by those who use it. Its past associations with royal absolutism, rather than the unsuitability of its connotation, facilitate the suppression of paternalism as a fundamental and its disguise in operative ideology. Thus: OI ((p 1)). Conversely, some official party ideology continues to contain general principles, although these have no direct operative significance. Thus:

F (p 1)
OI (—).

This in fact, brings our argument full circle. For while, in view of the fairly general reluctance to subject a party ideology openly to revision, we particularly need to remind ourselves of the way of evading adaptation by sticking to traditional principles and even particular specifications (nationalization or free enterprise) – even though policies in their spirit are no longer pursued or continue to diverge significantly from them – the same is involved as when things are done that contravene fundamentals. And the deviation in the operative dimension from fundamental principles is the decisive test of the existence of two-dimensionality and gives rise to the whole problem that concerns us here.

Much as the ubiquity of the problem (and the attitude towards it) is further evidence against the distinction of ideological and non-ideological politics, the specific content of an ideology accounts for quite important dissimilarities between ideologies in respect of the relationship between the two dimensions. This correlation needs clarification, because the question arises of the extent to which, and also of the situational context in which, the distance, and hence the tensions, between the two dimensions indicate the moderate or extremist character of an ideology. The clarification of this point leads to the further question of how the classification of ideologies according to the Left-Right polarity is affected by taking into account the two-dimensionality of ideologies. Only after dealing with these issues in the remainder of this chapter and in Chapter VII shall we illustrate and explain in Chapter VIII the attitudes towards ideological change and its mechanism.

3. THE CHARACTER OF THE IDEOLOGY AND THE DISTANCE BETWEEN ITS DIMENSIONS

At first sight it would seem that the more extremist an ideology in its claims for social and/or political reconstruction, the greater the degree of incongruence, dissonance or conflict between its fundamental and operative principles, and the more difficult the modification of fundamentals, or rather the acknowledgment of it. However, while it is true of communism, this chain of reasoning is not universally applicable.

The two dimensions may be relatively close to each other, even closer than in a moderate ideology, and the ideology nevertheless be extremist, as is the case in fascism(s). The reason is that ideologies do not bear on political action and organization alone, but also, among other spheres, on socio-economic action and organization; and different principles may be adopted for each of these spheres. Thus in fascism, unlike communism, the undue widening of the gap between the dimensions (vertical asymmetry) is forestalled by built-in asymmetry in the dimension of fundamentals inasmuch as not exactly the same principles are held to be applicable in politics and economics.

In the fundamental dimension of liberalism correspondence between principles is comparable to that in communism, yet in virtue of the nature of liberal principles inter-dimensional conflict does not seem to be greater than in fascism. Things are different when we consider what happens to ideologies in revolutions made in their name. This consideration is of general importance since no politically significant ideology can forego the right of revolutionary action,[56] so that each ideology may become involved in the specific conflict which such action creates between the two dimensions. Here, too, fascism fares differently from communism, but so long as revolutionary action lasts, inter-dimensional conflict in liberalism is much more like that in communism than in fascism.

I come now to the demonstration of the aforementioned points and of the conclusions they entail.

a. *Divergence in Liberal and Communist, and Proximity in Fascist Revolutions*

Extremism may refer to the way in which change is effected and in this sense even to the revolutionary seizure of power alone. This particular form of effecting change, like all other forms, is motivated by its objective, which may be the reinstatement of an illegally or legally ousted government; the restoration of the previous order; the instalment of a new government and of a moderately changed regime or of a radically new political and social order. The forceful seizure of power, is, as such, a principle not only of extreme leftist and extreme rightist ideologies but also of liberal and even of conservative ideologies. Once they are ousted from government and unwilling to give up their aspirations or any hope of realizing them, neither moderates nor conservatives can consistently disclaim the right to depose by force a government which in their view is illegitimate.[57]

As far as the revolutionary overthrow of a government and/or regime is concerned, therefore, counter-revolution is the same as revolution. In this technical sense of extremist action, revolution is thus one of the more neutral ideological principles. Much as the grounds and purposes of revolutionary action differ, its justification cannot but comprise the insistence on the right – as a rule or as a necessary exception to it – to bring about political change by force, which is necessarily effected by basically similar methods. The 'neutrality', or ubiquity, of fundamental and/or operative principles asserting or implying the right of revolution as such, and the methods of its first-stage implementation, are the counterpart of those parts of the institutional and value system which any revolution must momentarily challenge and which are likewise 'neutral' or ubiquitous. These are the mainstays of any known regime, namely the fundamentals of the rule of law and of the right to enforce its observation on the one hand, and the operative principles for the realization of these fundamentals on the other.[58]

If each revolution violates the order against which it is directed, things are different in respect of the order that the revolution is to bring about. Here, the specific contents of the ideology cause differences. A liberal as much as a communist revolution not only breaks the rules of the order it seeks to replace but violates even more the principles of the order it seeks to establish. The dichotomy here is greater than in the case of an old-type (anti-liberal and/or anti-democratic) conservative, and particularly a fascist, revolution. Once in power, communists, like fascists, claim, at least during the first post-revolutionary stages, that in conformity with their ideology, their form of government is revolutionary in so far as it is dictatorial. However, neither communists nor fascists on this account conduct government as they and others have conducted revolution. The pretence to the contrary would be in stark contrast to the rigidly hierarchical institutionalization and bureaucratization of such regimes.

There exists, however, a radical difference between the conduct of revolution intended to install either a liberal or a communist regime, and the conduct of liberal government or the management of a communist society as envisaged in the fundamental dimensions of liberal and communist ideologies. The resort to revolutionary methods on behalf of these ideologies therefore carries with it a more or less prolonged but in each case pronounced conflict between the operative and the fundamental dimensions of these ideologies. As long as rule by revolutionary methods lasts, the conflict will be of a similar magnitude.The longer the revolutionary situation is said to exist, the more marked the conflict will become.

It would be difficult, and in any case largely immaterial, to try to estimate whether or not the distance between the dimensions is smaller when, for instance, a revolution made to establish a liberal democracy issues in a provisional military dictatorship than when the revolution designed to realize maximal freedom and equality issues in the dictatorship of the leaders of a communist party. It is important, however, to note that what renders the two cases similar, despite the dissimilarity of the aims of a liberal and of a communist revolution, distinguishes them from fascism in spite of the similarity of communist and fascist methods of government. The simple fact is that, as distinct from both liberalism and communism, the form of government fascism aims at *is* a dictatorship. Notwithstanding the difference in each of the three cases between the revolutionary process and the envisaged form of the political process, in regard to both processes fascism preaches and practises the same fundamental principle of 'führerism', the dictatorial leadership of one man.[59]

The distance between the dimensions of fundamental and operative ideology is, therefore, smaller in a fascist than in a liberal or communist revolution. It continues to be smaller in fascism after the three regimes are established, just as it stays great, or even grows, in a communist regime. However, concerning the distance between the dimensions, the affinity during revolution between liberal and communist ideology gives way after revolution to the affinity between fascist and liberal ideology. Normally, liberal and fascist regimes deviate less from their ideological fundamentals than does a communist regime. All of which goes to show that by itself the disparity between the dimensions is no secure indicator of the extremism of an ideology. To be sure, great disparity results from the extremism of the ideological objectives. But not every extremist ideology entails great inter-dimensional disparity. In fascist extremism it is considerably reduced, or compensated for, by diversity within the dimension of fundamentals.

b. *Proximity in Liberal and Fascist, and Divergence in Communist Regimes*

Principles relating to the political and socio-economic spheres, as well as to others, figure in the two dimensions of every ideology. In the dimension of fundamentals these principles are usually complementary or attuned to one another, though full harmony hardly ever exists among all of them. Fascism combines not only some degree of political equality and a hierarchical conception of society, but also overall totalitarinaism, with a considerable, though ultimately state-controlled (or tolerated), degree of pluralism in the sphere of economic organization and social stratification. The 'saturation' method, permitting, if not calculated to perpetuate, diverse appeals for diverse needs,[60] is anchored in the dimension of fundamentals. Furthermore, the 'catch-all' party of Western post-war democracy, too, exhibits the 'saturation' method, which in fact originated in Bonapartism and has operated in the form of Michels's 'law of transgression' in all democratic parties since before World War I. In fascist parties and regimes the 'catch-all' appeal is often programmatically reduced to the principle of 'catch-all-except-some' (e.g., Jews), though not on the grounds of the pragmatic principle of the minimal winning coalition as practised in the democratic game of politics.[61] The fundamental principles of dictatorial leadership and the one-party system (partly bought at the price of allowances to socio-economic pluralism, attendant upon the existence of private enterprise even in big industry) distinguish a fascist from a democratic 'catch-all' party. Indeed, the overriding authority of the leader prevents any serious rift between the spheres of politics and economics, while differences between fundamentals relating to the political and economic spheres minimize discrepancies between the operative and fundamental dimensions of fascist ideology.

Despite the vastly different degrees of intensity and directions in which liberal and fascist ideologies relate socio-economic to political aims and organizations, in the dimension of fundamentals they agree in acknowledging the moral and practical predominance of politics over economics. This is ostentatiously displayed in fascist ideology and underlies liberal theory in that specific political institutions are devised both to guarantee the desirable socio-economic order and to preserve the limitations of government power. It is often ignored that to do so through an elaborate and efficient institutionalization of counterveiling powers attests the recognition of the prime importance of the sphere of politics in relation to all other spheres.[62] That liberalism and fascism share recognition of the instrumental primacy of politics, though on diametrically opposed grounds and in the light of no less divergent values, ensures in this respect a relatively low tension between their fundamental and operative dimensions. While this does not then minimize the difference between liberalism and fascism as moderate and extremist ideologies, it does nevertheless distinguish both from communism.

In communism the actual predominance of political activity and organization conflicts with fundamental principles and final goals. On the basis of the near-total implementation of the socialization of the means of production and distribution, communist regimes have assumed the institutional and even constitutional complexion of an etatism unsurpassed by fascism. Yet their spokesmen still present these regimes as a phase in the revolutionary transition towards the total disappearance of political coercion and organization. There is little in the fundamental principles and final goals of socialism and communism to justify the prolonged terrorist dictatorship of a tiny minority and the hecatombs of victims *ad majorem communismi gloriam.* Even the principle of class war does not provide an excuse, since during the socialist transition period class war was to be waged upon the relicts of the old regime. But like the terror of 1793–4 (over which the young Marx waxed enthusiastic in his supposedly humanistic-philosophical phase),[63] communist terror has for the most part hit a much greater number of ordinary people than members of the formerly privileged classes. This may still be true, although intellectuals, who already in Stalin's day aroused the suspicion of the dictator according to his alternately shrewd and hallucinatory, but always ruthless application of 'the law of anticipated reactions', have by now again become the target of persecution, despite the fact that they have by no means abandoned the socialist ideals (fundamentals), but have dared to uphold them over and against the official party line (operative ideology). The more salient and sordid political methods actually used under communist and fascist rule and defended in their operative ideologies are largely identical and they are likewise removed from the practice of Western-type welfare democracies. Yet, unlike the Marxist fundamentals of communist ideology, fascist fundamentals are fully attuned to such political practice and at the same time less removed in the socio-economic sphere than either communist ideology or practice from the conditions previously prevailing or in the process of unfolding.

Indeed in the social and economic spheres, fascist operative ideology accords with fundamentals, because a fascist programme represents a rather opportunistically fluid mean between bourgeois-liberal, corporative and statist principles. With the exception of generally less direct than indirect statism in the economic sphere, and concessions to welfarism (according to conceptions already applied by Bismarck and defended by Treitschke), fascist socio-economic operative ideology reflects, broadly speaking, the Hegelian relegation of liberal principles to 'civic society' under the aegis of an authoritarian government. Fascist fundamental ideology does not accord with Hegel's claim that the authoritarian government was to be guided by the idea of the realization of reason in law. His was not the explicit supposition that the *Rechtsstaat* is that which the monarch (*Führer*) holds state and law to be at any given moment. However, Hegel postulated no institutional safeguards to prevent such a degeneration. He did not demand that the representative institutions of Prussia be invested with the independent authority such institutions already possessed in England and America before his time.

According to fascist fundamental principles about human nature and the natural hierarchy of values, liberal democracy is unnatural, because it is inimical to the destiny of the nation-state. Therefore, the fascist radical break with a pluralistic political order, as in Italy and Germany, or with the political aspirations to achieve and consolidate a liberal-democratic order, as in Spain, has been effected in accord with fundamental ideology. If few divergencies between the two dimensions obtrude in the political as well as in the socio-economic sphere, a major reason is that fascist fundamentals are predominantly predicated on the ways in which society must be ruled to occupy its proper place among, and if possible over, other nations. The fascist vision is Machiavellian in that it is essentially political and, above everything else, concerned with the maintenance of power in the state and the power of the state as ends in themselves. Yet because the state is the modern nation-state, it permits the focusing of intense feelings upon the nation – or race – and has at its disposal the means of modern technology.

On these grounds, the fundamental of fascist authoritarianism issues in unequally high degrees of totalitarianism. The six criteria of a totalitarian dictatorship of Friedrich and Brzezinski, 'an ideology, a single party typically led by one man, a terroristic police, communications monopoly, a weapons monopoly, and a centrally directed economy' apply generally to fascism,[64] but require some qualification. This is first of all due to the fact that pluralistic economic organization exists by courtesy as much of the fundamental of direct control as of that which leaves untouched the principle of private ownership of the means of production and distribution. As a result, 'central control ... through bureaucratic co-ordination' cannot exclude and has not excluded co-ordination by genuine, though not much publicized, bargaining between governmental agencies and corporate bodies of private owners.[65] Fascism likewise complies with the elaboration of the first condition only if stress is laid not so much on the ideology's focusing on 'a perfect final state of mankind' as on a radically 'new' political organization of the state and, through it, of the world. I say 'new' in accord with Friedrich's view that only the sum-total of fascism's ingredients renders fascist, like communist, dictatorships totalitarian and hence a new phenomenon. But I do not think it right to equate this novelty with a 'perfect final state of mankind', because I find convincing that implication of Nolte's view which Rauschning anticipated in his *Die Revolution des Nihilismus* and which explains further the considerable congruence of the dimensions of fascist ideology. In this view, fascist radicalism made no pretence of transcending the human condition; it had no intention of redeeming the world and rendering it more humane but wished to heal it of all such visions of redemption.[66]

What distinguishes fascist from communist totalitarianism, as well as from liberal, democratic and socialist meliorism, is rooted in the postulate that the baser human instincts are unchangeable and, with the help of the most up-to-date techniques, can be utilized in the age-old pursuit of the domination of one group of men over others. The appeal not only to 'historic destiny' but to one of the oldest prejudices, the racialist, and in the most ill-founded way at that, was in consonance with the presupposition about human nature and the ideal of conquest.

Class envy is as old as the racialist superiority complex. But while German fascism wanted to re-order the world on a racialist base, communism draws is *raison dêtre* from its aim to overcome class and race distinctions altogether. Yet it is precisely the elevation of racial superiority to the rank of an overriding fundamental which at least partly embroiled Nazism in the typical conflict between fundamental and operative ideology. Nordic superiority and anti-semitism fitted ill with pro-Arabism and the Japanese alliance. Generally, the operative deviation from racialist fundamentals occurred only in foreign policy. But there were also other conflicts, for instance Feder's 'socialist' programme and the cooperation with big industry. However, the shifts between the often ill-assorted commitments typical of a 'catch-all' party were settled and re-settled as a matter of principle by the fiat of the leader. Disturbing effects of discrepancies in the dimension of fundamentals or between it and the operative dimension were also to a considerable extent provided against by professing the principle of anti-ideological realism, which was largely indistinguishable from cynicism. This fitted the intrinsically anti-transcendent aspects of the ideology, just as it was characteristic of the asymmetry of principles that fascism should at the same time make the most of the idealistic dedication to supra-individual values. Not only had decadent liberal individualism to be countered; cynicism had to be coated to remain other-directed.

Thus, in ways not entirely alien to those employed under communism, conflicts within the dimension of fundamentals and between it and the operative dimension were either decreed away or theoretically forestalled. Communist 'dialectics' fulfil the function of fascist 'realism', and terror is the mainstay of both. Despite these similarities, the proximity between the dimensions is far closer in fascism than in communism. As we have seen, this is due to the motley assemblage of socio-economic principles and their subjection, like everything else, to the fundamentals of the leader-principle and its concomitant, the concentration on aggressive power politics. Promise and fulfilment (fundamental and operative ideology) bore each other out in rabid nationalism and expansionism, or – where the country could not afford it – in the anti-democratic and anti-liberal commitment, which was equated with national solidarity and in the name of which ruthless internal oppression was justified. It remains the eternal shame of Germany to have let itself be guided by the amorphous socio-economic vision of a racially pure and world-dominating German society, and to have supported or condoned its realization by premeditated genocide, which although mainly carried out against Jews could have been directed against any other ethnic group which it might have been convenient to proclaim as racially inferior.[67] Towards Jews in particular, wantonly destructive extremism was carried out in the political sphere according to the letter of fundamental principles. Nothing could be more telling than that the enormity of the crime bears no relation to the effect it could have had on the socio-economic structure of society.

c. *Distance and Rigidity*

Between the inter-dimensional disparity caused in communist regimes by the nominally transitional revolutionary betrayal of fundamental principles and final goals, and the far-reaching inter-dimensional harmony which is far from being disturbed in fascism by the profanation of humanitarian values (differences of degree between varieties of fascism can be taken into account), lies the inter-dimensional relationship of liberalism. It shares the morally-founded aspiration of meliorism with the radicalism to its left and the easier confluence between the dimensions of ideology with the radicalism to its right. The affinity with the extreme Right in this point, as I have already said, is due also to its recognition as an ideological fundamental, however differently based, of the permanently regulatory function, and therefore practical prevalance, of politics over other spheres of social activity. While fascism and communism are equally unable to attain and maintain power through free competition for the consent of the citizens, the discrepancy between the political structure actually maintained and that which each communist government claims to bring about in the fullness of time is a measure only of communist extremism. Fascism and liberalism, unlike communism, can straightforwardly rely on specifications of their fundamental principles in the justification of their diametrically opposed attitudes towards principles like the freedom of political competition and their institutional implications. Indeed, on this kind of affinity in diversity rests the relatively low inter-dimensional tension in both liberalism and fascism and hence the impossibility of relying on the degree of inter-dimensional disparity as an indicator of the extremism of an ideology; an affinity, that is, in which the dissimilar outweighs the similar in all that is politically significant.

Pluralism is an essential characteristic of liberal democracy as a whole; it is more stringently maintained in the political than in the economic sphere and it is in the former that the limitations of competition in the economic sphere are determined; but the latter remains *au fond* pluralistic, despite (and thanks to) the limitations. Contrariwise, in fascism the explicit allowances for pluralism in the economic sphere are a contradiction in principle of the ban on pluralism in the political sphere. Inter-dimensional asymmetry is thus diminished at the cost of being domiciled in the dimension of fundamentals itself. Hierarchy in this dimension prevents the shift from inter- to intra-dimensional asymmetry from furnishing ground for open internal conflict. In reliance on some mutually supporting fundamentals which have priority over all others and are rigidly maintained, the shifting validity of subsidiary and partly deviant principles is justified.

If, then, extremism may involve either much or little discrepancy between the dimensions – and proximity between them is not always characteristic of moderate ideologies, or the measure of the inner unity of an ideology – in what sense can it be said that rigid adherence to dogmatic assertion of the cohesion of central fundamentals is the hallmark of extremist ideologies? In communism, this applies to principles and goals like the collective ownership of the means of production and distribution, the classless society, the dictatorship of the proletariat and the eventual withering away of the state, etc. Thus, in Soviet Russia, for instance, subordination and discipline in economic enterprises through managerial authority are not officially acknowledged to be inconsistent with the institution of the classless society and the eventual elimination of alienation in the process of work. Hierarchy of function is justified on the grounds that all workers are owners, and hence are subject only to their own authority.[68] In fascism the unchangeable interlocking principles are the hierarchy of men and nations; etatism-cum-nationalism as the excuse for anything; the rejection of Marxism and democracy; and, in Germany, the sanctification of racialism, etc. Here, one of the unchangeable specifications of a central fundamental – the wholesale extermination of Jews – remained sacred for Hitler.[69] Although he nevertheless conferred Aryan purity by fiat, he did so according to 'the curiously paradoxical doctrine that no one whom he proclaimed an Aryan could be a Jew'.[70]

Thus the (horizontal) asymmetry of fascist ideology in the dimension of fundamentals can be regarded as the quasi-programmatical equivalent of the definitely counter-programmatical (vertical) asymmetry in communism between its operative and fundamental dimensions. This near-equation of the two 'mechanisms' – the attenuation of conflict between the two dimensions as a result of the greater diversity of principles in the fundamental dimension and the sharpened conflict between the two dimensions by dint of the greater uniformity of principles in the fundamental dimension – is justifiable for two reasons. The 'mechanisms' constitute the same intellectual and eventually also political challenge that is apt to generate pressure for change, and they entail the same insistence on what is calculated to forestall the acknowledgment of ideological change.

We may, therefore, conclude that discrepancy between the dimensions or within the dimension of fundamentals gives rise in each case to the challenge of ideological change. Indeed, in moderate ideologies, the normally small but also widening distance between the dimensions entails at some point the readiness to face squarely the problem of discrepancies. The acknowledgment that one must allow for the mutual impact of the dimensions is a corollary of the readiness to draw the ideological consequences from the compartmentalization in practical politics of issues of principle, that is, to reassess the merits and demerits of certain principles according to changing circumstances and the trends of public opinion. An example is the coming to terms of conservative and liberal ideologies with the Welfare State. However guarded, and at times refractory and diffident the approach towards the development and the modification of fundamentals on the part of anti-totalitarian parties, the eventual willingness to adapt fundamental to operative ideology and acknowledge the former's change distinguishes them from the totalitarian parties in totalitarian regimes. (Matters have become different for totalitarian parties in the West.)

It would be wrong to conclude that rigidity and apprehension of the mutual involvement of fundamental principles are absent from the attitude of non-totalitarian parties to their ideologies. Yet they are unyielding on only some central fundamentals. They adhere, above all, to those principles which permit ideological adaptation to changing trends of opinion and situational requirements and the more or less explicit acknowledgment of such adaptation. At the same time, these parties stress those fundamentals which are conducive to the preservation of their ideological identity.

These two postures are mutually supplementary, but they also operate at a cost to each other. Identity may get lost in the process of adaptation, while adaptation in deference to changing trends of public opinion follows from the fundamentals of the rules of the democratic game. If those in charge of totalitarian regimes were to embrace openly even the more guarded attitudes of non-totalitarian parties towards adaptation, their ideologies might well share the fate of previous ones. Like royal absolutism, they might lose their identity and finally disappear. Cogent awareness that this could happen to communism if it were to change into parliamentary social democracy, together with the determination to preserve its hegemony as a communist super-power, seems to have been at the root of Russia's decision to intervene in the Hungarian revolution and in Czechoslovakia. The logic of empire and of communism have become a tangle – and not so very recently at that. What is more, because two-dimensional argumentation is still far more than merely a device to cloak unexceptional deviance from fundamentals, neither in the East nor in the West has the tangle of the logic of *imperium* (in its original sense of rulership) with ideology reached the point of entirely or largely effacing the profile of the major party ideologies.

The systematic and realistic assessment of the actually prevailing distance between the two dimensions of political argumentation alone enables us, therefore, to determine how different party ideologies remain from one another, and how far, therefore, the classification of parties according to the traditional Left-Right divide still applies.

Chapter VII

RECONSTRUCTION OF THE LEFT-RIGHT CONTINUUM

The relevance of suggesting a tolerably comprehensive yet parsimonious model of the Left-Right polarity in order to make possible a realistic evaluation (and re-evaluation) of the position of parties on the Left-Right continuum hinges on the presupposition that the effects on the policy-orientations of ideological considerations constitute one factor among the pressures obtaining in the political market. In accordance with the extensive demonstration in the previous parts of this study of the inseparability of ideology and politics, policy-orientations and their connection with the ideological principles traditionally upheld by parties are considered here also as informing short- and long-range objectives, for which the political contest is conducted, and not as mere props for maximizing votes.[1] Ideological objectives are held to determine, in association with the performance of the government, part of the feedback that causes re-evaluation of the strategies by which the political parties approach the electorate after hammering out these strategies in 'within-system', *qua* intra-party, conflict.

The inclusion of ideological objectives among the factors exercising pressure on the political market indicates the difference between the political and economic markets. If, for example, we consider with Hirschman that 'slack' is the inevitable concomitant in the functioning of organizations,[2] its counterpart in policy-orientation, the deviations of policy from traditionally upheld ideological principles, is only in a very limited sense, and in any case not invariably, identical with a deterioration of the quality of the products available on the economic market. Above all, in Western democracies, such changes of quality might be considered by influential and/or large segments of the activists of the party, as well as by the electorate, to be an improvement on the original article. For some, the limitation of free enterprise and for others that of nationalization qualifies as such an improvement. The different, and more often than not controversial, evaluation of the 'quality' of a political-cum-ideological product even within the ranks of the leadership and the supporters of the same party constitutes, then, a major difference between the economic and political contexts which is perhaps more incisive than the fact that on the political market people do not have to buy but can stay away, since this does not secure them against becoming affected by its trends and transactions.

The ideological quality of a given policy (the ideologically political product) is determined by its relation to the fundamental principles professed by the party, or parties, responsible for the inception and implementation of that policy. Since it is always in the operative dimension that the decision-making process and its outcome are accounted for, this dimension is therefore the indicator of whether a confrontation takes place between fundamentals in the course of their attempted realization, or between them and the principles underlying the actual choice between options for action. Evidently, the difference between the party ideologies and the continued usefulness of the classification of parties according to the traditional Left-Right divide can as little be determined realistically by basing our appraisals on what is reflected in the operative dimension alone as by relying on policies pertaining to a single issue.

I. TWO-DIMENSIONALITY IN A MULTI-ISSUE FRAMEWORK

If the only alternative criteria for classifying political orders are taken to be maximal liberty v. authority sustained by force, then communist and fascist politics can be placed together at the extreme right of the Left-Right continuum.[3] Such a judgment constitutes a short cut since it relies on a single issue and, as far as communism is concerned, on the operative dimension alone. It is by no means illegitimate to equate the various communist and fascist regimes because of their shared oppressive features. It does not follow that their differences are irrelevant, such as the fact that the oppressive traits correspond to the fundamental principles of fascism but not to those of communism. This difference, which seems to be of little practical import, nevertheless indicates that an ideology will be misrepresented as much by our concentrating solely on ritually reiterated fundamentals as by considering them to be immaterial in view of a salient operative feature, like terror as the *ultima ratio* of reducing open dissensus.

Of course, only those fundamentals ought to be taken into consideration which have retained a noticeable influence on socio-economic and/or political organization and inspire policies that affect the life-situation of large segments of the population. Likewise, fundamentals which are invoked as determining long-range goals or which are relied upon by adherents of the ideology in order to oppose a salient operative feature, like terror, need to be taken into account. Any adequate classification of applied ideologies – that is ideologies used to justify government action or opposition to it, as well as at least potentially influential opposition – should reflect the fact that operative and fundamental principles clash as well as conform with each other. Nor should it be ignored that ideological pluralism applies in each dimension. Ideologies of parties, and still more their policies, share principles, since they tend to the left on some issues and to the right on others. Hence, in order to approximate to an exact classification of ideologies and of the regimes or policies they are invoked to justify, we must rely on several issue scales. Indeed, electorates generally evaluate parties, and parties propose their policies, in regard to more than one issue. The analyst who wishes to use a spatial model in order to determine the ideological profile of a party and embark on comparison must thus use several continua to accommodate several issues.[4] Moreover, a multi-issue model is incomplete if each of the issue-continua is not divided into two sub-continua, one for the ranking of parties according to the principles upheld in the fundamental dimension and the other for registering the principles applied in action and used in its justification in the operative dimension. Consequently, the net position of a party's ideology on the Left-Right continuum will be determined according to the average of the ratings it scores in the fundamental and operative sub-continua on each issue chosen to form part of the multi-issue composite.

As in many other respects, the differences between two-party and otherwise multi-party systems are irrelevant for ascertaining a party's ideological position. In either system a party tends to appeal to a wide range of social strata and, in order to be able to rally behind it various group interests, it blunts the edges of divisiveness on quite a number of issues, at least in its operative ideology. This tendency is possibly stronger in multi-party systems with more than two major parties and where the need for coalition government arises. In these circumstances party programmes may be, as in Italy, better integrated in the fundamental dimension, but, as in Sweden, this need not to be so; programmes may also perhaps range over a wider ideological spectrum, although most of it can be found in a two- or other multi-party system. None of the possible differences between the two kinds of multi-party system applies to the operative dimension in which the policy of the coalition has to be justified.[5]

Generally, then, the mean between declared long-term intentions and proposals for the short term and policies that are actually being carried out, must be taken into account in comparing party ideologies in two- and multi-party systems and in comparing the ideologies in both systems to those in one-party or hegemonic party systems. The wide range of this comparison does not in any way diminish its pertinence, since the great controversial issues are variations of the same themes in the intra- and inter-nation context, at least as far as the more developed countries are concerned. This can be seen, and the need to adopt a two-tier (fundamental and operative) construct further illustrated, if we add another observation to the brief argument already adduced against the equation of fascism and communism according to one aspect of their operative ideology.

Consider what is still (rightly or wrongly) held to be the most basic ideological issue: the socialization of the means of production and distribution v. private ownership. According to their traditional fundamentals, communist, social-democratic, liberal and conservative parties and regimes can be more or less neatly placed along the Left-Right continuum. However, quite apart from the fact that in respect of this issue we cannot place fascism at the extreme right pole,[6] the universal coexistence of private and socialized ownership has to be justified in the operative dimension of all these ideologies. Each party does this in different terms, according to the very different valuation of the two forms of ownership in the fundamental dimensions of communist, social-democratic and 'bourgeois' ideologies, and according to the vastly different proportions in which private and socialized ownership coexist in communist and non-communist societies.

Thus, rather than blurring the basic differences between ideologies of ruling parties or those likely to attain power and/or to influence policies, the two-dimensional perspective facilitates the exact appraisal of the ideologies of such parties, by being focused on the fundamental postulates in conjunction with their actual or immediately envisaged realization.

In view of the need for a two-tier multi-issue construct, the important question, of course, is: how do we go about choosing the sets of alternative principles and aims which can serve as the poles of the several continua that will enable us to arrive at a realistically balanced conclusion as to the net position of each party? An assemblage of issues particularly salient at a given moment is likely to produce as lopsided a comparison as a concentration on one central issue. Even if it were possible, the construction of an exhaustive composite of issue-scales would require constant amendment, in view of the perpetual shifts of contingent issues between more marginal and more central positions. Yet such shifts are more often than not related to what I propose to call core-issues. A careful selection of these, therefore, will be conducive to a relatively representative and stable classification, the more so since deviations from central basic principles, forming the core-issues which are of a more enduring and hence more important character, will be duly noted in the operative dimension. Two-dimensional ranking thus compensates for possible shortcomings due to restriction of the number of core-issues, and makes it possible to construct a model at once representative and concise. And both ideological continuity and the major tendencies indicating, or pressing for, ideological change find their expression through the subdivision of each issue-scale into a fundamental and operative sub-scale.

Core-issues would be those fundamentals which the parties themselves continue to refer to in political debate as the important issues on which they are ideologically divided. These issues must be taken to embody the principles by which parties invite their policies to be judged, at least by their more steadfast followers. In their ideological self-portraits, parties for the most part attach less importance to short-term than to middle- and long-term effects of policies. Parties' self-valuations and their evaluation by the analyst meet on these grounds in so far as the analyst, too, will relate policies to the alternative principles declared by the parties to inform their stand on socio-economic and political organization. But in establishing ideological differentiation, the analyst will be concerned with revealing whether policies reflect enduring divisiveness and/or incidental convergence, and hence to what degree policies conform with or contravene the advertised alternative fundamental principles, whatever the party leadership does or does not admit on this particular point. These criteria of selecting the core-issues are illustrative rather than exhaustive. Similarly, the six sets of core-alternatives that I am now going to suggest as the poles of a composite of spatial linear scales are again indicative rather than definitive for determining the positions on the Left-Right continuum of a paradigmatic communist (CP), social-democratic (SDP), liberal conservative (LCP) and fascist party (FP).

One hardly needs to justify speaking paradigmatically of a 'liberal-conservative' party, inasmuch as the great conservative parties in the West, like the British Tories or the French Gaullists or Right-Centre parties such as the German CDU, have adopted central principles of classical liberalism, combined them *inter alia* with concessions to welfarism, and absorbed on this basis the greater part of the erstwhile liberal clientele. Where parties bear the name 'liberal' and, having held their own, are serious contenders for office, or actually hold it, more often than not they have settled on a similar platform and pass for conservative parties. In the USA, and in similar systems where there is no serious confrontation between a Labour Party (or parties) and a liberal or conservative party (or parties), then the parties competing for office tend more to the Left or Right concerning some central issues such as welfarism. In America, therefore, particularly since Roosevelt, and perhaps solely on the level of presidential-federal politics, the Republican Party would qualify as an actual specimen of the 'liberal-conservative' party I have in mind here, and the Democratic Party would be placed more to the Left.[7] Neither the smaller ideological distinctiveness of the two parties, nor its confusion by regional and other cross-cutting, causes controversy between them to be ordinarily less animated than between Labour and the Conservatives in Britain.[8]

2. THE TWO SETS OF CORE-ISSUES

The three pairs forming the first set of alternative principles of a tolerably representative six-issue composite of continua concern basic controversial issues of socio-economic organization and policy orientation: socialized v. private ownership of the means of production and distribution; the classless society and the disappearance of status-differentiation v. meritocratic (with some ascriptive) class- and status-differences; maximal v. minimal government interference in the economy.

These three pairs of alternative principles have one common characteristic: either a traditional goal or a prominent political stance of the Left furnishes the point of departure for construing its counterpart at the right pole. Principles denoting the right pole do not necessarily correspond in more extended historical perspective to basic fundamentals of the traditional Right(s). The logical and immediate historical reason for the derivation of modern right from left principles is the fact that socialism and communism were conceived in opposition not so much to the traditional Right as to its political neighbour to the Left: bourgeois liberal democracy. Private ownership, much less meritocratic stratification, are not traditionally rightist principles in the sense which they assumed in the bourgeois socio-political culture. However, that which distinguished traditional conservative from bourgeois conceptions of property, class and status, has become largely irrelevant, as my brief remarks on the adoption of liberal principles by conservative parties have indicated. Still, not all original rightist principles have become irrelevant in the dimension of fundamentals, let alone in the operative dimension.

The alternative principles of maximal and minimal interference in the economy have only fairly recently become a hallmark of Left-Right controversy, and the distinction in these terms between leftist and rightist politics is problematic in more than one respect. Leaving aside the turning of all economies into 'command' economies in modern warfare, minimal state intervention, which serves as the right pole, is logically proximate to the leftist principle of the stateless society – which on its part can be construed as the logical extension to the left of the liberal principle of minimal states intervention. Maximal intervention, which serves as the left pole, is logically derivable from the rightist principle of authoritarianism – epitomized in the probably apocryphal *l'état c'est moi* – when it has become authoritarian etatism. On both counts the adoption by conservative parties of the liberal principle of minimal intervention is logically, though not in all instances historically, a move to the left. It would seem, therefore, to be appropriate to place minimal intervention in the economy near the left pole and maximal intervention near the right pole of a continuum extending between the alternative principles of the stateless society and authoritarian etatism. To do so would also enable us to place fascism at the extreme right, as far as fundamentals are concerned, and to make allowance in the operative dimension for its pragmatic-opportunist attitude toward state intervention in the economy, which certainly falls below communist interventionism based on near-total nationalization. Yet here precisely is the nub of the matter. Minimal interference in the economy has become a rightist principle because, as the outgrowth of social-democratic revisionist theory and communist practice, interventionism in the economy has for all practical intents and purposes assumed the rank of a fundamental principle of the Left. It is the implement both of the realization of welfarism and of the transition to either a social-democratic classless, if not entirely stateless, society, or a communist classless and stateless society. And the two ideals still figure very prominently (though not in equally unqualified form) on the agenda of socialist and communist parties, even though the advocates of both ideals have ceased long ago to commit themselves to anything regarding the length of the transition period. If, therefore, maximal and minimal interference can be retained as the alternative left and right poles of a continuum, this, despite their being genuine alternatives, does not mean that they represent historical and intrinsically compelling Left-Right opposites.

Even if one were to assume with scholars such as Downs that all political questions can be reduced to their bearing upon the issue of the amount of government intervention, one would in fact be left with a criterion which is not particularly useful for ideological differentiation.[9] Surely, as long as it is neither near-total nor near-nil, it is not the amount of government intervention but its purpose which pre-eminently fulfils this function. Far-reaching interference in the economy might be used in order to mobilize national resources for foreign aggression or for expanding social security. Political non-interference in the economic objectives of some people has almost invariably meant interference in the interests of others. Government intervention has been used to interfere with the freedom of action of the majority of those involved in the processes of production in order to guarantee maximal non-interference with the exploitation of wage earners. Government has also interfered in order to prevent powerful minorities from combining and dominating the market or at least in order to curb such tendencies. Any of these objectives might well require similar 'amounts' of government interference. It is the objective rather than the degree of either interference or non-interference that is of primary ideological, and for that matter practical, relevance. Hence only in conjunction with specific objectives, and therefore with other core-issues, does it make sense to reserve a continuum for this issue-pair, which continues superficially to be treated also *per se* in political controversy.

The second set of alternative principles, more than the first, concerns specifically political issues. These, too, are controversial and important in terms both of world-wide ideological confrontation and of the day-to-day life of individuals everywhere. They are: freedom and repression of expression and association; independence of the judiciary as a safeguard of the constitutional rights of the individual v. dependence of the judiciary on the power-holders and the constant jeopardy of the constitutional rights of the individual; respect for the sovereignty of all states and the right of national self-determination of all nations v. infringements of sovereignty and the denial of national self-determination. In these sets of alternative principles, the first two are leftist by courtesy of the liberal heritage. In point of fact, in contrast to the first three pairs of alternative principles, of the three just listed, the first two, that mark the left pole, are derivate opposites of principles historically associated with typically European pre- and anti-liberal (that is, conservative and generally right-wing) regimes and ideologies.

Concerning the last issue, national self-determination and sovereignty, the polar alternatives of affirmation and negation logically extend the principles of free association and the prohibition of its effective exercise from internal relations to the relations between states and nations. Here, even more than with the other two issues, it is difficult to identify unequivocally the principles that denote the left pole with principles traditionally upheld by the Left. Like liberalism, the socialist Left has espoused generous other-regarding principles in foreign affairs without developing a specific theory of international relations, or rather one that is fully consistent with the principles adopted in internal politics.[10] It hardly needs to be recalled how rapidly the liberation of neighbouring countries by the French revolutionary armies was followed by annexation or the imposition of satellite status, making those at the receiving end pay heavily for the honour. Since then, the impact of ideology on foreign relations has generally been adjusted to the requirements of global confrontations, so that either side supports preferably regimes like its own but also states with regimes different from its own. The Western allies, whose political systems resemble most of the USA suffer incomparably less interference from their senior ally in their internal and external policies than the East European allies of the USSR by the latter. But here, too, there are gradations which are by no means insignificant. At any rate, from the outset, communist revolutionary internationalism has not been disturbed by reverence for national sovereignty, and quickly became equivocal about national self-determination. There is no great leap from Lenin to the 'Brezhnev doctrine'.[11]

3. TWO-DIMENSIONAL RANKING

a. *Method of Presentation*

I propose now to proceed, with the help of graphic illustrations based on the coordination of orientations with a numerical scale, to the ranking from left to right of our four paradigmatic parties, according to the weighted average of all the positions upheld in the two dimensions.

To begin with, in Table 1 the position of the four paradigmatic parties on each issue is expressed in numbers which refer once to the fundamental and once to the operative principles. The average of the two is compounded for each issue. A numerical scale running from 0 to 100 is used. As is customary in using this device, 0 presents the left extreme pole and 100 the right extreme pole. The numbers denoting a position are the equivalent of the percentage of the total distance between the left and right poles, of the distance, that is, that a party can be said to be removed from the left extreme and to approach the right extreme. The lower the number (percentage), the more a party is supposed to uphold leftist principles; the higher the number (percentage), the more a party is supposed to embrace rightist principles.

For example, in terms of fundamentals the position of CP regarding the socialization of the ownership of the means of production and distribution is given at zero (F : 0). Since socialization is for the most part not total, concessions to private ownership in a communist regime are estimated to amount to 20 per cent (OI : 20). The average of both positions is 10. The three positions are listed in Table 1 as follows:

$$\left.\begin{array}{r}\mathrm{F}: 0\\ \mathrm{OI}: 20\end{array}\right\} 10$$

As can be seen from this example, I coordinate the orientation in respect of each issue in the fundamental and operative dimensions with a number (percentage) according to a purely impressionist estimate based on what seems to me confirmed by generally verifiable observation of political events and processes.[12] I am aware that estimates on one or another issue are open to debate, just as is the evaluation of generally perceived phenomena, and I shall indicate this in some of my comments. I do not think, however, that differences of opinion are likely to go so far as to impugn the rankings of the parties, let alone the usefulness of the proposed model and the appositeness of its underlying assumptions.

The averages of all percentages scored by each party on all six issues in the fundamental and operative dimensions, as well as the overall (net) average for each party are listed in Table 2, but will be discussed only in the last section of this chapter.

In order to facilitate explanation of the significance of Table 1's content (and eventually also Table 2's), the parties will be re-ordered on numerical scales from left to right according to the percentages listed in Table 1. Each party's position will be indicated on three linear scales in regard to each issue: according to scoring in terms of fundamental principles; of operative principles; and according to the average of the first two scorings. Table 3 which gives these scales for all six core-issues, provides the over-view of the two-tier multi-issue linear composite. It appears as Appendix 5, for the overall picture it

Table 1

		CP	SDP	LCP	FP		
1. *Socialized Ownership* of the means of production and distribution	F: OI:	0 20 } 10	20 70 } 45	90 80 } 85	80 75 } 77·5	:F :OI	*Private ownership* of these means
2. *Classless society* and disappearance of class- and status differentiation	F: OI:	0 70 } 35	20 80 } 50	90 90 } 90	100 100 } 100	:F :OI	*Meritocratic* (with some ascriptive) class- and status-differentiation
3. *Maximal intervention* in economy	F: OI:	0 10 } 5	40 70 } 55	90 80 } 85	30 50 } 40	:F :OI	*Minimal intervention* in economy
4. *Freedom of expression* and association	F: OI:	0 90 } 45	10 10 } 10	10 10 } 10	90 90 } 90	:F :OI	*Unfreedom of expression* and association
5. *Independent judiciary* as safeguard of constitutional rights of individuals	F: OI:	0 100 } 50	0 0 } 0	0 0 } 0	100 100 } 100	:F :OI	*Dependence of judiciary* on power-holders and jeopardy of constitutional rights of individuals
6. *Observance of sovereignty* and national self-determination	F: OI:	50 70 } 60	0 10 } 5	20 20 } 20	80 70 } 75	:F :OI	*Infringement of sovereignty* and national self-determination

Table 2

	CP	SDP	LCP	FP
Average of Fs	8·33	15	50	80
Average of OIs	60	40	46·66	80·82
Overall averages	34·16	27·5	48·33	80·41

conveys can be appreciated only after the coordination of the positions of the parties on various issues with numbers (percentages) has been explained. For the convenience of the reader, the three linear scales which in Table 3 pertain to each issue will be reproduced in the text at the beginning of the comments I propose to offer on all core-issues. In the last section of this chapter, the averages of Fs and OIs and the overall averages listed in Table 2 will be presented likewise on linear scales.

I now proceed to comment on the positions allocated to the parties on each issue, especially on those numerical estimates which are not self-explanatory and which reflect the changes in the traditional left-right ranking of the parties that result from averaging their positions in the fundamental and operative dimensions.

b. *The Socio-economic Issues*

Issue 1: Socialized *v.* private ownership

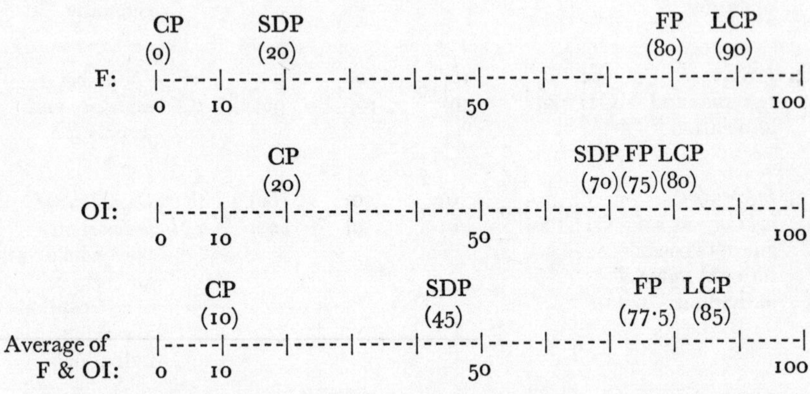

In the F dimension in Issue 1 we see the sharp polarization between the two parties of the Left over and against the other two parties. In the OI dimension SDP joins FP and LCP, whereas on the scale registering averages, SDP occupies a middle position between CP on the one hand and FP and LCP on the other.

The percentages in the F dimension reflect the reality that social-democratic parties have by now retreated from the principle of the total socialization of the means of production and distribution, although it is not quite clear where the retreat (or the advance newly heralded by the British Labour Party, for instance) is to stop. Equivocation in this respect is not new, as the examples adduced in the next chapter show. Moreover, socialization need not necessarily involve nationalization. For all these reasons the movement away from the extreme left pole has been rated at 20, which perhaps may be too low. In the West, nationalization as the realization of social ideals has practically come to a halt, for the time being at least.

I have rated the allegiance of LCP to the principle of private ownership higher than the allegiance of FP in view of the latter's etatism, though it bears on the principle of private ownership not directly, but indirectly through *dirigisme*. As a result of its fundamental commitment to private ownership, a deviation of LCP in the OI dimension slightly higher than that of FP from that principle had to be noted. In Britain, for instance, the Conservatives have not been able to undo as much of Labour's nationalization as they initially wished. As the irony of fate will have it, soon after Mr Heath's government had assumed power it saw itself forced to nationalize part of Rolls-Royce in order to save this prestigious and nationally important company from bankruptcy. In fact, like interventionism, nationalization had never been confined to socialist aspirations. It can serve very well as a prop to private enterprise if applied to nationally important but economically insufficiently profitable, or even unprofitable, services and economic sectors. Moreover nationalization, if profit-making, like the German Railways in the Weimar Republic, may be widely acceptable as being in the national interest (in this case as a security for international credit on account of the national debt), without any connection with socialist politics.

Issue 2: Classless *v.* meritocratic society

```
           CP        SDP                                                  LCP   FP
           (0)       (20)                                                (90) (100)
    F:     |-----|-----|-----|-----|-----|-----|-----|-----|-----|-----|
           0    10                       50                             100

                                                     CP   SDP   LCP   FP
                                                    (70)  (80)  (90)(100)
    OI:    |-----|-----|-----|-----|-----|-----|-----|-----|-----|-----|
           0    10                       50                             100

                             CP       SDP                          LCP  FP
                            (35)      (50)                        (90)(100)
Average of |-----|-----|-----|-----|-----|-----|-----|-----|-----|-----|
  F & OI:  0    10                       50                             100
```

The scores assigned to the parties on Issue 2 yield in both dimensions, and hence also on average, the traditional left-right progression.

The polarization in the F dimension is as sharp as on the previous issue, and despite the moving together nearer the right pole of all parties in the operative dimension within the span of 70–100, we get on average again a relatively high, though attenuated, cleavage between the parties of the Left and those of the Right. The result would be the same if we were to assume that a somewhat different rating in the OI dimension was in order.

Generally, it seems that FP must be rated higher, i.e. more to the right, on the issue under consideration, than LCP. True, in Western societies, unofficial vestiges of aristocratic privilege, alongside the very tangible advantages accruing to those born into the better-off strata, affect the meritocratic game and occasionally cause its dice to be loaded. This is not less true of proto-fascist and even fascist regimes. Despite the affirmation of formal political equality, religious and/or ethnic discrimination, together with political discrimination exists both in conservative societies of the more recent past and to a lesser degree, in liberal-democratic societies, and is usually intensified under fascism by the statutory denial of political equality to specific groups. This is why I place FP at the right pole and assume it to out-distance on this score all other parties in both the fundamental and operative dimensions. It is, of course, a moot point whether, on account of religious and racial discrimination (Jews are in this context more often than not supposed to fall under both categories), we ought not, in the operative dimension, to place CP (in a communist regime) to the right of SDP, if not even next to FP. Still, we cannot disregard the fact that in no branch of production and distribution does big enterprise exist in communist regimes, and its absence means the absence of strata obtaining influence and affluence from private enterprise and corporations. Academics, writers and top grades in the army and the various bureaucracies apart, workers and technical staff directly engaged in production have the opportunity to achieve higher incomes than doctors, lawyers and engineers (not directly connected with production).

On all these counts, a CP might be placed perhaps slightly more to the left in terms of operative ideology than the other parties, though it must be assigned a position vastly more to the right than any authentic interpretation of communist fundamentals would permit. Together with the first, this issue provides a striking example of the drastic diminution of the distance between F and OI as we move from parties of the Left to parties of the Right.

Issue 3: Maximal *v.* minimal intervention in the economy

```
      CP              FP  SDP                         LCP
      (0)            (30) (40)                        (90)
F:    |-----|-----|-----|-----|-----|-----|-----|-----|-----|-----|
      0    10                       50                          100

           CP                       FP        SDP  LCP
          (10)                     (50)      (70)  (80)
OI:   |-----|-----|-----|-----|-----|-----|-----|-----|-----|-----|
      0    10                       50                          100

        CP                  FP       SDP                LCP
        (5)                (40)      (55)               (85)
Average of |-----|-----|-----|-----|-----|-----|-----|-----|-----|-----|
  F & OI:  0    10                       50                          100
```

Despite the by-now quite generally accepted evaluation of maximal intervention as a leftist principle, FP could not be assumed to score zero on Issue 3 in the F dimension because fascism permits the functioning of a mixed economy in the framework of a state-directed economy. Therefore we can assign only 30 to FP, i.e. a place further to the left in the F dimension than SDP (40) but still far from CP(0). The rating of FP in the operative dimension is higher (50), i.e. more to the right, for here also ineffectiveness of state planning and control must be reckoned with. The discrepancy between the positions of FP in the fundamental and operative dimensions is 20, the highest on any issue. None the less it is perhaps under-stressed, since on the one hand fascist statism permits any degree of economic interventionism, and on the other, private property and big enterprise which remain untouched are capable to some extent of countering state *dirigisme*. Still, these considerations apply almost equally to both dimensions. It concerns the operative dimension more specifically that, in view of what has become known about the degree of inefficiency of 'totalitarian' planning and control, state intervention can be presumed not to be practised to the extent of CP's percentage in the OI dimension. Hence it may very well be that the difference between the ratings of CP on the F and OI dimensions is also not great enough; but one must remember that in this case interventionism from the centre is not significantly counteracted by non-state agencies. Contrariwise, while in Great Britain, for instance, inflation and industrial strife drove a Conservative government to pass legislation designed to ensure the enforcement of wage- and price-control, opposition to its implementation by the trade unions (more than by the Labour Party) led to elections that created a stalemate, turned by Labour into a marginal victory in the general elections of February 1974. In any event, interventionism as such has ceased to be (if it ever was) a monopoly of socialist or communist government. Indeed, this shows in the placing of the other parties, which also follows from the related changes of attitude towards nationalization and welfarism commented upon at various stages of my argument. The apparently bewildering disarray of the traditional ordering from left to right caused by placing FP nearer CP than SDP in the fundamental dimension follows from considering interventionism as a leftist principle. The appositeness of judging the ideological positions in terms of two-dimensionality is borne out by the fact that in the F dimension CP, FP, and SDP stand left of centre, whereas in the operative dimension all parties, except CP, need to be placed to the right of centre. Thus only the average of all positions in the two dimensions yields that relationship between the parties which conforms with a balanced judgment of all the factors involved.

c. *Specifically Political Issues*

Issue 4: Freedom *v.* unfreedom of expression and association

```
               CP SDP LCP                                              FP
               (0) (10) (10)                                          (90)
         F:    |-----|-----|-----|-----|-----|-----|-----|-----|-----|-----|
               0    10                      50                            100

                  SDP LCP                                          CP FP
                 (10) (10)                                       (90) (90)
        OI:    |-----|-----|-----|-----|-----|-----|-----|-----|-----|-----|
               0    10                      50                            100

                   SDP LCP                CP                           FP
Average of        (10) (10)              (45)                         (90)
   F & OI:     |-----|-----|-----|-----|-----|-----|-----|-----|-----|-----|
               0    10                      50                            100
```

As with the next issue (5), the main assumption in Issue 4 is that, apart from CP, the parties practise what they preach, or come very near to doing so. Contrary to what I have just pointed out in concluding the comment on intervention in the economy, the average of 45 for the CP's ideological position towards freedom of expression and association could be taken as evidence against the appositeness of averaging. However, this relatively low (= high leftist) average rating of CP takes into account the need for apologia, not incumbent on the other parties in regard of this issue. Although CP exercises oppression to the same degree at least as fascist regimes, these are not committed to the final goal of maximal freedom, as any CP on principle is. In rating CP on this issue, one should not discard, in my view, this fundamental commitment, since it forces a CP to engage in juggling formulae concerning the 'dialectical' relationship between freedom and necessity, or to resort also to the more conventional pretexts for oppression, such as the need to fend off capitalist conspiracy, or to seek excuse for draconic measures in most communist countries' initial backwardness which necessarily prolongs the transition to 'the reign of freedom'.

Thus, although on issues 4 to 6 the left poles have been derived as opposites of the right poles, it is justifiable to consider a CP as being committed in the fundamental dimension to freedom of expression and association, by virtue of the never-revoked postulate in the *Manifesto* of 'an association in which the free development of each is a condition of the free development of all'. Such was to be, above all, the free association of 'the immediate producers'. Naturally, the promise of these goals and the intellectual distortionism exercised to bridge the gap between promise and reality do nothing to ease repression. The ranking of CP in the operative dimension accounts for this fact. The question remains whether the fundamentals ought not to be discounted, since they are professed without having any appreciable bearing on actual social and political orientation. If for these reasons averaging is out of place, or the position on the F scale should be given less (more to the right) than even 50 per cent, this would merely accentuate the change in the left-right ordering produced by the net average of all positions on all issues. The same applies in connection with the next issue. Lastly, for reasons presumed to be self-evident, SDP and LCP have been assumed to hold the same position here and on the next issue.

Issue 5: Independent *v.* dependent judiciary

```
      CP SDP LCP                                              FP
      (0) (0) (0)                                           (100)
F:    |-----|-----|-----|-----|-----|-----|-----|-----|-----|-----|
      0     10                      50                        100

        SDP   LCP                                          CP   FP
        (0)   (0)                                     (100)(100)
OI:   |-----|-----|-----|-----|-----|-----|-----|-----|-----|-----|
      0     10                      50                        100

        SDP   LCP                   CP                          FP
        (0)   (0)                  (50)                       (100)
Average of |-----|-----|-----|-----|-----|-----|-----|-----|-----|-----|
F & OI:    0     10                      50                        100
```

In the dimension of fundamentals a total polarization has been assumed in Issue 5 between all parties and FP. As with the previous issue, FP is joined at the right pole by CP in the operative dimension. For reasons similar to those adduced on the previous issue, CP is assumed to be committed in principle to an independent judiciary and the safeguarding of individual rights within a stateless and classless society conceived as a self-directed but not unorganized society of 'the immediate producers'. Obviously, even 'the administration of things' requires a judiciary. As on the previous issue, CP's average here is half of the rating of FP and averaging is open to question. However, even if in both cases we were to decide against averaging because in either case commitment to the extreme left position is for the time being entirely irrelevant, and if we were to apply an equally high (right) rating to both dimensions, this would cause the net average of the positions of CP and SDP on all issues to change only in that SDP would merely have to be placed further to the left of CP than would be necessary anyway. CP's overall average of 34·16 as calculated in Table 2 (and graphically illustrated in Scale 3, p. 229) would rise to 40, and the distance between CP and SDP would grow by 5·84, but the net position of CP would still be 8·33 (instead of 14·57) to the left of LCP.

Issue 6: Observance *v.* infringement of sovereignty and national self-determination

```
             SDP        LCP               CP              FP
             (0)        (20)             (50)            (80)
F:           |-----|-----|-----|-----|-----|-----|-----|-----|-----|-----|
             0    10                      50                            100

                   SDP  LCP                          CP FP
                   (10) (20)                        (70) (70)
OI:          |-----|-----|-----|-----|-----|-----|-----|-----|-----|-----|
             0    10                      50                            100

               SDP      LCP                     CP       FP
               (5)      (20)                   (60)     (75)
Average of   |-----|-----|-----|-----|-----|-----|-----|-----|-----|-----|
F & OI:      0    10                      50                            100
```

According to what I have already said in explanation of the choice of core-issues, about the peculiar position of CP on this particular issue, I have coordinated its fundamental commitment to the observance of national sovereignty and self-determination with 50 (i.e. 50 per cent observance) and its operative ideology, like that of fascism, with 70 (i.e. 70 per cent infringement). I have not rated infringement higher, for even 70 might be too high (as for fascism in its heyday). There are not only the more or less blatant evasions, within limits, of Soviet control and directives in Eastern Europe, which the USSR could, at some cost, repress without risking a global confrontation; the same would seem to apply to the subversion of the regimes of some of its non-communist client-states. For instance, at the moment of first writing this passage (July 1972), it was highly improbable that in the event of a pro-communist or even communist palace revolution in Egypt the USA would intervene, unless as a result of such a revolution the USSR drastically increased its military presence and/or openly and massively took part in a military encounter between Egypt and Israel.[13] The latter possibility was not obviated by the departure from (and partial return to) Egypt of Russian military personnel.

Be that as it may, it is usually on this issue only that there is no considerable division between the fundamental and operative principles of a CP ruling a super-power and that of one ruling a smaller state, though in the latter case the percentage would resemble that of SDP and LCP. What applies to the USSR was true of a powerful expansionist fascist regime like Nazi Germany, except that there the fundamental principle was frankly expansionist-annexationist while the sound and fury also ran somewhat ahead of the operative principle, whereas in the case of the USSR the reverse seems to hold in both respects.

4. THE SUM TOTAL

As the coordination of orientations with a numerical scale exemplifies,[14] our paradigmatic communist, social-democratic, liberal-conservative and fascist parties can be ranked in this traditional order in both the fundamental and operative dimensions on one issue alone: classless society v. class differentiation. There is hardly an issue on which the position of a leftist party does not come very near to or actually overlap with one or even two parties to its right on one of the two sub-scales. Nevertheless, it is only to be expected that the average of all *fundamental* positions of all four parties on all six issues should yield the traditional left-right order. In the first place, in all but one instance (national sovereignty and self-determination), the CP has been held committed to the most extreme leftist principles. In addition, although reassessed, the fundamentals of the other parties, on the whole, comply with their place in the traditional left-right order more than they deviate from it.[15] Hence the average of the sum total of the positions of the four parties in terms of fundamentals (Fs) yields the traditional left-right ordering as in Scale 1.

Scale 1

```
                 CP  SDP                      LCP                   FP
               (8·33) (15)                    (50)                  (80)
Average of Fs |-----|-----|-----|-----|-----|-----|-----|-----|-----|-----|
              0    10                        50                         100
```

It is likewise not surprising that things are very different when it comes to operative principles. Apart from the issue of classlessness v. meritocratic class- and status-stratification, there is not a single issue in relation to which the operative principles of the four parties can be arranged in the traditional order, nor is there a complete reversal, even though on all three specifically political issues (freedom of expression and association, independent judiciary and observance of the sovereignty of other nations) the extreme left-wing party (CP) and the extreme right-wing party (FP) occupy respectively a position nearest to, and at, the right extreme. On two issues (freedom of expression and association and independent judiciary) the two other parties (SDP and LCP) occupy identical positions, and in the third instance (observance of sovereignty) they stand quite near the left pole.[16] Thus, the average positions of all four parties on all six issues in terms of operative ideology yield Scale 2.

Scale 2

```
                                      SDP  LCP    CP           FP
                                     (40) (46·66) (60)        (80·82)
Average of OIs |-----|-----|-----|-----|-----|-----|-----|-----|-----|-----|
               0    10                        50                        100
```

In comparison with the average of fundamentals, the average of operative standpoints exhibits, then, a spectacular slide to the right of the two leftist parties (CP and SDP). The shift is attendant upon their adoption of established institutions and practices, which CP particularly renders often more onerous. The move to the right reflected in the FP's average of operative principles is insignificant. Its position in both dimensions is only slightly less to the right than it would have been had not state intervention in the economy come to be regarded as a leftist principle (hence on this issue FP averages 40, i.e. a position left of centre), and the only significant disparity between the two dimensions of fascist ideology occurring on this issue and amounting to 20 (F:30, OI:50) does not affect the picture of practically complete inter-dimensional correspondence generally characteristic of FP. This tallies with the fact that in the decisive issues I have listed, the brutality of FP in practice largely tallies with its quite frank statements of principle. LCP alone moves on average leftwards in the operative dimension. This shows not only that the party comes to terms with welfarist principles in the fundamental dimension but also that it acts often in a more leftist way than it cares to admit.

If we compound the parties' net position as the averages of all their positions in the fundamental and operative dimensions, that is, if we average the percentages shown in Scales 1 and 2, we see, that, in comparison with the averages scored in the operative dimension, some left ground is recovered by CP and SDP and practically none by FP, while LCP moves again a little to the right (Scale 3).

Scale 3

```
                         SDP     CP     LCP                 FP
                        (27·5) (34·16) (48·33)            (80·41)
Net average   |-----|-----|-----|-----|-----|-----|-----|-----|-----|-----|
              0    10                       50                           100
```

The partial recoverage of left ground, which is quite considerable in the case of CP and far from negligible in the case of SDP, is due to their low (= high left) scoring on fundamentals. That SDP and LCP again move considerably away from each other is due to the high divergence between their fundamentals on the socio-economic issues. These divergences outweigh by far the equal or almost equal scoring of SDP and LCP on the political issues and hence also outweigh the small difference (6·66) between their averages in the operative dimension (Scale 2). The extreme leftist fundamentals attributable to CP on five out of six issues assure that party a relatively low (i.e. high left) average. Thus, the impact of fundamentals goes some way towards redressing the shift to the right in the operative principles. Yet while all but one party (FP) cluster on the left half of the scale and CP moves again to the left of LCP, CP does not regain its position nearest the left pole. That place is now taken by SDP. This outcome does not signify that the consideration of fundamentals is a mere academic exercise, even if they are counteracted by operative principles; on the contrary, this outcome fully justifies the procedure as being conducive to a realistic assessment of ideological party profiles.

As I have already argued, the only fundamentals that ought to be considered are those which are upheld as goals and which still play a part in policy orientation or in argument about it. These also comprise, then, the goals and principles that, though far removed from political reality, are invoked by the internal opposition, which challenges those who make concessions over goals and principles and/or declare that they are as yet not fully realizable. We have heard increasingly also of such opposition in communist countries, and no one can say that it is without influence. It therefore proves that the 'political' fundamentals especially, though trampled upon by communist governments, can be evaluated as leftist fundamentals and attributed as such to a CP, the more so as the opposition from within – so far – proclaims allegiance to socialism. The appositeness of weighing fundamental and operative ideologies against each other is demonstrated best, indeed, inasmuch as it entails altering the traditional ranking on the Left-Right continuum, without affecting adversely its further usefulness. It does make sense that according to the overall average, SDP should emerge in a position more to the left than CP. In the dimension of fundamentals, a social-democratic party is less extreme in its leftist principles than a communist party. But in the dimension of operative principles only on two issues – socialized ownership and intervention in the economy – does it move much more to the right than a communist party. On one issue – class differentiation – the difference is rather small, and concerning the remaining three issues, of freedom of expression and association, the independence of the judiciary and respect for other nations' sovereignty, a communist party vastly outdistances a social-democratic party in its movement to the right.

Lastly, the coordination with numerical scales of the fundamental and operative principles of our four paradigmatic parties illustrates the drastic diminution of distance between the two dimensions as we move towards the right.[17] Once again it is obvious that the distance between the dimensions is not the measure of their extremism. But it does not follow that, because in a rightist extremist party the distance between the dimensions is reduced as a result of the asymmetry within the dimension of fundamentals, such asymmetry creates less tension than the distance between dimensions. In fact, whether or not the distance is small on average, the operative dimension enhances, if not the asymmetry between fundamentals, then the weight of their practical significance, which otherwise might not be fully grasped.

Asymmetry in the dimension of fundamentals exists in all ideologies and reflects indigenous ideological pluralism. The manifestation, growth or changes in the asymmetry between the fundamental and operative dimensions add to that pluralism or highlight it so that the intra- and inter-dimensional tension becomes an indicator of ideological change, or at least of pressure in its direction. On the supposition that argumentation in terms of operative ideology can blur but not dissimulate the actual tendency and visible results of policies, such argumentation reflects, then, any of the following possibilities: the faithful implementation of fundamentals (which reveals the extent to which they are reconcilable); the impossibility of such implementation; or the fact that from the outset faithful implementation is evaded; and, if this tendency persists, that ideological change has occurred, whether or not it is acknowledged.

I hope I have demonstrated that the dynamics inherent in the relationship between party ideology and party politics can be assessed properly only in a conceptual framework whose visual illustration requires a two-tier multi-issue spatial model on the lines of the one proposed here. The varied orderings of the parties from left to right required and permitted by the model in respect both of various issues and of each issue on the fundamental and operative sub-scales – all this attests not swings of the pendulum between more and less ideological politics, but rather the movements of various party ideologies between the left and right extremes of the ideological continuum. In point of fact, since those who maintain the distinction between ideological and unideological politics identify as ideological the extremes of the Left and the Right, how in fact can they define as unideological what lies somewhere in between these extremes without denying the very idea of a continuum, that is, of debate and battle on the same issues between the moderate and the extreme parties? To use the notion of middle-of-the-road politics as the equivalent of unideological politics is to use an expression which implies the relatedness (to the left and to the right) of the positions it indicates. Political debate and decision-making nowhere conform only with fundamental principles or postulates, nor solely with operative principles determined by nothing but technical ends-means calculations, but with an ever-changing admixture of both. On this fact rests the ideological two-dimensionality of political argumentation, that is to say, the actual orientation and dynamics of politics.

Obviously, for the analyst to outline the possibilities of the adaptation of the dimensions to each other, to indicate the disparities and rearrange the parties on the Left-Right continuum, is one thing. The readiness of party leaders to acknowledge a change of fundamentals is something else, although in actual fact they are constantly engaged in making adaptations in one of the directions indicated in Chapter VI. In what way party leaderships and ideologues face asymmetries in their party ideologies and to what extent they face the implication, that is, ideological change, is for the most part a matter of squaring tactical considerations with both the commitment to traditional ideological fundamentals and the assessment of their practicability. The response to the challenge of ideological change is, of course, inhibited by the delusion that there can be politics – not just politicking – without ideology. Yet whether or not Western party leaders and political scientists continue to labour under that delusion, the fact that policy orientations have been changing everywhere is not denied by any party leaders; nor is it asserted that these changes do not imply movement towards and away from fundamental principles, entailing even the co-optation of once hotly contested principles.

The following documentation of the generally complex attitude towards ideological change and the exposition of its mechanism involves reasserting central points, just referred to again, as in previous chapters, and demonstrated in detail in Part I. The last chapter, therefore, fulfils also the purpose of a conclusion to this study.

Chapter VIII

IDEOLOGICAL CHANGE

More often than not the modification of fundamentals is equivocal for a considerable time, and it is doubtful whether it ever ceases to be so. The reduction of dissonance (among fundamentals, and between them and operative ideology) in politics is not dissimilar to the minimizing of dissonance in private affairs. Dissonance is not felt each time an individual actor encounters resistance or frustration in his private affairs.[1] Policy-makers, too, are not always bothered by dissonance, but its perception and the pressure to dissimulate or reduce it are part of the conduct of politics, and are imposed directly by some actors on others. Purists and diehards are normally bothered by dissonance between cherished and applied principles, and, in return, they worry the leadership with their rather articulate misgivings – which at least part of the leadership may share but choose to ignore.

This is due to the other factor which brings dissonance out into the open, political competition. Through this, the interplay of exit (its threat or actual exercise), voice (protest) and loyalty within the party links up with the interplay of exit, voice and loyalty among the party activists and the voting public at large. Party activists normally try to confound the clientele of other parties in order to cause exit from them whenever, among other things, they think they can show reason for blaming dissonance on their competitors.[2]

In all these instances the problem of ideological change arises, since, to remain effective signals, ideologies must change with policies,[3] or rather in some manner reflect their change. However, even though change is invariably evinced in the operative dimension of political discourse, it is far from certain that change will be acknowledged overtly there, let alone in the dimension of fundamentals. Hence we cannot simply infer actual policy from the dimension of final goals and fundamental principles – or vice versa.

Proclaimed aims often serve to cloud real intentions.[4] Also, the reduction, if not dissimulation, of dissonance between professed fundamental commitments and the explanation of deeds is often achieved in politics, as in individual behaviour, by magnifying aspects of the situation which justify the action generating 'cognitive dissonance'. Exaggerating the beauty of the girl you have taken to a restaurant much too expensive for your purse[5] is not dissimilar to underplaying an ideological turn-about by exaggerating its eventual prospect for achieving goals of the ideology. And just as the individual avoids information that increases dissonance and seeks information that reduces it,[6] so in politics the party leadership handles information (withholding it, supplying it, or exposing it as false) with a view to reducing dissonance between ideological commitments and actual policies. While cognitive dissonance may more easily become troublesome for political than for private actors by virtue of becoming a subject of public debate, weighty inconsistencies apt to cause cognitive dissonance may be actually useful in politics. Apart from the fact that conflicting principles can be invoked at different times for different purposes, and a 'two-tier' doctrine permits the reversal of everything,[7] 'the swallowing of an absurdity . . . in the acceptance of an ideology' is, as Gellner remarks, comparable to a tribal *rite de passage*.[8] Nevertheless, although double-talk, deception and ideological ritualization and degeneration cannot be ruled out, the disparity between the continued proclamation of traditional principles and the policies that are actually pursued is not primarily due to intentional deception. We cannot deny that genuine attachment to cherished ideals is an important cause of 'double-think'. Ideals, like conventional standards, are not easily renounced, however inconsistently professed and followed.

1. CONCESSIONS AND FIDELITY: THE UNIVERSAL MIX WITH A DIFFERENCE

If there is one general reason why parties are forced to make concessions over what they originally rejected or aspired to, it is the fact that, after attaining power or the chance of it, the maintenance of an effective body politic becomes the prime consideration. This also explains why 'at some point or other one always betrays'.[9] Lenin, who never forgave Kautsky and other socialists for backing their country, provides a striking example, but the rule does not apply to leftist parties alone.

In accordance with his attribution of pre-eminence to the political struggle during the years prior to the revolution, Lenin, once in power, moved steadily towards embracing statism as part of the transition to socialism and, equally, as a way of preserving the Russian state as a going concern. How much everything became geared to this purpose – as it had to be, if the revolution was to survive – is epitomized in Lenin's last published article. There he expressed his disgust with the inefficiency of the existing state machinery and wondered once more whether as much had been learned about 'state construction' – *pace State and Revolution* – as could have been expected.[10] At times, Lenin was extraordinarily frank in admitting errors of judgment, mistakes and reversals in the past. These were unavoidable, he argued, in a venture as new in world history as 'the creation of a state edifice of an unprecedented type'. The reversals and mistakes had been most severe in the economic field and, therefore, led to NEP after it had become clear that state (not commune!) production and distribution could not be organized on 'communist lines . . . by order of the proletarian state'. Hence without state capitalism, 'we shall never get to communism'. Typically, the deviations were not explained as derogating from but as conducive to the achievement of the unchanged goal, while being in any case temporary. In the evident effort to align operative and fundamental ideology, and perhaps not quite in full correspondence with the emphases of his earlier argument in *What is to be Done*?, he now asserted: 'We have always said that reforms are a by-product of the *revolutionary* class struggle'.[11] Accordingly, when dwelling in *The Tax in Kind* on the special severity of past mistakes in the economic field, he asserted that they concerned only the length of the period of transition to socialism. To strengthen this point he referred, a year later, to the belief of 1918 that six months of state capitalism would suffice for socialism to gain a permanent foothold, and remarked: 'We were more foolish than we are now.' Apparently he did not mean to say that 'foolish things' would cease to be done. By now, in summing up the achievements of NEP, he also confessed that its state capitalism was a doctrinal retreat despite its success. In this context he made the statement, already quoted in Chapter IV, that 'practical experience . . . is more important than all the theoretical discussions in the world'.[12]

Notwithstanding his occasional double-talk and retrospective readjustment of earlier perspectives, we learn from the outstanding architect of the greatest revolutionary venture between the French and the Chinese revolutions that coming to terms with immediate requirements, available resources, unforeseeable contingencies and complications, rather than premeditated deception, are the compelling reasons for ideological deviations. We also learn that these deviations are not acknowledged by a communist as amounting to ideological change. Indeed, when it becomes clear that the desired goals lie so far ahead that interim goals must suffice, and expedience requires exceptions to principles, it is quite credible that this does not affect the commitment to the final goals of a communist or social-democratic society. Thus, while Lenin suggested sending people to the West in order to learn about effective state control, he was as adamant as ever in branding the West as 'counter-revolutionary' and 'imperialist' and in setting against it 'the revolutionary and national East',[13] with which the future lay. This unwavering belief went together with the formation of the patterns for the future development of Soviet – and Chinese – foreign policy. Latter-day elaborations of Leninist 'zigzag' policies by the two communist super-powers therefore do not necessarily indicate a lessening of the commitment to the traditional final goals, especially in so far as they have merged with the aspiration of world predominance, if not domination. Only total military defeat, as in the case of Nazi Germany and Fascist Italy, has so far put an end to the commitment to fundamentals of totalitarian regimes, inasmuch as defeat put an end to the party.

Generally, some goals and fundamental principles are modified in practice as advances are made in their direction, just as much as doubts arise about their feasibility and desirability. This may eventually also be the fate of the ideal of a fully classless society. Communist experience has done nothing to reduce the striking contrast between the dogmatic certainty about its advent and the lack of systematic thought that Marx and Engels and their successors have given to the subject, except for the systematic misrepresentation of the 'commune state'.[14]

In the West, where the principles of free private enterprise and competition have been a myth all along, parties opposed to the Welfare State and those which have seen in it only an advance in the right direction have come to settle for it. Indeed, dissonance between traditional and actual aims is inflicted also by the realists and the more open-minded members in the leadership of parties on their purists and hard-liners in deference to the electorate and to inescapable requirements of social and economic developments. Even where socialist parties have been voted into power, so far they have not received an electoral mandate to effect the full-scale expropriation of the expropriators and the abolition of all differences of income. In point of fact, in free elections social-democratic parties have never asked voters for such a mandate. Not even at the height of its return to Marxist orthodoxy in the Erfurt Programme (1891) did the German SPD make such claims for the immediate future;[15] nor did the British Labour Party after having been ousted from office in 1951. The following quotations from the Report of its Annual Conference in 1956 reflect the dual commitment of the party to solving problems of the moment and to doing so in the light of the socialist ideal, as conceived in the spirit of the traditionally 'reformist' bulk of the party.[16]

> We have a double task; firstly to think out clearly and present to the electorate the policies we shall adopt when we are returned to power, and secondly to convince the electorate that these policies are sound. In other words, we need a programme which, as convinced socialists, we believe will take us significantly nearer our ultimate goal. But it must also be a programme that will show every thinking voter that Labour has a practical solution to the immediate problems that will confront *any* Government. We cannot doubt that only a Socialist approach can provide an answer to these problems. But in order to translate our Socialist faith into concrete policies of action, rigorous discipline of thought and an awareness of changing realities are needed . . . Our ideal is a community in which class struggle and bitterness, selfishness and greed, will be replaced by a spirit of brotherhood and kindness and an atmosphere of equality.

In support of this statement of principle, the chairman quoted from a speech by Keir Hardie of January 1906:

> Socialism has its message of hope for every section of the community; for the business man pressed with care and worry as well as for the ordinary working man. I do not say, no one has ever said, that socialism itself will solve all the problems of life; what we do claim, however, is that it will solve the material problem of how to obtain food, raiment and shelter, and transfer the struggle for improvement from the sordid materialism of the present time on to the higher moral and spiritual planes.

It will be noted that Clause Four (the socialization of the means of production and of distribution) is not mentioned in this context, nor is the abolition of classes and of inequality promised. These aims seem to reappear in the Labour Party's official resolutions, particularly when an attempt is made to have them officially modified.[17] Not one is stated in *Time for Decision,* the manifesto of the Labour Party for the 1966 general election, in which the party increased its slender majority, nor in Anthony Crosland's 'Social Objectives for the 1970s', a preconference statement published in *The Times* (25 September 1970) after Labour had suffered, as he put it, 'a narrow election defeat'. It seemed to him, tentatively at least, that 'the lessons of the last six years' confirmed that Labour's 'objectives in the social field remain broadly valid', while economic and industrial policies 'need drastic re-examination'. The four 'basic objectives' which distinguish Labour from the Tories were: 'an exceptionally high priority for the relief of poverty, distress and social squalor'; 'a more equal [note: not an equal] distribution of wealth'; 'a wider ideal of social equality', meaning in addition to educational reform, provision for the less well-off of access to housing and health 'of a standard comparable, at least in the basic decencies, to that which the better-off can buy for themselves ...'; and 'strict control over the environment'. If, as we may presume with Mr Crosland, 'these four objectives span the central area of party-political dispute on social policy', then the basic objectives of Labour as re-stated in 1970 by a former Cabinet minister were obviously not inspired by the fundamental of the socialization of the means of production and distribution, or by the fundamental of a classless society, or even by the ideal stated in 1956 of a community liberated from class struggle. Indeed, during Labour's years of office, the pursuit of the objectives which Mr Crosland suggested retaining in the future entailed not the abolition of class differentials and inequality of incomes, but the improvement of the lot of the working classes, and their position in the class struggle and the chances of mobility.

If concessions over fundamental principles in the conception and execution of policies have changed the overall complexion of social democracy and communism, although serious commitment at least to a few central fundamental principles or their toned-down specifications has not ceased, the same applies to the ideals of liberal and conservative parties. They stress individual freedom, natural hierarchy and individual excellence, but cannot refrain from making concessions over these in the spirit of egalitarian principles and leave the free-for-all scramble restricted by no more than an entirely nominal equality of opportunity.

As in other parties, so also in the debates of the British Conservative Party, the authority of former leaders is invoked. While the more progressively-minded normally invoke Disraeli's spirit of 'Young England' and the Primrose League,[18] reference to the party's traditions also involves for them the honouring of tradition as such. Generally, traditional values which are taken to provide the guide-line for meeting new requirements are also supplemented by once-contested values, and in this way the outlook as a whole undergoes change. 'Above all', as the Marquis of Salisbury stated in 1953, 'we made it our aim not to sweep away *all* our forefathers bequeathed to us, but to build on the strong foundations of the past, always adapting the ancient fabric to our social system to suit modern needs.'[19] Perhaps more overtly than Labour, though in very general terms, Tories acknowledge the need for some sweeping away, although they are as careful as Labour not to offend directly against specifications of central fundamental principles. In contemporary Tory ideology, for instance, such a specification is the unequal outcome of equality of opportunity. The concern with 'excellence', as the Tories like to eulogize inequality, derives both from their traditional reverence for hierarchy and from the liberal principle of socio-economic competitiveness. The marriage between the two already presents an ideological change, and one of long standing. It was made easy by the meritocratic tradition of elevating commoners into the ranks of the British aristocracy, while its younger sons descend into the ranks of the untitled. The Butler Education Act of 1944, the Health Service and then 'Butskellism' in general, symbolize breaches in the conservative ideology effected under the pressure of growing approval among the electorate of more egalitarian welfare principles. Although some backlash accompanied the reassertion of the party's distinctiveness, the debate about comprehensive education affords a particularly instructive illustration of restrictions on both the retreat from and the preservation of old fundamentals.

In 1967 Edward Heath attempted to reconcile the party's traditional preferences with a new educational policy. Like Lenin, he did not quite abide by the historical record. He declared: 'It has never been a conservative principle that in order to achieve [the classification of children according to their I.Q.], children have to be segregated in different institutions'. The motions moved by the Tories in 1952 and 1957 and the explanation of the policy of the Conservative Party by the Bow Group tell a different story.[20] In any case, Mr Heath was by now ready to condone the abolition of the 11-plus examination and the establishment of comprehensive schools. He revealed no intention of approving the abolition of selection, which was to be postponed until the sixth form, that is until 15-plus. New sixth-form colleges were to take over the function of grammar schools where old ones were abolished or no new ones established. Mr Heath concluded with a declaration of principle which is typical in so far as it illustrates the tendency of all parties to associate real changes of policy with the traditional fundamentals of the party. He said:

> But we must be sure that in concentrating on those who have not had a chance in the past, we do not neglect those who could and should be excelling. To the challenge of the revolution in education to which I referred . . . I add the other. . . . It is the challenge of widening opportunity without sacrificing the abilities of the best.

Mr Heath made his concessions to giving more substance to the principle of equal opportunity on the basis of his opposition to 'an undesirable trend toward egalitarianism . . .'.[21] He did the same again in a more general policy statement which is of particular interest since, as the leading article in *The Times* (11 September 1968) put it, the speech at Keith, Scotland, which 'sounded like plain common sense . . ., becomes interesting because of the contrast between his approach and the more strident approach of his right wing critics'.

As reported in the same issue of *The Times,* once in general terms and then in more specific reference to his six-point policy statement, Mr Heath formulated the 'fundamental divisions between Tory and socialist philosophy and beliefs' in rejecting plainly the claims of party critics, such as Mr du Cann and Mr Enoch Powell, who demanded tougher opposition and more distinctive alternative Tory policies. Mr Heath in his six points enunciated, on the whole less specifically than Mr Crosland in his four points, the distinctive social objectives of his party, although he based his policy statement as clearly as Mr Crosland on the specification of fundamentals which had guided his party during the post-war period. Mr Heath promised to cut down direct taxation ('we want people to earn more and keep more of what they earn'); to control government expenditure ('to wage war against waste in Whitehall and in local government'); to overhaul 'the antiquated system of industrial relations' ('The socialists . . . won't touch the reform . . . with a barge pole'); to enact 'a massive programme of industrial training and retraining'; to expand farming by restriction of government control and guidance; and 'to make sure that additional social service benefit goes to those who need it most', instead of 'indiscriminately dishing out more welfare benefits'.

Though easily discernible, the opposition to undesirable egalitarianism is somewhat hidden behind the attack on government intervention, but it is precisely on this issue, apparently not included in the six points, that Mr Heath's comment is most noteworthy in our discussion. While Labour to date has not formally renounced Clause Four and the goal of a classless society (figuring also in Mr Crosland's earlier writings), Mr Heath, as David Wood reported in *The Times,* 'challenged the vestigial Conservative attitude', which had enjoyed some revival in the years of opposition, 'that government intervention in shaping the life and economy of Britain is always to be regarded as suspect'. Wood quoted Heath hitting at his critics from within the party:

> That, although a century out of date, would certainly be a distinctive, different policy . . . . But it would not be a Conservative policy and it would not provide a Conservative alternative. For better or worse, the central Government is already responsible, in some way or another, for nearly half the activities of Britain.

Saying that to suspect government intervention as such 'would not be a Conservative policy' was in accordance with the more recent historical record. In the 1930s a group of Conservatives which had included Harold Macmillan had come out with a manifesto stressing that government cannot evade its increasing intervention in the economy. Sharing this insight is what 'Butskellism' had largely amounted to.

Quite generally, then, the will to keep faith with traditional fundamentals must be evaluated in conjunction with the practice of all major parties of detracting from or adding to their original fundamental ideology, no matter in what regime they operate. As a result, an appreciable measure of consensus within and between the various political systems prevails about objectives of social policies, not to mention principles of economic and external policies. In both communist and non-communist regimes actual ideological changes are much less admitted than they are permitted to affect fundamentals. Still, similarity between the regimes on the last point is greater than on the first since only in Western-type democracies can ideological change be exposed freely by purists, opponents and observers. Yet, in the West, the misapprehension that there are unideological politics and that these are evinced in the convergence of the political orientations of the major parties needs to be added to the factors which generally work against the admission of ideological change, whose nature is obscured by the equation of consensual with unideological politics.

2. CONVERGENCE AND ITS MISTAKEN EVALUATION

a. *The Politics of Consensus*

If the much-acclaimed politics of consensus, or convergence, is taken as proof of a rather recent de-ideologization of politics, the phenomenon of ideological change is evidently restricted to the shift from ideology to non-ideology and it is ignored that convergence is neither complete, nor stable, nor new. It bears witness to the pacification of some sectors on the ideological fronts and perhaps also their shortening, but not necessarily a general abatement of ideological fervour and commitment. While breakaways from convergence signify the reintensification of ideological conflict, the spread of consensus does not inevitably mean insipidity, nor, if correctly assessed as ideological, 'a total victory of ideology', in the sense that the masses have been manipulated to conform with the complacent views of certain intellectuals.[22] Rather, party ideologies which still differ in doctrinal postures and in the emphases of priorities reflect sooner or later the spread among part of their leaders and among mass publics of genuine agreement about formerly disputed principles and policies. Such ideological agreement is as much misconstrued by confusing it with de-ideologization as it is obscured by considering parties, at least in two-party systems, as moving ever closer to each other for no other purpose than to maximize votes.

Clearly, the convergence of the platforms of parties bent on maximizing votes presupposes that the majority of voters are (or can be made to believe that they are) ideologically close to one another on some key issues. Equally, the electorate may become, or may be initially, divided over platforms of serious reform and changes of policy, so that the electoral 'pay-off' lies as much, if not more, in divergence than in convergence. It is on the first of these assumptions that Downs's improvement of Hotelling's spatial market model chiefly rests. Hotelling suggested that voters are equally distributed along the ideological spectrum. According to Downs, the frequency distribution has one peak at the midpoint of a linear scale to fall steeply towards the left and right extremes.[23] On more than one occasion reality has disproved this hypothesis of the high concentration of voters within a centre area of ambiguity and insipidity and the dispersal of the sparse remainder in the space of increasingly sharply profiled orientations stretching from the centre area to the fringes. With the nomination of Senator Goldwater in 1964 as the Republican candidate, the cleavage between party platforms widened considerably just as it had previously widened over the New Deal with much more momentous consequences.[24] The ideological cleavage was not accompanied in either case by a polar split of the voters, but was reflected in a higher peak left of centre and a lower peak right of centre. Majority consensus had revealed itself each time in a definite ideological stance: once for radical reform in a left direction, and once against rightist radicalization.

Far-reaching agreement on political alternatives, including readiness to agree on the need for reforms, is obtained through the intermediacy of parties not only by electoral landslides or programmatic ambiguity but also through national exigencies for which each party receives a similar mandate and/or cannot but envisage similar solutions. Since 1858, Britain has been ruled for thirty-four years by coalition governments which have handled the important questions of Ireland, the depression of 1931, total mobilization and the foundation of the Welfare State.[25] With the exception of total mobilization, which normally requires and creates wide consensus, none of these was an issue over which the parties had customarily seen eye to eye. Another telling illustration of such *rapprochement* in specific areas is the initiation of social welfare policies by Bismarck. To the extent that they were a result of political calculation intended to forestall the growth of the Social-Democratic Party, his welfare policies can also be regarded as an adaptation of conservative patriarchial principles to the industrial age (and hence as an instance of ideological pluralism). Then there is the coming to terms of both the SPD and of more enlightened German conservatism with the rules of parliamentary democracy. The consensus reached in the mid-1950s on the rules of the game and, to varying degrees, on the Welfare State was the consummation of a trend first precipitated by the downfall of the Empire, then impeded by the post-war policies of the Allies which helped the conservative forces to foreclose the success of the Weimar Republic, and finally interrupted by Nazi dictatorship.

In short, there is no novelty in changing party orientations and their confluence on specific and important issues, a confluence attesting the impact of strong trends of public opinion and of the necessity of adopting similar standpoints in view of impracticable, undesirable or non-existent alternatives. What is new is the proliferation of the social basis of consensual public opinion and of the growth of substantial agreement on social and political ends even among the committed rank and file of parties.[26]

Relatively recent growth in America of 'the politics of consensus'[27] signifies not a retreat from ideology but, as elsewhere in the West, the diminishing appeal and suitability of diametrically opposed social values and goals, following success in the battle for raising the standard of living among large sections of the working classes and the spread of social security. As a result, moral *absolutes* may have lost much of their appeal in party politics, but they retained influence and issued in political change, even at the time when Lane had consigned them to the past. For instance, the SNCC (Student Non-Violent Coordinating Committee) was formed in 1960. After three years' campaigning for the desegregation of public accommodation, the Civil Rights Act of 1964 made free access a statutory right. SNCC workers took up the issue of voters' registration, which was at least partially removed from the agenda of radicalism with the passing of the Voting Right Act of 1965.[28] Contested applications of moral absolutes enshrined in the Constitution but balked at in practice had been enforced upon party politics and thus have secured legal status. These facts and others certainly do not suggest that the discussion of means has replaced that of ends or that politics in America are or were, even at that time, in the process of losing their ideological character.[29] Views to this effect, having put a premium on incrementalism, tended to exaggerate the extent of consensus or pacification within the system, and were, therefore, not unjustly considered to be manifestations of conservative ideology.[30]

If there was then, and perhaps there still is, some justification for maintaining that moral absolutes had lost their appeal, this is not only untrue of a number of specific issues, but should not entail the implication that moral appeals have ever been largely abandoned. We can see this in Bell's rejection of 'abstract absolutes' and his plea for orientation according to 'relative standards of social virtue and political justice'.[31] Bell does not really disconnect 'absolute' and 'relative' moral standards, since he need not be told that the preference for, and growing consensus on, the 'relative' standards he has in mind testify to the partial acceptance (and fulfilment) of the 'absolute' demands of the Left. Previously they could be formulated only as 'absolutes', or rather in connection with them, because the disagreement over them was absolute.

Even independently of the traumatic experience of communism, the retreat from socialist 'absolutes' such as the abolition of private property or the polarization of class conflict, is, therefore, easily understandable. These absolutes are now (and, in fact, have been for a long time) at odds with the attitudes towards the nature of class relations and class outlooks[32] of the majority of the public, and hence of mass parties and governments, whether socialist or not, because it is precisely under the impact of socialist demands that class relations and with them ideological outlooks have changed. Indeed, when Bottomore succumbs for once to the notion of non-ideological politics, speaking of 'the rejection of ideology, by the American new left in particular', he explains immediately that we face 'not so much the spurning of all ideology' but the rejection 'of those creeds inherited from the 1930s' which the facts have failed to bear out,[33] or, as one might also say, which have been overtaken by the facts. In other words, we face ideological change on the Left as we face it in the politics of consensus – and ordinary people are not unaware of this.

Lane's findings in *Political Ideology* do not support the conclusion of his later article about the non-ideological significance of the politics of consensus. The outlook of his fifteen men of Eastport shows that the opinions of such relatively ordinary and yet not uneducated men reflect principled stands on fundamental problems of political ideology. These stands represent slight variations on the principles of the common – or consensual – ideological elements and are influenced by the ups and downs of the social and political trends prevailing in the American polity.[34]

The common man's understanding of an ideology is easily misrepresented if the researcher fails to take into account ideological bifurcation or two-dimensionality in general, and in particular the difference between what an ideology means in quite general terms and its immediate practical significance. As I have already pointed out in Chapter V, this lack of discrimination leads Converse to misconstrue the significance of the answers of a respondent who, classifying himself as a strong socialist, identified socialism with being 'four square for the working man against the rich'[35] but was also of the opinion that the federal government should let private enterprise handle electric power and housing. Converse considers this to be a striking example of the lack of 'contextual grasp' of the 'chosen "ideology" ' by the less educated.[36] He assumes that if it had been explained to the respondent that 'standard socialist doctrine' requires preference for government intervention over private enterprise, he would have answered accordingly. There is reason to doubt this if the impression made by facts on people counts for anything.

Since government intervention has not always been 'standard socialist doctrine' in America and elsewhere,[37] and since in America the cultivation of socialist utopias has remained the preserve of sectarians, what Converse's respondent is reported to have identified as socialism squares with the ideology which, since Gompers, has taken shape and become preponderant in the influential organizations of labour. 'The working people', said Gompers 'are in too great need for improvement[s] in their condition to allow them to forego them in their endeavour to devote their entire energies to an end however beautiful to contemplate. . . . The way out of the wage system is through higher wages.'[38] The clear intention of this disarmingly illogical conclusion is to concentrate on enlarging the workers' share in the profits of private enterprise and on improving working conditions, deciding on government intervention according to whether it serves these aims or not. Never since its rise has the American Federation of Labour attacked the institution of private property and competitive advancement. This policy has prevailed with the overwhelming majority of American organizations of labour, although the workers had to fight bloodier industrial battles for the recognition of their unions than, for instance, French workers.[39]

To be, like Converse's working man, against the rich, identify with the working classes, and yet not automatically prefer government interference over private enterprise, does not therefore prove that members of mass publics are ideological scatterbrains. On the contrary, the example shows that they are quite capable of grasping what American 'standard socialist doctrine' is about. As one learns from Lane's study, his sample of differently educated men also thinks that business is the source of legitimately earned money and that government has become the source of relief, welfare and charity.[40] It follows that, unlike the researchers, the working man has not been misled by any knowledge of fundamentals which are politically irrelevant for the American scene. He reveals rather precise knowledge of the operative ideology which he knows as 'socialist' and which is not opposed to private enterprise as such, but banks on its success. Unlike others in Converse's important study, the case in hand affords no support to his thesis of the greater lack of 'constraint' in the beliefs of mass publics than in those of elites. The same conclusion would follow if a British socialist worker had answered like Converse's American respondent, although in British standard socialist doctrine the socialization of the means of production and distribution has never been repudiated. A British worker none the less could be well aware that the way Labour governments have dealt with nationalization leaves little doubt that, even if there is to be more of it in the foreseeable future, nothing forebodes the elimination of private enterprise.

Indeed, the substance of the appraisal of socialist doctrine in America reflected in the answers of Converse's working man is implicit in the discerning assessment by an educated British white-collar Labourite of both the fundamental and the operative significance of British socialism and of the difference between the Labour Party and the Conservatives. In accordance with the proclaimed aims of the Labour

Party, mentioned in the first section of this chapter, this 'well informed and participant citizen' said:[41]

> Ideally, socialism means what the word implies, that is, the requirement for people to live together, help each other, and to be just to each other. That's what socialism stands for, ideally. [Not specifically nationalization.] Unfortunately, socialists have to make short term decisions which are not truly socialistic.

The respondent evaluates the Conservatives as follows:

> Going back to the nineteenth century, they were always opposed to social progress, but the Conservative Party today – one must be just – is a good deal more liberal than it was. Indeed, the left wing of the Conservative Party is very similar to the right wing of the Socialist [meaning the Labour] Party. But in the last analysis, they stand in the way of progress.

Although this study is not directly concerned with the nature of the ideological outlook of mass and elite publics but with the ideology presented to them by political parties, in the present context reference to their attitudes is important not only in so far as the foundation of the politics of consensus in public opinion is concerned, but also in order to show that to avoid serious errors of judgment, any evaluation of 'constraint', and indeed of data pertaining to ideological trends in public opinion in general, must take into account the distinction – and interplay – between fundamental and operative ideology. As the case I have commented upon shows, the re-interpretation of data on this basis furnishes grounds for supposing that ideological change is 'taken in' on the grass-roots level and therefore that members of mass publics are discerning enough to support leaders they trust who press for the mutual adaptation of fundamental and operative ideology, i.e. ideological change, or even to induce leaders to adopt such a course of action.

Evidently, the failure to appraise the growth of consensus as ideological change manifested in the growth of ideological pluralism in conditions of relative affluence and changing class relations, or to mistake such consensus for the retreat from ideology or as evidence of the non-existence of ideology in American politics in the first place, are all ways of coping with ideological change by more or less conscious and self-contradictory evasion of the problem altogether. After all, to ignore the ideological foundation of the politics of consensus is not merely to abstract from its rootedness in the commonly accepted principles and rules which in Dahl's expression form 'the common ideology'. It is also to disregard, as we have seen in Chapter IV in connection with Dahl's views, the fact that no controversy on the basis of shared ideological elements can be considered unideological. It would not matter if political debate were to become, on the whole, less polarized, the 'fixed' elements more identically interpreted and applied and the differences between the policies of parties further diminished because neither repudiated all, or most, of the principles which the other pursued. None of this would demonstrate the independence of such policies from basic convictions concerning the content of policies, that is from ideology. To evade this conclusion is to cling to the initial *non sequitur* attendant upon the idea of the end of ideology, namely that the diminution of conflict over values indicates progress towards the vanishing of ideology. Yet since the generally observable relatedness of policies to values and the ultimate anchorage of the former in the latter render politics ideological, it certainly does not matter whether there is consensus or dissensus over values.

Moreover, distinctions in the orientations of political parties have so far not disappeared, precisely because the tendency of the politics of consensus is in general characterized by giving their due, within the political framework of liberal democracy, to the social values which the Left has found insufficiently realized, or contravened on principle, in liberal democracy or in the more or less democratized parliamentary monarchies.[42] The extent of the actual and of the ideological changes reflected in the postures of those involved in the politics of consensus, or, as I would call it, the politics of diminishing alternatives, is almost as much obscured when scholars and politicians designate such politics as unideological as when doctrinaire extremists of the Right and Left denigrate the same politics as ideologically insignificant. In fact, to justify this attitude the extremists have only to avail themselves of the widely accepted misinterpretation of the politics of consensus and of what follows from prevailing evaluations of policy-making and party competition in general.

b. *Vote-catching and Ideological Distinctiveness*

We are told that decisions in the United States, including those on old-age security, are normally made 'disjointly' or that problems in Britain like housing, education, washing-machines, taxes and the like are 'mundane' issues which 'extend the scope of politics beyond the confines of ideological debate'.[43] In one instance 'unideological' is identified with 'non-controversial'. It is ignored in both cases that decisions in favour of old-age security, better housing and schooling have been taken, and make some sense as a whole, because they embody a relatively coherent series of standpoints about society's obligations towards the aged, the needy and the less affluent – in sum, about social justice. The decisions are disjointed only inasmuch as they have been taken piecemeal, but they are not unideological, since to enable people with a relatively low income to purchase 'mundane' amenities which reduce toil and which are otherwise conducive to raising the standards of civilized existence is to abide by certain values – even if the ultimate aim of pursuing them be electoral success. However, policy decisions regarding old-age security, decent housing and the easier purchase of washing-machines have a more intimate connection with the fundamentals professed by one of the American or British parties than with those of the other. Furthermore, the connection between policy and ideology is not severed by distinguishing between 'moving *away* from social ills' and 'moving *toward* a known and relatively stable goal'.[44] Moral considerations can be carried in either direction. Besides, one never moves away from some point without moving towards another.[45] In short, it is impossible to get away from the connection between the normative components in operative and fundamental ideology as a root-cause of the remaining differences between parties.

While it is maintained that parties offer 'only incrementally different policies' on the basis of 'agreeing on fundamentals',[46] it is also recognized that there are fundamentals, however contradictorily maintained and whether or not concessions are made over them, with which a party is identified and wishes to be identified.[47] To add another specific example to those adduced in the first section of this chapter, the American Republican Party traditionally opposes the expansion of government regulation, but supports its extension over trade unions;[48] and this is true of the British Conservatives as well. The fact that votes representing different interests must be caught to achieve a majority makes for the dilution of fundamentals, yet also for restricting that dilution. Voters must be able to distinguish between the parties, if we do not want to presuppose that entirely irrational loyalty determines all voting. And in any case such loyalty would not apply to the non-committed vote which often tips the scales. While commitments to social responsibilities that were once hotly contested have become espoused by the main parties and the majority of the public, this has often been a matter of degree, and the different emphases and applications of similar principles still reflect allegiance to different central fundamentals. The situation is still very much the same as the leader of the German SPD described it when he wrote in 1961 that it has become the rule in a working democracy that the parties approach the voter with 'similar, even identical demands in a number of fields', while priorities, methods and accents remain controversial.[49] Although performance as such has become a more decisive criterion than ever, what remains controversial is also clearly related to the basic principles traditionally upheld by the parties. For instance, the CDU had already in 1953 coined the concept 'social market economy' in order to remove the cut-throat connotations of the term 'market economy'. The SPD adopted the new concept and some of its leftists went further and spoke of a 'socialist market economy'.[50] Then, convergence notwithstanding, Willi Brandt fell back on the traditional attitude and sharply condemned the ideas of competition and private initiative as 'demagogic phrases', insisting instead on 'skill, knowledge and individual capacity' within the framework of the prevention of the concentration of economic power in the hands of a minority.[51]

Since in order to increase or retain membership and, above all, votes, any mass party must appeal to, and can only somehow coordinate, a variety of interests, asymmetry in political commitments is as inevitable as the overlapping of party programmes and policies.[52] Thus whether they call themselves socialist, liberal or conservative, all great contemporary parties in the West have moved from being class parties (and/or denominational parties) towards being 'people's parties'. Far from being intrinsically new and anti-ideological, the 'catch-all' appeal has ideological roots. As originally in Bonapartist Caesarism, this appeal is expressed in the (nominal) rejection, especially by conservative parties, of abstract innovation and class perspective, for which the socialists were blamed. Marx rightly disclaimed class perspective as a socialist invention.[53] Moreover, quite apart from Marx's universalistic conception of the proletarian class, social-democratic parties quickly widened their electoral appeal without, as Michels admitted when he analysed the process, letting ideological dilution run its full course.[54] If, then, the principle of the 'catch-all party' is adaptable to, if not a requirement of, the rules of the two-party and multi-party game in general, a significant ideological difference remains between its applications by a democratic and a non-democratic party. Fascist parties turn the 'catch-all' into the 'catch-all-but-some' principle.[55] A democratic party, though open to all denominational and ethnic groups, practises not strictly the 'catch-all' principle but only the 'catch-all-you-need' principle. As Riker says, parties seek to maximize votes only 'up to the point of subjective certainty of winning' and after that 'to maintain themselves at the size . . . of a minimum winning coalition'.[56] The rule is in accordance with Michels's presuppositions, in so far as it implies, like Michels's law of transgression, its own limitation by each party. This is to say that the appeal to variegated group, regional and other interests, which conflict as often as they intersect, and consequently the dilution of the party's ideological hard core, must be bounded somehow and somewhere. For if it is generally applicable, as I think it is, the strategy of the winning coalition can hardly be supposed to succeed and win the minimum number of voters needed for victory by exceeding the minimum number of concessions over those ideological convictions that hold party leaders and activists together.

The decision as to which ideas will appeal most to the majority of voters may be made according to opinion polls. The decision about the composition of party platforms and policies is a somewhat different matter. The ideological concessions a party can make, and for which opinion polls provide important information, are prescribed by three intertwined calculations: (a) to attract the minimum of non-committed voters who will tilt the scales; (b) to keep the maximum of its committed members and voters; (c) to keep election platforms somehow in tune with the fact that more often than not the choice of alternative policies is limited anyway.

Obviously, the attempt to adjust the three kinds of calculation arouses internal dispute. Although the first two objectives are equally attractive for the party as a whole and the third might well be rather generally acquiesced in, dissension is to be expected. Quite apart from dispute about which ideas are the better vote-getters,[57] it is almost certain that (a) may require more concessions than is reconcilable with (b), so that (a) and (b) are unequally attractive to groups within the party. Deciding on an electoral platform, therefore, entails for different groups in the party a choice between unequally attractive alternatives for the sake of equally attractive aims. Here subsists a difference in the nature and the extent of cognitive dissonance in an individual actor and in a group of groups, that is in a collective body like a political party.

In the individual's feeling and thought dissonance is assumed to be small when objectives are far apart in attractiveness. Dissonance is assumed to be great when the objectives are almost equally appealing.[58] To some extent, in politics the reverse easily becomes true because objectives both close and apart in attractiveness to the different groups are involved. The activists of a party who are most concerned over its ideological image and heritage will often find it highly unattractive to make the ideological concessions necessary for achieving the attractive aim of a minimum winning coalition. Yet neither do they find it attractive to antagonize the activists most concerned over winning. The latter group, for its part, might find it relatively easy to make the necessary ideological concessions but at the same time inopportune to antagonize thereby the first group. Each group is faced with equally unattractive alternatives if both assume that victory will be out of reach if one simply overrules the other.

In a situation where a relatively drastic trimming of the ideological sails is required in order to secure electoral success, and where the more purist groups refuse to comply, the stands of the two groupings are far apart; dissonance in the party is great. Unlike the individual case, the cause of great dissonance is the conviction that objectives are far apart, inasmuch as they are felt to be achievable only at the expense of each other. The adjustment of opinions to action is regarded as most likely in the individual case when the promised rewards and the threatened unpleasantness which induce action are relatively small. In politics, however, only the prospect of much unpleasantness and the expectation of a significant reward provide the inducements for the mutual adaptation of opinions and actions, i.e. of opinions reflecting fundamentals and actions that run counter to the former and are defended in operative ideology.

It is possible that the majority of the leadership of a party may decide on preserving a purer ideological image than accords with 'subjective certainty of winning'. Such a reduction of ideological dissonance within a party may be necessary to safeguard the dedication of the activist hard-core of the party which rallies round the policy orientation of an established leadership or its successful challenger. A more distinct range of commitments which is presented to the public may have been endorsed by the party in the knowledge that thereby its electoral chances are likely to be adversely affected. But the attempt to maximize votes by a wishy-washy platform addressed to the middle-of-the-roaders at large may also prove counter-productive. Not only may it dampen the enthusiasm of the activists who might otherwise have been able to sway the indifferent and undecided vote,[59] but it may also disappoint too many voters who expect precise commitments on pressing issues. 'Irrational motives such as loyalty' may cause success in any case, in the form of a minimum or an oversize winning coalition.[60] According to many American theorists, the loyalty of the bulk of a party's members has little to do with ideological consistency or the precise comprehension of principles of policy. Despite the awareness of vagaries caused by elastic demand and concomitant uncertainty, as well as of ideological in-fighting, the coalition principle remains for Riker, like the maximising of votes for Downs, the measuring-rod of the ideological behaviour of parties – that is, the criterion of their rationality[61] and hence their normalcy.

At least for the construction of models, it is assumed that, through elections, the same rationality prevails in politics as in a parlour-game, and that adherence to convictions is a function of the electoral 'pay-off' they promise. As Downs asserts, party members 'choose an ideology which will win votes, not one they believe in, since their objective is the acquisition of office, not the creation of a better society'. The all-out drive for office is 'the larger end' and the maximizing of votes plays 'a larger role' than any ideal. The maximizing of votes may become a subsidiary to the implementation of ideological doctrines, but though quite common, 'this irrational development' is an exception and does not affect the rule.[62] However, to admit that voters' preferences may and do count with parties indirectly contravenes the assumption that elections have no significance beyond replacing the holders of office. After all, most voters have no office to gain whichever way they vote. Since, then, some other common denominator between them and the minority of contestants for office must be found, voters' preferences – even for a better society – cannot be discounted. In point of fact, nobody denies that in order to maximize votes convictions are often modified and certain principles are even adopted for electoral purposes. This is only natural because the will of the voters must count, if the system is to be democratic. Yet if it is rational for candidates to maximize votes, it is not irrational to try to persuade voters to support certain policy orientations and/or to remain faithful to convictions traditionally upheld by a party, even if thereby electoral success is imperilled. Even those who postulate that vote-getting is the foremost consideration concede that under some circumstances parties will not adjust ideologically to major changes in the distribution of voters but will try to move voters towards the positions of the party.[63] And, if we keep to the parallel between maximizing profits and maximizing votes, as is the wont of democratic theories fashioned after economic theory, measures designed to reduce discontent about the quality of a party's policy might be conducive to maximizing votes only in the long run, as may be steps taken to reduce discontent about the quality of a firm's product in respect of profits.[64]

Parlour-games are played for fun and to win. Politics cannot be reduced to that. In adhering to his Vietnam policy, President Johnson did what he thought was right morally and strategically, knowing full well that not only he himself but his party too might have to pay for the consequences. Very much the same applied to Senator Goldwater and many activists who worked for him in 1964. Senator Eugene McCarthy also fought for his beliefs without much illusion about getting the Democratic nomination in 1968. Since such behaviour is irrational by the standard of the pay-off, the standard is insufficient as the criterion of rationality in politics. Bare goal-achievement is a wider but hardly more satisfactory criterion, since by that standard Hitler's and Stalin's elimination of their real and imaginary adversaries would qualify as the height of 'pure' rationality. If the British Labour Party could win another election by changing Clause Four or by clamouring in its spirit for more nationalization, the chance of the pay-off would certainly not be the sole, and hardly the decisive, consideration. In short, it seems highly unrealistic to consider purposes other than winning the election only as means.[65] The evidence furnished in word and deed by the leadership of parties – evidence to which I have constantly referred, especially in the first section of this chapter – does not confirm that the rule and the opposition of parties never serve, or even only occasionally serve, as the means for the realization of ideological fundamentals. The two opposite ends-means relationships – of ideology as a means of achieving power and of power as a means of realizing ideology – are not always sharply and consistently distinguishable, since they are inseparable in, because they are of the essence of, democratic politics. As the guiding-star only of election politics, even the principle of maximizing votes or the winning coalition with no other purpose than gaining office presupposes a criterion of rationality in the most restricted, not to say empty, utilitarian sense.

Our examples have shown that politics in the real world exhibit together with the rationality of winning for winning's and office's sake, the rational defence of more or less different principles of social organization and justice, of more or less different specifications of the same principle. The conflict and interdependence between these two kinds of rationality, manifested in the two kinds of ends-means relationship between parties and their ideologies are as perpetual as the two-dimensionality of ideology, because they are joined to it. Inter-dimensional tension is almost uninterruptedly acute because parties have to reckon with the reactions of mass publics to changing conditions brought about by a party's own or its opponents' policies and by the impact on the political system of change in other sub-systems (the educational, technological, etc.)

So far, parties have explained their attitudes toward issues of national importance almost always by reference to their fundamental principles and never by reference only to those which have become largely consensual. In this way they have preserved their identity not merely because for strategic reasons they have no 'incentive to absolute ambiguity',[66] but by virtue of the adherence of sizeable parts of the party's leadership and activists to traditional commitments of the party, or genuine concern over ideological reconstruction through the reformulation of fundamentals and their specification. Parties have not ceased to stress their care for the lot of distinct strata, nor have they ever done so otherwise than by explaining (and believing) that such emphases of orientation are in the long run beneficial to other groups and the national interest as a whole. In East and West alike, the integration of interests rather than the subjugation of the interests of one class to those of another is the generally proclaimed aim, held not to preclude, but rather to require, specific priorities in the consideration of class- or group-interests.

As long as the dimension of fundamentals and their authorized specifications does not reflect a consistent change in orientation to which policies testify, the party lays itself open to the charge of dissimulating ideological change, of incoherence and double-talk. Yet sometimes it looks as if there existed a tacit gentleman's agreement between parties not to accuse one another too much of dissimulating ideological change. Not only does restraint in this respect absolve parties from investing undue intellectual efforts in the renewal of their basic polemical armoury; from the point of view of party propaganda it would also be counter-productive to accuse one's competitors of far-reaching ideological change and thus to highlight how far they had moved with the times, and all major parties drifted towards one another, thereby revealing how little there was to choose between them.

3. THE PRESSURE FOR ACKNOWLEDGMENT OF CHANGE AND ITS MECHANISM

a. *The Ubiquity of the Quest and the Limitation*

In order to justify their *raison d'être,* ideologically and otherwise, political parties of all persuasions in or near power quite naturally stress convergence less than divergence and relate even consensual policies as far as is possible (and feasible in view of the tendencies presumed to prevail among the citizenry) to their distinctive goals and fundamental principles. A lingering belief in and hope for their future realization by the party is a reason why those concerned about its ideological consistency, too, are not invariably eager to press for hammering out a programme reflecting the real extent of ideological change which demonstrated their party's operative ideologies. Still, a minority is usually ready for a consistent revision and renovation of the party's fundamental principles, while hardliners complain about the betrayal of principles and press for a reversion to fundamentals – or what they have come to present as such. Normally, neither minority gets its way, but in actual practice things go more the way of reformers than that of dogmatists. *Mutatis mutandis*, this is true also of Eastern Europe,[67] particularly in connection with the basically universal tension between political and professional elites. In its specific, though not uniform, manifestations in communist regimes, the contest between 'red' on one side and 'expert' and 'intelligentsia' on the other, at once mitigated and exacerbated by the need for cooperation, is not only a supplement of the play of forces within the sealed walls of the decision-making bodies, but also to some extent reflects and expresses critical trends of public opinion. No doubt we have here a weak substitute for public and democratically decided ideological dispute – but a substitute it is.

If we consider communist fundamental and operative ideologies generally in their bearing on the life-situation of individuals and groups, we may probably assume that, apart from some general fundamentals concerning socialist society, some operative features have enjoyed of late a certain (or rather uncertain) degree of majority consensus, if for no other reason than that some socio-economic policies are directed towards that end and go some way to respond to pressures from below: take, for instance, shifts in the concern with the production of consumer goods in the USSR or the fall of Gomulka in Poland. A very small, though perhaps not quite insignificant, part of official operative ideology would seem to respond to the aspirations for freedom of expression or the impartial administration of justice, etc. The ever so slight loosening of the dictatorial and terrorist grip on one side, and courageous manifestations of defiance on the other, cause expectations of liberalization to rise. The demands of the left (liberal revisionist) activist fringe play into the hands of the right wing, which, being posted in the corridors of power, can achieve retreats from liberalization. The right wing, however, can also be contained by the less orthodox elements of the leadership in reliance on the presumably more leftist (liberal) inclined, largely politically silent but not entirely impassive majority. While any straightforward demand to modify fundamental implements – the dictatorship in the name of the proletariat, nationalization (with some temporary exceptions) – so far remains tantamount to betrayal, the cost of even minor heresy is heavy, but no longer as prohibitive as it used to be, at least not in all cases.

After all, no political domain is an island, not even one upon which a single ideology is enforced. Notwithstanding the powerful apparatus of oppression and the monopoly of manipulation, there is no denying that comparisons with other political ideologies and systems are being drawn and that those which are proffered officially are being viewed critically by some segments of the population. Moreover, especially in communism, pressure from within feeds on the very tension between promise and fulfilment. In affording the tools for relating policies to fundamentals by the crudities rather than the niceties of dialectics, the philosophical foundations of Marxism at the same time provide the grounds on which such official promulgations of the unity of theory and practice constitute a challenge to, because they become an insult to, the intellectuals and the common sense of ordinary people. (Does the burden of enforced silence or dissimulation really weigh more heavily on the intellectual and the artist than on the common man? Does the restriction of intellectual and artistic creativity tell more heavily on the thoughts and feelings of human beings than the repression of freedom of expression imposed on common people as to their working and living conditions, material and spiritual?)

One may doubt also whether reaction to the oppression of free expression is less strong under fascist systems. Their intrinsic anti-intellectualism and the resulting intellectual poverty – exception being made for some founding fathers of the French variety – constitute the same challenge as the pseudo-scientism of degenerated Marxism. If under communism opposition is *inter alia* a corollary of the particularly stark contradiction which results from the betrayal in practice of fundamentals grounded in humanitarian messianism, its denial in fascism may provide the same incentive for opposition and the quest for ideological change. It is a measure of its explosive potential that so far any tolerated liberalization in literature, philosophy and social science, including theoretical discussions of political issues, has had a similar fate in all illiberal regimes. Renewed restriction has been neither complete nor equally far-reaching, nor has there been a full reversal even in the USSR, although the same probably does not apply to China.

In the West, besides revisionist pressures for change from within the parties and from the larger segments of public opinion, dissatisfaction at widening consensus has gathered momentum at the fringes: on the left because of the absence, for the time being, of substantial support for going beyond intermediate goals; on the right because many consensual objectives are considered excessive concessions to the Left. Leftist minority groups and intellectuals rejecting on principle what the major parties do and stand for have increased the pressure for reorientation within the major parties in respect of specific issues – segregation, the war in Vietnam, the conflict in the Middle East, university reform, etc. Pressure for reorientation in a definite direction is also a corollary of the demands of conservative right-wingers who, unlike many leftist extremists, do not defame the parliamentary system but wish to use it for reverting to politically less liberal and economically less welfarist and interventionist policies than their parties practise or condone. Pressure for radical structural, and (concomitantly) for systematic ideological change is advocated by people who attack 'the system' but, again unlike leftist extremists, demand its thoroughgoing reform rather than smashing it *à tout prix*. For instance, in England an unorganized group of critics with varied political affiliations and ideological orientations finds prevailing policies to be wanting inasmuch as they are neither clearly nor efficiently directed towards the modernization of institutions and attitudes.[68] The issue of the machinery of government is crucial here, as is the plea for a consistent public policy inspired by the right kind of doctrinal values.[69] In conjunction with administrative renovation, a new ideology apparently is expected to emerge through the adaptation and the revitalization of current doctrinal values conducive to modernization. Since this also means accepting ideological criteria which are professed but not, according to these critics, efficiently and consistently implemented by the parties in power, these critics are at one on this point with the criticism parties now increasingly level against one another – the failure to carry out their own policies.

In contradistinction to these constructive and systematic critics, the radicals of the New Left are uncompromising in their total rejection of what is practised and professed by all parties, including the great communist parties of the West, in Italy and in France, which indeed have become part of the 'establishment'. Although the radicals of the New Left claim that their indiscriminate condemnation of Western policy orientation is matched by their rejection of communism as practised hitherto, they rely heavily upon the goals and principles of the old

Marxist Left (making due allowance for the embroidery with anarchist, psychologist and 'communitarian' slogans). Their fervour is no indicator of systematic ideological innovation.[70]

So far the new Lefts have provided neither a coherent and comprehensive nor any democratically authentic and trustworthy alternative which would justify their deprecation of the perhaps not excitingly momentous, but by no means irrelevant, differences between the more leftist and more rightist establishment parties. Nevertheless, a more or less general 'establishment-weariness' created an atmosphere of tolerance in wider circles towards intolerance and violence under left-wing banners borne by a minority of the material, no less than the ideological, beneficiaries of the welfare state, who (for a while) constantly raised their demands both for benefits for the deprived and for their own influence in academic, national and world affairs.[71]

No doubt, extra-parliamentary opposition adds substance to the principle of participation. In Britain such agitation and intense moral crusades are neither new nor, for the most part, unconnected with parliamentary opposition.[72] The rejection of parliamentary in favour of extra-parliamentary opposition – *l'élection c'est trahison* – is also no novelty. It squares with the traditional Marxist contempt – shared by fascists – for 'formal' democracy[73] and their attempts today, as in the 1930s in Europe, to weaken primarily the forces which within the rules of the game strive to advance the realization of humane and democratic values. Anti-parliamentarism is also evidence of the awareness of a privileged group's inability to acquire such influence within the system and by its rules as would be commensurate with the groups' – or rather the *groupscules'* – pretensions to leadership. Like their predecessors of the officially non-communist old extreme Left, members of such groups arrogate to themselves, if not the leadership, then the role of spokesmen of the under-privileged, without the latters' consent. While there is no assurance at all that the militants outside social-democratic parties will stay left, or, if they do, that it will distinguish their methods less from those of fascists, experience has already shown that tolerance and empathy towards them in the wider public is short-lived.

The sound and fury of militancy and its corollary, the eruptions of anti-intellectualism, in the end estrange the former progressive mentors of the militants from the latter and frighten the *marrais*, the cautious and more balanced. Outbursts of violence, vandalism and wallowing in obscenity (the pillars of Nazi shock-tactics) have so far tended to secure the more conservative forces of 'law and order' in power and kept a Wallace, a McCarthy or a McGovern away from it. Even where

New Leftists have joined social-democratic parties, as in Germany, they are likely to contribute to bringing about the same result.

At the same time, more or less extreme leftist radicalism has made its impact on the majority and in all probability has induced it to support the acceleration and widening of gradual reform and forthwith re-assessments of the ideological 'superstructure' of the parties. For instance, while America did not experience a 'Revolution of 1968', the latter actually had a smaller general political effect than the students' revolts in the United States. Although, in 1972, the American electorate gave a conservative president an overwhelming majority for his second term of office, not only did his party remain in the minority, but it also seems quite certain that the impact of the empathy of a considerable part of the public and the mass media with some specific demands of the militants made its mark as much in some of the more spectacular steps and apparent resoluteness of Mr Nixon's and Dr Kissinger's foreign policy (though its practical results admit of quite divergent evaluations) as in the general thrust of Mr Nixon's internal policies. At least there is ground for asking whether these conformed more with the tradition of his party than with the orientation of his democratic predecessor. It seems safe to assume that there would have been less room for asking this question, let alone for the nomination of Mr McGovern as the presidential candidate of the Democratic Party, if there had not been the all-out attack from the Left on 'the system' and the reinforcement of its public echo through the Vietnam war.

So far such ideological change as we witness within the established political parties takes the form of issue-reassessment rather than systematic ideological reconstruction which is not provided either in the New Left's rehashes of Marxist formulae or the combination of these with some more topical and not always highly controversial issues.

b. *Scriptures and Books*

The manner and degree of responding to the challenge of ideological change depend considerably upon whether or not a party views its ideology as embodied in holy writ and canonical books and allows only a centrally censored exegesis. True, it does not require much time for any orthodoxy to be faced with demands for reform and accusations of heresy. Orthodoxy actually takes shape and is reshaped in warding the two off. Very much like founders of religions, Marx himself had to fight his battles against 'reformists', and did not win them all. The quarrel continued between those demanding the de-radicalization of theory in accordance with actual policies, and purists in the German

SDP who pressed for the abandonment of reformist practice.[74] For Lenin the apostate was Kautsky; for Trotsky it was Stalin. Although 'revisionism' allows a greater variety of opinions, socialist parties nevertheless generally find it difficult to revise basic fundamentals of their creed.[75] One of the more obvious reasons seems to be that they see the ideals of socialism grounded in modern industrial society as distinct from the pre-industrial provenance of conservative and liberal ideals.

However, when socialists and communists suggest their new form of social organization, they wish to substitute it for that which on its part has evolved and developed together with industrialization. Their pre-industrial origin has not prevented modern liberal and conservative ideologies from being conducive to the proliferation of industrial society. Rather, adaptation especially of liberal principles to changing conditions seems to have been facilitated because they, like the more modern conservative principles, have been developed in a number of 'classical' writings by men who were neither founders nor leaders, nor even official ideologues of a party. None of these writings was ever canonized *in toto*. Even when the Philosophical Radicals acted as a group inside and outside Parliament, the doctrinaire ideology they adopted was not the work of one person, or of a few; nor was it expounded with one voice.[76] Yet whether authorized communist exegesis of canonized writings affords ideological legitimation of either adherence to fundamentals or deviation from them; or for the extreme Right, the living word of the leader suffices for the purpose; whether the dialectics and/or the wisdom and realism of the leader serve to label as deviationist the opponents who have lost out; or whether the need for doctrinal change is eventually openly admitted by parties considering themselves to be pragmatic – commitment to some traditional principles remains a universal feature, as is the reluctance to tamper with them. As Mannheim has observed, flexibility of methods of thought and readiness to accept the findings of researchers is not characteristic of political parties.[77] By and large the attitude is still that of Thomas Aquinas to natural law: you may admit additions but must not detract from it.

The following example is characteristic, and epitomizes what is inherent in the examples adduced in the first section of this chapter, and earlier. After 1945, the Conservative Party in Great Britain reacted to what until then had been their 'one great defeat in modern times'[78] by overhauling the party's organization and redrafting its policies. The Conservative coming to terms with the Welfare State was under way. Labour's three successive defeats in the fifties prompted chiefly re-organization and an attempt, as tardy as it was inept, by the party leader, Hugh Gaitskell, to void Clause Four of the party's statutes. The venture failed in such a way that one might also say it succeeded. Clause Four embodies the central principle of 'the common ownership of the means of production, distribution and exchange'. The Labour Party retained the clause, but the 1960 Party Conference approved also as 'a valuable expression of the aims of the Labour Party' an 'amplification and clarification' adopted by the National Executive. The Executive had expressed the conviction that the social and economic objectives of the party could 'be achieved only through an expansion of common ownership substantial enough to give the country power over the commanding heights of the economy'. In addition to thus qualifying Clause Four, the statement not only speaks of 'varying forms' of common ownership but also assures private enterprise a place in the economy, expressing the belief 'that further extensions of common ownership should be decided in the light of these objectives and according to circumstances, with due regard for the view of the workers and consumers concerned'.[79] The same standpoint was reiterated in *Signposts for the Sixties* (1964). Evidently, Gaitskell's attempt had not been in vain. Long-practised principles of operative ideology which were out of tune with a central fundamental had gained conditioned legitimation by reference to the same fundamental principles which in theory had been left unimpaired. In accordance with Aquinas's rule concerning natural law, the principle in question had become programmatically qualified by its 'amplifications and clarifications', that is by additions. As a result it had been rendered less definite and less obligatory.

Gaitskell's success-in-failure resembles *au fond* the fate of Bernstein's similar, yet more wide-ranging, attempts at revisionism more than half a century earlier. Revisionist practice and to some extent also its programmatic acceptance preceded Bernstein, as they preceded Gaitskell. The compromise between the Eisenachers and the Lassallians in the Gotha Programme (1875) aroused the criticism of Marx who went so far as to point out what was hardly conducive to his stand on basic principles, namely that the toiling masses in Germany were not workers but peasants. Liebknecht and Bebel rejected Marx's critique of the programme, and the newly fused Sozialistische Arbeiterpartei Deutschlands henceforth refused to accept direction from 'the old men'.[80] Nevertheless the readjustment of fundamental to operative ideology remained ambiguous. The Erfurt Programme (1891), prepared with the help of Engels, repudiated the Gotha compromise. However, as far as party politics were concerned, the return to orthodox fundamentals was more theoretical than practical. The programme endorsed no other line of immediate action than the one proposed later by Bernstein and again repudiated in theory (that is in the dimension of fundamentals) by the party at its congress in Lübeck (1901).[81] Under the circumstances it is not surprising that the censure of Bernstein was mild and that he was permitted to continue the debate in the party. As Cole concludes, 'the Congress voted Revisionism down, but did not vote it out'.

Bernstein's great hour came at the congress in Görlitz (1921), but the unification of the SPD with the USPD (Independent Socialists) in 1925 caused a return to the rhetoric of the Erfurt Programme, that is, to more sharply accentuated two-dimensional argumentation. Yet it is worth remembering, as Kautsky explained, that at Görlitz those moot points which, like class war, touched on Marx's teachings were 'temporarily' omitted. Kautsky himself did not recommend an uncritical return to orthodoxy, and stressed the need to clarify on which points the Erfurt Programme and hence Marx's teachings were dated. He recalled that already in Erfurt he had rejected the third part of the programme, dealing with the proletarian revolution, because adherence to revolutionary models of the past obfuscated the perception of that which was new. Only precise knowledge of what is happening, he argued, allows us to choose the action which fits the occasion.[82] However, not until 1959 in Bad Godesberg did the SPD coordinate theory and practice in clearly admitting ideological change, as Bernstein had demanded all along.[83] This change has again come under attack from the party's left-wing radicals.

If, even in a social-democratic party as intrinsically reformist as the British Labour Party, it is difficult to modify in a straightforward manner a central fundamental, albeit *the* central fundamental, as in Gaitskell's attempt, this is perhaps all the more characteristic of the mechanism of ideological change in general, because the attempt to align fundamentals and principles of actual policy as spelled out in operative ideology was initiated in a party more bound by scriptural texts than its rivals, the Tories and Liberals, yet much less so than communists or even than its German counterpart.

c. *The Mechanism: Explication and Implication*

Change which first evolves in the operative dimension is, then, usually restricted to it for a long time and explained as an inevitable temporary concession to specific circumstances. If such measures as high wage differential in a communist regime or welfarism under a liberal-conservative government persist and entail other measures, like the prevention of public dissensus in the first case and renunciation in practice of de-nationalization in the second, the respective fundamentals of the classless society and the restoration of free enterprise and competition remain as remote as ever. An approximation to the long-rejected principles of another ideology (e.g. concessions to the market-economy on one side and statism on the other) takes place. Social-democrats, liberals and conservatives in the West elaborate on those specifications of fundamentals which permit them to strike some balance between the acknowledgment of ideological change and continuity. In communist regimes this is achieved by presenting changes as purely transistory measures, calculated to pave the way for achieving the ultimate goals. Such specifications are stipulated to be derivations from fundamentals deemed to provide the justification for a prolonged period of transition and (so long as pursued) of coexistence with other political systems.

Deviousness in the legitimation of operative principles is not the preserve of communist orthodoxy. Others practise it, too, as in the case of Clause Four, or when the limitation of liberty by state interference is castigated while strenuous efforts are made to ensure, legally or otherwise, the defence of privileges which curtail the opportunities of many individuals to enjoy in practice the liberties allowed in principle. Nevertheless, only in Western-type democracies does the cumulative effect of the *rapprochement* of competing ideologies in the operative dimensions find its public expression and eventually lead to the straightforward acknowledgment of ideological change.

The German SPD achieved in its Bad Godesberg resolutions of 1959 what Hugh Gaitskell failed to induce his party to do. So did other social-democratic parties in Europe. Similarly, conservative and liberal parties have progressed from endorsing specific measures of social security to accepting the idea of the Welfare State. This represents a good deal more than what conservatives and liberals (in the European sense) would willingly have asked for but much less than what social-democrats had hoped for. In deference to His Majesty the Voter conservative-liberals can as little go back on the Welfare State as socialists can go much beyond it. (As I have already intimated, a similar stalemate may well obtain on a rather different level in the communist countries of Eastern Europe.[84]) Even acknowledged adaptation removes neither all differences nor all ambiguity. Not all specifications of fundamentals are adjusted to operative ideologies, or adjustments are incomplete. Moreover, not all fundamentals need adaptation; and operative ideology also needs, and is subjected to, readjustment to fundamentals. Enough remains of traditional goals and principles to account for what continues to distinguish the policies of parties and permits their identification by the voter. If there were no rational grounds for honest differences of opinion about means *and* ends, it would be unreasonable to bank on the survival of multi-party democracy.[85]

Given that in Western societies goals of social policy once hotly disputed have become widely accepted in practice, so politics have beome more concerned with the technicalities and intricacies of economic growth, and the differences between the policies carried out by different parties have been reduced. Through the overlapping of policy orientations and the resultant approximation of operative ideologies, the inter-dimensional relationships of various party ideologies become connected with another. When the differences between the actual contents of the operative ideologies of different parties tend to decrease, the tension within each party between its operative ideology and its unchanged fundamental principles increases. As long as it does not cause a change of fundamentals and amount to either less or more than is demanded by fundamentals, the approximation between parties in the operative dimension is matched by a growing disparity between the two dimensions of each party's ideology. This is illustrated in Figure 7, where Pa and Pb designate two different parties.

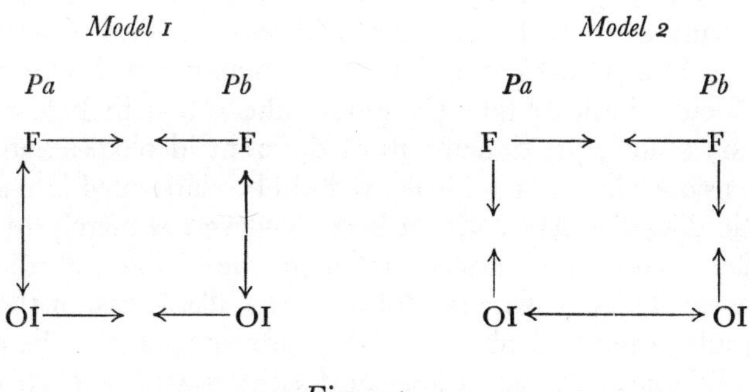

Figure 7

Model 1 shows the ideal-type congruence inside each of the two parties between their characteristic fundamental and operative principles ($\overset{F}{\underset{OI}{\updownarrow}}$: vertical correspondence between F and OI under headings Pa and Pb) and ideal-type disparity between the characteristic fundamental and operative principles upheld by the two parties

($F \rightarrow\leftarrow F$: F under the heading Pa clashes with F under the heading Pb, and $OI \rightarrow\leftarrow OI$: OI under Pa clashes with OI under Pb). In Model 2, we assume congruence or rather far-reaching approximation of the two parties. ($OI \leftrightarrow OI$: horizontal correspondence between OI under heading Pa and OI under heading Pb.) If no corresponding modification of the fundamentals has taken place and they remain opposed as in Model 1, the result is that now fundamental and operative principles conflict *within* the ideology of each party ($\overset{F}{\underset{OI}{\updownarrow}}$: F clashes with OI under the heading Pa as well as under the heading Pb). To 'translate': as we have seen, many policies look more and more alike, irrespective of which party is in power. To the extent that parties continue to declare fidelity to opposed fundamentals while engaging on more and more similar policies, the disparity between the dimensions of their ideology increases.

Needless to say, the two models are the ideal-type poles of a continuum. There is never full congruence between the dimensions of any party's ideology, nor absolute discongruence between different party ideologies. Neither is there ever *full* congruence between operative ideologies, i.e. never between all, and rarely even between some, policies of competing parties, nor *complete* inter-dimensional asymmetry within the ideological argumentation of a party. In Chapter VI, I have indicated what seem to me the more characteristic forms of conflict and adaptation and the more typical complexities attendant upon them. The schemes of Figures 4–6, where the respective Fs and OIs are broken up into the principles which compose them (p 1, p 2 etc.), indicate how the global illustration in Figure 7 of the interaction among the dimensions of different ideologies and between the dimensions within each ideology could be elaborated into a detailed schematic diagram. My concern here, however, is merely to illustrate the basic phenomenon attendant upon the politics of diminishing alternatives: the approximation of operative ideologies, in the wake of considerable agreement about social improvements and the spread of relative affluence, causes strains and stresses within each ideology. These constitute the challenge of ideological change. Neither movement between the poles designated by Models 1 and 2 nor adaptations between the dimensions are in only one direction, so that ideological change and development are also straightforwardly acknowledged, in the West at any rate.

As for communist and fascist one-party states, including the communist states which formally have more than one party, the schematization of the processes illustrated by Models 1 and 2 can serve also in its broad outlines either for comparing the policies of these systems with those of pluralist systems or for indicating what occurs within a communist or fascist system. To use Models 1 and 2 for comparing a communist totalitarian and a Western-type non-totalitarian system, we can subsume under the heading CG, instead of under Pa, the F and OI dimensions of the ideology of one of the European communist governments, and under the heading NTG, instead of Pb, the F and OI dimensions of the ideology of the party, or parties, which sustain a Western non-totalitarian government. In Figure 8, the same ideal-type congruence within each ruling party between F and OI and the likewise ideal-type opposition between both dimensions of the respective ideologies of the ruling parties of the two systems can be assumed as in Model 1 of Figure 7 for the parties facing each other in the same system.

The assumption of approximation between the policies of the ruling parties in the two types of regime is as well-founded in fact as the assertion of similarities between the policies of parties within a pluralist system. The approximation between the operative ideologies of the different regimes is to some extent mutual. Totalitarian systems adopt principles current in the West, like hierarchial or conflict-reducing production-increasing patterns of industrial organization. 'Leftist' principles have become operative in liberal and fascist regimes and all meet on the grounds of welfarism and global competition. Not a few of these approximations involve the parties in inter-dimensional conflict. The processes shown in Figure 7 therefore apply broadly in inter-system comparison. Allowance has to be made, however, for greater contradiction between the F and OI dimensions in communist totalitarian systems, though not on all issues.[86] Enhanced contradiction is indicated in Model 2 of Figure 8.

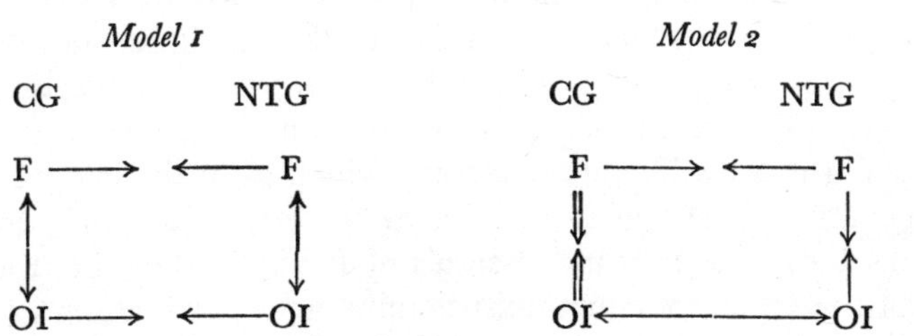

(CG = communist government, NTG = non-totalitarian government)

Figure 8

Figure 8 illustrates a paradigmatic inter-system comparison predicated on internal policies. But the scheme can be used also for inter-system comparison in respect of foreign policy. Briefly, if we compare a communist party in power (CP) with a non-totalitarian party or coalition (NTP) in power, Model 1 in Figure 7 would again show ideal-type congruence within each government party or coalition between fundamental and operative principles of a given foreign policy and full-scale opposition between both the fundamental and the operative principles of the different government parties. Inter-dimensional congruence would mean, for instance, that a communist power supported another communist regime and a liberal welfare democracy another pluralist regime. As in Figure 7, Model 2 would show approximation in the operative dimensions between the different ruling parties and tension between fundamental and operative principles within the ideology of each such party. This is the case when, for example, the principle of peaceful coexistence determines foreign relations to some extent, while eventual victory of one system over the other remains on the agenda of fundamentals. The same pattern (Model 3 in Figure 9) emerges (by the standard of merely functional, as distinct from substantive, equivalence), both when a communist power exercises 'fraternal' supervision over, and, when necessary, intervention in, other communist states, and when a liberal welfare democracy would do the same in other such democracies allied with it.

When the two super-powers support non-communist regimes, as they do, for instance, in the Middle East, then the substantive equivalence of their operative ideology, justifiable in terms of global strategy, causes a clash between the operative and fundamental dimensions only in the ideology of the communist super-power (Model 4 in Figure 9) which, however, may be considered as transient and necessary in view of long-term ideological strategy. The same applies to a non-totalitarian super-power which supports communist regimes allied with the communist super-power or otherwise authoritarian regimes in developing countries or elsewhere (Model 5 in Figure 9). A similar clash occurs between operative ideology and fundamentals largely shared by the major parties of a liberal democracy when, as in the case of Vietnam, the government supports an illiberal regime, although it does so for reasons justifiable by fundamentals of foreign policy, i.e. the prevention of the spread of communist domination. The inter-system correlation between the dimensions is different in so far as, despite the substantive disparity of operative ideologies, there is no conflict between the dimensions in the ideology of the communist power which in the

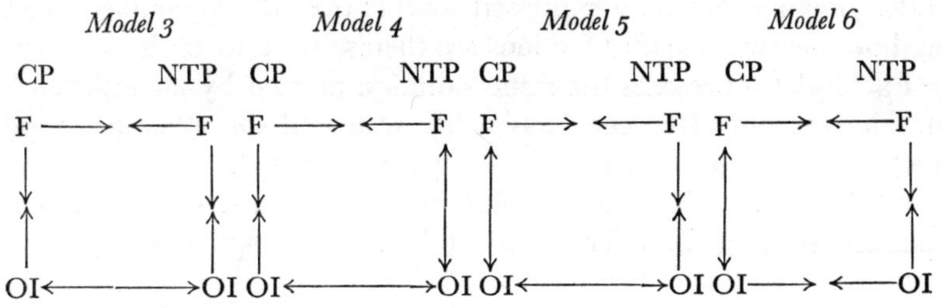

Figure 9

same conflict (Vietnam) supports a communist regime and movement. (This inter-system comparison is schematically illustrated in Model 6 in Figure 9.)

The schematization of the interaction of opposition and approximation in the two dimensions of ideologies within a Western system can also be used to illustrate what goes on within a communist or fascist regime, due allowance being made for the fact that the processes similar to those in the West do not operate publicly and in the main operate only in some of the hegemonic party's institutions and between them and those of that party's tolerated partners. Model 7 in Figure 10 illustrates a situation as evaluated by an objective outsider, in which there exists agreement on fundamentals, but an opposition faction (FO) challenges the government faction (FG) over deviations of operative from fundamental ideology and fights for a policy consonant with fundamentals. Pending a major crisis likely to culminate in a purge, the opposing forces within the influential party institutions conceal possible conflict over fundamentals and confine open dispute largely to the operative dimension. Model 8 in Figure 10 shows the clash of opinions in the operative dimension (OI →← OI) and the

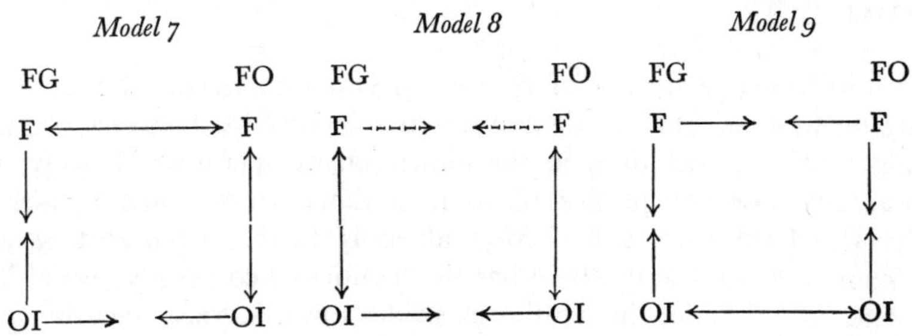

Figure 10

underlying and not fully expressed conflict over fundamentals, indicating how the two warring factions see themselves and each other (F ⇢ ⇠ F). Model 9 presents the same situation as seen by an independent outside observer after one faction has won and the other has yielded temporarily to the winner but is not (yet) eliminated.

We have already assumed that in a communist or fascist system opposition on a broader basis underlies the opposition that can operate within limits in a narrowly institutionalized arena but without publicity, and that the intentions of the opposition outside the official institutions tend to be more far-reaching than, say, those entertained by the group or groups of the leadership inclined towards liberalization and peaceful coexistence with the West. To exemplify schematically this process, we can include also the whole ruling apparatus under FG and oppose to it as FO those trends and pressures which, in the spirit of Western political democracy, express themselves in clandestine publications and corresponding organization, in a recalcitrant public opinion which has influence not only through its own unorganized force but also through the ambition of the regime to compete economically and otherwise with the achievements of the West. Complicated models or diagrams can be constructed to illustrate these processes in totalitarian regimes.

However, the essential point is not their schematic presentation but the fact that, though very different, these processes are not entirely incomparable with those in the West, and that it is essentially through the same mechanism of inter-dimensional interaction that the pressures for ideological change build up and can be contained, though much less so in Western-type democracies than in authoritarian and totalitarian systems. There the rigidity and capriciousness of official ideology which help to create these pressures at the same time provide the evidence of the degree of their containment by the system the ideology serves.

Despite the universality of relying on two dimensions of ideological argumentation and the demonstrated relationships between them, it might well appear that, in the dimension of operative ideology, the *rapprochement* of parties of some national importance applies to developed countries alone. After all, only there do pluralist systems predominate, and only there has the 'politics of consensus', which has found its expression in significant strides towards social security, prevailed in conditions of spreading affluence, or at least advanced industrialization.

In what is at once an epilogue and a prelude to another theme, I propose to intimate that, precisely because ideologies are two-dimensional, the politics of consensus on a pluralistic base is possible in developing countries.

Epilogue

The area of freely achieved consensus seems to be more limited in developing countries, because the final goals of competing modernizing ideologies are so much farther ahead of reality than in developed countries. However, although the discrepancy may accentuate the conflict about fundamentals, this does not necessarily make the convergence of operative ideologies more difficult. Experience does not confirm that only where ideological conflict about fundamentals has receded before growing saturation is a tolerable measure of freely achieved consensus possible, i.e. that economic modernization must precede Western-type democracy.

Gradualism prevailed in the modernization of the West,[1] and, while no industrial revolution has been effected unaided by government, by no means all have been advanced by authoritarian government. In England and America they were preceded by multi-party regimes, which, although not democratic at the outset, were based on principles which enabled progress to be made towards democratic government. More recent examples are India and my own country, Israel. In the latter, democratic procedures accompanied the initial stages of the building of a Jewish nation and economy in former Palestine and continue to distinguish the Jewish State. From the beginning and until quite recently, sharp ideological conflict rent the Labour movement. Even the Kibbutzim crystallized into several competing associations of settlements, in a division perpetuating that of the Labour parties.[2] Marxism and later the attitude towards the Soviet Union were the divisive issues. The increasing hostility of the Soviet Union towards Israel finally helped to unite as much as re-unite three Labour parties, and to create an 'alignment' with the fourth. But consensus on 'first things first' in the political and economic spheres had been hammered out of dissensus from the very beginning. Ideological conflict all around was violent, but there was no violence in politics, for compromise reigned on the operative level, as far as the overwhelming majority was concerned. Thus intensely expressed ideological commitment and conflict do not necessarily either disrupt or endanger the freedom of political minorities,[3] nor do they invariably fail to create pressures towards bargaining and compromise. Rather, acute ideological alertness is apt to nourish dedication not only to different social ends and political means but also to the pursuit and preservation of national independence, as well as to an all-round effort to catch up with modernization – and keep it humane.

The relatively huge influx of capital and the permanent emergency conditions which exist in Israel are widely held to be the prime reasons why – despite considerable party fragmentation – there prevails that broad measure of consensus which permits free democratic institutions to survive. The influx of capital has indeed contributed significantly to the success of the Israeli venture, but capital is also flowing into other developing countries; the proportions are in Israel's favour, but it ought to be borne in mind that many developing countries are richer than Israel in natural resources – and in no other country is the budget burdened by defence expenditure of comparable magnitude.

When it is argued that emergency conditions keep Israeli democracy alive despite the deep fragmentation of its political culture (in the dimension of fundamentals), it tends to be forgotten that usually it is military emergency conditions, above all, which provide the excuse for suspending democratic institutions. However, to the extent that emergency conditions strengthen solidarity, it also needs to be remembered that they are not necessarily and primarily the corollary of actual or imminent war. In some newly created African and Asian states emergency conditions may be said to exist, since they face the danger of disruption and of the actual or virtual loss of independence, so long as they do not achieve national cohesion, modernization and a welfare society. In fact, although modernization is a necessary condition of the military proficiency essential to Israel's survival, the political system of a fully modernized society may be geared to working in a way that permanently averts imminent dangers from within to its existence as a state in its present size. Swiss democracy, for instance, is operated to safeguard the claims of minorities and to forestall separatism.[4] Though exposed to different emergency pressures, both in Switzerland and Israel democracy has not only proved viable but may be said to have ensured the viability of the two states. In the process, no small role has been played by the will to bridge gaps between fundamentals or to circumvent their divisiveness through mutual concessions in the operative dimension.

The leading role of educated Europeans in the establishment and maintenance of Israeli pluralist welfare democracy does not constitute an insurmountable difference from other developing countries. 'Western' Jews and their descendants by now have become a minority. The cultural differences between Western and Oriental Jews – and within each sector – have not affected the non-ethnic party map. The prevailing political and cultural standards have remained Western, and through education will probably ensure that their hitherto unchallenged universality will endure. In other developing countries the main difficulty is not that the formally educated are a relatively new and tiny minority but that they permit their divisions to become disruptive, not always for purely ideological reasons.

Experience confirms that differences of opinion and the temptations of power and enrichment can be restrained in order to ensure the achievement by agreement of nationally and socially imperative goals – goals which are intermediate in regard to more than one final goal, but of such relevance that none of the competing elites can ignore them even if it 'goes it alone'. For the elites in developing countries, however small and variegated they are, to achieve a truce and to agree on what is and what is not immediate and of crucial relevance in nation-building and modernization, is to a considerable extent a matter of will. At any time and place, ideology, fundamental and operative, is produced by the few for the many.

Indeed, similar operative principles for the achievement of economic growth and welfarism, and a certain degree of ideological pluralism on the fundamental level, impose themselves under different political regimes. Notwithstanding the breakdown of imported parliamentary institutions in some developing countries, similar institutional mechanisms may achieve similar objectives in different conditions, with some degree of adaptation. Bureaucracy, for instance, is a necessary correlate of modernization. Controlling and countervailing mechanisms check it in developed states: as Eisenstadt concludes, the same result could be achieved in developing states by strong political elites and a high degree of articulation of both traditional and modern groups.[5] Although the conditions for checking are optimal in developed countries of the Western type, they can be created, and function, in developing societies.

In short, democracy (consociational and otherwise) is not a matter of pre-existing conditions, but a matter of the will to create and maintain the proper conditions. Democracy is historically 'the fruit of an *ideocracy*', of the power of men's belief in ideas.[6] In this century, the Soviet Union has furnished an example on the grandest scale of radically changing a society and modernizing it according to a preconceived ideology, adapting the latter in the operative dimension to the winds of change, in peculiar ways certainly not to everyone's taste.

I have noted a few reasons why African and Asian leaders who opt for refashioning – not just copying – the Western tradition of gradualism and freedom of competition for different ideologies affront neither logic nor historical experience. I have also tried to suggest why approximation in the dimension of operative ideology, on the basis of political pluralism, is not dependent on the stage of social security and affluence achieved in the West, but actually is one of the means of achieving them.

Two-dimensional political argumentation has been shown to be a universal phenomenon which has to be acknowledged in order to be conducive to improving – alas, also to corrupting – ideology. The degree of persisting inter-dimensional strain is commensurate with the nature and strength of the pressures for ideological adaptation and re-orientation. Two-dimensionality also enables us to evade ideological change, since it permits the coexistence of consensus and dissensus alongside, within and between party ideologies. Although ideological bifurcation is likely to remain a permanent concomitant of political argumentation, it would be mistaken to consider attempts to coordinate the two dimensions as futile. There is no virtue and only short-lived gain in double-talk. If one cannot say in good faith that concessions over ways and means do not impinge upon fundamentals, or that they do so only temporarily, professions of adherence to fundamentals in such conditions, especially where these questions cannot be adjudicated in public and free debate, would indicate the corruption of ideology. Yet while ideological intransigence has caused excesses, particularly in these circumstances, the pretension to unideological politics is certainly not the remedy, if for no other reason than that such politics have proved to be impossible.

If in industrially advanced Western-type democracies, though not in them alone, controversy today turns more upon the 'how' than the 'what', sooner or later one also asks 'why'? When differences between policies become those of degree rather than of kind, they do not cease to evoke internal and external debate and to call for public judgment in terms both of efficiency and of ethics. The view that political discussion could be reduced to argument over technicalities once more finds the believers in the classless society and a body of behavioural political scientists in agreement, though again on different grounds. The first promised that ideology and the struggle for power will evaporate; the second claim that the ideological emptiness of the struggle for benefits and power might well form the sole content of politics. Our present knowledge and experience do not support either conclusion. Rather they suggest that, instead of attempting the liberation of politics from ideology, we should stop treating ideology as if it were the subject-matter of demonology rather than of political science. Just as ideology is likely to profit from the systematic exploration of its nature and function by political science, so will such exploration not only help to evade the fetters of ideology, but will make it possible to exploit ideology fruitfully. For when all is said and done, ideology is one of the mainsprings for enlarging the horizons of political science.

Notes*

INTRODUCTION

1. K. Mannheim, *Ideology and Utopia—An Introduction to the Sociology of Knowledge* (Harvest Books, New York, n.d. Translated by L. Wirth and E. Shils from the German *Ideologie und Utopie* [1929], with the addition—as Part V—of Mannheim's article 'Wissenssoziologie' originally published in Vierkandt's *Handwörterbuch der Soziologie* [1931], and Part 1 which was especially written for the English edition first published in 1936 in the International Library of Psychology, Philosophy and Scientific Method.)

2. N. Birnbaum, 'The Sociological Study of Ideology (1940–60), A Trend Report and Bibliography', *Current Sociology*, Vol. IX, 2 (1960), 91.

3. *Ibid.*, 92, 116.

4. H. Barth, *Wahrheit und Ideologie* (Zürich, 1945), p. 9, C. Geertz, 'Ideology as a Cultural System', in D. E. Apter (ed.), *Ideology and Discontent* (New York and London, 1964), p. 51.

5. R. Bendix, 'The Age of Ideology: Persistent and Changing', in Apter, *op. cit.*, pp. 295–6.

6. S. Hampshire, *Thought and Action* (London, 1959), p. 91.

7. For the terms quoted, see R. E. Lane, *Political Ideology* (New York and London, 1962; paperback repr. 1967), p. 16.

8. For the explanation in these terms of the tensions permeating the Marxian theory of ideology and of its fate, see my *The Marxist Conception of Ideology*.

9. 'Ideology and Elections', *Molad* [in Hebrew] (October 1960) and 'Ideologie und Politik in Israel', *Geschichte in Wissenschaft und Unterricht*, Vol. XVIII, 9 (September 1967), 513–41. For a shorter and revised version, see 'Positions and Predispositions in Israeli Politics', *Government and Opposition*, Vol. III, 4 (Autumn 1968), 465–84.

10. See below, note 19, Chapter VII.

11. As asserted by H. M. Drucker, *The Political Uses of Ideology* (London, 1974), p. xii, in disregard of abundant evidence to the contrary, some of which is already contained in the following section.

12. See my *The Marxist Conception of Ideology* from which the points stated in the following survey have been chosen and where their demonstration can be found. No specific references to that study are given here, since its detailed table of contents and the index provide easy guidance.

13. The view of Drucker, *op. cit.*, pp. xii, 5–9, of an intimate connection between the new science of ideas and the art of government is neither new (it is upheld in a 'programmed' basic textbook by E. Brand, *Ideologie* [Düsseldorf, 1972], pp. 33–6), nor is it convincingly substantiated by Drucker's evidence. If such substantiation should prove feasible, one would still want proof of the logical validity of the connection in the writings of the *idéologues*. My doubts in this respect emanate from Destutt de Tracy's oversight of the deterministic implications of *l'idéologie* and their significance for his claim of freedom (see my *The Marxist Conception of Ideology*, Chapter 1). The merit of Drucker's book lies in

* All quotations from works published in languages other than English are offered in my translation, except when the title is given in English.

indicating varieties of ideological style in the writings of Milton, Paine, Comte and Koestler (Chapters 5–8).

14. The conclusions indicated here are based on a detailed study of their writings in my doctoral dissertation *The Conception of History of the French Historians of the Restoration (1815–1830) in their Treatment of French History* (unpubl. doctoral thesis [in Hebrew], The Hebrew University of Jerusalem, 1956). On the aspect of historical and social causation to which Marx and in his wake Plekhanov and Lenin referred, the relationship between leading individuals and the masses, see my 'Napoleonic Authoritarianism in French Liberal Thought', in A. Fuks and I. Halpern (eds), *Studies in History Scripta Hierosolymitana*, Vol. VII (1961), pp. 254–95.

PART I

1. Z. A. Jordan, *Philosophy and Ideology, The Development of Philosophy and Marxism-Leninism in Poland since the Second World War* (Dortrecht, 1963), pp. 452 ff., 474 ff., 491 ff.; D. Joravsky, 'Soviet Ideology', *Soviet Studies*, Vol. XVIII, 1 (1966), 5 ff.; G. Fischer, 'Sociology', in Fischer (ed.), *Science and Ideology in Soviet Society* (New York, 1967).

2. E. Nolte, *Der Faschismus in seiner Epoche* (München, 1963), p. 509.

3. 'Ideology and Terror, A Novel Form of Government', *The Review of Politics*, Vol. XV, 3 (1953), included as Chapter XIII in *The Origins of Totalitarianism* (2nd edn, Meridian Books, New York, 1958), p. 469.

4. The same argument is taken up by Sartori (see below, pp. 50 ff.); he repeats its second part in almost the same words (see below, p. 125).

5. Arendt, *op.cit.*, pp. 469, 470, 468.

CHAPTER I

1. See Appendix 1.

2. J. Benda, *The Betrayal of the Intellectuals* (Paris, 1927. Transl. by R. Aldington; introduction by H. Read [Boston, Beacon Press, 1955]), pp. 36, 9, 21–3, 63 respectively.

3. *The Web of Government* (New York, 1947), p. 454.

4. *The Social System* (Glencoe, 1951), p. 349.

5. T. W. Adorno, E. Frenkel-Brunswick, D. J. Levinson and R. N. Stanford, *The Authoritarian Personality* (New York, 1950), p. 151, note. K. W. Deutsch, *Nationalism and Social Communication, An Inquiry into the Foundations of Nationalism* (New York and London, 1953), pp. 17, 50, 55, 166.

6. Ed. by R. McKeon with the assistance of S. Rokkan (Chicago, 1951).

7. A. Naess and associates, *Democracy, Ideology and Objectivity* (Oslo and Oxford, 1956).

8. *Ibid.*, pp. 4, 236.

9. This tendency is characteristically reflected in W. Stark, *The Sociology of Knowledge* (London, 1958), and L. S. Feuer, 'Beyond Ideology', from *Psychoanalysis and Ethics* (Springfield, Ill., 1955), pp. 126–30, in Waxman, *op.cit.*, pp. 64–8.

10. Barion, *Was ist Ideologie?*, p. 23 (cf. also pp. 45, 90f.); Corbett, *Ideologies*, pp. 51, 88, 104, 118; 138; Feuer, *op. cit.*, p. 66. See also below, p. 34.

11. H. M. Johnson, 'Ideology and the Social System', *The International Encyclopedia of the Social Sciences*, Vol. 7 (1968), p. 77. Ideologies are also designated by Johnson, however, as 'more or less coherent systems of ideas' (81) and consistency is not restored by the *caveat* that 'ideology, properly speaking, is a variable element in such [conservative, counter-reform and revolutionary] doctrines'. Barion, *op.cit.*, p. 102, eventually agrees that ideologies must not be understood necessarily in a pejorative sense (102). Similarly, H.-G. Assel, *Ideologie und Ordnung als Probleme politischer Bildung* (München, 1970), pp. 8, 19, 30, 65 ff., 74–5, though with greater emphasis on distortion and deception. For Corbett, *op. cit.*, pp. 161, 162, 'co-operative discussion . . . [which] is the alternative to doubt and dogma', permits us (particularly the philosophers *qua* sceptics) to dismiss on rational grounds what is 'irrelevant and silly'.

12. *Rationalism in Politics and Other Essays* (London, 1962, paperback 1967), p. 8.

13. *Ibid.*, pp. 6–7.

14. J. L. Talmon, *Political Messianism* (London, 1960). L. Schapiro, 'The Concept of Totalitarianism', *Survey*, No. 73 (Autumn 1969), 103–4, restricts ideology proper still further, i.e. to the dictatorships of Mussolini, Stalin and Hitler. Commitment to social and political change is considered one of the hallmarks of an ideology in such thematically different works as J. Hamburger, *Intellectuals in Politics, John Stuart Mill and the Philosophic Radicals* (New Haven and London, 1965), pp. 1, 276–7; M. Walzer, *The Revolution of the Saints, A Study in the Origins of Radical Politics* (1st edn, Cambridge, Mass., 1965; repr. New York, 1968), p. 27; D. Germino, *Beyond Ideology: The Revival of Political Theory* (New York, Evanston, and London, 1967), pp. 46 ff., 51; M. Cranston, 'Ideology and Mr. Lichtheim', *Encounter*, Vol. XXXI (October 1968), 72.

15. H. Arendt, 'Race-Thinking before Racism', *The Review of Politics*, Vol. VII, 1 (1944), 37–9. The logical and empirical validity of these two reasons are very much open to question.

16. *The Origins of Totalitarianism*, p. 469.

17. *Ibid.*, pp. 470, 472.

18. In T. W. Adorno and W. Dirks (eds), *Sociologica* (Frankfurt, 1955), 219–33. (Reprinted in Aron's *L'opium des intellectuels* [Paris, 1955]; unchanged new edn, 1968), pp. 411–35.

19. *Ibid.*, 415–16, 421. On the relationship between class, party and convictions, see below, Chapter IV.

20. S. M. Lipset, *Political Man* (New York, 1960), pp. 403–4 and the literature cited there. See also Aron's account of the post-war situation in *op. cit.*, Chapter VIII and the account of the Milan Conference by E. A. Shils, 'End of Ideology', *Encounter*, Vol. V (November 1955), in Waxman *op. cit.*, pp. 49–63.

21. Shils, *op. cit.*, 49, 52.

22. O. Kirchheimer, 'The Waning of Opposition in Parliamentary Regimes', *Social Research*, Vol. XXIV, 2 (1957), 128–56. See also below, pp. 264, 54. Similar aspects were also discussed under the name of 'de-politization', although in this case the focus was on whether and how far behavioural criteria such as electoral participation could be taken as indices of public interest in politics. Cp. G. Vedel (ed.), *La dépolitisation, mythe ou réalité?* (Paris, 1962). For connections between de-politization and de-ideologization see, e.g., Vedel's introduction and the contributions by J. Touchard (pp. 28 ff), J. Y. Calvez (pp. 35 ff), S. Hurtig (p. 67) and especially Meynaud, *op. cit.*, pp. 60 ff.

23. Shils in Waxman, *op. cit.*, p. 60, and 'Ideology and Civility: On the Politics of the Intellectual', *The Sewanee Review*, Vol. LXVI, 3 (1958), 453–4.

24. Aron, *op. cit.*, p. 329.

25. *Ibid.*, pp. 422, 416, 423, 424. My italics.

26. Shils in Waxman, *op. cit.*, p. 52. As against his later articles, Shils, too, did not unequivocally stipulate here the indiscriminate identification of 'ideology' with these properties but spoke of 'authoritarian' (52) and 'ideological' radicalism (62).

27. Feuer, *op. cit.*, pp. 64–5, 66. See also 'Ideology & No End, Some Personal History', *Encounter*, Vol. XL (April 1973), where Feuer gives a survey of his contribution to the subject since 1942. He seems to hold now the same view as in 1955, for he says 'ideology, among other things [a qualification?], is a matter of the group unconscious and the irrational' (85). Cp. below, note 6, Chapter VIII, for Erikson's definition.

28. Peter Worseley as quoted in H. J. Steck, 'The Re-emergence of Ideological Politics in Great Britain: The Campaign for Nuclear Disarmament', *The Western Political Quarterly*, Vol. XVIII, 1 (1965), 98.

29. O. Brunner, 'Das Zeitalter der Ideologien', *Neue Wege der Sozialgeschichte* (Göttingen, 1956), pp. 201, 199, 204–5, E. Spranger, 'Wesen und Wert politischer Ideologien', *Vierteljahresschrift für Zeitgeschichte*, I (1954); and Hölzle, *op. cit.*, p. 162, respectively.

30. C. Kerr in R. Bendix, *Work and Authority in Industry, Ideologies of Management in the Course of Industrialization* (New York and London, 1956), p. xii.

31. R. Milliband, 'Théorie et pratique du travaillisme', *Res Publica*, Vol. II, 3 (1960),

216, speaks of 'ce refus de l'idéologie' on the part of the British Labour Party.

32. V. Poussin (sénateur), 'Suis-je un homme de droit?', *ibid.*, 255, 253.

33. *Ibid.*, 276.

34. *Ibid.*, 278.

35. *Ibid.*, 279.

36. *Ibid.*, 286.

37. E. Shils, 'Ideology and Civility', 450–80. This is no more than nominally a review article of the English edition of Aron's *The Opium of the Intellectuals* and N. Cohn's, *The Pursuit of the Millenium* (London, 1957). The few comparative and critical comments refer, as elsewhere in this chapter, in the main to questions of consistency or to distinctions whose arbitrariness seems to me immediately evident. Detailed criticism of the main assumptions will be made in connection with the defence of the inclusive definition in Chapters III and IV.

38. *Ibid.*, 450.

39. *Ibid.*, 452.

40. *Ibid.*, 451.

41. *Ibid.*, 452, 475.

42. 'The Concept and Function of Ideology', in *The International Encyclopedia of the Social Sciences*, Vol. VII (1968), p. 68, henceforth referred to as 'Ideology'.

43. *Ibid.*, p. 66. In 'Ideology and Civility' (e.g. 450), he could use 'ideological outlook' since at the time he made no distinction between the two terms. In the *Encyclopedia* article, Shils also forgets his distinctions when he speaks of 'a prevailing outlook'. This is a pleonasm since 'outlooks and their subsidiary creeds' are defined as 'the characteristic patterns of belief in those sections of society which affirm or accept the existing order of society' (66).

44. *Ibid.*, p. 71.

45. 'Ideology and Civility', 460, 477, 479. My italics.

46. 'Ideology', p. 68. My italics. A similar half-prepared turn-about—though in the opposite direction—occurs in connection with Protestantism. In 'Ideology' it is an 'outlook' and in the earlier article a fount of ideological politics (459), the bridge to 'civility' likewise being established at the end of the article (480).

47. 'Ideology and Civility', 473, 471–2.

48. *Ibid.*, 454–5, 480.

49. *Ibid.*, 459–63.

50. *Ibid.*, 464–9, 475.

51. *Ibid.*, 477.

52. *Ibid.*, 476, 475, 470, 471.

53. 'Ideology', pp. 66–8.

54. *Ibid.*, pp. 66.

55. *Ibid.*, p. 70.

56. *Ibid.*, p. 68.

57. *Ibid.*, pp. 67–81, 67–8. Shils seems to adopt here a line of argument developed by Marcuse who speaks of the rational choice between 'realized' and 'arrested' alternatives as a guide to the conception and realization of 'the transcendent project'. See my 'Herbert Marcuse's One Dimensionality—The Old Style of the New Left', in K. von Beyme (ed.), *Theory and Politics, Festschrift zum 70. Geburtstag für Carl Joachim Friedrich* (The Hague, 1971), pp. 213 ff., 221 f.

58. 'Ideology', pp. 67–8.

59. *Ibid.*, p. 71.

60. *Ibid.*, pp. 74, 75.

61. 'Ideology and Civility', 470, 471 and 'Ideology', p. 67.

62. *Ibid.*, 469, 480.

63. 'Ideology', p. 75.

64. 'Ideology and Civility', 458.

65. See his articles in *Encounter* (1955) and in *The Encyclopedia* (1968). In 'Ideology and

Civility' (1958) the use of 'the end of the ideological age' seems to have been accidental also, because in his article in the *Encyclopedia* he spoke of the idea of 'the end of ideology' while arguing that it had been misunderstood by its adversaries.

66. 'Ideology and Civility', 473 and 475–6. There is, of course, no contradiction between an anti-political attitude evinced in political withdrawal and the possibility also mentioned by Shils of being anti-political without being ideological.

67. See above, text to note 46.

68. *Ibid.*, pp. 475–6.

69. S. M. Lipset, 'Ideology & No End, The Controversy Till Now', *Encounter*, Vol. XXXIX (December 1972), 17–8, and H. Marcuse, *One Dimensional Man* (London, 1964; repr. 1968), pp. 11–12. That Marcuse, besides retaining the Marxist connotations of ideology as being deceptive (51) and dissociated from material practice (134), also equated ideology with being embedded in facts (217) and appeared to oppose it to critical philosophy but also equated his own 'project' with ideology is another matter. Lipset is also imprecise in saying that in his essay on Feuerbach, Engels was the first to use 'the famous phrase', viz. 'the end of ideology'. Engels did not use exactly these words and, more importantly, the words he did use do not pertain to the attainment of true consciousness, as Lipset and D. Bell, 'Ideology and Soviet Politics', *Slavic Review*, Vol. XXIV, 4 (1965), 592, intimate. True, Marx and Engels envisaged an end of ideology with the cessation of the division of labour in the classless and stateless society. However, in the essay on Feuerbach, Engels did not address himself to this issue. Commenting on the nature of ideology to occupy itself increasingly 'with thought as with independent entities, . . . subject only to their own laws', he continued: 'That the material life conditions of the persons inside whose heads this thought process goes on in the last resort determine the course of this process remains of necessity unknown to these persons, for otherwise there would be an end to all ideology' ('*denn sonst wäre es mit der ganzen Ideologie am Ende*'—perhaps better rendered as: 'for otherwise the whole of ideology would be at an end'). (E. Engels, 'Ludwig Feuerbach and the End of Classical German Philosophy' [1888], in L. S. Feuer, *Basic Writings on Politics and Philosophy—Karl Marx and Friedrich Engels* [New York, Anchor Books, 1959], pp. 237–8. For the German source, see Karl Marx and Friedrich Engels, *Werke* [Berlin, 1969], Vol. 21, p. 303.) Engels's clear intention to restate the nature of ideology and the conditions of its existence is not conveyed by Lipset's reading: 'Engels argued that there would be "an end to all ideology", unless the material interests underlying all ideologies remained "of necessity unknown to these persons" '.

70. *Political Man*, p. 408. The italics here are mine but not in the quotations taken from (and quoted in that order): 'Ideology & No End', 21, and 'The Changing Class Structure and Contemporary European Politics', *Daedalus*, Vol. 93 (Winter 1964), 298.

71. *Ibid.*, 271, 273, 278, 284 and 290.

72. M. Rejai, 'Political Ideology: Theoretical and Comparative Perspectives', in Rejai (ed.), *Decline of Ideology?* (Chicago, 1971), p. 23. Indeed, if this were true, why does Rejai blame those he defends for their confusion of 'the end' with 'the decline' of ideology (18)?

73. M. Rejai, W. L. Mason and D. C. Beller, 'Empirical Relevance of the Hypothesis of Decline', in *op. cit.*, pp. 271–4. Thus already Lipset, 'The Changing Class Structure and Contemporary European Politics', 271–303, and in special reference to studies on Norway, Japan and the Netherlands, in 'Some Further Comments on "The End of Ideology" ', *The American Political Science Review*, Vol. LX, 1 (1966), 18.

74. H. Tingsten, 'Stability and Vitality in Swedish Democracy', *Political Quarterly*, Vol. XXVI, 2 (1955), 145–7; U. Himmelstrand, 'A Theoretical and Empirical Approach to Depolitization and Political Involvement', *Acta Sociologica*, Vol. VI (1962); A. Hoogerwerf, 'Latent Socio-Political Issues in the Netherlands', *Sociologica Neerlandica*, Vol. II (1965). For Lane, see below, in the framework of the section whose title indicates what is at stake: 'Convergence and Its Mistaken Evaluation'.

Since Rejai and co-authors defend the continued empirical significance of the decline hypothesis, it is perhaps worth mentioning that some evalautions of the processes observed seem to have been over-optimistic. Have status gaps, differences in the style of life and tensions of stratification dwindled, and has increased education made for tolerance to the extent Lipset ('The Changing Class Structure . . .', 272, 274) has assumed would be the case? Indeed, he himself is aware that in all countries, impoverished or affluent, the more deprived strata give vent to their resentments and their wish for further redistribution of goods by voting largely for leftist parties (299, 285) and suffer from 'cultural deprivation' (294). Still, on Lipset's view, these facts do not speak against the decline of ideological differences and the rise of ideological moderation (280, 295).

75. See below, p. 76.

76. D. Bell, *The End of Ideology—On the Exhaustion of Political Ideas in the Fifties* (New York, 1960; rev. edn paperback Colliers, 1961), pp. 16, 393, 161, and Bell in D. Bell and H. D. Aiken, 'Ideology—A Debate', *Commentary*, Vol. XXXVIII (October 1964), in Waxman, *op. cit.*, p. 271. As is indicated in one of the passages following in the text, Bell is aware that he does not adopt the Marxian conception of ideology in spite of making use of the principal Marxian connotations of the term. For reasons for objecting to Bell's contention that only in its Bolshevik crusading phase Marxism became 'a total ideology' (in Waxman, *op. cit.*, p. 261), see my *The Marxist Conception of Ideology*, Chapters II and III.

77. Bell, *op. cit.*, 265, 269, *The End of Ideology*, pp. 385 ff., and pp. 391–2 respectively.

78. *Ibid.*, pp. 37, 287.

79. Meynaud, *Destin des Idéologies*, pp. 16, 28, 52 ff., 61, 112, 121.

80. *New Left Review*, V (1960), in Waxman, *op. cit.*, pp. 129, 130. Similarly S. W. Rousseas and I. Farganis, 'American Politics and the End of Ideology', *The British Journal of Sociology*, Vol. XIV, 4 (1963) for whom 'ideology need not be equated with chiliastic fanaticism' (in Waxman, *op. cit.*, p. 216) and who evaluate the New Deal as one of the 'supreme examples [*sic*!] of . . . non-committed, non-ideological . . . political expediency' (223).

81. Mills, *op. cit.*, 127, 129–30. On the first point, see above, p. 33, Shils in Waxman, *op. cit.*, p. 56 and his 'The Intellectuals and the Powers: Some Perspectives for Comparative Analysis', *Comparative Studies in Society and History*, Vol. I, 1 (1958), 5–22 and Bell, *The End of Ideology*, p. 397. On the second point, see above, p. 32.

82. R. H. Haber, 'The End of Ideology as Ideology', (1962) in F. V. Lindenfeld. *Reader in Political Sociology* (New York, 1968), repr. in Waxman, *op. cit.*, p. 183.

83. *Ibid.*, pp. 186, 191.

84. *Ibid.*, pp. 213, 196.

85. *Ibid.*, p. 205. The stance has been maintained by Aron in his *Dix-huit leçons sur la société industrielle* (Paris, 1962) up to the 'Note pour la réédition' of *L'opium des intellectuels* in 1968, pp. 9 ff.

86. H. D. Aiken, 'The Revolt Against Ideology', *Commentary*, Vol. XXXVII (April 1964) in Waxman *op. cit.*, pp. 251, 236, Bell and Aiken, 'Ideology—a Debate', *ibid.*, p. 276–7. The italics are mine.

87. *Ibid.*, pp. 264, 276 and H. D. Aiken, *The Age of Ideology* (New York, Mentor Books, 5th printing, 1961), p. ix, respectively.

88. In Waxman, *op. cit.*, pp. 274, 253, 250.

89. For example, Partridge, *op. cit.*, p. 34, MacRae, *op. cit.*, pp. 64 f.; J. Gould, in Gould and Kolb (eds), *A Dictionary of the Social Sciences*, p. 315, and Harris, *op. cit.*

90. B. Williams, 'Democracy and Ideology', *The Political Quarterly*, Vol. XXXII, 4 (1961), 384. Cp. pp. 375 f., 378. This reflects Hannah Arendt's first conception. See above, p. 32. H. McClosky, 'Consensus and Ideology in American Politics', *The American Political Science Review*, Vol. LVIII, 2 (1964), 362, applies Williams's view to American 'democratic ideology'.

91. B. Crick, *In Defence of Politics* (1st edn 1962; rev. edn Harmondsworth, repr. 1966), p. 34. Cp. Germino, *op. cit.*, p. 45. F. Neumann, *Behemoth: The Structure and Practice of National Socialism* (New York, 1942).

92. Crick, *op. cit.*, p. 21.

93. *Ibid.*, pp. 32, 33, 170 ff., 22.

94. *Ibid.*, pp. 33, 40, 47, 55, 164, 171.
95. *Ibid.*, p. 67.
96. *Ibid.*, pp. 34, 39, 44. Germino, *op. cit.*, p. 51, follows Crick in this respect too. For an earlier distinction between 'doctrines' and 'ideologies' and of the orders which they characterize, see H. Freyer, *Theorie des gegenwärtigen Zeitalters* (Stuttgart, 1955), p. 117.
97. Crick, *op. cit.*, p. 194.
98. *Ibid.*, pp. 39, 45 f.
99. *Ibid.*, pp. 34, 49.
100. *Ibid.*, pp. 46.
101. B. Crick, 'Britain's "Democratic" Party', *The Nation*, Vol. CXI, 20 (December 1960), 453.
102. 'European Political Parties', in J. LaPalombara and M. Weiner, *Political Parties and Political Development* (Princeton, 1966), pp. 158–9. Sartori here adopts Duverger's view of the correlation between ideologization and the proliferation of small parties and of the 'brokerage' function of parties in a two-party system. Sartori does not consider that these views had already been convincingly criticized by H. McClosky, P. I. Hoffman and R. O'Hara, 'Issue Conflict and Consensus among Party Leaders and Followers', *The American Political Science Review*, Vol. LIV, 2 (1960), 407 ff.
103. Sartori, *op. cit.*, 172.
104. G. Sartori, 'Politics, Ideology and Belief Systems', *The American Political Science Review*, Vol. LXIII, 2 (1969), 402.
105. *Ibid.*, 403.
106. *Ibid.*, 411.
107. *Ibid.*, note 23 to p. 402.
108. J. P. Diggins, 'Ideology and Pragmatism: Philosophy or Passion?', *The American Political Science Review*, Vol. LXIV, 3 (1970), 899–906, with whose critical comment on Sartori I largely agree, relies perhaps too exclusively on self-definition.
109. See also below, pp. 100 ff., 125 ff.
110. Sartori, *op. cit.*, 402 and note 22.
111. Rokeach, *The Open and the Closed Mind*, pp. 4–5, 14, 16. Cp. 395 ff.
112. Sartori, *op. cit.*, 399 and note 8. The last phrase is Bell's as noted by Sartori (*ibid.*, note 7).
113. *Democratic Theory* (Detroit, 1962), p. 455. 'Ideocracy' was already used by Heinrich Leo, *Studien und Skizzen zu einer Naturlehre des Staates* (Halle, 1833), who had the rule of Savonarola, Thomas Münzer and Robespierre in mind as well as the ideas of Saint-Simon, should they be realized. See Brunner, *op. cit.*, 216. For 'guarantism', see Sartori's 'Constitutionalism: A Preliminary Discussion', *The American Political Science Review*, Vol. LVI, 4 (1962), 855.
114. Sartori, 'Politics, Ideology and Belief Systems', 404 and 401 respectively, and W. Weidlé 'Sur le concept d'idéologie', *Le Contrat Social* (March 1959), reprinted in *Res Publica*, Vol. II, 3 (1960). Weidlé stresses that he means thinking 'dans le sens fort du mot', i.e. rethinking (191), and that in rejecting its indefinite suspension he is concerned with setting ideology apart from *Weltanschauung* and philosophy. Moreover, in distinguishing between 'idéologies totalitaires et partielles' (192), Weidlé says specifically of the former that they are no longer thought because they prevent everybody from thinking, obviously meaning critical re-thinking.
115. Sartori, *op. cit.*, 399.
116. See below, pp. 124 ff.
117. Sartori, *op. cit.*, 400.
118. Not all the critics of 'ideological politics', let alone its advocates, do then not bear out the assertion of Drucker, *The Political Uses of Ideology*, p. xii, that despite general disagreement about ideologies, it is agreed that they 'are nasty things'.
119. R. A. Dahl (ed.), *Political Opposition in Western Democracies* (New Haven and London, 1966).

120. A. Potter, p. 29; M. Sternquist, pp. 132, 141; V. R. Lorwin, pp. 142 ff.; F. C. Engelmann, p. 262; A. Grosser, p. 291; S. H. Barnes, pp. 304, 317 ff.

121. Dahl, 'Epilogue', *op. cit.*, p. 399.

122. Dahl, 'The American Opposition: Affirmation and Denial', in *op. cit.*, pp. 39, 46. I discuss the ideological base of a pragmatic style of politics in connection with Dahl's views below, pp. 131 ff.

123. Dahl, *op. cit.*, p. 63.

124. *Ibid.*, p. 64. My italics.

125. R. A. Dahl, 'Ideology, Conflict and Consensus, Notes for a Theory', Paper submitted to the Seventh World Congress of the International Political Science Association (Brussels, September 1967), 7.

126. Dahl, in *Political Opposition*, pp. 338, 401.

127. Reprinted in Dahl, *Political Opposition*, p. 249. Kirchheimer admits exceptions also in his 'The Transformation of the European Party System', in LaPalambora and Weiner, *op. cit.*, p. 169, or rather limits 'de-ideologization' to a drastic reduction of ideological 'baggage' (190). This, of course, was also Lipset's intention and is at the root of LaPalombara's explanation of his self-contradiction. See above, p. 43 f., and below, p. 64 f.

128. 'Ideology, Conflict and Consensus . . .', 2.

129. This applies not only to scholars who will be referred to in this section but also to some scholars listed in the first part of Appendix A. For example, S. P. Huntington and Z. K. Brzezinski, in 'Ideology in the U.S.A. and U.S.S.R.', originally part of their *Political Power: U.S.A./U.S.S.R.* (1963), reprinted in N. Guild and K. T. Palmer, *Introduction to Politics, Essays and Readings* (New York, London and Sidney, 1968), prefer to speak of 'Soviet ideology' and 'American political beliefs', despite using 'ideology' for both in the title of their chapter and in spite of the view that the two 'perform each functions of conservation and innovation' (72). Indeed, in the first section entitled 'The Function of Ideology and Political Belief', the authors indirectly justify what otherwise would be a pleonasm by saying that 'the American beliefs lack the overt and doctrinal elements of the Soviet ideology' and use 'ideological' for the American scene particularly in connection with strong issue salience and deep-reaching controversy, like slavery. Apter, in contrast to the inclusive conception he uses in his *Introduction to Ideology and Discontent*, distinguishes in his *The Politics of Modernization* (Chicago and London, 1965; 3rd impr. 1967), p. 170, between theorist, ideologist, pragmatist and compromiser. Lane, too, uses the term in different senses. Cp. *Political Ideology*, p. 16, and as referred to below p. 244. I should like to record that during a conversation in Yale in March 1968, with Professor Dahl, he not only gave me permission to discuss his 'Ideology, Conflict and Consensus', but also seemed inclined to accept my objections to the juxtaposition of ideological and pragmatic politics.

130. R. D. Putnam, 'Studying Elite Political Culture: The Case of "Ideology" ', *The American Political Science Review*, Vol. LXV, 3 (1971), 654, 677, 678. For earlier expressions of my views on these points elaborated below in Part III, see my 'Ideologie und Politik in Israel', esp. 515 f. and 540 f. and 'Fundamental and Operative Ideology: The Two Dimensions of Political Argumentation', *Policy Sciences*, Vol. I (1970), 325–38; see p. 326.

131. Putnam, *op. cit.*, 651.

132. *Ibid.*, 661.

133. *Ibid.*, 657.

134. *Ibid.*, 673.

135. *Ibid.*, 656.

136. *Ibid.*, 661. For the central place accorded to Shils's criterion see pp. 665, 674.

137. Shils, 'Ideology', 68, and Putnam, *op. cit.*, 666–7. From Shils's article in the *Sewanee Review*, Putnam deduces what the latter explicitly states in the *Encyclopedia* article.

138. Putnam, *op. cit.*, 660.

139. *Ibid.*, 661.

140. *Ibid.*, 662.

141. *Ibid.*, 657, 659, 677.

142. *Ibid.*, 665.

143. Putnam, *op. cit.*, 668–9, 671–3. The generational difference expressed in the greater militancy of older politicians which Putnam's findings confirm merits comparison with the greater militancy of older workers. Work on this subject has been noted already in Birnbaum's 'Trend Report', 1107.

144. Christoph, 'Consensus and Cleavage in British Ideology', 631 and 629–30, note 4, respectively.

145. *Ibid.*, 635.

146. P. King, 'The Ideological Fallacy', in P. King and B. C. Parekh, *Politics and Experience, Essays presented to Professor Michael Oakeshott on the occasion of his retirement* (Cambridge, 1968), pp. 371, 344.

147. *Ibid.*, pp. 352, 356, 360, 369, 367, 358.

148. The interesting treatment of 'the ideological fallacy' (386 ff.) issues in its definition as 'a universal, non-contextual [not related to a given existential context] recommendation which claims to be true' but cannot be true in virtue of its claim to be 'non-contextual both in space and time' (392). Underlying this formulation is a restrictive conception since King assumes that, unlike prescriptions, recommendations require justification, proof and refutability (390), and that recommendations can be so formulated as to meet this condition to a satisfactory degree. It would seem to follow that in this case recommendations and the policies grounded on them are non-ideological.

149. *Ibid.*, p. 352.

150. *Ibid.*, p. 366.

151. King apparently means something less drastic and more in the vein of his assertion that a government may have a programme but no ideology when it observes no commitment to specific metaphysical principles and is not abstract (367; see also 360). It will be observed that the distinction of ideology and programme here is sharper than in Shils's conception, though not any better founded.

152. *Ibid.*, pp. 361, 363.

153. *Ibid.*, p. 359.

154. *Ibid.*, p. 347.

155. Rejai, Mason, Beller, in *op. cit.*, pp. 2, 3, 7, 17 ff., 278.

156. *Ibid.*, p. 278. This applies to Lipset from whom Rejai apparently takes his cue without noticing that Lipset also gets himself involved in semantic equivocation. (See above, pp. 43–4).

157. Similarly, R. M. Christenson (ed.), *Ideologies and Modern Politics* (London, 1972). In his introduction, he quotes in evident agreement with them a number of inclusive definitions and at the same time adopts Shils's distinction between ideology on the one hand and creeds, doctrines, outlooks, programmes 'and other words used to denote political ideas active in the arenas of politics' on the other. *Ibid.*, pp. 5–6; 9 ff. If Rejai and Christenson have been misled by Sartori to whom they refer more than once and who is himself misleading in his reliance on other scholars (see above, pp. 51–2), they have in addition missed the whole point of Sartori's argument, which is certainly not flawed by any lack of lucidity. Even when Rejai and co-authors object to what they consider to be the excessive 'broadness' of LaPalombara's and Aiken's definition and style their own definition as 'a more restricted definition' of ideology (279), they do not reveal awareness of what I have shown to be the nature of the restrictive conception. Apart from failing to notice the restrictive denominator common to Aiken and Bell (see above, p. 47), they consider as an excessively 'broad' definition one according to which 'any set of propositions held by anyone would qualify for inclusion'. This is certainly not what either Bell or Aiken say and mean, as even the passages quoted by their critics testify.

158. Rejai, *op. cit.*, pp. 8, 25. This vestige of the restrictive conception is also retained by Friedrich (see below, pp. 67–8) and it reverberates more weakly in LaPalombara's view (see below, pp. 64–5). See also Plamenatz, *Ideology*, p. 143, where the association of ideology with 'extremist change' is suddenly asserted after the inclusive definition has been used throughout the book. Similarly, Drucker, *op. cit.*, p. 77, who also in still stronger contrast

to his for the most part inclusive use opposes ideology as 'intolerant political thinking' to liberalism and conservatism (136).

159. Rejai, *op. cit.*, pp. 14, 15, 275, 278, respectively. On the inconclusiveness of the intensity of commitment as a mark of distinction between political beliefs, see below, p. 107 and especially pp. 136 ff.

160. W. A. Mullins, 'On the Concept of Ideology in Political Science', *The American Political Science Review*, Vol. LXVI, 2 (1972), 498.

161. *Ibid.*, 503, 504. Those who advance this view, like Oakeshott, *Rationalism in Politics*, p. 28, D. Bell, 'Reply', *Slavic Review*, Vol. XXIV, 4 (1965), 618, H. Zeltner, *Ideologie und Wahrheit, Zur Kritik der politischen Vernunft* (Stuttgart, Bad Canstatt, 1966), pp. 12 ff., and others, fail to make the distinction, which is appositely restated in the opening sentence of Lenk's introduction (*Ideologie*, p. 17), between the existence already in the oriental and classical world of 'ideologies providing theoretical sanction of social forms of rule' (and providing grounds for their criticism) and the 'systematic inquiry into ideologies' which began in the modern age only. See also Barion, *Was Ist Ideologie?* p. 9 and Corbett, *Ideologies*, p. 9, Still, even accepting the distinction implies drawing a sharper line than is warranted between political philosophy and ideology. See below, p. 112 ff.

162. Mullins, *op. cit.*, 504, note 40.

163. For my exception to this view, see below, pp. 91–2.

CHAPTER II

1. See note 74 of Chapter I, and E. Allardt, 'Finland: Institutionalized Radicalism' in Rejai, *op. cit.*, pp. 116–39. While Allardt designated Finland as a 'deviant case with many qualifications' (118), Lipset, 'The Changing Class Structure and Contemporary European Politics' (273, 276 f., 282, 292), also acknowledges 'deviant cases' in the opposite direction, represented by whole countries or socio-economic and political groups within given societies.

2. Helenius, *The Profile of Party Ideologies*, pp. 15–17, 337–8. The language and style of the English version, which certainly do no credit to The English Centre to whom the author feels indebted for corrections, may be responsible for the impression that the valuable material the author has collected is often treated in a not particularly refined manner. I discuss 'the law of transgression' in the following section.

3. For a detailed documentation and discussion of Helenius's distinction between 'manifest' and 'latent' ideology, see Appendix 3.

4. Helenius, *op. cit.*, pp. 8–9.

5. *Ibid.*, p. 205.

6. *Ibid.*, p. 57.

7. *Ibid.*, p. 31. Cp. also p. 128.

8. Cp. also *ibid.*, note 1, p. 131 and p. 34.

9. 'Ideology and Political Behaviour', 318 ff.

10. *Ibid.*, p. 323.

11. *Ibid.*, p. 331.

12. 'Decline of Ideology: A Dissent and an Interpretation', 7.

13. LaPalombara and Weiner, *Political Parties and Political Development*, pp. 36 f., 405. When I drew Professor LaPalombara's attention to the contradiction, he acknowledged the fact without ado in his reply of 28 July 1969 but suggested that, in view of what he and Weiner had had in mind, the contradiction was not 'as massive as may appear at first glance'. I readily agree and I have formulated the following passage almost in the words used by LaPalombara in his attenuation of the self-contradiction. Yet precisely if the ground for contradiction is slender, it is all the more imperative to abide consistently by one conception of ideology.

14. G. A. Almond, in Almond and J. S. Coleman, *The Politics of Developing Areas* (Princeton, New Jersey, 1960), p. 43.

15. 'Reply' to comments on D. Bell, 'Ideology and Soviet Politics', 619. Bell says that this view caused Friedrich not to relate ideology to governments. While I can see that, as Bell complains, neither Friedrich nor Lichtheim in their comments address themselves particularly to any of Bell's arguments, I fail to see how one can accuse somebody of not relating ideology to government if he includes among the functions of ideology the preservation of 'a given body politic' (C. J. Friedrich, 'Ideology in Politics: A Theoretical Comment', *Slavic Review*, Vol. XXIV, 4 [1965], 613). Evidently such preservation is, above all, a concern of governments.

16. 'Ideology and Soviet Politics' and 'Reply', 591, 618. This stance is reproduced by Mullins. See above, p. 61.

17. 'Ideology and Soviet Politics', 593.

18. *Ibid.*, 549.

19. *Ibid.*, note 6, 595.

20. *Ibid.*, 593–5.

21. *Ibid.*, 596.

22. *Ibid.*, 601. How this 'base' can be distinguished from 'official ideology' and both from the value system *qua* 'established doctrine' as embodied, for instance, in the American Constitution, remains unexplained.

23. *Ibid.*, 603.

24. See above, pp. 44 f. and below, pp. 141 ff.

25. C. J. Friedrich and Z. K. Brzezinski, *Totalitarian Dictatorship and Autocracy* (Cambridge, Mass., 1956), p. 74.

26. *Man and His Government*, p. 89.

27. 2nd edn rev. by C. J. Friedrich (New York, Washington and London, 1965; paperback 1966), p. 77.

28. Friedrich, 'Ideology in Politics', 612, 613.

29. For Shils, see above pp. 41 f., and R. Aron, 'Remarques sur le nouvel age idéologique,' in von Beyme, *Theory and Politics*, pp. 226–41.

30. R. Michels, *Zur Sociologie des Parteiwesens in der modernen Demokratie* (2nd edn, Leipzig, 1925), pp. 25–6. Only the first italics are Michels's. As I have alreday mentioned, Helenius, *op. cit.*, pp. 16 f., has drawn attention to this law. As he points out, it appears only in the second edition of the original and is omitted from the English translation.

31. Michels, *op. cit.*, p. 27.

32. See below, Chapter VIII, 2b.

33. Michels, *op. cit.*, p. 465. My italics.

34. *Ibid.*, p. 481. According to Roth, in R. Bendix and G. Roth, *Scholarship and Partisanship: Essays on Max Weber* (Berkeley, Los Angeles and London, 1971), pp. 248–9, Max Weber, who since the nineties had been strongly influenced by Ostrogorski's analysis of party organization in England and the United States, also believed, like Michels, that the German SPD had 'something like a Weltanschauung'. In fact, Weber communicated this view to Michels in 1906, as Roth notes in his attempt to disprove that Weber's views of the German SPD were shaped by Michels. As Roth shows, and as Michels himself acknowledged with some qualification, Michels approached the broader problems of the issue 'at least in part under Weber's influence' (248), notwithstanding some basic differences between the two men (246, 248, 251).

35. Michels, *op. cit.*, pp. 482, 473, 475–6, 222–4.

36. *Ibid.*, pp. 495, 496–7; 498.

37. Helenius does not seem to be aware of the difference between Michels's 'law of transgression' and the latter-day thesis of the decline and/or end of ideology. Since he reads the former in the spirit of the latter, the detailed evidence he adduces does indeed disprove the former but it does not disprove Michels's law.

38. *Ibid.*, pp. 464, 500.

39. *Ibid.*, pp. xxiv, 479.

40. *Ibid.*, pp. 464–5, 471–2.

41. *Ibid.*, pp. 162 *passim*; 465–70, 474 ff., 479 ff.

42. *Ibid.*, pp. 500–10.
43. As Lipset assumed in *Political Man*, p. 406.
44. 'Ideology', *op. cit.*, pp. 69, 70, 72. It seems that for this reason Shils has not referred to Chapter IX (*Charismatismus*) as well. Chapters IX and X of *Wirtschaft und Gesellschaft*, half-volumes I and II (2nd enlarged edn, Tübingen, 1925), are an extension of Chapter III, paras 10–12b, pp. 140–8.
45. E. Shils, 'Charisma, Order and Status', *American Sociological Review*, Vol. XXX, 2 (1965), 197.
46. On Weber's use of the term see Hölzle, *Idee und Ideologie*, pp. 144–5.
47. Weber, *op. cit.*, p. 753.
48. W. J. Mommsen, 'Universalgeschichtliches und politisches Denken bei Max Weber', *Historische Zeitschrift* (1965), 588, quoted by Hölzle, *op. cit.*, p. 145, whose comment is referred to in the text.
49. Weber, *op. cit.*, p. 763.
50. *Ibid.*, p. 758.
51. *Ibid.*, pp. 753, 756, 759, 761, 763.
52. *Ibid.*, p. 754.
53. *Ibid.*, pp. 760, 763–4.
54. K. Loewenstein, *Max Webers staatspolitische Auffassungen in der Sicht unserer Zeit* (Frankfurt a/M and Bonn, 1965), p. 77, dwells on the difficulty of drawing a line between 'the mysterious impact' of charisma and 'other forms of socio-psychological behaviour'. His denial to Churchill or any modern English prime minister or American president of genuine charisma leads him to conclude that 'in politics the charismatic is a phenomenon of the pre-Cartesian world' (84) which today is still evident only where, as in Asia and Africa, mythical-religious elements form part of the political milieu (78–9). Yet here, too, Loewenstein relies on the impressions of 'reliable Western observers' without pretending to solve thereby the vexed question of an objective foundation for distinguishing charisma from the popularity of leaders. In 'Charismatic Leadership', in Bendix and Roth, *op. cit.*, pp. 170–87, Bendix highlights the ambivalence of the terms of definition of charismatic leadership, particularly when the relations between leader and followers are considered in practice, as Bendix illustrates in his sketches of four Asian leaders.
55. Weber, *op. cit.*, pp. 758, 759.
56. See above, p. 40.
57. Weber, *op. cit.*, p. 762.
58. *Ibid.*, p. 768.
59. *Ibid.*, p. 760.
60. *Ibid.*, pp. 769, 770.
61. 'Ideology', p. 70.
62. Weber, *op. cit.*, pp. 762, 755.
63. *Ibid.*, pp. 773–7.
64. *Ibid.*, p. 766.
65. S. N. Eisenstadt, *Max Weber on Charisma and Institution-Building* (Chicago and London, 1968) p. xxxvi. In his Introduction, Eisenstadt refers to progress made since Weber and indicates subjects of further investigation. In his view, the relating to each other of the charismatic and the ordinary-regular affords the key to the understanding of Weber's work in general and of its importance for modern sociology in particular (ix). If correct, my objections to the degree of Shils's 'dispersion' show that the understanding of Weber's work is not served by blurring whatever boundaries remain between the charismatic and the ordinary. If the latter, too, is imbued with charisma to the extent Shils asserts, to begin with, one might well doubt the relevance of the attempt to distinguish between charismatic and successful leadership. See above, note 54.
66. Eisenstadt, *op. cit.*, p. xxix, insists in the wake of Shils on the necessity to go beyond 'the semi-conspiratorial' theory of charisma or of ideology (xxix). By this formulation Eisenstadt does not wish to imply (as confirmed by him orally) awareness of a connection between Weber's charisma in its pathological and normal manifestations and conceptions

of ideology like Shils's. He follows Shils in considering the exercise of the charismatic only in respect of ideological institutionalization and orientation.

67. Shils, 'Charisma, Order and Status', 205, 206, 207, 212, 213.

68. *Ibid.*, 208, 207. 'Whatever expresses or symbolizes the essence of an ordered cosmos or significant sector thereof awakens the disposition of awe and reverence, the charismatic predisposition' (202). ' . . . secularly, the constitution and the legal system, effective governmental institutions and the moral opinions in which they are embedded, provide such meaningful orders' (204).

69. *Ibid.*, 204 and note 8.

70. *Ibid.*, 208, 204, 207.

71. H. D. Lasswell and A. Kaplan, *Power and Society—A Framework for Political Inquiry* (New Haven, 1950, 3rd pr. 1957), p. 123. The italics in the following quotation are mine. D. C. Hodges, 'The End of "The End of Ideology" ', *The American Journal of Economics and Sociology*, Vol. XXVI, 2 (1967) in Waxman, *op. cit.*, 344, 374, is one of the exceptions I have come across.

72. Mannheim, *Ideology and Utopia*, p. 118.

73. *Ibid.*, p. 125.

74. Cp. my *The Marxist Conception of Ideology*, Chapter IV, 3.

75. Mannheim, *op. cit.*, pp. 129, 130.

76. *Ibid.*, p. 194.

77. *Ibid.*, p. 192. See also p. 40.

78. *Ibid.*, pp. 192–3, 194, 195–6, 146, 193 respectively.

79. See my *The Marxist Conception of Ideology*, for the demonstration of this interpretation.

80. Mannheim, *op. cit.*, pp. 204, 203.

81. *Ibid.*, pp. 194, 199.

82. *Ibid.*, pp. 40, 204 respectively. So defined, the distinction is certainly of no use for application by contemporary scholars to contemporary problems, as Connolly, *Political Science and Ideology*, p. 77, points out.

83. Mannheim, *op. cit.*, p. 203.

84. *Ibid.*, pp. 229, 230, 232, 208 respectively.

85. *Ibid.*, p. 233.

86. *Ibid.*, and p. 219, 249 etc. Mannheim adopts here Michels's view of the function of the democratic ideal, See above, p. 72.

87. *Ibid.*, p. 224.

88. *Ibid.*, pp. 137, 134. Moreover, for Mannheim fascism was as yet an undeveloped doctrine and 'itself lays no particular weight upon integrally knit theory' (note 26, p. 135).

89. *Ibid.*, p. 193. Barion, *Was ist Ideologie?* pp. 24–44, offers a useful analysis of recent discussions of the concepts 'ideology' and 'utopia', though not in connection with the problem I am concerned with here.

90. Delany, 'The Role of Ideology', in Waxman *op. cit.*, p. 313. This is the more surprising since Delany notices that to identify ideology 'with desire for change reverses with Marxian use of the term' (307).

91. Shils, 'Ideology', 67.

92. Shils, 'The End of Ideology?' (1955), p. 61.

93. Mills, 'Letter to the New Left', pp. 137 ff.

94. Bell, *The End of Ideology*, pp. 401, 402. See Mannheim, *op. cit.*, pp. 262–3, where he speaks of 'the decline of ideology' as of the crisis affecting only some strata as the result of 'the objectivity which comes from the unmasking of ideologies', whereas the disappearance of the utopian element from human thought is seen to result in the paradox that 'at the highest stage of awareness . . . man would lose his will to shape history and therewith his ability to understand it'. For a perspective account of the decay of utopianism, see J. N. Shklar, *After Utopia, the Decline of Political Faith* (Princeton, 1957). Shklar also agreed on the desirability of some renewal of utopianism, but at the same time saw hope only for 'a reasoned scepticism' (272–3).

95. The inadequacy of Aiken's riposte, in Waxman, *op. cit.*, p. 255, can be gauged from

the fact that he does not refer to the specific examples that served Bell as the basis of his demand. Some of these were: that Lenin undertook socialization without any notion of what it implied; that the costs of Stalin's ruthless collectivization in 1929 were unjustifiable; and that even projects of slum-clearance must be subject to social cost-benefit calculation (*ibid.*, 266). See also Bell, *op. cit.*, pp. 367–73, on the lack of any idea from Marx down to Lenin about what the setting free of rationality by the abolition of private property specifically implied.

96. Naess, *Democracy, Ideology and Objectivity*, p. 168.

CHAPTER III

1. Hampshire, *Thought and Action*, p. 186.

2. Montesquieu, *De L'Esprit Des Lois* (Classiques Garnier, 1949), 2 Vols, I, Bk XI, Ch. VI, p. 168.

3. I see no reason for distinguishing in modern societies, between conservative and traditionalist ideologies, as does Mullins, 'On the Concept of Ideology in Political Science', 504, note 40. To assume that for traditionalists the question of change constitutes no 'political and intellectual problem', is to ignore the fact that, when in opposition, traditionalists certainly raise the problem of change, and that it poses a constant practical and intellectual challenge when they are in power.

4. Huntington, 'Conservatism as an Ideology', 457, 461, 463, respectively.

5. See above pp. 56–7.

6. Huntington, *op. cit.*, 458. This is an adaptation of Mannheim's view that utopia is alien to the conservative mentality. (See above, p. 84.)

7. *Ibid.*, 660, 672–3.

8. Williams, 'Democracy and Ideology', 384, despite his hesitation as to the extent to which liberalism fully equals an ideology, is aware of the relativity caused by the situational factor. For instance, he points to the 'dynamics', otherwise less apparent, which liberal ideals can acquire in the face of colonial rule and totalitarian regimes.

9. For an anthropologist's view, see M. Gluckman, *Politics, Law and Ritual in Tribal Society* (1965; 2nd impression, Oxford, 1967), pp. 36 ff. See also *idem*, *The Ideas in Barotse Jurisprudence* (New Haven, 1965), pp. 75 ff.

10. For the claims of African leaders on the socialist, in the sense of communitarian ('communaucratic') nature of the traditional African economy as the basis of an African humanist socialism, see C. F. Andrain, 'Democracy and Socialism: Ideologies of African Leaders', in Apter, *op. cit.*, esp. pp. 172 ff.; Mamadou Dia, *Contribution à l'etude du mouvement cooperatif en Afrique noir* (Paris, 1958); L. Senghor, *Nation et voie africaine du socialisme* (Paris, 1961); K. A. Busia, *Africa in Search of Democracy* (London, 1967), Chapter 5; and P. E. Sigmund (ed.), *The Ideologies of the Developing Nations* (rev. edn, New York, 1967), pp. 32 f., 36, 52. On Sékou Touré's condemnation of individualism and liberalism, on Julius Nyerere's reference to traditional African politics, and its comparability to that of the Greek city-states, and the opposed – federalistic – conception, equally based on African tradition, of Chief Awolowo, see Andrain, *op. cit.*, pp. 158 ff., 164 ff., 167 ff. On the rather general inclination to copy neither bourgeois capitalism nor proletarian communism, see *ibid.*, pp. 172 ff, and Macpherson's evaluation that the revolutionary ideologies in the developing countries have bypassed Marxism and Leninism, as well as liberal democracy. ('Revolution and Ideology', in Cox *op. cit.*, pp. 304 ff., 309 f.)

11. Cp. G. D. H. Cole, *A History of Socialist Thought*, 4 vols (London and New York, 1959–60), III, I, pp. 411–12.

12. The question of the universality of the Left-Right polarity has been raised by R. Rémond, *La Droite en France* (Paris, 1955; 2nd edn, 1968), pp. 253–6. He has checked for France the test of 'conservative-radicalism' carried out in England by H. J. Eysenck, 'Social Attitudes and Social Class', *The British Journal of Sociology*, Vol. I, 1 (1950), 55–66. Rémond found that each statement would have evoked similar responses from the French

population. Since the contents of the test reflect the ideological issues bequeathed by the French Revolution, Rémond concludes that where these issues play a role, the (by now traditional) Left-Right divide can be applied. My view that, notwithstanding their different contextual complexion, the similarities of the content of conservative and radical ideals extend by now also beyond Europe is based not only on the epoch- and culture-transcending comparability of basic social problems but on the fact that the Bolshevik Revolution, and later the Chinese, have considerably extended what S. Rokkan, *Citizens, Elections, Parties* (Oslo, 1970) p. 335, calls 'the relative universality' of the Left-Right polarity.

13. This is asserted by A. Naess, 'The Function of Ideological Convictions', in H. Cantril (ed.), *Tensions that Cause War* (Urbana, 1950), pp. 275–6.

14. Putnam, *op. cit.*, 666, who makes both assertions, is unaware that he takes up Naess's assumption. Similarly Harris, *Beliefs in Society*, pp. 104, 106, 139–40, 145, 234 ff., who argues that concern with compromise, harmony and the absence of the intent to subject an existing social structure to serious radical challenge, require no 'formal theorization', general analysis or theory.

15. Connolly, *Political Science and Ideology*, p. 53.

16. Geertz, 'Ideology as a Cultural System', 47–76, deals most perceptively with the question of 'boundaries' in general cultural contexts. On the specific issue of the difference and relationship between political philosophy and ideology, see below, Section 3,c.

17. This is the limitation of T. Geiger, *Ideologie und Wahrheit, Eine Soziologische Kritik des Denkens* (Stuttgart and Wien, 1953). See also Naess, *Democracy, Ideology and Objectivity*, pp. 183, 190, for going beyond this limitation.

18. R. E. Lane and D. O. Sears, *Public Opinion* (Foundations of Modern Political Science Series, Englewood Cliffs, 2nd printing, 1965), p. 69.

19. On this basis, the distinction between ideology and myth can be made. Cp. Mullins, 'On the Concept of Ideology in Political Science', 506. B. Halpern, ' "Myth" and "Ideology" in Modern Usage', *History and Theory*, Vol. I, 2 (1961), 136 and 139 ff., bases his distinction on Sorel, Mannheim and Max Weber and ascribes to myth an integrating and to ideology a segregating function. Yet ideology may be viewed as predominantly integrative on the social and personal level (Apter, *op. cit.*, pp. 18 f.). I would not agree with D. G. MacRae, *Ideology and Society*, p. 65, that each ideology is a myth, nor with L. Kolakowski, *Der Mensch ohne Alternative* (München, 1960, rev. edn 1967) p. 23, that myth is a special case of ideology. I would argue rather that each ideology contains myths, i.e. irrational elements pertaining to values which keep a group together. One may, therefore, consider myths as the functional equivalent of ideology in a pre-rationalistic culture. On these grounds one can imagine ideology to become entrusted with two functions of religion: to defend ultimate purposes and to ensure social consensus. (L. Dion, 'An Hypothesis Concerning Structure and Function of Ideology', originally published as 'Political Ideology as a Tool of Functional Analysis . . .' *The Canadian Journal of Economic and Political Science*, Vol. XXV, 1 [1957], repr. in Cox, *op. cit.*, pp. 322 ff.)

20. Gluckman, *Politics, Law and Ritual in Tribal Society*, p. 235. Gluckman follows Evans-Pritchard in contrasting 'mystical' and 'empirical' beliefs (216). Gluckman also argues convincingly in favour of the comparability of tribal and developed societies (xxii, 17 f., 111 ff., 165, 185, 292) and as a matter of course uses the term 'ideology' for their sets of beliefs (56, 274) or for specific levels of their meaning (258).

21. For a recent incisive treatment of this specific issue, see W. W. Bartley III, *The Retreat to Commitment* (London, 1964).

22. MacRae, *op. cit.*, p. 53. For a discussion of parallels on method and substance between Soviet philosophy and Catholic scholasticism, see G. Wetter, *Dialectical Materialism: A Historical and Systematic Survey of Philosophy in the Soviet Union* (trans. from the German by P. Heath, London, 1958). To conceive, like Dion (note 19), the relationship between ideology and religion primarily in terms of a takeover of functions should thus not obscure their continuing coexistence and the tensions between them. On the transformation-cum-secularization in and through ideology of religious concepts, see below p. 165.

23. For the introduction of the term by S. N. Eisenstadt, see his 'Post-Traditional

Societies and the Continuity and Reconstruction of Tradition', *Daedalus*, Vol. 102, 1 (Winter, 1973), 1–27 and the editor's 'Preface to the Issue "Post-Traditional Societies" '.

24. See, for instance, S. E. Finer, H. B. Berrington and D. J. Bartholomew, *Backbench Opinion in the House of Commons, 1955–59* (Oxford, 1961), pp. 48 ff., 56 ff., on the Early Day Motions sponsored and consistently supported by about fifty Labour backbenchers.

25. J. Hersch, *Idéologie et Réalité, Essai d'Orientation politique* (Paris, 1956), pp. xx, 5 Cp. also pp. 78 ff.

26. E. Gellner, *Words and Things, A Critical Account of Linguistic Philosophy and a Study in Ideology* (London, 1959), pp. 232, 164.

27. Sartori, 'Politics, Ideology and Belief Systems', 401.

28. Converse, 'The Nature of Belief Systems in Mass Publics', in Apter, *op. cit.*, p. 207.

29. The correlation is disregarded by Sartori (*op. cit.*, 402), who associates the rationalistic way of believing with the coherence theory of truth and the empirical way with the correspondence theory. However, indirectly, though not in relation to his main argument, he seems to imply convergence (*ibid.*, note 24). For what is understood by facts and the demonstration of the indispensability of the factual base, see below, pp. 158–9.

30. Sartori, *op. cit.*, 401.

31. See above, pp. 50 ff. and below, 124 ff.

32. Rokeach, *The Open and the Closed Mind*, p. 45; my italics.

33. I agree on these points with Diggins, as well as with his criticism that Sartori leaves a gap between his 'philosophical categories' on the one hand and actual political performance and its underlying principles on the other. ('Ideology and Pragmatism', 901.) I would add that whether he uses them in a philosophical or psychological sense, Sartori takes it for granted that his categories denote actual behaviour. I cannot see, however, that this has anything to do with a lack of interest on Sartori's—or anybody else's—part 'in the intellectual and psychological genesis of belief', unless it is demonstrated that one cannot show 'how', or for that matter 'what', people believe without knowing 'why' they believe 'what' they believe.

34. Sartori, *op. cit.*, 403.

35. Rokeach, *op. cit.*, p. 4. See Appendix 2, 1.

36. Sartori, *op. cit.*, 401.

37. See above, pp. 50 ff., and for further disproof below, pp. 124 ff. On the context in which Sartori's 'structural elements' acquire an authentic differentiating quality, see below, pp. 111–12.

38. See above, p. 98.

39. I use the term as defined by W. J. M. Mackenzie, *Politics and Social Science* (Harmondsworth, 1967), p. 196. A society is meant which 'may be politically organized yet stateless, in that it lacks a distinguishable state apparatus', but for resolving conflicts it possesses the 'institutions of statelessness' existing in every society (205). The idea of statelessness does not exclude personal prominence and influence in war and peace. Cp. M. Fortes and E. Evans-Pritchard (eds), *African Political Systems* (London and Oxf rd, 1940), Introduction. Indeed, Gluckman, *op. cit.*, p. 83, raises the question whether differentiated societies are necessarily more complicated than 'the segmentary and stateless ones'.

40. Cp. M. Weber, 'Der Sozialismus—Rede zur allgemeinen Orientierung von österreichischen Offizieren in Wien (1918)', in *Gesammelte Aufsätze zur Soziologie und Sozialpolitik* (Tübingen, 1924), p. 501.

41. Loewenstein, 'Political Systems, Ideologies and Institutions: The Problem of their Circulation', 696.

42. On the distinction between the two 'oughts' see my *The Liberal Politics of John Locke* (London, 1968; New York, 1969), pp. 28–9.

43. Connolly, *op. cit.*, pp. 54, 43. Cf. also pp. 49, 143 and similarly, on the last point, Geertz, in Apter, *op. cit.*, p. 46. This is an elaboration on Aron's view that, in times of *désagrégation*, fanaticisms thrive (*L'opinion des intellectuels*, p. 433) and, of course, of Shils's

adaptation to ideology of Weber's view of the circumstances propitious for charismatic leadership. See above, pp. 74 ff.

44. As asserted by King, 'The Ideological Fallacy', 342.

45. R. M. MacIver, *The Web of Government*, p. 217, uses this formulation to denote the nature of the democratic party-system, probably in reliance on D. E. Davidson, *Ballots and the Democratic Class Struggle* (Stanford, 1943).

46. Rokeach, *op. cit.*, pp. 32 ff., 46 ff.

47. Since, in ideologies, norms are in the main turned into prescriptions, I have chosen the latter term. Unlike King, in *op. cit.*, p. 390, I include recommendations in prescriptions. In accordance with what I have said already (above, p. 104), it seems to me unwarranted to equate prescriptions with propaganda and to assume that, unlike recommendations, prescriptions are beyond justification, proof and refutability.

48. Mostly to avoid a second 'D', I have used 'rejection' where Rokeach uses 'disbelief'.

49. Apter, *The Politics of Modernization*, pp. 320–1, considers as the stages in which ideologies are formed: 'multiple images', 'selective recall', 'relative threshold', 'horatory realism' and 'political fantasy'. However, Apter not only construes into a sequence what in my view reflects a continuous flux of emphasis of components within the same configuration of formal content, but his examples (Khrushchev's revelations and China's attacks on the Soviet Union) are in fact indicative not of stages in the formation of ideologies but of the changes of ideological attitudes.

50. Rejai, 'Political Ideology: Theoretical and Comparative Perspectives', 3–10, in his typology of ideologies, and Mullins, *op. cit.*, 507, in his classification of their elements according to what they respectively call dimensions or components, criteria and features, do not set components of formal content apart from overall characteristics which, on my showing, presuppose the former. Among the dimensions which Rejai adds to the cognitive and evaluative dimensions (which pertain to formal content), he includes in addition to the 'affective' the 'programmatic' dimensions, that is the specific content of the ideology which *is* the ideology and unites in itself all dimensions. As one of these Rejai also designates 'social base' on the undemonstrated (and in my view undemonstrable) assumption that 'ideology, to be ideology must have a mass base' (9). Rejai also maintains that constraint, coherence, centrality, richness, openness and closedness (4) are dimensions along which elements of belief systems, or belief systems as a whole, vary. For my objections to, and qualifications of, the differentiating quality of these criteria, including the use of 'affective' in order to make a distinction between 'high-intensity and low-intensity belief systems'(14), see, in addition to what I have already said on some of them in the present chapter, below pp. 126 ff. and 136 ff. Mullins, who besides logical coherence and action-orientation, considers as components 'cognitive power' and 'evaluative power' (507) (why 'power'?), actually treats logical coherence as a prerequisite of 'cognitive power' since he connects the two via constraint. Eventually, he also admits that he could not avoid dealing with logical coherence in connection with all his other components (510).

51. Sartori, *op. cit.*, 403.

52. V. I. Lenin, *Left-Wing Communism, An Infantile Disorder* (1920), *Selected Works* (Moscow, 1946), II, p. 584.

53. Hersch, *op. cit.*, p. 86.

54. MacRae, *Ideology and Society*, pp. 159, 177.

55. C. E. Lindblom, *The Intelligence of Democracy* (Glencoe, New York and London, 1965), pp. 137–8.

56. *Ibid.*, pp. 143 f. See also, D. Braybrooke and C. E. Lindblom, *A Strategy of Decision, Policy Evaluation as a Social Process* (Glencoe, New York and London, 1963), pp. 44 f., 69–70 and *passim*.

57. See below, pp. 248–9.

58. Sartori, *op. cit.*, 402.

59. This will be exemplified in the following chapter.

60. Seliger, *op. cit.*, pp. 26–31, where the formal content is divided into three strands. These comprise, however, those added here. It hardly needs to be pointed out that the

question why we should not identify the operative dimension with the factuality of science does not arise. The greater immediate impact of the exigencies of action-orientation on the operative dimension relates it more intimately to the facts of politics but not for this reason to the factual insights of science. The relationship to the latter is a problem concerning ideology as such and I shall deal with it in Chapter V, section 2.

61. B. Barry, *Political Argument* (London, 1965; 3rd impr., 1968), 37–8.

62. *Ibid.*, p. 36.

63. K. Jaspers, *Psychologie der Weltanschauungen* (Berlin, 1922), pp. 1, 2, 12 f.

64. Weidlé in the introduction to *Res Publica* (1960), 190, and Cranston, 'Ideology and Mr. Lichtheim', 73.

65. Apter, *op. cit.*, p. 17.

66. Touchard, *Histoire des Idées Politiques*, Préface, I, p. vi. To some extent this view underlies Apter's words quoted in the text to note 65.

67. I. Jenkins, 'Justice as Ideal and Ideology', in C. J. Friedrich and J. W. Chapman (eds), *Justice*, *Nomos* VI (New York, 1963), pp. 217–20.

68. *Ibid.*, pp. 222–4.

69. Cp. Dion, *op. cit.*, p. 323, who designates natural law as the first political ideology.

70. T. S. Kuhn, *The Structure of Scientific Revolutions* (2nd enlarged edn, 3rd impr., Chicago, 1973), Chapter V.

71. Jenkins, in *op. cit.*, pp. 227–8.

72. Germino, *Beyond Ideology*, p. 13. For the term and for the argument, see pp. 7–13, 89 and *passim*.

73. D. D. Raphael, *Problems of Political Philosophy* (London, 1970), p. 5 and *passim*. Raphael concedes no more than that critical evaluation can indirectly support a belief 'by the elimination of alternatives' (9). The assertion renders historically inexact Raphael's admittedly 'individual interpretation' of his 'account of the primary aims of traditional [political] philosophy'. The assertion also entails considering as 'ideological' the direct support of, or setting up of, norms and ideals. Raphael's definition of ideology as a 'prescriptive doctrine that is not supported by rational argument' (17) does not to my knowledge reflect what ideology 'is usually taken to mean' but is akin to what those scholars mean by ideology who identify it as entirely irrational and generally enlarge in un-Marxian fashion on the Marxist notion of 'false consciousness'. (See above, notes 9 and 10 to Chapter I.) I hope my previous discussions have amply shown that such a definition is rather idiosyncratic. For the argument against a truth-distorting and in this sense irrational conception of ideology, see below, Chapter V, 2.

74. Seliger, *op. cit.*, pp. 343 ff.

75. On the first issue, see, for instance, J. Plamenatz, *German Marxism and Russian Communism* (London, 1954; 3rd impr., 1961), pp. 144 ff., 156 ff., and on the second issue see G. Lichtheim, *Marxism, An Historical and Critical Study* (London, 1961), Chapters 4 and 5 respectively.

76. See my *The Marxist Conception of Ideology*.

77. Seliger, *The Liberal Politics of John Locke*, pp. 331–3, 364, 372.

78. Naess and associates, *Democracy, Ideology and Objectivity*, pp. 161–7, classify the uses of the term according to the following chief *definiens* key words: Static key terms (A), dynamic key terms (B), stress of value orientation (C), causation finality (D), negative but sincere evaluation (E), negative but insincere evaluation (F) and borderline cases (G). The detailed specifications under these headings inevitably involve much overlapping which I have tried to avoid without, I hope, having curtailed any essential components of ideological thought. Neither this procedure nor the criticism of Naess and associates' definition are meant to detract from the importance of their outstanding pioneer study in the field. Minar, 'Ideology and Political Behaviour', 318 ff., also offers a more restricted typology than Naess and succeeds in capturing salient characteristics.

79. Naess, *op. cit.*, pp. 181, 183, 189, 195.

80. *Ibid.*, pp. 187–9.

81. *Ibid.*, p. 189.

82. See above, pp. 100 ff.
83. Naess, *op. cit.*, p. 190.
84. *Ibid.*, pp. 199, 218 ff, 228 ff.
85. The two are not necessarily the same when, say, communist party membership or the communist vote is concerned. In the first instance, what is possible might be (and has been) considered to be more than the desirable, whereas in the second instance, as much as possible is desirable.
86. See my *The Marxist Conception of Ideology*.

CHAPTER IV

1. Thus, for example, in his historical judgment of the American parties, R. Hofstadter, 'Goldwater and His Party', *Encounter*, Vol. XXIII (October 1964), 3. Cp. also Lipset, *Political Man*, pp. 403, 415; Bell, *The End of Ideology*, pp. 121, 308, and the works referred to in the present chapter.
2. W. Scott, *The Life of Napoleon Buonaparte, Emperor of the French* (Edinburgh, 1827), 9 Vols, VI, p. 251.
3. Sartori, 'Politics, Ideology and Belief Systems', 408.
4. See Appendix 2, 2.
5. L. Hartz, *The Liberal Tradition in America* (New York, 1955), p. 79.
6. *Ibid.*, p. 137. Even if pure representation is the hallmark of the pressure-group world, it does not represent the world of politics. The former is politically imperfect by virtue not only of the unequal occurrence of conflicting pressures and influences but as a result of being counterbalanced by the sum total of the prevalent institutional and value system. See, S. E. Finer, *Anonymous Empire* (London, 1966, 2nd edn), p. 111, and Ch. 9.
7. H. D. Aiken, 'The Revolt against Ideology', *Commentary* (April 1964) in Waxman, *op. cit.*, p. 248. See also *ibid.*, pp. 257–80, on the ideological principles of the Declaration of Independence and the Constitution and particularly Y. Arieli, *Individualism and Nationalism in American Ideology* (Cambridge, Mass., 1964) on the strength and significance of ideology in America and its intimate links with Europe.
8. Aiken, *op. cit.*, pp. 247 ff., and 'Ideology—A Debate', 274.
9. 'Politics, Ideology, and Belief Systems', 408. Cp. also Diggins's reference to the *Federalist* ('Ideology and Pragmatism: Philosophy or Passion', 902) and other examples of the applicability of Sartori's criteria across his cultural divide.
10. *Two Treaties of Government*, II, 103. Cp. Seliger, *The Liberal Politics of John Locke*, pp. 230–7.
11. Locke, *op. cit.*, II, 108.
12. W. H. Greenleaf, *Order, Empiricism and Politics: Two Traditions of English Political Thought* (London, New York and Toronto, 1964), p. 165.
13. Sartori, *op. cit.*, 403.
14. Lenin, *Selected Works*, II, p. 185.
15. K. Popper, *The Open Society and Its Enemies* (Princeton, 1950) and M. Ginsberg, 'Facts and Values', *The Advancement of Science*, Vol. XIX (1962), 12.
16. Amended and supplemented on these lines—including specifically the use of the two sets of cognitive processing-coding elements within the framework of the two-dimensionality of political argumentation, and excluding the distinction between 'fixed' and 'firm' elements and the indiscriminate application of the same criteria to personal belief systems and 'isms'—the schemata Sartori develops in his 'framework of analysis' are very useful for the theoretical clarification and formal illustration of the process of change within belief systems.
17. G. A. Almond and S. Verba, *The Civic Culture—Political Attitudes and Democracy in Five Nations* (Princeton, 1963), pp. 4, 484.
18. *Ibid.*, pp. 14 f., 9 and 440 respectively.
19. G. A. Almond and G. Powell, Jr., *Comparative Politics, A Developmental Approach* (2nd edn, Boston and Toronto, 1966), p. 61.

20. W. H. Riker, *The Theory of Political Coalitions* (New Haven and London, 1962), pp. 97 ff.

21. W. H. Riker, *Democracy in the United States* (2nd edn, New York and London, 1965), p. 287.

22. *Ibid.*, pp. 49, 110, 119. Riker enlarges on this position and the evidence in W. H. Riker and P. C. Ordeshook, 'A Theory of the Calculus of Voting', *The American Political Science Review*, Vol. LXII, 1 (1968), 25–42. Cp. also V. O. Key, Jr., *The Responsible Electorate* (Cambridge, Mass., 1966). For a recent reassessment in this spirit on the basis of taking into account both the change in awareness according to circumstances and the question of articulating preferences, see G. M. Pomper, 'From Confusion to Clarity: Issues and American Voters, 1956–1968', *The American Political Science Review*, Vol. LXVI, 2 (1972), 415–28, and the literature on the various evaluations of the problem.

23. Riker, *Democracy in the United States*, pp. 324, 329, 335–6.

24. See, for instance, McClosky, Hoffman and O'Hara, 'Issue Conflict and Consensus among Party Leaders and Followers', 406, 410, 414 ff., 418, 420.

25. *Ibid.*, 422, 426, 424; A Campbell *et al.*, *The American Voter;* and A. Leiserson, *Parties and Politics, An Institutional and Behavioural Approach* (New York, 1958), pp. 162–8.

26. Dahl, 'Some Explanations', in *Political Opposition*, p. 384, and A. Downs, *An Economic Theory of Democracy*, Chapter 3. I discuss in Chapter VIII the necessary limitation by ideological considerations of Downs's vote-maximizing and Riker's winning coalition principle as the criterion of the rational behaviour of parties.

27. See below, note 30.

28. McClosky *et al.*, *op. cit.*, 407, 410, 415, 418.

29. D. E. Stokes, 'Spatial Models of Party Competition', in A. Campbell, P. E. Converse, W. E. Miller and D. E. Stokes, *Elections and the Political Order* (New York, London and Sidney, 1966), pp. 170–2.

30. In fact, according to Pomper, *op. cit.*, 416–17, party identification, the awareness of differences between the parties and consensus among the electorate on the position of the parties have increased between 1956 and 1968 in respect of 'the six precise policy questions which have been asked consistently . . . since 1956'. These turn largely on bread-and-butter issues, i.e. federal aid to education, government responsibility for medicare, full and fair employment, fair housing, school integration and foreign aid.

31. Thus Polsby and Wildavsky, *Presidential Elections*, pp. 9 ff. (in reliance on the standard works in the field) on the basis of the different standpoints revealed by the majority of Democrats and Republicans in Congress on economic and welfare issues (256–6) and on party policy in general (29 f., 197).

32. This position is critically appraised by Eldersveld, *op. cit.*, p. 182, who deals with the problems mentioned in the text in Chapter VIII of his book.

33. See, for instance, Campbell, Converse, Miller and Stokes, *Elections and the Political Order*, pp. 76, 176 ff., 253, 277, 284.

34. Almond and Powell, Jr, *loc. cit.*

35. Dahl, 'Ideology, Conflict and Consensus', 2, and *Pluralist Democracy in the United States* (Chicago, 1967), pp. 356 f.

36. *Pluralist Democracy*, p. 369.

37. Partridge, 'Politics, Philosophy, Ideology', p. 43.

38. Dahl, 'Ideology, Conflict and Consensus', 3, 5. On the abortive distinction between 'fixed' and 'firm' elements, see Appendix 2, 2.

39. Dahl, *Political Opposition*, p. 39.

40. *Ibid.*, p. 341.

41. *Pluralist Democracy*, p. 357, and *Political Opposition*, p. 48.

42. *Pluralist Democracy*, pp. 356, 368, 369.

43. Dahl, 'Ideology, Conflict and Consensus', 7. See also *Political Opposition*, pp. 357, 367, on the problem of parochial schools and 'social conflict' generally, and *Pluralist Democracy*, p. 357, on the American as 'an ideologist . . . when he talks about international politics and especially when he talks about America in relation to the rest of the world'.

44. *Political Opposition*, p. 399.

45. H. Eckstein, *A Theory of Stable Democracy* (Princeton, 1961), pp. 30–1.

46. Bell, *op. cit.*, p. 279.

47. R. R. Alford, *Party and Society, The Anglo-American Democracies* (London, 1964), p. 2. See also Bell, *op. cit.*, pp. 121, 279–80, 302, 309. This is probably still the most widespread assumption if we remember that the prevalence of pragmatic over ideological politics does not in many cases entail the denial of the existence of ideological politics as well.

48. T. Parsons, 'The Political Aspect of Social Structure and Process', in D. Easton (ed.) *Varieties of Political Theory* (Englewood Cliffs, 1966), pp. 87, 89, 92. See also Harris, *Beliefs in Society*, pp. 9–10, 22, and particularly Eduard Bernstein, on the connection between motivation by interest and by 'ideal forces' in 'Das realistische und das ideologische Moment im Sozialismus' (The Realistic and the Ideological Component in Socialism), *Die Neue Zeit* (1897–8), repr. in *Zur Geschichte und Theorie des Sozialismus* (2nd edn, Berlin and Bern, 1901), pp. 270–1. Cp. my *The Marxist Conception of Ideology*, Chapter 5, Section III.

49. The second pair of terms are those used by John Stuart Mill in *On Liberty*, the first pair by Barry, *Political Argument*, pp. 38–40. In using the terms 'material and ideal interests' I follow Max Weber. See H. H. Gerth and C. W. Mills, *From Max Weber: Essays in Sociology* (New York, 1946; repr. 1969), p. 63, and R. Bendix, *Max Weber, An Intellectual Portrait* (New York, 1960), p. 260.

50. *De l'Esprit des lois* (ed. Garnier), III, vii.

51. Barry, *op. cit.*, pp. 202 ff.

52. Adorno, Frenkel-Brunswick, Levinson and Sanford, *The Authoritarian Personality*.

53. Lane and Sears, *Public Opinion*, p. 106.

54. The views advanced here are a corollary of my argument in Chapter III, especially pp. 92 ff.

55. Eldersveld, *Political Parties*, p. 183. In this common-sense observation is implicit what Putnam, 'Studying Elite Political Culture: The Case of Ideology', 668, 671, finds out about the division within extremist right-wing and left-wing party representatives between those who are and those who are not willing to engage in bargaining and compromise.

56. M. I. Ostrogorski, *Democracy and the Organization of Political Parties*, Vol. II, *The United States* (Anchor Books, 1964), pp. 173, 233 f., 305 f.

57. Almond and Verba, *The Civic Culture*, p. 172.

58. R. Rose, 'The Political Ideas of English Party Activists', *The American Political Science Review*, Vol. LVI, 2 (1962), 364.

59. For the term, see E. Hoffer, *The True Believer* (Mentor Books, 1958) and N. Cohn, *The Pursuit of the Millenium*, p. 312. The pair 'concerned citizen' and 'true believer' is discussed by Lane and Sear, *op. cit.*, pp. 94 ff., though not in the respect on which my argument rests.

60. Rokeach, *The Open and the Closed Mind*, pp. 4 ff., 13 ff., 394, as in part quoted above, p. 52.

61. As Loewenstein, 'Political Systems, Ideologies and Institutions', 705, intimates. For reasons contained in Chapter VII, I think, like others, that it is misleading to use 'totalitarianism' indiscriminately for both fascism and communism. Still, having intimated in the preceding passages the more appropriate semantics, in a general discussion I shall, for convenience's sake, occasionally use 'totalitarianism' for fascism and communism, in view of what both have in common.

62. Williams, 'Democracy and Ideology', 384. The same view is implicit in Shils' 'articles of faith of ideological politics'. See above, p. 36.

63. Sartori, *op. cit.*, 402, note 32, 402, 403.

64. King, 'The Ideological Fallacy', 344, 352, 369, thinks that liberalism is superior on these grounds to racialism but not quite equal to Marxism. Rejai, 'Political Ideology: Theoretical and Comparative Perspectives', 4, goes the whole way in the opposite direc-

tion and maintains that, 'the more "extreme" a belief system, the less logical and coherent it will tend to be'.

65. Bell, *End of Ideology*, p. 121.

66. See above, p. 87.

67. Bell and Aiken, 'Ideology—a Debate' 263; *The End of Ideology*, p. 120; and Aiken's rejection of Bell's defence in Waxman, *op. cit.*, p. 277.

68. See above, p. 45.

69. Seliger, *The Liberal Politics of John Locke*, pp. 69 f.

70. John Locke, *Two Treaties of Government* (ed. with an introduction by P. Laslett, Cambridge, 1960), II, 135.

71. O. H. von der Gablentz, 'Kant's politische Philosophie und die Weltpolitik unserer Tage', *Schriftenreihe der Deutschen Hochschule für Politik* (Berlin, 1956), pp. 11, 12.

72. Cp. Seliger, *op. cit.*, pp. 45–8.

73. *On Liberty* in *Utilitarianism, Liberty and Representative Government* (New York and London, Everyman's Library, 1951), pp. 91–2. In this and in the following quotations, the italics are mine. Mill's view reverberates in Harris's rejection (*op. cit.*, pp. 25, 43, 49, 105) of the attribution of a set of beliefs to society as a whole. Like Mill and Marx, but unlike Lenin and Gramsci, Harris proceeds as if the attribution were self-evident in respect of classes.

74. For an apposite rejection of such an assumption, see e.g., D. Dahrendorf, *Gesellschaft und Freiheit* (München, 1962), pp. 95 ff.

75. Mannheim, *Ideology and Utopia*, pp. 56, 77, 78 respectively. See also pp. 58, 93, 104. For a fuller treatment, also of the significance of Mannheim's 'conceptions' of ideology, see my *The Marxist Conception of Ideology*, Chapter 8, I and II.

76. Weber, *Wirtschaft und Gessellschaft* p. 633.

77. Bendix, *Work and Authority*, pp. 13–14, notes 3 and 4, and p. 199, is aware of the difference but concludes that it is impossible 'to keep the two meanings verbally apart'. I belive that one can and ought to do this, particularly in scholarly discourse. Take the case of G. Gurvitch, *Le Concept de Classes sociales de Marx à nos Jours* (Paris, 1954), p. 120, who suggests that we consider a class as a particularist 'supra-functional formation' because no one organization expresses the whole reality of the group. On these terms it is improper to say that a class is 'preparing to assume power' (92), nor is it impossible to say what Gurvitch means in a proper way, e.g.: 'Party x is preparing to assume power on behalf of the working classes.'

78. K. Marx and F. Engels, *Gesamtausgabe*—henceforth abridged as MEGA—(Frankfurt, Moskau and Leningrad, 1927–), VI, p. 534, and *Der 18. Brumaire des Louis Bonaparte* in K. Marx and F. Engels, *Werke* (Berlin, 1960), Vol. VIII, pp. 201, 198, respectively, as quoted in my *The Marxist Conception of Ideology*, Chapter 9, I.

CHAPTER V

1. Birnbaum, 'The Sociological Study of Ideology', notes the 'surprising and indirect influence' (100) on American sociology in quite general terms and without specific reference to the problem of ideology. As far as I know, such reference is likewise absent in later and more specific exemplifications of the impact of Marxist conceptions on behavioural studies.

2. Alford, *Party and Society*, pp. 249, 165–6, 365–6, 326, respectively.

3. *Ibid.*, pp. 156, 305, 2.

4. Dahl, 'The American Opposition, Affirmation and Denial', in *Political Opposition in Western Democracies*, p. 68.

5. See above, pp. 130, 135. The juxtaposition of interest-conditioned and ideological postures is not consistently upheld (cp. Dahl, *op. cit.*, p. 40), which is not surprising in view of the prevarications I have commented upon in Part I.

6. Cp. especially Walter Scott's reading of the Napoleonic intention. See above, p. 125.

7. K. Marx, *Die deutsche Ideologie* (*The German Ideology*), MEGA, V, p. 177, and K. Mannheim, 'Das Konservative Denken (I–II), Soziologische Beiträge zum Werden des politisch-historischen Denkens in Deutschland', *Archiv für Sozialwissenschaft und Sozialpolitik*, Vol. 57, 1 and 2 (1927), pp. 80, 108–9.

8. S. M. Lipset, 'Religion and Politics in the American Past and Present', in R. Lee and M. E. Marty (eds), *Religion and Social Conflict* (New York, 1964), pp. 92 ff. On the general importance of the Catholic vote in these elections, see Polsby and Wildavsky, *Presidential Elections*, pp. 19 ff.

9. For an early presentation of this view by Lukács and a detailed account of the following summary of Mannheim's ideas, see my *The Marxist Conception of Ideology*, Chapters 7, I and 8, II, respectively.

10. For the necessary corrective of this view, see A. Arblaster, 'Ideology and Intellectuals', in Benewick *et al.*, *Knowledge and Belief in Politics*. Granting that there is something to be said for Mannheim's belief in education, Arblaster, within the context of well-known ideological (anti-establishment) assertions, points to the concern of the members of academia—representing 'the institutionalization of intellectual life' ignored by Mannheim (117)—with their status in the class structure and the income commensurate with that status (118). This concern, of course, ties intellectuals, like the professions as a whole, directly to the distributive side of the economic process. Whether this necessarily reduces cognitive detachment and tolerance is another matter. The assertion to this effect, together with Arblaster's accusation of servility caused by crushing free expression and dissent, obviously are refuted by the very publication of Dr Arblaster's views and by the fact that he holds an academic position in a university which, like his publisher, he would certainly call 'bourgeois'.

11. Bernstein, 'Das realistische und das ideologische Moment im Sozialismus', 270–1, 278.

12. There is a basic similarity between the argument in favour of the likeness of interest-based and other beliefs and the argument for considering Locke's right of property as a natural right like all other natural rights. See my *The Liberal Politics of John Locke*, pp. 159 ff.

13. Neither Marx nor any of his disciples has been able to uphold this position consistently. See my *The Marxist Conception of Ideology*.

14. See Seliger, *op. cit.*, Chapter 9, on Mannheim's disregard of Burke's class position in his accounting for the social roots of Burke's thought.

15. M. Abrams, 'Party Politics after the End of Ideology', in E. Allardt and Y. Littunen, *Cleavages, Ideologies and Party Systems* (Helsinki, 1964), pp. 57 ff; G. C. Moodie, *The Government of Britain* (New York, 1961), pp. 19, 61, and R. T. McKenzie and A. Silver, 'Conservatism, Industrialism and the Working Class Tory in England', in R. Rose (ed.), *Studies in British Politics* (London, 1966, repr. New York 1967), pp. 24 ff. Regarding self-identification, the percentage of the population was 60 per cent in 1948, the same as in Norway. That America comes second among nine nations (51 per cent) demonstrates that most Americans do not think of themselves as middle-class. (W. Buchanan and H. Cantrill, *How Nations See Each Other* [Urbana, 1953, p. 13]). For a seminal case study on the asymmetric relationship between sociological and ideological differentiation, see S. M. Lipset, 'Working Class Authoritarianism' (1955) repr. in *Political Man*, Chapter IV; see also Chapter V, 'Fascism Left, Right and Centre'.

16. V. O. Key Jr, *Public Opinion and American Democracy* (New York, 1961), p. 124.

17. Mill, *Representative Government*, p. 247.

18. For the presentation of their views and comment, see my *The Marxist Conception of Ideology*, Chapter 5.

19. Naturally, opinion surveys are extremely important to establish how effective propaganda and indoctrination are, as well as to verify or debunk assertions about 'manipulation'. See below, pp. 159 ff.

20. E. Topitsch, *Sozialphilosophie zwischen Ideologie und Wissenschaft* (2nd edn, Neuwied, 1966), pp. 27–9, adopts a position quite similar to Mannheim in maintaining that scientific truth is not absolute truth. Yet while Topitsch admits the existence of descriptive

elements in ideologies, he tends to identify ideological exclusively with pseudo-argumentation, repeating in circular conclusions and empty formulae (*Leerformeln*) what is maintained by definition (pp. 21, 33, 39 ff., 60 ff.).

21. Aiken, 'The Revolt against Ideology', 255.

22. Geiger, *Ideologie und Wahrheit*, pp. 139, 141, and E. Topitsch, *op. cit.*, p. 32.

23. L. Althusser and E. Balibar, *Reading Capital* (1968, transl. by E. Brewster, London, 1970), p. 52.

24. Hampshire, *Thought and Action*, p. 68.

25. According to E. Voegelin, *The New Science of Politics* (Chicago, 1952), pp. 29–31, ideology is only partially homologous with *doxa* because *doxa* enabled Plato to distinguish the symbols used in actual politics from the symbols of theory concerned with the 'representation' of transcendental truths. However, it is precisely the 'representation' by Plato and Aristotle of the true or best possible order which in my view is permeated with ideology.

26. John Locke, *An Essay Concerning Human Understanding*, 2 vols (ed. with an introduction by J. W. Yolton, Everyman's Library, 1961), I, i., 2, 4.

27. See my *The Liberal Politics of John Locke*, pp. 26 ff.

28. Geertz, 'Ideology as a Cultural System', 48.

29. Detailed discussions on the scope and limits of objectivity in the social sciences are fairly numerous. The more balanced, and in my view pertinent, approaches to the problem in hand still reflect Rickert's distinction, and its elaboration by Weber, between valuation and value-relatedness (*Wertbeziehung* and *-bezogenheit*), the latter being instrumental in setting the problem for scientific inquiry without necessarily affecting the results. See H. Rickert, *Die Grenzen der naturwissenschaftlichen Bergriffsbildung* (Freiburg and Leipzig, 1896; 5th edn, Tübingen, 1929), pp. 245 ff., and M. Weber, 'Die "Objektivität" sozialwissentschaftlicher und sozialpolitischer Erkenntnis' (1904) in *Gesammelte Aufsätze zur Wissenschaftslehre* (Tübingen, 1922), pp. 146–214. Evidently, this is not to deny that, even if we attribute to Weber the substitution of theoretical pre-suppositions for value judgments so that social theories are comparable to natural-scientific theories in this respect as well (W. G. Runciman, *A Critique of Max Weber's Philosophy of Social Science* [Cambridge, 1972] Sec. III), the social sciences contain propositions as 'scientific' as those of the natural sciences, as well as propositions of a different kind. For examples, see W. G. Runciman, 'Ideology and Social Science', in Benewick *et al.*, *op. cit.*, pp. 16 ff.

30. Apter, *op. cit.* p. 17. On the twofold function of 'reflective' social science to determine and to interpret, see Topitsch, *op. cit.*, pp. 151, 162 f., 173 ff., 297 ff., 302, 330 ff.

31. B. de Jouvenel, *The Pure Theory of Politics* (Cambridge, 1963) p. 37.

32. Connolly, *Political Science and Ideology*, pp. 137, 143 ff., 152 ff.

33. As does Apter, *op. cit.*, p. 39. Cp. pp. 28, 29, 17. Similarly, R. E. Lane, 'The Decline of Politics and Ideology in a Knowledgeable Society', *The American Sociological Review*, Vol. XXXI, 5 (1966), 649 ff., who maintains that scientific thought and knowledge could replace politics. If so, opinion surveys could replace elections. For an instructive analysis of the plebiscitarian assumptions of commercial polling and its connection with the principles of representative democracy, see W. Hennis, *Meinungsforschung und repräsentative Demokratie* (Tübingen, 1957).

34. T. B. Bottomore, *Elites and Society* (London, 1964; Harmondsworth, 1966), p. 20, and Mills, *The Sociological Imagination*, p. 80 respectively. See also *ibid.*, p. 84.

35. Bottomore. *ibid.* On this confrontation through the exercise of 'rational criticism' or 'critical rationality', as the essence of political education, see the attempt of Assel, *Ideologie und Ordnung*.

36. Cp. Naess, *Democracy, Ideology and Objectivity*, pp. 149 ff., 158, 172, 195, 199 ff., 226 and Wiatr, 'Sociology-Marxism-Reality', 427–8, from a communist point of view. See also Macpherson, in 'Revolution and Ideology', 302.

37. Gellner, *Words and Things*, p. 223.

38. Althusser, *Reading Capital*, p. 44, and Kolakowski, *Der Mensch ohne Alternative*, p. 27. Kolakowski's preoccupation with institutionalized Marxism surely leads him to make the

exaggerated generalization that 'political organization as such' has a 'destructive effect . . . in scientific thought' (25).

39. What Kolakowski, *op. cit.*, pp. 26 ff., says in this respect of Marxism must be taken to apply generally, for he considers social action to require ideology (22, 26). He contradicts himself, therefore, when he says that the Left has an ideology and the Right only tactics.

40. The criteria represent a combination of those of the 'correspondence theory' and of the 'coherence theory' as set out by W. H. Walsh, *An Introduction to Philosophy of History* (3rd rev. edn, London, 1967), p. 79, and Chapter 4 *in toto*. On this basis we cannot vouch either for the establishment of only unquestionable historical statements or for equal probability for all historical statements (*ibid.*, 86, 83).

41. *Ibid.*, p. 76.

42. I adopt 'experiential' from Germino, *The Revival of Political Theory*, pp. 6, 13, without confining it to inner experience or opposing it to 'experimental' and testability in the way Germino seems to be doing. I mean simply that which can be safely inferred about men's relation to their own and others' experiences from their words and/or deeds.

43. E. Gellner, *Thought and Change* (London, 1964), p. 79.

44. Lane, *Political Ideology*, p. 427.

45. See my 'Herbert Marcuse's One-Dimensionality—The Old Style of the New Left', in von Beyme, *op. cit.*, esp. pp. 202 ff., on the *contre-sens* implications of Marcuse's talk of 'repressive freedom' and his overstatements concerning the mass media. On the 'middlemen', see E. Katz and P. F. Lazarsfeld, *Personal Influence* (New York, 1955).

46. Lane, *op. cit.*, p. 426.

47. Bartley, *The Retreat to Commitment*, pp. vii, 18, 31 f. For the attempts of liberal Protestants to rely on the historical Jesus, as against the one on whom Calvinist claims were based, see pp. 105 ff., 139 ff., 147, 158 ff. See also W. H. Greenleaf, *Order, Empiricism and Politics*, pp. 169 ff., on the mutual reinforcement of simple observation and theological authority in the two traditions of thought prevailing between 1500 and 1700.

Bartley separates the justification from the tenability of a position, holding only tenability to be open to criticism and testing (147–8). It seems to me that the critical question—'How can we best arrange our political institutions so as to get rid of bad rulers . . . or at least restrict the harm they can do?' (137)—must inevitably lead to or proceed from justificatory questions, which according to Bartley beg an 'authoritarian answer', i.e. 'who should rule?' and 'what is supreme authority?' (136).

48. Mill, *Representative Government*, p. 236.

49. Riker, *Democracy in the United States*, pp. 319–20.

50. See Merton, *Social Theory and Social Structure*, pp. 474–5, who refers to the relationship between ideas and conceptualization in M. Granet's study of the Chinese language (*La pensée chinoise* [Paris, 1934]).

51. Hampshire, *op. cit.*, pp. 121–2. The point has often been made. See, for instance, G. Ryle, *The Concept of Mind* (London, 1949); L. Wittgenstein, *Philosophical Investigations*, (2nd edn, Oxford, 1958); and Nietzsche, who said: 'Aber ein Anderes ist der Gedanke, ein Anderes die Tat, ein Anderes das bild der Tat. Das Rad des Grundes rollt nicht zwischen ihnen.' (But one thing is the thought, another the deed, [and] another the picture of the deed. The wheel of causality does not roll between them.) *Also sprach Zarathustra*, *Werke*, Vol. VII, p. 53.

52. Converse, 'The Nature of Belief Systems in Mass Publics', 227–8. The problem of differences of constraint has also been dealt with in the earlier study by A. Campbell, P. E. Converse, W. Miller and D. Stokes, *The American Voter*. For a more recent restatement, see A. Campbell, P. E. Converse, W. E. Miller and D. E. Stokes, *Elections and the Political Order*, pp. 174 ff. For studies on discrepancies in political behaviour, see Lane-Sears, *Public Opinion*, pp. 13 ff. In their great study *The Civic Culture*, Almond and Verba concentrate on educational attainment as the demographic variable most significant and best able to explain differences within and among nations as far as political attitudes and involvement are concerned (e.g. pp. 67, 150 ff., 176, 205, 304 ff., 338 etc.). Rokkan,

Citizens, Elections, Parties, p. 321, reminds us of sources of political education other than formal education.

53. 'The Nature of Belief Systems in Mass Publics', 216–17.

54. For a fuller account of the following exemplification of contemporaneous ideological pluralism and of the few hints concerning the epoch-transcending variety, see, in special reference to Marx and Marxism, my *The Marxist Conception of Ideology*, Chapters 10 and 11.

55. Lichtheim, 'The Concept of Ideology', 193.

56. K. Marx, *Das Kapital, Kritik der politischen Okonomie*, ed. by F. Engels (Hamburg, Vol. I, 4th edn, 1893; Vol. II, 2nd edn, 1893; Vol. III [in 2 vols] 1894), I, pp. vii–viii, 23. Cp. Preface to 2nd edn, p. xii. See also K. Marx, *Zur Kritik der politischen Ökonomie*, ed. by K. Kautsky (7th edn, Stuttgart, 1907), p. 148.

57. MEGA, VI, pp. 407–8 and Abt., 3, III, p. 46.

58. As noticed by Mannheim, 'Das konservative Denken', 84, 101, 106. Despite this awareness of ideological pluralism, Mannheim did not use the term, nor consider the significance of the phenomenon for a theory of ideology.

59. *Representative Government*, pp. 242, 244–5, 247, and Lenin, S. W. II, pp. 177–8.

60. F. Schurman, *Ideology and Organization in Communist China* (Berkeley and Los Angeles, 1966), pp. 97, 111 ff.

61. R. D. Lukić, 'Political Ideology and Social Development', in Allardt and Littunen, *op. cit.*, pp. 67–9.

62. See above, p. 103. Cp. R. Aron, *Dix-huit leçons sur la société industrielle*, for critical exemplifications.

63. Bendix, *Work and Authority in Industry*, p. 209 and Chapter 4. See also Schurman, *op. cit.*, pp. 298 ff., on the degree of relevance of the managerial practices of General Motors for communist China and that of Ford for the Soviet Union and the ensuing dilemmas and confusion in both instances.

64. For the demonstration of this point, see my *The Marxist Conception of Ideology*, Chapter 10, II.

65. Greenleaf, *op. cit.*, pp. 10 ff.

66. Cp. Seliger, *The Liberal Politics of John Locke*, pp. 46 ff., for this point and the following remarks. These, and those already mentioned, seem to me to disprove what is implied by Topitsch, *op. cit.*, pp. 39–40, namely that, because the same basic assumptions are being used in sharply divergent valuational conclusions, such assumptions are pseudo-arguments and empty formulae.

67. Cp. R. C. Tucker, *Philosophy and Myth in Karl Marx* (Cambridge, 1961), and Chapter 11, I, of my *The Marxist Conception of Ideology*.

68. Topitsch, *op. cit.*, p. 37; Tucker, *op. cit.*, pp. 25, 299. On the assumption of the unity of theory and practice in romanticism, see Mannheim, 'Das Konservative Denken', 493.

69. Topitsch, *op. cit.*, note 38 to p. 274; 248. The religious origins of integral components of modern (secular) political value and institutional systems is, besides the socio-political role of religion *per se*, an essential part of Leo Moulin's preoccupation during more than twenty years. See especially *Le Monde vivant des Religieux* (Paris, 1964), his numerous articles cited in his 'Les origines Electorales et délibératives contemporaines', *Res Publica*, Vol. XV, 4 (1973), 787, note 4, and the succinct overview in 'Le Religion comme facteur d'intégration, de non-intégration et de desintégration Politique', Moulin's contribution to the IPSA Round Table, Jerusalem, 9–12 September 1974, on Political Integration.

70. E.g. L. Goldmann, *The Hidden God* (trans. by P. Thody, London, 1964), pp. 278, 94–5, *idem*, *Recherches Dialectiques* (3rd edn, Paris, 1959), p. 18, and Kolakowski, *op. cit.*, pp. 224 ff., 227 ff. On the relationship between ideology as 'false consciousness' and the Christian teachings on the consequences of the Fall and theodicy, see my *The Marxist Conception of Ideology*, *loc. cit.*

71. E. G. Touchard in his Preface to *Histoire des idées politiques*, I, p. viii. Harris, in *Beliefs in Society*, points to thematic continuities, culture-transcending similarities and contemporaneous overlapping of ideologies.

72. E.g. M. Leroy, *Histoire des idées sociales en France, 3 Vols* (3rd ed, Paris, 1946–54), II (1950), p. 124, and among political scientists, Meynaud, who uses the term frequently, but connects it particularly with political pluralism in the West as manifested in 'ideological appeasement' or 'de-ideologization' there (e.g. pp. 43–5).

73. W. G. Runciman, *Social Science and Political Theory* (Cambridge, 1963), p. 143.

PART III

1. A. O. Lovejoy, *The Great Chain of Being* (New York, 1960), quoted in Greenleaf, *Order, Empiricism and Politics*, p. 15.

2. 'Ideology in Politics', 612.

CHAPTER VI

1. L. Binder, 'Ideological Foundations of Egyptian-Arabian Nationalism', in Apter, *Ideology and Discontent*, pp. 150–1. See also generally, M. Duverger, 'Où en sont les nationalismes?' *Res Publica* (1960), 267 ff.

2. S. H. Beer, *Modern British Politics* (London, 1965), pp. 12, 9–10.

3. Crick, *In Defence of Politics*, p. 44, who uses 'operative theory' (49) in the same sense as 'operative ideology', and Harris, *Beliefs in Society*, p. 77, respectively.

4. F. J. Fleron Jr and R. MacKelly, 'Personality, Behaviour and Communist Ideology', *Soviet Studies*, Vol. XXI, 3 (1970), 302 and 312. Since their subject is the extent of ideological together with other motivations, the authors are well aware of the inconsistencies in the application of official ideology. They do not, however, associate them with operative ideology'.

5. McClosky, Hoffman and O'Hara, 'Issue Conflict and Consensus among Party Leaders and Followers', 410.

6. D. Marquand, 'The Politics of Deprivation, Reconsidering the Future of Utopianism', *Encounter*, Vol. XXXII (April 1969), 39.

7. R. A. Scalapino, 'Ideology and Modernization—The Japanese Case', in Apter, *op. cit.*, pp. 113, 121, 124.

8. Harris, *op. cit.*, p. 124. See Appendix 3, 1.

9. T. Lowi, 'The Public Philosophy: Interest-Group Liberalism', *The American Political Science Review*, Vol. LXI, 1 (1967), 18.

10. *Ibid.*, 8, 12, 22 ff.

11. C. Bay, 'Politics and Pseudopolitics', 41.

12. *Ibid.*, 40–1.

13. See above, pp. 111–12.

14. Huntington, 'Conservatism as an Ideology', 467 ff.

15. Christoph, 'Consensus and Cleavage in British Political Ideology', 629.

16. See above, pp. 58–9.

17. Christoph, *op. cit.*, 631 ff. and 638 ff., respectively.

18. See Appendix 3, 2 and 3.

19. Bernstein, 'Das realistische und das ideologische Moment im Sozialismus', 283–4.

20. N. Leites, *The Operational Code of the Politburo* (New York, 1951), and the discussion in Meyer, *Leninism*, Chapter 4.

21. *Left-Wing Communism*, S.W. II, pp. 601, 603. Similarly in connection with England, *ibid.*, p. 620.

22. Joravsky, 'Soviet Ideology', 6, 8, 11.

23. L. Schapiro, as he points out in his classic *The Communist Party of the Soviet Union* (London, 1962), p. xi, and throughout the book demonstrates, has 'as yet not discovered a single instance in which the party was prepared to risk its own survival in power for considerations of doctrine'. But this does not, in Schapiro's own view, mean that the theories and the action which the party purportedly implemented had never anything to

do with each other, or that the clash between them never caused serious difficulties. See, for instance, Chapters XI and XVI.

24. R. V. Daniels, 'The Ideological Vector', *Soviet Studies*, Vol. XVIII, 1 (1966), 72.

25. While the sovietologist Meyer, 'The Function of Ideology', 242, also sees a parallel with the West, in a gloss in the manuscript Leonard Schapiro objects to the parallel on the grounds that 'we are dealing with two distinct mental processes' and in a letter to me of 16 August 1973 argues in the vein of H. Arendt (see above, p. 32), that the use which Stalin and Hitler made of ideology 'introduced an entirely new dimension into the meaning and significance of ideology' after it 'became through the work of Lenin not only a guide to action but also an instrument for the manipulation of spontaneity'. Since in his *Totalitarianism* (London, 1972), see especially pp. 45–58, Schapiro also used 'ideology' for doctrines other than those characteristic of his three prototypes of totalitarian rule, he therefore reverted in his letter, without otherwise shifting ground in any way, to his rejection of the inclusive use in his *Survey* article of 1969 ('The Concept of Totalitarianism', 103–4). For he asserts in that article that the concept 'ideology' becomes 'totally useless' if not applied solely to a situation in which rulers can ensure a monopoly for the official doctrine and where, as an instrument of manipulation, it creates a cleft between the ideology and what people really believe.

Two main considerations impugn not so much the premises of Schapiro's argument, and certainly not the perceptive analysis of the nature of his prototypes of totalitarian rule, as the use he makes of these premises in stipulating the distinctiveness of totalitarianism to the point of excluding any significant comparability between it *qua* ideology and other doctrines and their role in the political process. In the first place, Schapiro himself does not discount belief to varying degrees in totalitarian doctrines by their chief manipulators and their immediate associates, and this applies still more to the willing supporters of the regime. Surely there is a propinquity here between the stalwarts and other supporters of both totalitarian and pluralist doctrines and regimes, a propinquity which precludes the assumption of 'entirely distinct mental processes'. Moreover, although there is an enormous difference between manipulation by one central (terrorist) agency and by several competing agencies, it is undeniable that in both totalitarian and pluralist regimes, and not only in the first, as Leonard Schapiro maintains, doctrines are at once a guide to action and the instrument used to justify policies and institutions and thus ensure consent (not universal belief); as such, doctrines generally are an instrument for the manipulation of spontaneity. The *monopoly* of manipulation, and the *universally and overtly enforced* pretence of belief and dissimulation of disbelief and dissent, constitute a qualitative difference between totalitarian and pluralist doctrines in so far as these characteristics derive from the specific content of totalitarian doctrines: the association of the rejection inherent in all doctrines of the validity of all others with the denial of the right to propagate any other doctrine. It does not follow that, because these characteristics form part of the concurrent symptoms of a relatively new ideological syndrome, they obviate all important grounds of comparability and call for a new (restrictive) conception of ideology. Indeed, the demonstrable bifurcation into two dimensions is clearly further evidence of their structural and functional likeness, as well as of the general need and practice of manipulation.

26. For an example of argumentation in these terms by Ber Borochov at the beginning of the century in Russia, to make Zionism square with Marxism, see my 'Ideologie und Politik in Israel', 517–18.

27. *Kautsky, Die proletarische Revolution und ihr Programm* (Stuttgart and Berlin, 1922), p. vi. Kautsky also juxtaposed 'theoretical and action programme' (2). The former refers to '*die dauernden Grundsätze*' (the lasting fundamentals). For his use of '*Endziel*', and its pairing with '*Gegenwartsarbeit*' and '*Kleinarbeit*', see e.g. 'Die Revision des Parteiprogrammes der Sozialdemokratie in Österreich', 69.

28. 'Certain features in the Historical Development of Marxism', *Zvezda* (January 1911–23 December 1910), S.W.I., p. 481.

29. 'On Co-operation', *Pravda* (26/27 May 1923), S.W. II, pp. 830, 831, 832.

30. Lenin acknowledged, like Bernstein, that much in reality confounded the premises of the theory (*ibid.*).

31. N. Rotenstreich, *Basic Problems of Marx's Philosophy* (Indianapolis, New York and Kansas City, 1965), p. 49.

32. S. Avineri, *The Social and Political Thought of Karl Marx* (Cambridge, 1968), p. 138.

33. Schurmann, *Ideology and Organization in Communist China*, p. 22. The common-sense use of 'practical' can in all probabliity be attributed to the founders themselves. Kautsky, *Die proletatische Revolution*, p. 64, used 'practical' in respect of that part of the party programme which, unlike the theoretical part, is concerned not with final goals but with immediate steps.

34. Schurmann, *op. cit.*, p. 493.

35. S. H. Barnes, 'Italy: Opposition on Left, Right and Centre', in Dahl, *Political Opposition*, pp. 317–33.

36. Schapiro, *op. cit.*, pp. 206, 198, 208, 215 ff. See also the account of NEP in E. H. Carr, *The Bolshevik Revolution* (London, 1950–3), Vol. II, Chapter XIX; and R. V. Daniels, *The Conscience of the Revolution* (New York, 1960), who deals with the revolutionary opposition to the Revolution.

37. Schurmann, *op. cit.*, p. 349.

38. A. G. Meyer, *Communism* (New York, 1960; 4th repr. 1962), p. 3, seems to make the assumption alongside his otherwise well-balanced judgments. But in *Leninism*, pp. 81, 86, Meyer also avers that the 'minimum programme' and 'the pre-occupation with methods of control' (even though these, too, flow from ideological considerations) entail that 'the means' turn into absolutes, and the end, at least for the time being, becomes a mere myth. On the confusion and contradictions concerning the relationship between the official ideological system and the decisions of the Soviet leaders, see also Fleron Jr. and MacKelly *op. cit.*, 297, and the literature cited there.

39. R. Loewenthal, 'Ideology and Power Politics: A Symposium', *Problems of Communism*, Vol. VII, 2 (1957), 10 ff.

40. The terms are adopted from Dahl's 'Patterns of Opposition', in *Political Opposition*, p. 341.

41. The reader who does not find the abstract-formal explanation of figures and diagrams helpful, especially the more complex ones 5a-b, 6a-b, can disregard them and skip the text between Figures 5a and 5b.

42. Birnbaum, 'The Sociological Study of Ideology', 95, reports that the distinction has been considered as a possible model for the analysis of the internal structure of ideologies. There is also the analogy drawn by Piaget between his genetic epistemology and the analysis of ideology (sociocentric thought) (*ibid.*, 101, 137). The snare here again lies in not paying sufficient attention to the different structure and function of ideology in the personality system and in the activity of groups. See above, pp. 100–2. For a brief comment on the bearing of certain elements of Freud's theories on problems arising in the theory of ideology, see Lenk, *Ideologie*, pp. 30 ff.

43. L. Festinger, 'The Theory of Cognitive Dissonance', in W. Schramm (ed.), *The Science of Human Communication* (London and New York, 1963), p. 18, and L. Festinger, *A Theory of Cognitive Dissonance* (Evanston, Ill., 1957), pp. 4, 7.

44. S. Ossowski, *Class Structure in the Social Consciousness* (London, 1963), pp. 154, 152, 98 ff., 110 ff., 136 ff.

45. Bendix, *Work and Authority*, p. 4.

46. A principle may be the same in both dimensions, but in the operative dimension it underlies, and is in this sense part of, detailed measures of policy.

47. *The Politics of Aristotle*, III, ix, 1–4 (1280a, 22).

48. C. A. R. Crosland, 'The Transition from Capitalism', in R. H. S. Crossman (ed.), *New Fabian Essays* (London, 1952), p. 63. See also, *ibid.*, R. Jenkins, 'Equality', p. 76.

49. For details and analysis see V. O. Key, Jr, *Southern Politics in State and Nation* (New York, 1949), and more recently, Riker, *Democracy in the United States*, pp. 38 ff., 51 ff., 82.

50. Braybrooke and Lindblom, *A Strategy of Decision*, pp. 44 f., 69–70. For a more recent treatment see Y. Dror, 'Comprehensive Planning: Common Fallacies Versus Preferred Features', in F. van Schlagen (ed.), *Essays in Honour of Professor Jac. P. Thijsee* (The Hague, 1967), pp. 85–99, and Dror's comprehensive *Public Policymaking Re-examined* (San Francisco, 1968).

51. Lowi, *op. cit.*, 9, 10. On the problem in general, see H. S. Kariel, *The Decline of American Pluralism* (Stanford, 1961). For the proliferation and dispersion of 'sites' in which democratic bargaining is practised, see S. Rokkan, 'Numerical Democracy and Corporate Pluralism', in Dahl, *Political Opposition*, pp. 70 ff.

52. For the fact that, on principle, as yet undemocratic liberalism admitted of doing the same, see Seliger, *The Liberal Politics of John Locke*, pp. 179 ff.

53. Lowi, *op. cit.*, 22, 20, and *loci* referred to in note 10.

54. Further examples of adaptation and re-adaptation including direct and indirect restoration of coherence, will form part of the discussion in Chapters VII and VIII.

55. See above, pp. 177–8.

56. See above, pp. 92–4, and the next sub-section.

57. On Locke's awareness of this and on his attempt to enlist the support of conservative theorists for his defence of the right revolution, see Seliger, *op. cit*, pp. 254–6.

58. I have somewhat enlarged on these points in my 'Locke and Marcuse—Intermittent and Millennial Revolutionism', *Festschrift für Karl Loewenstein* (Tübingen, 1971), pp. 427 f., 430–1, 434–5, and also in S. E. Finer and M. Seliger, 'Political Roles of Violence', Position Paper of the General Reporters, Commission 1.10, IXth IPSA World Congress (Montreal, 1973).

59. The term 'führerism', introduced by R. C. Tucker, 'Towards a Comparative Politics of Movements-Regimes', *The American Political Science Review*, Vol. LV, 2 (1961), 281–9, not only refers to fascist rule but is also intended to denote one polar type of the relationship between a communist party and its leader. The other polar type is the 'Bolshevik' party in which a disciplined elite is connected with an elaborately organized mass following, and the party is not reduced to a mere tool in the hands of the leader. For an application of Tucker's distinction to the categorization of the roles of Lenin, Mussolini, Stalin, Hitler and Mao in relation to their parties, see L. Schapiro and J. B. Lewis, 'The Role of the Monolithic Party under the Totalitarian Leader', *The China Quarterly*, No. 40 (October-December 1969), 39–63.

60. Cp. H. Toch, *The Social Psychology of Social Movements* (Indianapolis, 1965), pp. 13 ff., 87 f.

61. On Michels's 'law of transgression', see above pp. 68 ff., and on 'the minimal winning coalition' below, pp. 251 ff.

62. I think that my findings on Locke in this point (see *loc. cit.*, in note 52) are almost universally applicable to the major liberal philosophers after him, with the possible exception of Herbert Spencer.

63. *Zur Judenfrage*, MEGA, I, I, p. 584. By way of compensation Marx commented critically in the same context upon 'the flagrant contradition' between revolutionary practice and its theory in regard to the declaration of the freedom of the press and its destruction by Robespierre, and other examples.

64. *Totalitarian Dictatorship and Autocracy* (2nd edn) p. 21. The 'syndrome' is elaborated on p. 22 and its components are then demonstrated in detail in separate chapters. In C. J. Friedrich, M. Curtis and B. R. Barber, *Totalitarianism in Perspective: Three Views* (New York, 1969), Friedrich's classic formulation is likewise discussed and defended in his contribution, where it is slightly altered (126) to account for recent changes and analyses. See also Schapiro, *Totalitarianism*, for an appreciation and criticism of the 'six-point-syndrome' for which he substitutes five 'contours' (general features) and three 'pillars' (instruments). See pp. 18–20, Chapters 2 and 3.

65. Friedrich points to de-bureaucratization as a result of loyalty to *Führer* and party being 'made the ultimate tests of official conduct' (*Totalitarian Dictatorship*, p. 214), and he is aware of the ineffectiveness of Nazi planning (277). But he does not accept (240–1) the

significance of Franz Neumann's distinction in *Behemoth* between a capitalist 'monopolistic' and 'command' economy in Nazi Germany.

66. *Nolte, Der Faschismus in seiner Epoche*, p. 504. 'National socialism was . . . the practical and violent resistance against transcendence', i.e. 'against the "beyond" in the nature of man' (507). See pp. 515 ff. on the problem of 'transcendence'.

67. See K. von Beyme, *Vom Faschismus zur Entwicklungsdiktatur—Machtelite und Opposition in Spanien* (München, 1972), p. 57, on 'the fascist drive of aggression', which in the absence of Jews turns against other minorities. Von Beyme creates, however, the impression that certain political postures adopted by Jews or their social role are sufficient explanation, if not reason, for countering with anti-semitism. Thus he says that, although the number of Jewish anti-fascists in Italy was well above the average, anti-semitism played a subordinate role. Must we infer that the opposite would have been more understandable? We learn also that 'for Germany Hitler exaggerated from his Austrian point of view the Jewish question as a social problem', as if, as far as Austria was concerned, Hitler's views were not 'exaggerated'. Knowing von Beyme personally and thinking of him as a friend, I find these probably inadvertent implications somewhat disturbing, since they have their inverted companion-piece in his earlier underplaying of the significance of the 'antiquated' anti-semitism of the brothers Mohl. Despite their anti-semitism and general racialist tendencies, von Beyme regards their liberalism as 'beyond any doubt' and draws the puzzling conclusion that, if realized earlier, their liberalism (albeit allied with racialism) might have nullified these precedents of 'later manifestations of the degeneration of political thought in Germany'. Robert von Mohl, *Politische Schriften, Eine Auswahl*, ed. by K. von Beyme (Koln-Opladen, 1966), pp. xxvii–viii.

68. Bendix, *Work and Authority*, pp. xviii, 191–2.

69. As revealed in *Hitler's Secret Conversations*, 1941–4 (ed. by H. R. Trevor-Roper, New York, 1953).

70. Friedrich and Brzezinski, *Totalitarian Dictatorship and Autocracy*, p. 114.

CHAPTER VII

1. The untenability of this proposition is demonstrated in Chapter VIII, 2b.

2. Hirschman, *Exit, Voice and Loyalty* (Cambridge, Mass., 1970), pp. 1 ff., 6 ff., and especially pp. 10–15.

3. As Hersch, *Idéologie et Réalité*, pp. 6 ff., suggests. In fact the author is aware of the contrasts between 'le front idéologique et le front de la lutte pratique' (5) and even between the real ideological fronts and the political divide between the parties (86).

4. Stokes, 'Spatial Models of Party Competition', in Campbell *et al.*, *Elections and the Political Order*, p. 170, in the course of his argument against Downs's unidimensional model (146 ff). Instead of 'multidimensional' I use 'multi-issue' model, since I have in the main reserved the term 'dimension' for my distinction between the strands of ideological argumentation.

5. In distinguishing between clarity on the programmatic level and ambiguity on the level that takes into account the prospect of joining a coalition, Downs, *An Economic Theory of Democracy*, p. 160, comes near the distinction between fundamental and operative ideology. Yet in making it only in the context of his treatment of coalition systems, the essential point of two-dimensionality is missed.

6. See above, pp. 203 ff.

7. Reasons for the justifiability of this particular distinction, despite well-known facts about the reactionary South etc., are implicit in the evidence and its judgment by political scientist that I have relied upon in Chapter IV, 1b. On cross-national comparability in general see above, note 12, Chapter III. See also Rokkan, *Citizens, Elections, Parties*, p. 335, who takes 'the relative universality' of the Left-Right polarisation as his cue in his appraisal of sample surveys carried out in 1953 of teachers' attitudes in seven Western countries. Rokkan points to the difficulties which the right-centre-left classification entails

where religious parties disturb cross-national comparability (337). Nevertheless, he concludes that the findings concerning some basic ideological orientations are comparable to the findings for both the United States and Great Britain. One can only support Rokkan's plea for more co-ordinated investigations in order to specify further correlations and varations. Even so, the applicability of the Left-Right divide seems in Rokkan's view to be serviceable in establishing cross-national, including cross-Atlantic comparability of broad but fundamental differences of party orientations. This much is confirmed by data which are already available, as well as by common-sense observation and historical evidence (which, after all, provide the basis for the questions we hope to answer by testing), as can be concluded from Rokkan's comprehensive and recently composed 'Nation-Building, Cleavage Formation and the Structuring of Mass Politics', 72–144. See also the indirect confirmation of cross-national comparability on this basis in variations of the Left-Right divide in the studies of J. A. Laponce, 'Note on the Use of the Left-Right Dimension', in *Comparative Political Studies*, Vol. II, 4 (1970), 481–502; 'The Use of Visual Space to Measure Ideology', in J. A. Laponce and P. Smoker (eds), *Experimentation and Simulation in Political Science* (Toronto, 1972), pp. 46–58, and 'In Search of the Stable Elements of the Left-Right Landscape', *Comparative Politics*, Vol. IV, 4 (1972), 455–75.

8. If averages and not extremes as well as frequency distribution of positions within parties are considered, the distance between the two American parties need by no means be assessed as smaller than the distance between the two British parties. See D. Butler's short remarks in 'The Paradox of Party Difference', in R. Rose, *Studies in British Politics* pp. 266–70.

9. Downs, *op. cit.*, p. 116, proposes the reduction and follows economic theory in so far as his model of 'rational' behaviour is predicted on means and never on ends (15). Nevertheless, the reduction is assumed to be ideologically meaningful. Since, notwithstanding qualifications concerning the unexceptional primacy of the nexus of self-interest and vote-maximizing, and despite admissions of the incongruence of the model with the real world, Downs adheres to vote-maximizing as the standard of rationality in a democracy, he offers not a theory of democracy but a sophisticated reductionist theory of voting and vote-getting. Moreover, his reduction of all issues to one, in his use of Hotelling's famous model of the spatial market, does not prevent him from arguing on a multi-issue basis even when he expands on the one-issue model (Chapter 8). However, he does not show how 'the many issues' in relation to which a party's net position on the left-right scale emerged as 'a weighted average of the positions occupied by each of its policy decisions' (141) can be equated with the position of a party regarding the one crucial issue of government intervention to which, he argues, all political questions can be reduced (116). Contrariwise, when Downs distinguishes between issues and ideological axioms on the basis that there are more of the former than of the latter (100), he does not allow for the possibility that this quantitative distinction need not mean a thing. Several issues—wage and race conflicts, for instance—are, after all, logically related to, and can be subsumed under, the same axiom, namely social equality or inequality.

10. Locke provides an example of such inconsistency in his justification of colonial conquest and slavery (see my *The Liberal Politics of John Locke*, pp. 114 ff.). He also shows that prominent features of the rationale of nationality and nationalism are embedded in the liberal theory of civil society (see my 'Locke, Liberalism and Nationalism', in J. W. Yolton (ed.), *John Locke: Problems and Perspectives* [Cambridge, 1969], pp. 19–33).

11. Cp. Lenin, *The Right of Nations to Self-Determination* (1914). Lenin here takes Rosa Luxemburg to task in what, to my mind, is a deliberate and entirely unfair (to her) confusion of issues, with the obvious aim of keeping all the options open for the Great Russian proletariat. 'We cannot vouch for any particular path', and it is not foreseeable what will happen to the Ukraine, although its right to form a state 'is beyond doubt'. Every national demand must be valued from the angle of the class struggle and 'the alliance of the proletarians of all nations'. S.W.I, pp. 576, 578–9.

12. See Appendix 4.

13. The last part of the statement has been confirmed meanwhile by the non-events of the *Yom-Kippur* War in October 1973.

14. Table 3 in Appendix 5 contains all issue scales.

15. This can be seen in detail in Table 1 (see above, p. 219), on which the other tables are based, whereas Table 2 (p. 219) contains the averages reproduced graphically on scales 1, 2, 3 and commented upon in the text.

16. See comment on issues 4–6.

17. The difference between the average of Fs and OIs of each party as listed in Table 2 and used in Scales 1 and 2 yields the average distance between the dimensions as follows: CP: 51.66—SDP: 25—LCP: 3.33—FP: 0.82.

CHAPTER VIII

1. Festinger, *A Theory of Cognitive Dissonance*, p. 278.

2. These intra- and inter-group relationships, which are most characteristic of politics and what is known about them even in hegemonic party systems, permit us to assume for certain that the hypothesis suggested by Hirschman, *Exit, Voice and Loyalty*, pp. 94–6, and Appendix E (written in collaboration with P. G. Zimbardo and M. Snyder), will prove true. Hirschman suggests an investigation of whether there are in normal conditions, or only under certain circumstances, ways other than self-deception for reducing or overcoming dissonance. He points to exit from the group or 'voice' (protest and incitement to remedial action for reorganization) as alternatives to self-deception. I hope it will emerge from this chapter that 'voice' and 'loyalty' are often joined in politics both to press for ideological change and to keep it within limits.

3. Downs, *An Economic Theory of Democracy*, p. 102.

4. M. Duverger, *Introduction à la politique*, p. 19. See also Downs, *op. cit.*, and W. H. Riker, *The Theory of Political Coalitions*, p. 99, who speaks of 'an artistically devised mixture of ambiguity and clarity'. Mackenzie's succinct account (*Politics and Social Science*, pp. 288, 290, 292) of language as a tool of politics and Bentham's view that vagueness might be a trick which occasionally can be as much of a virtue as precision, deserve special mention.

5. 'The Theory of Cognitive Dissonance', 18.

6. *Ibid.*, 22, and *A Theory of Cognitive Dissonance*, pp. 18–24. It would seem that the resolution of dissonance underlies the definition of ideology by E. H. Erikson, *Young Man Luther: A Study in Psycho-Analysis and History* (London, 1958), p. 22. Erikson defines ideology as 'an unconscious tendency ... to make facts amenable to [religious, scientific and political] ideas, and ideas to facts ... to support the collective and individual sense of identity' by a convincing world-image. Similarly Parsons, *The Social System*, p. 357, in regard to social movements. Cp. above, p. 30, and notes 9, 10, 27, and p. 34.

7. Gellner, *Words and Things*, pp. 164, 223 and 174. 'Two-tier' in Gellner's sense refers to the asymmetry between principles of equal standing (such as fundamentals), and is therefore not identical with my 'two-dimensional'. In his use of 'double-think' (*Thought and Change*, p. 79), he comes near a crucial aspect implicit in the notion of two-dimensionality mainly when he applies 'double-think' to change. On the one hand, he states that in 'the post-transitional' condition, that is, after a revolution, no totally new outlook emerges which would be in accordance with the deviations from the revolutionary creed, because old beliefs are nominally retained (81). On the other hand, he finds that in modern society there exists a dualism or a division of labour between 'symbolic unifying ideas ... once full-bloodedly cognitive' and 'the cognitively effective but normatively not very pregnant or insistent beliefs about the world' (125).

8. *Words and Things*, p. 223.

9. Hersch, *Idéologie et Réalité*, p. 88. I have somewhat modified the premises of Mme Hersch's conclusion.

10. 'Better Fewer, But Better', *Pravda*, 4 May 1923 SW, II, 844. *The Tax in Kind* (1921), SW, II, pp. 713–14, 717.

11. 'The Fourth Anniversary of the October Revolution', *Pravda*, 8 October 1921, SW, II, pp. 750, 752, 753, 749. My italics.

12. *Five Years of the Russian Revolution and the Prospects of World Revolution*, Report delivered at the fourth Congress of the Communist International, 13 November 1922, SW, II, pp. 810, 811, 819, 815. Already in 1919 Lenin admitted publicly that 'a long schooling side by side' with bourgeois experts would be necessary (II, p. 572). Eventually, he also conceded that the transition period would last years (II, 711–12).

13. 'Russia, India, China', SW, II, 854.

14. See G. Ionescu, 'Lenin, The Commune and the State—Thoughts for a Centenary', *Government and Opposition*, Vol. V, 2 (1970), 139 ff.

15. On the inherent reformism of the Erfurt Programme, see below, pp. 262–3.

16. 'The Chairman's Address', Report of the 55th Annual Conference (Blackpool, 1–5 October 1956, Transport House, London), p. 67. The italics are mine. For the relatively late change to such a pronounced reformist stance in the official party statements of the German SPD or the Swedish SAP, see Helenius, *The Profile of Party Ideologies*, pp. 39–48. Indeed, the first part of the SAP programme of 1960 quoted by Helenius (40–1) reads like a paraphrase of Keir Hardie's words of 1906.

17. See the NEC statement of 1960, approved by the Conference in the same year as a result of the attempt to annul Clause Four. See below, pp. 261–2, in connection with Crosland's article, referred to in the passages following in the text.

18. See, for instance, R. A. Butler, 'A Disraelian Approach to Modern Politics', in *Tradition and Change* (London, Conservative Political Centre, 1954), and *The Conservative Opportunity, Fifteen Bow Group Essays on Tomorrow's Toryism* (London, CPC, 1965).

19. *The New Conservatism* (London, CPC, 1955), p. 15. My italics. This quotation is taken from R. Bilski, *The Relations between Ideologies and Policies in the Debate about Comprehensive Schools, 1944–1970* (unpublished doctoral dissertation, The University of Glasgow, 1971), p. 325. Miss Bilski has also supplied me with the British material referred to in note 16 and the first item of note 18. In the text, the further examples of the ideological significance of the Conservatives' attitude towards education also come from her dissertation. I owe a debt of gratitude to Professor W. J. Mackenzie, who was Miss Bilski's supervisor, and who was interested enough in the conceptual framework of two-dimensional argumentation, which I had worked out by the end of 1967, to set Miss Bilksi, a former student and present colleague of mine, the task of testing in her case study the applicability and utility for comparative policy analysis of the detailed theoretical conclusions I had drawn from my more wide-ranging but more fragmentary observations. Miss Bilski's study provides all the detailed confirmation I could wish for. However, the merit of her work goes far beyond that. It presents a fascinating analysis of the application by the two parties—and the camps within them—of their conceptions of equality and social justice to the issue of education, which has become one of the most sensitive and crucial areas of the interplay between ideology and politics. See her articles: 'Ideology and the Comprehensive Schools', *The Political Quarterly* (March-April 1973), 197–211; 'Secondary Education and British Party Ideology', *Res Publica*, Vol. XVII (1975) and, with Y. Gal-Nur, 'Values and Ideologies in National Planning', in G. Sheffer (ed.), *Towards More Systematic Thinking on Israel's Future* (Jerusalem, 1974 [In Hebrew]).

20. E. Heath before the National Advisory Committee on Education, 17 June 1967. News Service, Central Office (unpublished), p. 6. 'Conservatives and Comprehensives', A Bow Group Memorandum by Simon Jenkins (London CPC, 1967), p. 8. For both items, see Bilski, *op. cit.*, p. 433.

21. Heath, 19, 2–3, respectively in Bilski. *op. cit.*, pp. 435, 431.

22. D. C. Hodges, 'The End of "The End of Ideology" ', Waxman, *op. cit.*, pp. 385, 387, on the basis of an inclusive conception of ideology, though in the sense of what I have tried to reveal elsewhere as the untenable Marxist dogmatic conception of ideology, i.e. 'the more or less conscious deception and disguises of human interest groups' (374).

23. Downs, *op. cit.*, pp. 117 ff.

24. See Hirschman, *op. cit.*, pp. 67–72, and S. M. Lipset, *Revolution and Counterrevolution: Change and Persistence in Social Structures* (New York, 1968).

25. Rose, 'Parties, Factions and Tendencies', 45.

26. M. Abrams, 'Party Politics After the End of Ideology', in Allardt and Littunen, *Cleavages, Ideologies and Party Systems*, p. 58.

27. R. E. Lane, 'The Politics of Consensus in an Age of Affluence', *The American Political Science Review*, Vol. LIX, 4 (1965), 882, 888. As to the consequences: 'the Age of Affluence produces, with occasional regression, political contests which do not jeopardise a person's income or economic security' (882). For a succinct evaluation of what the contents of consensus comprise in general terms and for its leaving room for ideological controversies, see Partridge, 'Politics, Philosophy, Ideology', 37–8.

28. On these and other fights and achievements, see P. Jacobs and S. Landau, *The New Radicals, A Report with Documents* (1st publ. 1966; Harmondsworth, 1967).

29. Lane, *op. cit.*, 893, and 'The Decline of Politics and Ideology in a Knowledgeable Society', 649 ff.; A. Campbell and H. Valen, 'Party Identification in Norway and the United States', in Campbell, Converse, Miller and Stokes, *Elections and the Political Order*, p. 267; and the majority of American political scientists, at least during the last decade, have so argued. So have many, if not most, British political scientists, and Mark Abrams (see note 26) is a much more characteristic example than Rose (see note 25). The view of Brunner ('Das Zeitalter der Ideologien', 201–18) of party programmes and coalitions as indicators of de-ideologization appears to be quite characteristic of the tendency prevailing in Germany during the fifties and sixties.

30. Meynaud, *Destin des Idéologies*, pp. 49, 126; and see above, pp. 45–6.

31. Bell, *The End of Ideology*, p. 283.

32. Bottomore, *Critics of Society*, p. 130.

33. *Ibid.*, pp. 130–1. This is another example of the pervasiveness of the semantics of 'the end of ideology'—and of its inherent illogicality, discussed in Chapter I.

34. Lane, *Political Ideology*, pp. 60 ff., for instance, on equality and liberty; on the connection between democracy, industrialization and government responsibility (246 ff.), and utopianism (202 ff.). See also *ibid.*, Chapters 25–7.

35. Converse, 'The Nature of Belief Systems in Mass Publics', 216.

36. *Ibid.*, p. 217.

37. See above, p. 161.

38. Quoted in Bell, *op. cit.*, p. 288, in the excellent chapter (12): 'The Failure of American Socialism'. See also Dahl's succinct account in *Pluralist Democracy*, Chapter 17, and for more extensive treatment, P. Taft, *Organized Labour in American History* (New York, 1964), and *The AFL in the Age of Gompers* (New York, 1957).

39. V. R. Lorwin, 'Reflections on the History of the French and American Labour Movements', *Journal of Economic History*, Vol. XVII, 1 (1957), 37.

40. Lane, *op. cit.*, p. 26.

41. See Almond and Verba, *The Civic Culture*, p. 456. The quotation is on p. 457.

42. In 1942, J. A. Schumpeter, *Capitalism, Socialism and Democracy* (1st edn, 1942; 3rd edn, Harper Torchbooks, 1962), p. 66, tried to show that 'if capitalism repeated its past performance for another half century starting with 1928', that is, maintained a rate of economic growth of 2 per cent, not only would poverty be eliminated but all reformist desiderata 'would be fulfilled automatically' (69). In general terms Auguste Comte anticipated the standpoint that class conflicts can be resolved without challenging the insitution of private property, a view which causes Marcuse to prefer Hegel to Comte. See my 'Locke and Marcuse—Intermittent and Millenial Revolutionism', 445–6.

43. Braybrooke and Lindblom, *A Strategy of Decision*, p. 72, and Abrams, *op. cit.*, 62. Since Abrams is aware of sharp differences among voters, on a very limited number of issues (59), and agrees that the parties in Britain are committed to conflicting positions that offer the voter a genuine choice (63), his distinction between 'mundane' and 'ideological' issues and politics (60, 62) must be said to imply the identification of 'ideological' with 'controversial'.

44. Braybrooke and Lindblom, *op. cit.*, p. 71. Cp. also p. 102.

45. Substantially the same objection applies to Braybrooke and Lindblom's view that we are able to agree on what we are against without agreeing on what we are for (134). One can do the first without the second about some issues, but certainly not about all.

46. *Ibid.*, p. 73.

47. Thus, for instance, also Dahl, *Pluralist Democracy*, pp. 357 ff., 368, 488 ff., and Campbell *et al.*, *The American Voter*, p. 203.

48. McClosky *et al.*, 'Issue Conflict and Consensus', pp. 411, 415.

49. W. Brandt, *Pladoyer für die Zukunft* (Frankfurt, 1961), p. 71.

50. Helenius, *The Profile of Party Ideologies*, pp. 251–2.

51. W. Brandt, *Das Regierungsprogramm der SPD* (Bonn, 1961), p. 11, as reported in Helenius, *op. cit.*, p. 230.

52. Downs, *op. cit.*, p. 133, and Riker, *op. cit.*, p. 98.

53. See above, p. 162.

54. See above, pp. 70 f.

55. See above, pp. 200 f.

56. Riker, *op. cit.*, p. 33, See also p. 100.

57. Downs, *op. cit.*, p. 111.

58. Festinger, *A Theory of Cognitive Dissonance*, p. 20.

59. Hirschman, *op. cit.*, p. 72.

60. Riker, *op. cit.*, p. 33. Cp. also p. 100.

61. Riker, *op. cit.*, p. 23.

62. Downs, *op. cit.*, pp. 111–12, 145. Cp. pp. 26, 51, 96, 101. '. . .clearly [*sic*!] if everyone knew which type of ideology would win, all parties would adopt it . . .' (145). '. . . if elections are preference polls, voting is irrational. . .' (154). Downs, who insists on self-interest as the motivation of seeking office (287), merely does not exclude the possibility that self-interest can take the form of competing for reputation for service, altruism and social responsibility (291–2).

63. *Ibid.*, p. 140. As emerges from the comments of Polsby and Wildavsky, *Presidential Elections*, Chapter 4, the successful efforts to get the Republican Party to nominate Goldwater were sustained by his 'purist' supporters' aim to move voters towards the principles maintained by Goldwater, even at the risk of losing the election. Moreover, although Polsby and Wildavsky adduce a number of specific circumstances in order to explain how Goldwater succeeded in securing nomination, they also conclude that the image of politicians is changing, greater stress than hitherto being laid on 'idealism and issue orientation' (191). Cp. above, p. 130.

64. Hirschman, *op. cit*,, pp. 64–5.

65. Riker, *op. cit.*, p. 100, is aware of the problems raised by the existence of other factors but holds that opinion leaders 'can easily slip between the horns of the dilemma' (112). This tactical view of the matter is different from the texture of the view pervading his *Democracy in the United States*. He effects some realignment, for after concluding that 'no rules of balance can be formulated for n-persons zero-sum games' (169), he also stresses that moral and institutional restraints are needed to moderate instability and to prevent the elimination of losers (175). Yet this is actually to evade the kernel of the whole problem, which is the relationship between the criterion of maximizing votes, i.e. of 'the larger pay-off', and the extent of ideological stability in terms of fidelity to some fundamentals and policies that reflect them.

66. Riker, *ibid.*, Cp. Downs, *op. cit.*, pp. 97 ff., 136.

67. On the all-too-often neglected differences between the East European regimes, see G. Ionescu, *The Politics of the European Communist States* (New York, 1967), especially Part III on trends of dissensus.

68. On this group see the apt summary of Christoph, 'Consensus and Cleavage in British Ideology', pp. 640–2.

69. B. Chapman, *The British Government Observed* (London, 1963).

70. The brothers G. and D. Cohn-Bendit, *Obsolete Communism, The Left-Wing Alternative*

(transl. by A. Pomerans, Penguin Special, 1969), can lay no claim to any novel conclusions except for the role assigned to students in the revolutionary process. On Marcuse in this context, see my 'The One-Dimensionality of Herbert Marcuse—The Old Style of the New Left', *passim.* I do not deny that Marcuse and others also face new problems and modify old dogmas. But more often than not they are at pains to present on the basis of highly selective textual evidence what are modifications of the original doctrine as its essential meaning. Leftist ideologies of the Third World are different in this respect. See, for instance, F. Fanon, *The Wretched of the Earth* (transl. by C. Farrington, London, 1965), pp. 32–3. For perhaps even more striking examples see Andrain, 'Democracy and Socialism: Ideologies of African Leaders', 115–205.

71. As a leader of the students' majority in Britain remarked, 'no society could tolerate a selfish, educational elite, supported by the tax-payer and protected from the realities of life, parading a cause of self-interest, imagined grievances, in the pursuit of power for power's sake. . . . More has been done over the last ten years by student leaders quietly fighting the battle . . . than by any of the head-line makers of recent months . . .' quoted in J. Gould, 'Politics and the Academy', *Government and Opposition*, Vol. III, 1 (1968), 40–1. See also *ibid.*, K. Sontheimer, 'Student Opposition in Western Germany', and the literature cited in both articles. See further K. Hermann, 'The End of the Revolt?', *Encounter*, Vol. XXXI (September 1968), 57–60; R. Nisbet, 'Who killed the Student Revolution?', *ibid.* Vol. XXXIV (February 1970), 10–18, and E. Gellner, 'Myth, Ideology and Revolution', in B. Crick and W. A. Robson (eds), *Protest and Discontent* (Harmondsworth, 1970), pp. 204–20.

72. Steck, 'The Re-emergence of Ideological Policies', 92 ff.

73. Regarding the Weimar Republic, Sontheimer, 51, concludes: 'Had it been left to the German students to decide the course of German politics, democracy in Germany would long before Hitler . . . have had some kind of authoritarian regime.' As to the present, Sontheimer stresses the coincidence of democracy, welfare and national prestige in Western Germany. Since this applies elsewhere it is likewise of general significance, and connects the present and the past, that the activism of students in countries like the USA, Britain and Western Germany is directed against a liberal-democratic establishment. Therefore, the findings of the Frankfurt Institute of Social Research that the democratic potential of German students is not reliable enough need as little be unqualifiedly restricted to Western Germany as Sontheimer's conclusion that the students 'do not constitute a democratic elite . . . although they like to raise that claim' (*ibid.*, 61) and that it is not at all certain that 'student power' will stay predominantly left-wing (67).

74. R. C. Tucker, 'The Deradicalization of Marxist Movements', *The American Political Science Review*, Vol. LXI, 2 (1967), 350, 352.

75. C. A. R. Crosland, 'The Future of the Left', *Encounter*, Vol. XIV (March 1960), 11. For Crosland's allegiance to the goal of the classless society, see his *The Future of Socialism* (London, 1956), p. 115. The goal, which is not mentioned in Crosland's 'Social objectives for the 1970s' (see above, pp. 237–8), is not precluded by these objectives from serving as a long-range commitment.

76. Hamburger, *Intellectuals in Politics*, p. 53.

77. Mannheim, *Ideology and Utopia*, p. 53.

78. R. T. McKenzie, *British Political Parties, The Distribution of Power Within the Conservative and Labour Parties* (1955; 2nd edn, paperback, London, 1967), p. 606. The data used in the following analysis are on pp. 607–12. On the controversy in the Labour Party over the nationalization of the means of production, see W. A. Robson, *Nationalized Industry and Public Ownership* (London, 1960), esp. pp. 460–94.

79. For the text of the NEC statement, see Helenius, *op. cit.*, p. 90.

80. Stadler, *Karl Marx: Ideologie und Politik* (Göttingen, Frankfurt and Zürich, 1966), pp. 121 f.

81. Cole, *A History of Socialist Thought*, II, pp. 425–34, III, I, pp. 276, 295 f.

82. *Die proletarische Revolution*, pp. 3, 64.

83. On the Bad Godesberg Programme in the context of West German post-war

politics, see A. Grosser, *L'Allemagne de notre temps, 1945–1970* (Paris, 1970), pp. 267 f.

84. See above, pp. 256–7. In Britain, E. Powell, *A New Look at Medicine and Politics* (London, 1966), criticizes as his wont, the defects typical in his view of a nationally organized and financed institution, such as the Health Service. But, acknowledging that people have become used to it, he refrains from suggesting something radically different.

85. The emphasis here is, of course, on democracy, since multi-party systems can coexist with an oligarchic order, and parliamentarism preceded modern democracy.

86. As shown above, pp. 199 f., 227 ff., respectively.

EPILOGUE

1. Lipset, 'Political Change in "Developed" and "Emerging" Polities', in Allardt and Littunen, *op. cit.*, p. 40.

2. See my 'Ideologie und Politik in Israel'. The points mentioned here, and others, have been treated at some length in that paper and also in 'Positions and Dispositions in Israeli Politics'.

3. The obverse view is presented by Lipset, 'Some Further Comments on "The End of Ideology" ', 117, as one of the 'specific testable propositions' emerging from the literature by experts from various countries.

4. This is the main reason why 'tous les partis de quelque importance sont incorporé en permanence à la coalition gouvernementale, tant à l'échelon fédéral que cantonal' (R. Girod, 'Le Système des Partis en Suisse', *Revue Française de Science Politique*, XIV, 6 [1964], 1114). See also *idem*, 'Geography of the Swiss Party System', in Allardt and Littunen, *op. cit.*, 132–52, and the particularly enlightening case-study of E. Gruner, 'Die Jurafrage als Problem der Minderheit in der Schweizerischen Demokratie', *Civitas*, Vol. XXIII, 7 (March 1968), 523–37.

5. S. N. Eisenstadt, 'Bureaucratization, Markets, and Power Structure', in Allardt and Littunen, *op. cit.*, 248 ff., 254. See also Eisenstadt, *Essays on Sociological Aspects of Political and Economic Development* (The Hague, 1961).

6. Sartori, *Democratic Theory*, p. 455.

Appendix 1
A Bibliographical Sample

For definitions of ideology as action-oriented irrespective of the nature of its aims, see, for instance: K. Loewenstein, 'Political Systems, Ideologies, and Institutions: The Problem of their Circulation', *The Western Political Quarterly*, Vol. VI, 4 (1953), 691; S. P. Huntington, 'Conservatism as an Ideology', *The American Political Science Review*, Vol. LI, 2 (1957), 454; J. Touchard (ed.), *Histoire des Ideés Politiques* (Paris, 1959); M. Rokeach, *The Open and the Closed Mind—Investigations into the Nature of Belief Systems and Personality Systems* (New York, 1906), pp. 4 ff., 13 and *passim*; J. Meynaud, *Destin des Idéologies* (Lausanne, 1961), pp. 11–12, 14; K. Lenk, *Ideologie, Ideologiekritik und Wissenssoziologie* (Neuwied and Berlin, 1961; repr. 1967), Introduction and Epilogue; D. G. MacRae, *Ideology and Society* (London, 1961), pp. 64 f; D. Minar, 'Ideology and Political Behaviour', *The Midwest Journal of Political Science*, Vol. V, 4 (1961), 326, 330; P. H. Partridge, 'Politics, Philosophy, Ideology', *Political Studies*, Vol. IX, 3 (1961), repr. in A. Quinton (ed.), *Political Philosophy* (Oxford, 1967), pp. 34, 42–5; E. R. Lane, *Political Ideology*, pp. 14–15; C. J. Friedrich, *Man and His Government* (New York, San Francisco, Toronto and London, 1963), p. 89; Apter, Bendix and Geertz, in D. E. Apter (ed.), *Ideology and Discontent*, pp. 16–17, 297 and 53, 63, 71 respectively; J. Barion, *Was ist Ideologie?* (Bonn, 1964), pp. 8, 45, 90 ff.; J. Gould and W. L. Kolb (eds) *A Dictionary of the Social Sciences* (New York, 1964), p. 315; W. Delany, 'The Role of Ideology: A Summation' (1964), in C. I. Waxman, *The End of Ideology Debate* (New York, 1968), pp. 296, 300; M. Duverger, *Introduction à la politique* (Paris, 1964), pp. 138 ff; J. Dunner (ed.) *Dictionary of Political Science* (New York, 1964), pp. 250–1; F. M. Watkins, *The Age of Ideologies—Political Thought, 1750 to the Present* (Englewood Cliffs, 1964), pp. viii, 7 ff., 103; C. Bay, 'Politics and Pseudopolitics: A Critical Evaluation of Some Behavioural Literature', *The American Political Science Review*, Vol. LIX, 1 (1965), 40, 42, 44; J. B. Christoph, 'Consensus and Cleavage in British Political Ideology', *The American Political Science Review*, Vol. LIX, 3 (1965), 629–30; P. Corbett, *Ideologies* (London, 1965), pp. 11–13, 138; A. G. Meyer, 'The Functions of Ideology in the Soviet Political System', *Soviet Studies*, Vol. XVII, 3 (1966), 272 f.; Joravsky, *ibid.*, Vol. XVIII, 1 (1966), 3, 4, 7, 15–16 (his controversy with Meyer does not seem to extend to the inclusiveness of the term ideology); J. LaPalombara, 'Decline of Ideology: A Dissent and an Interpretation', *The American Political Science Review*, Vol. LX, 1 (1966), 7; W. E. Connolly, *Political Science and Ideology* (New York, 1967), pp. 2, 49, 50–4, 78; S. H. Barnes, 'Political Ideology and Political Behaviour', originally publ. as 'Ideology and the Organization of Conflict . . .', *The Journal of Politics*, Vol. XXVIII (1966), repr. in R. H.

Cox (ed.), *Ideology, Politics and Political Theory* (Belmont, Cal., 1969), p. 349; C. B. Macpherson, 'Revolution and Ideology', in C. J. Friedrich (ed.), *Revolution. Nomos* X (New York), in Cox, *op. cit.*, p. 301–2, and J. J. Wiatr, 'Sociology—Marxism—Reality', *Social Research*, Vol. XXXIV, 3 (1967), 426–7 (for the acceptance respectively by a Western and a Polish Marxist scholar of the inclusive conception in acknowledged deviation from Marx); A. J. Gregor, *Contemporary Radical Ideologies—Totalitarian Thought in the Twentieth Century* (New York, 1968), p. 8; N. Harris, *Beliefs in Society, The Problem of Ideology* (London, 1968), pp. 22, 41 f., 266; Cox, *op. cit.*, pp. 79 ff., 179 ff. (In his introduction Cox also quotes political statements made in the USA during the 1950s. Although they are not adduced for this purpose, these statements reveal the use of the inclusive conception.); R. Helenius, *The Profile of Party Ideologies* (Helsinki, 1969), pp. 3 f., 8 ff. and *passim*; E. Hölze, *Idee und Ideologie, Eine Zeitkritik aus universalhistorischer Sicht* (Bern and München, 1969), pp. 141 ff., 161 ff., for the situation in Germany; J. Plamenatz, *Ideology* (London, 1970), pp. 15, 31, 72, 76. Drucker, *The Political Uses of Ideology*. Some of these scholars show ambivalence or changes of position, as will be noted in the course of our discussion.

For some scholars who as a matter of act presuppose the inclusive definition, see, in Britain, R. T. McKenzie, *British Political Parties* (1st edn, 1955; paperback edn, London, 1967) p. v, and R. Rose, 'Parties, Factions and Tendencies in Britain', *Political Studies*, Vol. XII, (1964), 39, and the contributors to R. Benewick, R. N. Berki, B. Parekh (eds), *Knowledge and Belief in Politics, The Problem of Ideology* (London, 1973). As to American scholars, see, for instance, A. Downs, *An Economic Theory of Democracy* (New York, 1957; paperback repr., 1965), p. 96; P. E. Converse, 'The Nature of Belief Systems in Mass Publics', in Apter, *op. cit.*, pp. 211, 220, 222, 234, 237, as well as other contributors; or such standard works as A. Campbell, P. E. Converse, W. Miller and D. Stokes, *The American Voter* (New York, 1960); S. J. Eldersveld, *Political Parties: A Behavioural Analysis* (Chicago, 1964); V. O. Key, Jr, *The Responsible Electorate* (Cambridge, Mass., 1966), and N. W. Polsby and A. B. Wildavsky, *Presidential Elections, Strategies of American Electoral Politics* (New York, 1964; 2nd edn, 1968). See also R. E. Agger, D. Goldrich and B. E. Swanson, *The Rulers and the Ruled—Political Power and Impotence in American Communities* (New York, London and Sidney, 1964), for an examination of American local politics in terms of ideological controversy. For a Scandinavian scholar of international standing, see the former associate of Naess, S. Rokkan, *Citizens, Elections, Parties: Approaches to the Comparative Study of the Processes of Development* (Oslo, 1970), e.g. Chapter X (originally prepared in 1956) and *passim*.

I need perhaps not stress that, even in the first part of this note, the references are intended to be representative only but not exhaustive. In the absence of agreement, or rather a systematic clarification of the issue, it has become a habit for many writers to define what they mean by ideology without justifying the definition. Even to locate all those who use the inclusive definition would therefore involve a very extended and intrinsically unprofitable search. The same applies to a still greater extent to the documentation of the use of the restricted definition. References to both usages, to scholars who have elaborated on the restrictive definition, and to characteristic methods of its application, will be made during our discussion in Part I.

Appendix 2
Rich and Poor Belief Systems – Fixed and Firm Beliefs

1. Considering the belief systems of organized groups, one cannot, like Sartori *op. cit.*, 407, in following Dahl, 'Ideology, Conflict and Consensus', 3, simply take it for granted that belief systems *qua* 'isms' are classifiable, like the belief systems of individuals, as relatively rich or poor, according to the number of belief elements they contain. My conjecture is that quantitative comparison of political doctrines would as little confirm such a distinction as a closer look at liberalism and Marxism confirms the former's inferiority in terms of comprehensiveness, etc. (See text, pp. 139 ff.)

2. I use 'fixed' principles for the fundamentals of all political belief systems. Sartori's distinction between 'fixed' and 'firm' principles, which refers to the emotive as distinct from the cognitive plane, is untenable. In the first place, it is of interest to note that Dahl ('Ideology, Conflict, and Consensus', 3), who associates *cognitively* 'open' with 'firm' elements and *cognitively* 'closed' with 'fixed' elements, neither gives a detailed explanation of the nature of 'firm' elements, nor refers to them again after having placed them in different positions in a figure. Here and elsewhere, Dahl uses only 'fixed' in connection with all ideologies. Sartori produces no example of doctrinal principles for which his purely definitional elaboration on Dahl (*op. cit.*, 404, 409) could be seen to apply. I can think only of examples which controvert the distinction. 'Fixed elements' said to distinguish ideological belief systems (i.e. those which are 'rigid, dogmatic, impermeable to argument and evidence', and 'subject only to traumatic change under conditions of great stress' (404) are to be found not only in ideologies like Marxism, but also in liberalism, which Sartori considers as a near non-ideology. If doctrinal propositions like the socialization of the means of production and distribution represent a 'fixed element', as I take it Sartori would confirm, there is no earthly reason why we should not claim the same for the sanctity of private property. To classify the latter as one of the 'firm' elements (i.e., those which are 'firmly held . . . open to evidence and/or argument . . . tend to be persistent', but 'are not impermeable and are, therefore, changeable at least in principle'), does not really establish a difference. Where either of the two forms of ownership is preponderant there have been deviations from it; and if this involved 'traumatic change' in the case of NEP, it is hard to see why the same did not apply to British Conservatives' cessation of wholesale reversal of Labour's nationalizations. According to Dahl and Sartori's terms of definition, a deviation from a 'fixed' element turns it into a 'firm' element. This transformation invalidates the definition, for if 'fixed elements can become 'firm', then they are, by definition, not 'fixed'. Hence,

unless concrete examples are produced or different doctrinal principles which have been consistently maintained by a political party in or near power according to the definitions of either 'fixed' or 'firm' elements, the distinction (which in any case has little lexicographical foundation) does not provide any support for opposing in the emotive context open-pragmatic and closed-ideological belief systems.

Appendix 3
Ideology: Operative and Inoperative, by Purpose and Function, Manifest and Latent

1. In contrast to Scalapino's reference to Japanese conservatism, Harris approaches his treatment of British conservatism, as well as his examination of the similarities between the latter and developments in Marxism-Leninism (*Beliefs in Society*, pp. 143 and *passim*), with the Hegelian-sounding proposition that in conservative thought, 'the ideal is broadly the real' (*op. cit.*, 124). He improvidently stipulates that, unlike radical ideals, conservative ideals are 'inoperative, they entail no specific action' (141). Obviously, quite specific actions are required to maintain any version of the ideal = real, and these are clearly the subject matter of the specific problems which, according to Harris, 'generate tensions within the orthodoxy' and 'conflicting prescriptions within the common inheritance' which, if they persist, cause 'inconsistent positions' to be advanced simultaneously (141). Harris does not show anywhere in his book that the purpose of any kind of political prescription and position is not specification of desirable action, nor that, unlike radical ideals, conservative ideals never, or only rarely, require formalized theoretical exposition. He eventually qualifies this thesis by saying that 'the distinction between passive or "non-operative" and "operative" beliefs *partly* [my italics] relates to conservative and radical' (232), and even admits that 'in practice, our imaginary conservative and radical do not exist' (243). The distinction between 'passive and operational beliefs' is not given up altogether but is seen to apply clearly to personal beliefs, whereas 'in the context of ideologies which presuppose beliefs shared by a social group', it is in practice 'impossible to separate passive and operational very clearly' (233). Harris then modifies the initial proposition and attributes 'a peculiarly high proportion of non-operative beliefs' to conservative doctrines, and 'a high proportion of operative beliefs' to radical theories (233). He demonstrates the modified proposition as little as his initial one, but the former permits us to attribute to him awareness of the the coexistence of operative and inoperative beliefs in all ideologies —in different proportions, though. For my objections to Harris's unacknowledged elaboration on Mannheim and Huntington's view, that conservatism requires no general social theory, or if so, then not as an essential part of it, see above, pp. 60, 92, 95–6.

2. King suggests calling a system of political ideas 'ideology by purpose', and a programme of government or of political action designed to criticize the government 'ideology by function' ('The Ideological Fallacy' 350–2, 355). What King has in mind is not accurately conveyed in these terms, for he wishes to distinguish between intended and actual application, which, as he says, are ordinarily both comprised in the term 'ideology'. He notes that he uses it in this sense except when

he wishes to distinguish between intended and actual application. Obviously, a programme of political action may be nearer to action than a system of political ideas, but strictly speaking intended action applies to both, since a system of political ideas is usually intended for actual application. Moreover, there is no actual without intended application, only intended without actual. Still, a distinction is indicated which could be considered similar to that between a fundamental dimension (intended application) and an operative dimension (actual application), the more so as King takes into account the manipulations and explanations which are required to show that practice conforms with principles and goals (354). King does not engage in any systematic elaboration of the interaction between the two 'applications'. Indeed, his advance towards the notion of two-dimensionality, like his advance towards the inclusive conception of ideology (see text pp. 59–60), is blocked by assertions which are as inconsistent as they are ill-founded. While the possibility of their contradiction is implicit within the terms (if it be not one of the reasons) of King's distinction of intended and actual application—what he calls 'ideology by purpose' and 'ideology by function'—he suddenly asserts that contradictoriness is an indication of unideological attitudes (365). (He says this after having castigated H. Arendt for her pre-occupation with logical coherence [345], without making clear that she is, in fact, preoccupied with a logic of ideology different from the logic of science.) Colonial government is King's example for contradictoriness's signifying an unideological attitude. Having appraised nationalism as an ideology (366), he would be all the more hard put to it to demonstrate that justifications of colonial rule, like 'the white man's burden' and 'indirect rule' (not to mention 'fraternal intervention'), are unideological because (or rather if) they are inconsistent with the attitudes and doctrinal postures the colonialists or imperialists otherwise practise and/or profess. King also maintains that explanatory manipulation and its smokescreen effect arise only when states or groups become fissiparous (357). The evidence already referred to in connection with the notion of two-dimensionality, and the elaborations in the present and following chapter, confirm what any common-sense observation indicates, that explanatory smokescreening is part of political activity and argumentation in all known situations of *vis politica*.

3. Apparently unaware that Feuerbach used 'manifest' and 'latent' to designate respectively the surface meaning of Hegelianism and its underlying esoteric meaning (*Kleine philosophische Schriften*, p. 58), Helenius uses these terms in order to distinguish between 'the manifest party ideology', appearing in 'programmes and documents of principle of a more formal character', and 'the latent party ideology', revealed in the ' "unofficial" party literature in the form of conference reports, pamphlets, speeches, etc.'. While the use of 'official' and 'unofficial' is not quite precise (a conference report is, after all, an official party document), Helenius means that views are 'latent' as long as they are not officially adopted by the party (*The Profile of Party Ideologies*, pp. 8–9. Cp. pp. 149 ff., 157 ff., 180, etc.). 'Manifest' and 'latent' thus essentially designate the programmatic positions on specific policy issues sanctioned by the leadership, and other positions adopted by groups of a party.

Helenius's distinction is not focused on the relationship between officially maintained principles and those actually underlying policies. Therefore, while he does not assert that officially adopted principles are invariably translated into policies, his 'manifest ideology'—officially approved positions—partakes, in my terms, of both fundamental and operative ideology, though perhaps more of the latter than of the former. Helenius's 'latent' ideology—the views voiced by groups that disagree with official party ideology—may also be in the spirit of either fundamental or operative principles, and may exhibit, as much as its 'manifest' counterpart, the existence of discrepancies between fundamental and operative principles. According to whether the latter conform with or deviate from the former, 'latent' and 'manifest' ideology is purist or not. Indeed, for Helenius, 'latent', like my 'operative', is less 'rigid', 'freer', more 'dynamic' and 'transformative', and yet, at the same time, like my 'fundamental' ideology, 'purer' than 'manifest' ideology, which reflects the convergence of party ideologies, or rather programmes (139, 299, 123). Helenius can regard 'latent' ideology as at once purer, less rigid and more transformative than 'manifest' ideology because the former is the welter of the diverse unofficial and counter-official views, some of which may eventually gain official recognition (or re-recognition); and such opinions can be rigid, pure, transformative and what not. Only when Helenius also calls the short-range decisions of party executives 'latent' (140), does his 'latent' correspond to my 'operative' ideology.

However, no precise parallel can be drawn, owing to the imprecision of Helenius's appraisals of what, following Jansson (note 3, p. 25), he calls two kinds of 'undervegetation'—*nomen est omen*, as the appraisal of short-range decisions of party executives as 'latent' ideology shows. Since the latter is assumed to be different from official party programmes, but decisions of party executives cannot be said to be unofficial, they cannot, on Helenius's own terms, represent 'latent' ideology. That he commits the lapse is connected with the view that 'the foremost function of the manifest party ideology' reveals itself in the discussions and resolutions concerning the revision of party programmes (28), for he stipulates, to my mind unconvincingly, that even where changes of 'the programmes of principle' are not only systematic but frequent, they can guide long-range party activity but 'seldom as such unilaterally . . . daily politics in a more direct way' (27). Apparently on this assumption he bases the assertion that short-range decisions of party executives belong to 'latent' ideology. The self-contradictoriness of this is supplemented by the implication that, although party programmes register changes of formerly held positions (and 'manifest' rather than 'latent' ideology reflects conformity between the parties [123]), daily politics converge less than the ever-changing and ever more converging 'programmes of principle' indicate. This hardly makes sense. One also wonders whether it is on the grounds that 'latent' ideology bears in the main on matters of 'practical politics' rather than of principles that the Fabian Society and left-wingers can be styled typical representatives of 'latent' ideology (149–53, 293).

Helenius's failure to relate 'manifest' and 'latent' ideology uniformly to actual party policies parallels his failure to adhere consistently to the inclusive conception (see above pp. 63–4). This is of interest here, since in distinguishing policies from ideology and speaking of the relation between 'practical ideology' and 'ideological practice' (he means and eventually uses 'political practice' [285]), Helenius comes nearest to discussing what I understand to be the problems arising out of the relationship between operative and fundamental ideology. For he comments in this context on the extent to which questions are and should be considered as 'tactical' or 'ideological', 'practical', 'urgent' or 'great' (287–97). However, precisely in facing such problems he falls back on the simple distinction between party ideology and political practice, i.e. on the separation of politics from ideology.

The distinction between 'manifest' and 'latent' ideology is purely formalistic, pertaining in the last resort neither to what is argued nor to what is done, nor to the relationship between the two, but to whether an issue is argued in official or unofficial party quarters. It is a measure of its lack of significance as an analytical tool that inconsistent applications of the distinction (which Helenius himself admits to be superficial [9]) do not in any way affect his convincing demonstration of the changes between 1920 and 1960 in the ideologies of the social-democratic parties and of their competitors in Sweden, Great Britain and Germany, or of the view that, although these ideologies converge on one another and consequently have become fissiparous, they have not ceased to be divided on matters of principle (e.g. pp. 100 ff., 119, 125, 130, 177, 246 ff., 299, 366, 376).

Appendix 4
The Co-ordination of Orientations with Numbers – a Caveat and a Justification

I wish to make it clear beyond any doubt that no attempt whatsoever at arithmetical quantification is involved. Were it possible to use scales and mark positions and their averages on them without using numbers expressing percentages, I should have done so. I am aware of the fact that at least specific objectives of governments which can be stated in economic terms 'in principle are capable of measurement (either ordinal or cardinal)' (E. D. Kirschen [ed.], *Economic Policy in Our Time*, 3 vols [Amsterdam, 1964], I, p. 3. I am indebted to Professor B. Frei of Konstanz-Basle who at a conference at Bellagio drew my attention to this book, as well as to Professor D. Rae of Yale who on the same occasion made suggestions concerning the concluding part of this note.)

Kirschen in the main deals with preferences as they show in actual policies (OI in my terms). At some point, he considers also 'a priori preferences' (which come near to my Fs) of three 'political families', i.e. Socialists, Centre and Conservatives (I, pp. 224 ff.), of the then eight Common Market countries (Luxemburg being often omitted) Norway, the UK and the USA. However, as against my concerns, the relationship between the two kinds of preference is not of central importance for Kirschen, nor is it the basis for reconsidering the Left-Right polarity. In the Appendix to Chapters I and IX, Kirschen suggests examples of mathematical formulations of objectives of economic policy. Yet in showing how 'a priori preferences', with which the various classes of policy-makers had to cope in eight countries, are related to the three 'political families', to which he adds three interest groups, Kirschen also uses the symbols + and – for affirmation and negation, = for indifference and ± for being divided on an issue (Table IX, 5, p. 242). In the synthesis of the preferences of objectives of economic policy as they were pursued in the several countries by the 'three families', he again uses symbols in order to demote the importance attached by the parties to each objective (D = dominant, S = significant, M = minor, N = negligible, H = hostile, pp. 226–7 and Table IX, 2).

J. Meisil, 'Recent Changes in Canadian Parties', in L. G. H. Thorburn (ed.), *Party Politics in Canada* (2nd edn, Scarborough, 1957), p. 43, in an admittedly tentative outline of 'a general descriptive schema which will permit the comparison of parties' in 'their full splendour . . . within one or more political systems' (42), applies, like myself, 'a very rough quantitative expression' (43). He scores 'on a scale from 1 (low) to 5 (high)' party ideology (one of six 'aspects' of comparison) under four sub-headings. Only one, 'Role of State' i.e. Downs's criterion, is taken to indicate whether 'a party is on the left or right' (42). Scorings are allocated according to three criteria: the degree of correspondence between 'the party's avowed position' and its performance, the degree of consensus within a party on an issue, and the intensity of a party's concern over an issue. Only the first criterion, which could comprise the third, poses the problem underlying the notion of two-dimensionality, but in terms which imply that a politically significant performance need not be connected with some kind of 'avowal', i.e. explanation and justification. Meisil does not follow the same procedure in expressing assessments of the six general 'aspects' of inter-party comparison. Even for the 'aspect' ideology he uses symbols (+, −, o) in conjunction with numbers, to indicate change and trend (44). The symbols are used only once more for another 'aspect', yet not with the numerical scale. Its quantitative measures are applied to three out of six 'aspects' but not according to the same criteria, although, as Meisil admits, 'some of the categories overlap' (43). Thus no ground is provided for overall ranking and, while Meisil anyway does not find a left-right ranking useful, it is hard to see what methodological advantage acrues from his partial and non-uniform use of numbers and symbols over and against a purely verbal description of the 'physiognomies of parties'. To eschew a consistent and generally applied use of numbers (percentages) for the purpose of illustrating assessments seems to be justified only in a case like Kirschen's, where genuinely mathematical expressions of policy objectives are probed.

Indeed, in using numbers consistently in my two-tier multi-issue spatial illustrations, I was guided by the belief in the basic appositeness of the method and, above all, by the hope of providing an inducement to scholars versed in measurement theory to test the feasibility of constructing arithmetically exact scales also for other socio-economic issues. Such constructs might prove to be rather costly. Precise quantification, even in the economic sphere, is often difficult (Kirschen, *op. cit.*, pp. 8, 253 and *passim*). Moreover, it is easily conceivable that the result will be the same as an informed impressionist assessment of clearly observable processes. But this would not render precise and properly calculated percentages superfluous. Given, then, that I have not intended to offer a mathematical determination of ideological positions, let alone a 'mathematization' of ideology, and that my numerical allocations of space on the various continua must be read with this caveat in mind, it should be self-evident that my averages are not mathematically proved either, but reflect the result of less formal, though not necessarily incorrect, conjectures. The principle of averaging need not in itself create any difficulty if one finds that different degrees of salience ought to be attributed to core issues and the respective continua. If so, no more is required than to allocate a different weight (percentage) to the average scoring on one issue or more when it comes to compounding the net average of the positions of all parties in respect of all issues.

Appendix 5

Table 3 Spatial Overview of the Two-tier Multi-issue Left-Right Ranking

(The reader need hardly be reminded that the Average Continuum does not count as a separate tier.)

```
                    CP        SDP                                     FP    LCP
                    (0)       (20)                                   (80)   (90)
1. Socia-   F:  |-----|-----|-----|-----|-----|-----|-----|-----|-----|-----|  Private
   lized        0    10                      50                           100  owner-
   ownership                                                                   ship

                              CP                            SDP FP LCP
                             (20)                          (70) (75) (80)
            OI:  |-----|-----|-----|-----|-----|-----|-----|-----|-----|-----|
                 0    10                      50                           100

                         CP                SDP                   FP     LCP
                        (10)               (45)                (77·5)   (85)
   Average       |-----|-----|-----|-----|-----|-----|-----|-----|-----|-----|
                 0    10                      50                           100
```

```
                 CP          SDP                                                  LCP     FP
                 (0)         (20)                                                 (90)   (100)
2. Class-   F:  |------|------|------|------|------|------|------|------|------|------|------|   2. Merito-
   less          0     10                                 50                                100   cratic
   society                                                                                         society
                                                                   CP     SDP     LCP     FP
                                                                  (70)    (80)    (90)   (100)
           OI:  |------|------|------|------|------|------|------|------|------|------|------|
                 0     10                                 50                                100
                                           CP           SDP                       LCP     FP
                                          (35)          (50)                      (90)   (100)
   Average      |------|------|------|------|------|------|------|------|------|------|------|
                 0     10                                 50                                100
                 CP                    FP    SDP                                  LCP
                 (0)                  (30)   (40)                                 (90)
3. Maxi-    F:  |------|------|------|------|------|------|------|------|------|------|------|   3. Mini-
   mal           0     10                                 50                                100   mal
   inter-                                                                                          inter-
   vention                                                                                         vention
   in                                                                                              in
   economy                                                                                         economy
                       CP                                 FP               SDP     LCP
                      (10)                               (50)              (70)    (80)
           OI:  |------|------|------|------|------|------|------|------|------|------|------|
                 0     10                                 50                                100
                    CP                        FP            SDP                 LCP
                    (5)                      (40)           (55)                (85)
   Average      |------|------|------|------|------|------|------|------|------|------|------|
                 0     10                                 50                                100
```

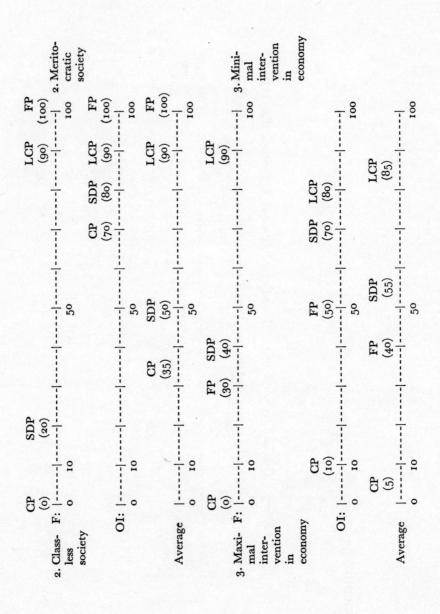

```
                 CP   SDP LCP                                          FP
                 (0)  (10) (10)                                        (90)
4. Free-     F:  |-----|-----|-----|-----|-----|-----|-----|-----|-----|-----|  4. Unfree-
   dom of        0     10                      50                          100     dom of ex-
   expression                                                                      pression
   and asso-                                                                       and asso-
   ciation                                                                         ciation

                    SDP  LCP                                        CP   FP
                    (10) (10)                                       (90) (90)
            OI:  |-----|-----|-----|-----|-----|-----|-----|-----|-----|-----|
                 0     10                      50                          100

                    SDP  LCP                 CP                        FP
                    (10) (10)                (45)                      (90)
   Average       |-----|-----|-----|-----|-----|-----|-----|-----|-----|-----|
                 0     10                      50                          100

              CP SDP LCP                                                     FP
              (0) (0) (0)                                                    (100)
5. Inde-     F:  |-----|-----|-----|-----|-----|-----|-----|-----|-----|-----|  5. Depen-
   pendent       0     10                      50                          100     dent
   judiciary                                                                       judiciary

              SDP LCP                                                 CP     FP
              (0) (0)                                                 (100) (100)
            OI:  |-----|-----|-----|-----|-----|-----|-----|-----|-----|-----|
                 0     10                      50                          100

              SDP LCP                          CP                            FP
              (0)  (0)                         (50)                          (100)
   Average       |-----|-----|-----|-----|-----|-----|-----|-----|-----|-----|
                 0     10                      50
```

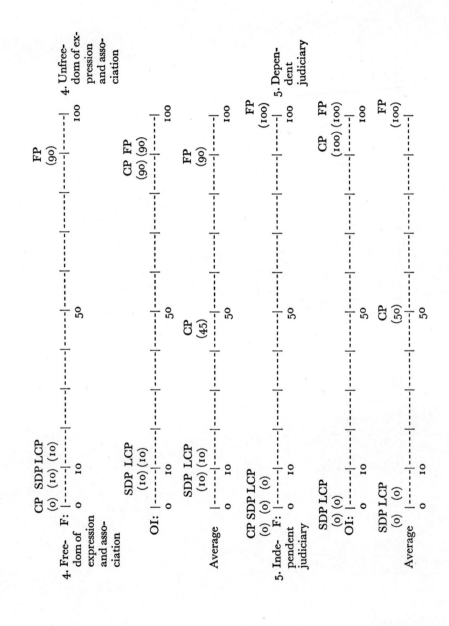

6. Observance of sovereignty — 6. Non-observance of sovereignty

F: SDP (0), LCP (20), CP (50), FP (80)

|------|------|------|------|------|------|------|------|------|------|
0 10 50 100

OI: SDP (10), LCP (20), CP (70), FP (70)

|------|------|------|------|------|------|------|------|------|------|
0 10 50 100

Average: SDP (5), LCP (20), CP (60), FP (75)

|------|------|------|------|------|------|------|------|------|------|
0 10 50 100

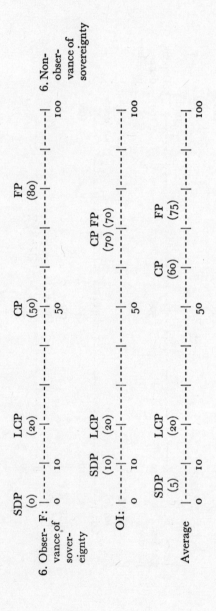

Bibliography

Only the books and articles referred to in the text are listed here. When more than one essay of a collection of essays has been used, the volume is listed separately and only this volume entry gives place and date of publication.

Abrams, M. 'Party Politics after the End of Ideology', in Allardt and Littunen, *Cleavages, Ideologies and Party Systems.*

Adorno, T. W., Frenkel-Brunswick, E., Levinson, D. J., and Stanford, R. N. *The Authoritarian Personality* (New York, 1950).

Agger, R. E., Goldrich, D., and Swanson, B. E. The Rulers and the Ruled—*Political Power and Impotence in American Communities* (New York, London and Sidney, 1964).

Aiken, H. D. *The Age of Ideology* (New York, 5th printing, 1961).

Aiken, H. D. 'The Revolt Against Ideology', *Commenatry*, Vol. XXXVII (April 1964), in Waxman, *The End of Ideology Debate.*

Alford, R. R. *Party and Society, The Anglo-American Democracies* (London, 1964).

Allardt, E. 'Finland: Institutionalized Radicalism', in Rejai, *Decline of Ideology?.*

Allardt, E., and Littunen, Y. (eds). *Cleavages, Ideologies and Party Systems* (Helsinki, 1964).

Almond, G. A., and Coleman, J. S. *The Politics of Developing Areas* (Princeton, New Jersey, 1960).

Almond, G. A., and Powell, G. Jr, *Comparative Politics, A Developmental Approach* (Boston and Toronto, 1966; 2nd printing).

Almond, G. A., and Verba, S. *The Civic Culture—Political Attitudes and Democracy in Five Nations* (Princeton, 1963).

Althusser, L. *For Marx* (1965; trans. B. Brewster, London, 1969).

Althusser, L., and Balibar, E. *Reading Capital* (1968; trans. B. Brewster, London, 1970).

Andrain, C. F. 'Democracy and Socialism: Ideologies of African Leaders', in Apter, *Ideology and Discontent.*

Apter, D. E. (ed.). *Ideology and Discontent* (London and New York, 1964).

Apter, D. E. *The Politics of Modernization* (Chicago and London, 1965; 3rd impression, 1967).

Arblaster, A. 'Ideology and Intellectuals', in Benewick *et al.*, *Knowledge and Belief in Politics.*

Arendt, H. 'Race-Thinking before Racism', *The Review of Politics*, Vol. VI, 1 (1944).

Arendt, H. 'Ideology and Terror, A Novel Form of Government', *The Review of Politics*, Vol. XV, 3 (1953).

Arendt, H. The Origins of Totalitarianism (1951; 2nd enlarged edn, New York, 1958).

Arieli, Y. *Individualism and Nationalism in American Ideology* (Cambridge, Mass., 1964).

Aristotle, *The Politics* (trans. with an introduction, notes and appendices by E. Barker, Oxford, 1946; corrected reprint, 1952).

Aron, R. *L'opium des intellectuels* (Paris, 1955; repr., 1968).

Aron, R. *Dix-huit leçons sur la société industrielle* (Paris, 1962).

Aron, R. *La lutte des classes, nouvelles leçons sur la société industrielle* (Paris, 1964).

Aron, R. 'Remarques sur le nouvel âge idéologique', in von Beyme, *Theory and Politics.*

Assel, H.-G. *Ideologie und Ordnung als Probleme politischer Bildung* (Munich, 1970).

Avineri, S. *The Social and Political Thought of Karl Marx* (Cambridge, 1968).

Barion, J. *Was ist Ideologie?* (Bonn, 1964).

Barnes, S. H. 'Italy: Opposition on Left, Right and Centre', in Dahl, *Political Opposition in Western Democracies.*

Barnes, S. H. 'Political Ideology and Political Behavior', originally publ. as 'Ideology and the Organization of Conflict . . .', *The Journal of Politics,* Vol. XXVIII (1966), repr. in Cox, *Ideology, Politics and Political Theory.*

Barry, B. *Political Argument* (London, 1965; 3rd impression, 1968).

Barth, H. *Wahrheit und Ideologie* (Zürich, 1945).

Bartley III, W. W. *The Retreat to Commitment* (London, 1964).

Bay, C. 'Politics and Pseudopolitics: A Critical Evaluation of Some Behavioural Literature', *The American Political Science Review,* Vol. LIX, 1 (1965).

Beer, S. H. *Modern British Politics* (London, 1965).

Bell, D. *The End of Ideology—On the Exhaustion of Political Ideas in the Fifties* (New York, 1960; rev. edn, New York, 1961).

Bell, D., and Aiken, H. D. 'Ideology—A Debate', *Commentary,* Vol. XXXVIII (October 1964), repr. in Waxman, *The End of Ideology Debate.*

Bell, D. 'Ideology and Soviet Politics', *Slavic Review,* Vol. XXIV, 4 (1965).

Benda, J. *The Betrayal of the Intellectuals* (Paris, 1927. Trans. by R. Aldington; introduction by H. Read [Boston, 1955]).

Bendix, R. *Work and Authority in Industry, Ideologies of Management in the Course of Industrialization* (New York and London, 1956).

Bendix, R. *Max Weber, An Intellectual Portrait* (New York, 1960).

Bendix, R. 'The Age of Ideology: Persistent and Changing', in Apter, *Ideology and Discontent.*

Bendix, R., and Roth, G. *Scholarship and Partisanship: Essays on Max Weber* (Berkeley, Los Angeles and London, 1971).

Benewick, R., Berki, R. N., Parekh, B. (eds). *Knowledge and Beliefs in Politics, The Problem of Ideology* (London, 1973).

Bernstein, E. 'Das realistische und das ideologische Moment im Sozialismus', *Die Neue Zeit* (1897–8), repr. in *Zur Geschichte und Theorie des Sozialismus* (2nd edn, Berlin and Bern, 1901).

Beyme, K. von. *Robert von Mohl, Politische Schriften, Eine Auswahl* (Cologne and Opladen, 1966).

Beyme, K. von. *Theory and Politics, Festschrift zum 70 Geburtstag für Carl Joachim Friedrich* (The Hague, 1971).

Beyme, K. von. *Vom Faschismus zur Entwicklungsdiktatur—Machtelite und Opposition in Spanien* (Munich 1972).

Bilski, R. *The Relations between Ideologies and Policies in the Debate about Comprehensive Schools, 1944–1970* (unpublished doctoral dissertation, the University of Glasgow, 1971).

Bilski, R. 'Ideology and the Comprehensive School', *The Political Quarterly* (March–April 1973).

Bilski, R. 'Secondary Education and British Party Ideology', *Res Publica*, Vol. XVII (1975).

Bilski, R., and Gal-Nur, Y. 'Values and Ideologies in National Planning', in G. Sheffer (ed.), *Towards More Systematic Thinking on Israel's Future* (Jerusalem, 1974 [in Hebrew]).

Binder, L. 'Ideological Foundations of Egyptian-Arabian Nationalism', in Apter, *Ideology and Discontent.*

Birnbaum, N. 'The Sociological Study of Ideology (1940–60), A Trend Report and Bibliography', *Current Sociology*, Vol. IX, 2 (1960).

Bottomore, T. B. *Elites and Society* (London, 1964; Harmondsworth, 1966).

Bottomore, T. B. *Classes in Modern Society* (London, 1965).

Bottomore, T. B. *Critics of Society, Radical Thought in America* (London, 1967).

Brand, E. *Ideologie.* Studientreine Sozialwissenschaften, programmiert. (Düsseldorf, 1972).

Brandt, W. *Plädoyer für die Zukunft* (Frankfurt/M., 1961).

Brandt, W. *Das Regierungsprogramm der SPD* (Bonn, 1961).

Braybrooke, D., and Lindblom, C. E. *A Strategy of Decision, Policy Evaluation as a Social Process* (Glencoe, New York and London, 1963).

Brunner, O. 'Das Zeitalter der Ideologien', *Neue Wege der Sozialgeschichte* (Göttingen, 1956).

Buchanan, W., and Cantril, H. *How Nations See Each Other* (Urbana, 1953).

Busia, K. A. *Africa in Search of Democracy* (London, 1967).

Butler, D. 'The Paradox of Party Difference', in Rose, *Studies in British Politics.*

Butler, R. A. 'A Disraelian Approach to Modern Politics', in *Tradition and Change* (London, Conservative Political Centre, 1954).

Butler, R. A. *The New Conservatism* (London, Conservative Political Centre, 1955).

Campbell, A., Converse, P. E., Miller, W. E., and Stokes, D. E. *The American Voter* (New York, 1960).

Campbell, A., Converse, P. E., Miller, W. E., and Stokes, D. E. *Elections and the Political Order* (New York, London and Sydney, 1966).

Campbell, A., and Valen, H. 'Party Identification in Norway and the United States', in Campbell *et al.*, *Elections and the Political Order.*

Carr, E. H. *The Bolshevik Revolution* (London, 1950–3).

Chapman, B. *The British Government Observed* (London, 1963).

Christenson, K. M. (ed.). *Ideologies and Modern Politics* (London, 1972).

Christoph, J. B. 'Consensus and Cleavage in British Political Ideology', *The American Political Science Review*, Vol. LIX, 3 (1965).

Cohn, N. *The Pursuit of the Millenium* (London, 1957).

Cohn-Bendit, G., and D. *Obsolete Communism, The Left-Wing Alternative* (trans. by A. Pomerans, Penguin Special, 1969).

Cole, G. D. H. *A History of Socialist Thought*, 4 vols (London and New York, 1959–60).

Connolly, W. E. *Political Science and Ideology* (New York, 1967).

Conservative Opportunity, The: Fifteen Bow Group Essays on Tomorrow's Toryism (London, Conservative Political Centre, 1965).

Converse, P. E. 'The Nature of Belief Systems in Mass Publics', in Apter, *Ideology and Discontent.*

Corbett, P. *Ideologies* (London, 1965).

Cox, R. H. (ed.). *Ideology, Politics and Political Theory* (Belmont, Cal., 1969).

Cranston, M. 'Ideology and Mr. Lichtheim', *Encounter*, Vol. XXXI (October 1968).

Crick, B. 'Britain's "Democratic" Party', *The Nation*, Vol. CXI, 20 (1960).

Crick, B. *In Defence of Politics* (1962; rev. edn, Harmondsworth, repr. 1966).

Crosland, C. A. R. 'The Transition from Capitalism', in Crossman, *New Fabian Essays.*

Crosland, C. A. R. *The Future of Socialism* (London, 1956).

Crosland, C. A. R. 'The Future of the Left', *Encounter*, Vol. XIV (March 1960).

Crosland, C. A. R. 'Social Objectives for the 1970s', *The Times*, 25 September 1970.

Crossman, R. H. S. (ed.). *New Fabian Essays* (London, 1952).

Dahl, R. A. (ed.). *Political Opposition in Western Democracies* (New Haven and London, 1966).

Dahl, R. A. 'Ideology, Conflict and Consensus, Notes for a Theory', paper submitted to the Seventh World Congress of the International Political Science Association (Brussels, September 1967).

Dahl, R. A. *Pluralist Democracy in the United States* (Chicago, 1967).

Dahrendorf, R. *Class and Class Conflict in Industrial Society* (Stanford and London, 2nd edn, 1961).

Dahrendorf, R. *Gesellschaft und Freiheit* (Munich, 1962).

Daniels, R. V. *The Conscience of the Revolution* (New York, 1960).

Daniels, R. V. 'The Ideological Vector', *Soviet Studies*, Vol. XVIII, 1 (1966).

Davidson, D. E. *Ballots and the Democratic Class Struggle* (Stanford, 1943).

Delany, W. 'The Role of Ideology: A Summation' (1964), in Waxman, *The End of Ideology Debate.*

Deutsch, K. W. *Nationalism and Social Communication, An Inquiry into the Foundations of Nationalism* (New York and London, 1953).

Dia, Mamadou *Contribution à l'étude du mouvement coopératif en Afrique noir* (Paris, 1958).

Dictionnaire classique de la Langue Française avec des Examples tirés des meilleurs Auteurs Français et des notes puisés dans les Manuscrits de Rivarol, par quatre professeurs de l'université (Paris, 1827).

Diggins, J. P. 'Ideology and Pragmatism: Philosophy or Passion?', *The American Political Science Review*, Vol. LXIV, 3 (1970).

Dion, L. 'An Hypothesis Concerning Structure and Function of Ideology', originally publ. as 'Political Ideology as a Tool of Functional Analysis. . .', *The Canadian Journal of Economics and Political Science*, Vol. XXV, 1 (1959), repr. in Cox, *Ideology, Politics and Political Theory.*

Downs, A. *An Economic Theory of Democracy* (New York, 1957; paperback repr., 1965).

Dror, Y. 'Comprehensive Planning: Common Fallacies Versus Preferred Features', in F. van Schlagen (ed.), *Essays in Honour of J. P. Thijsee* (The Hague, 1967).

Dror, Y. *Public Policymaking Reexamined* (San Francisco, 1968).

Drucker, H. M. *The Political Uses of Ideology* (London, 1974).
Dunner, I., (ed.). *Dictionary of Political Science* (New York, 1964).
Duverger, M. 'Où en sont les nationalismes?', *Res Publica*, Vol. II, 3 (1960).
Duverger, M. *Introduction à la politique* (Paris, 1964).
Eckstein, H. *A Theory of Stable Democracy* (Princeton, 1961).
Eisenstadt, S. N. *Essays on Sociological Aspects of Political* and *Economic Development*, (The Hague, 1961).
Eisenstadt, S. N. 'Bureaucratization, Markets, and Power Structure', in Allardt and Littunen, *Cleavages, Ideologies and Party Systems.*
Eisenstadt, S. N. *Max Weber on Charisma and Institution-Building* (Chicago and London, 1968).
Eisenstadt, S. N. *The Political Systems of Empires: The Rise and Fall of the Bureaucratic Empires* (New York and London, paperback, 1969).
Eisenstadt, S. N. 'Post-Traditional Societies and the Continuity and Reconstruction of Tradition', *Daedalus*, Vol. 102, 1 (1973).
Eldersveld, S. J. *Political Parties: A Behavioural Analysis* (Chicago, 1964).
Encyclopédie ou Dictionnaire Raisonné des Sciences, des Arts et des Métiérs, Vol. VIII (Neufchâtel, 1765).
Engels, F. *Der Ursprung der Familie, des Privateigentums und des Staates* (2nd edn, Stuttgart, 1886).
Engels, F. 'Ludwig Feuerbach and the End of Classical German Philosophy', in L. S. Feuer, *Basic Writings on Politics and Philosophy—Karl Marx and Friedrich Engels* (New York, 1959).
Erikson, E. H. *Young Man Luther: A Study in Psycho-Analysis and History* (London, 1958).
Eysenck, H. J. 'Social Attitudes and Social Class', *The British Journal of Sociology*, Vol. I, 1 (1950).
Fanon, F. *The Wretched of the Earth* (trans. by C. Farrington [London, 1965]).
Festinger, L. *A Theory of Cognitive Dissonance* (Evanston, Ill., 1957).
Festinger, L. 'The Theory of Cognitive Dissonance', in W. Schram (ed.). *The Science of Human Communication* (London and New York, 1963).
Feuer, L. S. 'Beyond Ideology', *Psychoanalysis and Ethics* (Springfield, Ill., 1955), repr. in Waxman, *The End of Ideology Debate.*
Feuer, L. S. *Basic Writings in Politics and Philosophy—Karl Marx and Friedrich Engels* (New York, 1959).
Feuer, L. S. *The Scientific Intellectual* (New York, 1963).
Feuer, L. S. 'Ideology & No End, Some Personal History', *Encounter*, Vol. XL (April 1973).
Feuerbach, L. *Kleine philosophische Schriften* (1842–5) (ed by H. G. Lange, Leipzig, 1950).
Finer, S. E., Berrington, H. B., and Bartholomew, D. J. *Backbench Opinion in the House of Commons, 1955–59* (Oxford, 1961).
Finer, S. E., *Anonymous Empire* (2nd edn, London, 1966).
Finer, S. E., and Seliger, M. 'Political Roles of Violence', Position Paper of the General Reporters, Commission I. 10, IXth IPSA World Congress (Montreal, 1973).
Fischer, G. 'Sociology', in Fischer (ed.), *Science and Ideology in Soviet Society* (New York, 1967).
Fleron Jr, F. J., and Mackelly, R. 'Personality, Behaviour and Communist Ideology', *Soviet Studies*, Vol. XXI, 3 (1970).

Fortes, M., and Evans-Pritchard, E. (eds). *African Political Systems* (London and Oxford, 1940).
Freyer, H. *Theorie des gegenwärtigen Zeitalters* (Stuttgart, 1955).
Friedrich, C. J. *Constitutional Government and Politics* (New York and London, 1937).
Friedrich, C. J. *Man and His Government* (New York, San Francisco, Toronto and London, 1963).
Friedrich, C. J. 'Ideology in Politics: A Theoretical Comment', *Slavic Review*, XXIV, 4 (1965).
Friedrich, C. J., and Brzezinski, Z. K. *Totalitarian Dictatorship and Autocracy* (Cambridge, Mass., 1956).
Friedrich, C. J., and Brzezinski, Z. K. *Totalitarian Dictatorship and Autocracy* (2nd edn, rev. by C. J. Friedrich, New York, Washington and London, 1965; paperback, 1966).
Friedrich, C. J., Curtis, M., and Barber, B. R. *Totalitarianism in Perspective: Three Views* (New York, 1969).
Gablentz, O. H. von der. 'Kants politische Philosophie und die Weltpolitik unserer Tage', *Schriftenreihe der Deutschen Hochschule für Politik* (Berlin, 1956).
Geertz, C. 'Ideology as a Cultural System', in Apter, *Ideology and Discontent*.
Geiger, T. *Ideologie und Wahrheit, Eine Soziologische Kritik des Denkens* (Stuttgart and Vienna, 1953).
Gellner, E. *Words and Things, A Critical Account of Linguistic Philosophy and a Study in Ideology* (London, 1959).
Gellner, E. *Thought and Change* (London, 1964).
Gellner, E. 'Myth, Ideology and Revolution', in B. Crick and W. A. Robson (eds), *Protest and Discontent* (Harmondsworth, 1970).
Germino, D. *Beyond Ideology: The Revival of Political Theory* (New York, Evanston and London, 1967).
Gerth, H. H., and Mills, C. W. *From Max Weber: Essays in Sociology* (New York, 1946; repr. 1969).
Ginsberg, M. 'Facts and Values', *The Advancement of Science*, Vol. XIX (1962).
Girod, R. 'Le Système des Partis en Suisse', *Revue Française de Science Politique*, Vol. XIV, 6 (1964).
Girod, R. 'Geography of the Swiss Party System', in Allardt and Littunen, *Cleavages, Ideologies and Party Systems*.
Gluckman, M. *The Ideas in Barotse Jurisprudence* (New Haven, 1965).
Gluckman, M. *Politics, Law and Ritual in Tribal Society* (1965; 2nd impr., Oxford, 1967).
Goldman, L. *Recherches Dialectiques* (Paris, 3rd edn, 1959).
Goldman, L. *The Hidden God* (trans. by P. Thody, London, 1964).
Gould, J. 'Politics and the Academy', *Government and Opposition*, Vol. III, 1 (1968).
Gould, J., and Kolb, W. L. (eds). *A Dictionary of the Social Sciences* (New York, 1964).
Granet, M. *La pensée chinoise* (Paris, 1934).
Greenleaf, W. H. *Order, Empiricism and Politics: Two Traditions of English Political Thought* (London, New York and Toronto, 1964).
Gregor, A. J. *Contemporary Radical Ideologies—Totalitarian Thought in the Twentieth Century* (New York, 1968).
Grosser, A. *L'Allemagne de notre temps, 1945–1970* (Paris, 1970).
Gruner, E. 'Die Jurafrage als Problem der Minderheit in der Schweizerischen Demokratie', *Civitas*, Vol. XXIII, 7 (March 1968).

Gurvitch, G. *Le concept de classes sociales de Marx à nos Jours* (Paris, 1954).
Haber, R. H. 'The End of Ideology as Ideology' (1962), in Waxman, *The End of Ideology Debate.*
Halpern, B. ' "Myth" and "Ideology" in Modern Usage', *History and Theory*, Vol. I, 2 (1961).
Hamburger, J. *Intellectuals in Politics, John Stuart Mill and the Philosophic Radicals* (New Haven and London, 1965).
Hampshire, S. *Thought and Action* (London, 1959).
Harris, N. *Beliefs in Society, The Problem of Ideology* (London, 1968).
Hartz, L. *The Liberal Tradition in America* (New York, 1955).
Helenius, R. *The Profile of Party Ideologies* (Helsinki, 1969).
Hennis, W. *Meinungsforschung und repräsentative Demokratie* (Tübingen, 1957).
Hermann, K. 'The End of the Revolt?', *Encounter*, Vol. XXXI (September 1968).
Hersch, J. *Idéologie et Réalité, Essai d'orientation politique* (Paris, 1956).
Himmelstrand, U. 'A Theoretical and Empirical Approach to Depolitization and Political Involvement', *Acta Sociologica*, Vol. VI (1962).
Hirschmann, A. O. *Exit, Voice and Loyalty* (Cambridge, Mass., 1970).
Hodges, D. C. 'The End of "The End of Ideology" ', *The American Journal of Economics and Sociology*, Vol. XXVI, 2 (1967), in Waxman, *The End of Ideology Debate.*
Hoffer, E. *The True Believer* (New York, 1958).
Hofstadter, R. 'Goldwater and His Party', *Encounter*, Vol. XXIII (October 1964).
Hölzle, E. *Idee und Ideologie, Eine Zeitkritik aus universalhistorischer Sicht* (Bern and Munich, 1969).
Hoogerwerf, A. 'Latent Socio-Political Issues in the Netherlands', *Sociologica Neerlandica*, Vol. II (1965).
Huntington, S. P. 'Conservatism as an Ideology', *The American Political Science Review*, Vol. LI, 2 (1957).
Huntington, S. P., and Brzezinski, Z. K. 'Ideology in the U.S.A. and U.S.S.R.', in N. Guild and K. T. Palmer, *Introduction to Politics, Essays and Readings* (New York, London and Sydney, 1968).
Ionescu, G. *The Politics of the European Communist States* (New York, 1967).
Ionescu, G. 'Lenin, the Commune and the State—Thoughts for a Centenary', *Government and Opposition*, Vol. V, 2 (1970).
Jacobs, P., and Landau, S. *The New Radicals, A Report with Documents* (1966; Penguin edn, 1967).
Jaspers, K. *Psychologie der Weltanschauungen* (Berlin, 1922).
Jenkins, I. 'Justice as Ideal and Ideology', in C. J. Friedrich and J. W. Chapman (eds), *Justice, Nomos* VI (New York, 1963).
Jenkins, R. 'Equality', in Crossman, *New Fabian Essays.*
Jenkins, S. 'Conservatives and Comprehensives', *A Bow Group Memorandum* (London, Conservative Political Centre, 1967).
Johnson, H. M. 'Ideology and the Social System', *The International Encyclopedia of the Social Sciences*, Vol. 7 (1968).
Joravsky, D. 'Soviet Ideology', *Soviet Studies*, Vol. XVIII, 1 (1966).
Jordan, Z. A. *Philosophy and Ideology, The Development of Philosophy and Marxism-Leninism in Poland since the Second World War* (Dortrecht, 1963).
Jouvenel, B. de. *The Pure Theory of Politics* (Cambridge, 1963).
Kariel, H. S. *The Decline of American Pluralism* (Stanford, 1961).

Katz, E., and Lazarsfeld, P. F. *Personal Influence* (New York, 1955).
Kautsky, K. *Die proletarische Revolution und ihr Programm* (Stuttgart and Berlin, 1922).
Key, Jr, V. O. *Southern Politics in State and Nation* (New York, 1949).
Key, Jr, V. O. *Public Opinion and American Democracy* (New York, 1961).
Key, Jr, V. O. *The Responsible Electorate* (Cambridge, Mass., 1966).
King, P. 'The Ideological Fallacy', in P. King and B. C. Parekh, *Politics and Experience, Essays presented to Professor Michael Oakeshott on the occasion of his retirement* (Cambridge, 1968).
Kirchheimer, O. 'The Waning of Opposition in Parliamentary Regimes', *Social Research*, Vol. XXIV, 2 (1957).
Kirchheimer, O. 'The Transformation of the European Party System', in La-Palombara and Weiner, *Political Parties and Political Development*.
Kirschen, E. S. (ed.). *Economic Policy in Our Time*, 3 vols (Amsterdam, 1964).
Klugmann, J., and Oestreicher, P. (ed.). *What Kind of Revolution? A Christian-Communist Dialogue* (London, 1968).
Kolakowski, L. *Der Mensch ohne Alternative* (Munich, 1960, rev. edn, 1967).
Kuhn, T. S. *The Structure of Scientific Revolutions* (2nd enlarged edn, 3rd impr., Chicago, 1973).
Lane, R. E. *Political Ideology* (New York and London, 1962; paperback repr., 1967).
Lane, R. E. 'The Politics of Consensus in an Age of Affluence', *The American Political Science Review*, Vol. LIX, 4 (1965).
Lane, R. E. 'The Decline of Politics and Ideology in a Knowledgeable Society', *The American Sociological Review*, Vol. XXXI, 5 (1966).
Lane, R. E., and Sears, D. O. *Public Opinion* (Foundations of Modern Political Science Series, Englewood Cliffs, 2nd printing, 1965).
LaPalombara, J. 'Decline of Ideology: A Dissent and an Interpretation', *The American Political Science Review*, Vol. LX, 1 (1966).
LaPalombara, J., and Weiner, M. (eds). *Political Parties and Political Development* (Princeton, 1966).
Laponce, J. A. 'Note on the Use of the Left-Right Dimension', in *Comparative Political Studies*, Vol. II, 4 (1970).
Laponce, J. A. 'In Search of the Stable Elements of the Left-Right Landscape', *Comparative Politics*, Vol. IV, 4 (1972).
Laponce, J. A. 'The Use of Visual Space to Measure Ideology', in J. A. Laponce and P. Smoker (eds), *Experimentation and Simulation in Political Science* (Toronto, 1972).
Larousse. *Grand Dictionaire Universel du XIXe Siècle*, Vol. 9 (Paris, 1873).
Lasswell, H. D., and Kaplan, A. *Power and Society—A Framework for Political Inquiry* (New Haven, 1950; 3rd printing, 1957).
Leiserson, A. *Parties and Politics, An Institutional and Behavioural Approach* (New York, 1958).
Leites, N. *The Operational Code of the Politburo* (New York, 1951).
Lenin, V. J. *Selected Works*, 2 vols (Moscow, 1946).
Lenk, K. *Ideologie, Ideologiekritik und Wissenssoziologie* (Neuwied and Berlin, 1961; repr. 1967).
Leo, H. *Studien und Skizzen zu einer Naturlehre des Staates* (Halle, 1833).
Leroy, M. *Histoire des idées sociales en France*, 3 vols (3rd edn, Paris, 1946–54).
Lichtheim, G. *Marxism. An Historical and Critical Study* (London, 1961).

Lichtheim, G. 'The Concept of Ideology', *History and Theory*, Vol. IV, 2 (1965).

Lichtheim, G. 'Comment', *Slavic Review*, Vol. XXIV, 4 (1965).

Lindblom, C. E. *The Intelligence of Democracy* (Glencoe, New York and London, 1965).

Lipset, S. M. *Political Man* (New York, 1960).

Lipset, S. M. 'Political Cleavages in "Developed" and "Emerging" Polities', in E. Allardt and Y. Littunen, *Cleavages, Ideologies and Party Systems*.

Lipset, S. M. 'The Changing Class Structure and Contemporary European Politics', *Daedalus*, Vol. 93, 1 (1964).

Lipset, S. M. 'Religion and Politics in the American Past and Present', in R. Lee and M. E. Marty (eds), *Religion and Social Conflict* (New York, 1964).

Lipset, S. M. 'Some Further Comments on "The End of Ideology" ', *The American Political Science Review*, Vol. LX, 1 (1966).

Lipset, S. M. *Revolution and Counterrevolution: Change and Persistence in Social Structures* (New York, 1968).

Lipset, S. M. 'Ideology & No End, The Controversy Till Now', *Encounter*, Vol. XXXIX (December 1972).

Locke, J. *Two Treaties of Government* (ed. with an introduction by P. Laslett, Cambridge, 1960).

Locke, J. *An Essay Concerning Human Understanding*, 2 vols (ed. with an introduction by J. W. Yolton, Everyman's Library, 1961).

Loewenstein, K. 'Political Systems, Ideologies and Institutions: the Problem of their Circulation', *The Western Political Quarterly*, Vol. VI, 4 (1953).

Loewenstein, K. *Max Weber's staatspolitische Auffassungen in der Sicht unserer Zeit* (Frankfurt/M. and Bonn, 1965).

Loewenthal, R. 'Ideology and Power Politics: A Symposium', *Problems of Communism*, Vol. VII, 2 (1957).

Lorwin, V. R. 'Reflections on the History of the French and American Labour Movements', *Journal of Economic History*, Vol. XVII, 1 (1957).

Lovejoy, A. O. *The Great Chain of Being* (New York, 1960).

Lowi, T. 'The Public Philosophy: Interest-Group Liberalism', *The American Political Science Review*, Vol. LXI, 1 (1967).

Lukić, R. D. 'Political Ideology and Social Development', in Allardt and Littunen, *Cleavages, Ideologies and Party Systems*.

McClosky, H., Hoffman, P. J., and O'Hara, R. 'Issue Conflict and Consensus among Party Leaders and Followers', *The American Political Science Review*, Vol. LIV, 2 (1960).

McClosky, H. 'Consensus and Ideology in American Politics', *The American Political Science Review*, Vol. LVIII, 2 (1964).

MacIver, R. M. *The Web of Government* (New York, 1947).

Mackenzie, W. J. M. *Politics and Social Science* (Harmondsworth, 1967).

McKenzie, R. T. *British Political Parties, The Distribution of Power within the Conservative and Labour Parties* (1955; paperback edn, London, 1967).

McKenzie, R. T., and Silver, A. 'Conservatism, Industrialism and the Working Class Tory in England', in Rose, *Studies in British Politics*.

McKeon, R. *Democracy in a World of Tension* (Chicago, 1951).

Macpherson, C. B. 'Revolution and Ideology', in C. J. Friedrich (ed.), *Revolution, Nomos*, X (New York, 1966), repr. in Cox, *Ideology, Politics and Political Theory*.

MacRae, D. G. *Ideology and Society* (London, 1961).

Mannheim, K. 'Das konservative Denken (I–II), Soziologische Beiträge zum Werden des politisch-historischen Denkens in Deutschland', *Archiv für Sozialwissenschaft und Sozialpolitik*, Vol. 57, 1 and 2 (1927).

Mannheim, K. *Ideology and Utopia—An Introduction to the Sociology of Knowledge* (new expanded version of *Ideologie und Utopie* (1929). Trans. (1936) by L. Wirth and E. A. Shils, New York, n.d.).

Marcuse, H. *One-Dimensional Man* (London, 1964; repr. 1968).

Marquand, D. 'The Politics of Deprivation, Reconsidering the Future of Utopianism', *Encounter*, Vol. XXXII (April 1969).

Marx, K. *Zur Kritik der politischen Ökonomie*, ed. by K. Kautsky (7th ed, Stuttgart, 1907).

Marx, K. *Das Kapital, Kritik der politischen Ökonomie*, ed, by F. Engels (Hamburg, Vol. I, 4th edn, 1893; Vol. II, 2nd edn, 1893; Vol. III (in 2 vols) 1894).

Marx, K., and Engels, F. *Gesamtausgabe* (Frankfurt, Moscow and Leningrad, 1927–).

Marx, K. and Engels, F. *Werke* (Berlin, 1960, 1969), Vols VIII, XXI.

Meisil, J. 'Recent Changes in Canadian Parties', in L. H. G. Thornburn (ed.), *Party Politics in Canada* (2nd edn, Scarborough, 1957).

Merton, R. K. *Social Theory and Social Structure* (rev. edn, Glencoe, 1957).

Meyer, A. G. *Communism* (New York, 1960; 4th repr., 1962).

Meyer, A. G. 'The Functions of Ideology in the Soviet Political System', *Soviet Studies*, Vol. XVII, 3 (1966).

Meyer, A. G. *Leninism* (Cambridge, Mass., 1957; 6th repr. 1971).

Meynaud, J. *Destin des Idéologies* (Lausanne, 1961).

Michels, R. *Zur Soziologie des Parteiwesens in der modernen Demokratie* (2nd edn, Leipzig, 1925).

Michels, R. *Political Parties* (trans. by E. and C. Paul, 1915; Dover edn, New York, 1959).

Mill, J. S. *Utilitarianism, Liberty and Representative Government* (New York and London, Everyman's Library, 1951).

Milliband, R. 'Theorie et pratique du travaillisme', *Res Publica*, Vol. II, 3 (1960).

Mills, C. W. *The Sociological Imagination* (New York, 1956; paperback edn, 1967).

Mills, C. W. 'A Letter to the New Left', *New Left Review*, V (1960), repr. in Waxman, *The End of Ideology Debate*.

Minar, D. 'Ideology and Political Behaviour', *The Midwest Journal of Political Science*, Vol. V, 4 (1961).

Mommsen, W. J. 'Universalgeschichtliches und politisches Denken bei Max Weber', *Historische Zeitschrift* (1965).

Montesquieu, C. L. de Secondat de. *De L'Esprit Des Lois*, 2 vols (Paris, Classiques Garnier, 1949).

Moodie, G. C. *The Government of Britain* (New York, 1961).

Moulin, L. *Le Monde vivant des Religieux* (Paris, 1964).

Moulin, L. 'Les Origines électorales et déliberatives contemporaines', *Res Publica*, Vol. XV, 4 (1973).

Mullins, W. A. 'On the Concept of Ideology in Political Science', *The American Political Science Review*, Vol. LXVI, 2 (1972).

Naess, A. 'The Function of Ideological Convictions', in H. Cantril (ed.), *Tensions that Cause War* (Urbana, 1950).

Naess, A., and associates. *Democracy, Ideology and Objectivity* (Oslo and Oxford, 1956).

Neumann, F. *Behemoth: The Structure and Practice of National Socialism* (New York, 1942).

Nietzsche, I. *Jenseits von Gut und Böse, Werke,* 10 vols (Taschenausgabe, Leipzig, 1906).

Nisbet, R. 'Who Killed the Student Revolution?', *Encounter,* Vol. XXXIV (February 1970).

Nolte, E. *Der Faschismus in seiner Epoche* (Munich, 1963).

Oakeshott, M. *Rationalism in Politics and Other Essays* (London, 1962; paperback, 1967).

Ossowski, S. *Class Structure in the Social Consciousness* (London, 1963).

Ostrogorski, M. I. *Democracy and the Organization of Political Parties.* Vol. II, *The United States* (New York, 1964).

Parsons, T. *The Social System* (Glencoe, 1951).

Parsons, T. 'The Political Aspect of Social Structure and Process', in D. Easton (ed.), *Varieties of Political Theory* (Englewood Cliffs, 1966).

Partridge, P. H. 'Politics, Philosophy, Ideology', *Political Studies,* Vol. IX, 3 (1961), in A. Quinton, *Political Philosophy* (Oxford, 1967).

Picavet, F. C. *Les Idéologues: Essai sur l'histoire des idées et des théories scientifiques, philosophiques, religieuses etc., en France depuis 1789* (Paris, 1891).

Plamenatz, J. *German Marxism and Russian Communism* (London, 1954; 3rd impr., 1961).

Plamenatz, J. *Ideology* (London, 1970).

Polsby, N. W., and Wildavsky, A. B. *Presidential Elections, Strategies of American Electoral Politics* (New York, 1964; 2nd edn, 1968).

Pomper, G. M. 'From Confusion to Clarity: Issues and American Voters, 1956–1968', *The American Political Science Review,* Vol. LXVI, 2 (1972).

Popper, K. *The Open Society and Its Enemies* (Princeton, 1950).

Popper, K. *The Poverty of Historicism* (London, 1957).

Poussin, V. 'Suis-je un homme de droite?', *Res Publica,* Vol. II, 3 (1960).

Powell, E. *A New Look at Medicine and Politics* (London, 1966).

Putnam, R. D. 'Studying Elite Political Culture: The Case of "Ideology" ', *The American Political Science Review,* Vol. LXV, 3 (1971).

Raphael, D. D. *Problems of Political Philosophy* (London. 1970).

Rejai, M. 'Political Ideology: Theoretical and Comparative Perspectives', in Rejai, M. (ed.), *Decline of Ideology?* (Chicago, 1971).

Rejai, M., Mason, W. L., and Beller, D. C. 'Empirical Relevance of the Hypothesis of Decline', in Rejai (ed.), *Decline of Ideology?*

Rémond, R. *La Droite en France* (Paris, 1955; 2nd edn, 1968).

Report of the 55th Annual Conference of the British Labour Party (London, 1956).

Rickert, H. *Die Grenzen der naturwissenschaftlichen Begriffsbildung* (Freiburg and Leipzig, 1896; 5th edn, Tübingen, 1929).

Riker, W. H. *Democracy in the United States* (2nd edn, New York and London, 1965).

Riker, W. H. *The Theory of Political Coalitions* (New Haven and London, 1962).

Riker, W. H., and Ordeshook, P. C. 'A Theory of the Calculus of Voting', *The American Political Science Review,* Vol. LXII, 1 (1968).

Robson, W. A. *Nationalised Industry and Public Ownership* (London, 1960).

Rokeach, M. *The Open and the Closed Mind—Investigations into the Nature of Belief Systems and Personality Systems* (New York, 1960).

Rokkan, S. 'Numerical Democracy and Corporate Pluralism', in Dahl, *Political Opposition in Western Democracies.*

Rokkan, S. *Citizens, Elections, Parties: Approaches to the Comparative Study of the Processes of Development* (Oslo, 1970).

Rose, R. 'The Political Ideas of English Party Activists', *The American Political Science Review*, Vol. LVI, 2 (1962).

Rose, R. 'Parties, Factions and Tendencies in Britain', *Political Studies*, Vol. XII, 1 (1964).

Rose, R. (ed.). *Studies in British Politics* (London, 1966; repr. New York, 1967).

Rotenstreich, N. *Basic Problems of Marx's Philosophy* (Indianapolis, New York and Kansas City, 1965).

Roth, G. 'Critique and Adaptation', in R. Bendix and G. Roth, *Scholarship and Partisanship.*

Rousseas S. W., and Farganis, I. 'American Politics and the End of Ideology', *The British Journal of Sociology*, Vol. XIV, 4 (1963), repr. in Waxman, *The End of Ideology Debate.*

Rousseau, J. J. *Du Contrat Social, Oeuvre Choisies* (Paris, Classiques Garnier, 1954).

Runciman, W. G. *Social Science and Political Theory* (Cambridge, 1963).

Runciman, W. G. *A Critique of Max Weber's Philosophy of Social Science* (Cambridge, 1972).

Runciman, W. G. 'Ideological and Social Science', in Benewick *et al.*, *Knowledge and Belief in Politics.*

Ryle, G. *The Concept of Mind* (London, 1949).

Salisbury, The Marquis of. *The New Conservatism* (London, Conservative Political Centre, 1955).

Sartori, G. *Democratic Theory* (Detroit, 1962).

Sartori, G. 'Constitutionalism: A Preliminary Discussion', *The American Political Science Review*, Vol. LVI, 4 (1962).

Sartori, G. 'European Political Parties', in J. LaPalombara and M. Weiner, *Political Parties and Political Development* (Princeton, 1966).

Sartori, G. 'Politics, Ideology and Belief Systems', *The American Political Science Review*, Vol. LXIII, 2 (1969).

Scalapino, R. A. 'Ideology and Modernization—The Japanese Case', in Apter, *Ideology and Discontent.*

Schapiro, L. 'The Concept of Totalitarianism', *Survey*, No. 73 (Autumn 1969).

Schapiro, L. *The Communist Party of the Soviet Union* (London, 1962).

Schapiro, L. *Totalitarianism* (London, 1972).

Schapiro, L., and Lewis, J. B. 'The Role of the Monolithic Party under the Totalitarian Leader', *The China Quarterly*, No. 40 (October-December 1969).

Schumpeter, J. A. *Capitalism, Socialism and Democracy* (1942; 3rd edn, Harper Torchbooks, 1962).

Schurmann, F. *Ideology and Organization in Communist China* (Berkeley and Los Angeles, 1966).

Scott, W. *The Life of Napoleon Buonaparte, Emperor of the French*, 9 vols (Edinburgh, 1827).

Seliger, M. *The Conception of History of the French Historians of the Restoration (1815–1830) in their Treatment of French History* (unpubl. doctoral thesis (Hebrew), The Hebrew University of Jerusalem, 1956).

Seliger, M. 'Ideology and Elections', *Molad* (Hebrew), (October 1960).

Seliger, M. 'Napoleonic Authoritarianism in French Liberal Thought', in A. Fuks and I. Halpern (eds), *Studies in History, Scripta Hierosolymitana*, Vol. VII (1961).
Seliger, M. 'Ideologie und Politik in Israel', *Geschichte in Wissenschaft und Unterricht*, Vol. XVIII, 9 (1967).
Seliger, M. *The Liberal Politics of John Locke* (London, 1968; New York, 1969).
Seliger, M. 'Positions and Predispositions in Israeli Politics', *Government and Opposition*, Vol. III, 4 (1968).
Seliger, M. 'Locke, Liberalism and Nationalism', in J. W. Yolton (ed.), *John Locke: Problems and Perspectives* (Cambridge, 1969).
Seliger, M. 'Fundamental and Operative Ideology: The Two Dimensions of Political Argumentation', *Policy Sciences*, Vol. 1, 3 (1970).
Seliger, M. 'Herbert Marcuse's One-Dimensionality—The Old Style of the New Left', in von Beyme, *Theory and Politics, Festschrift zum 70 Geburtstag für Carl Joachim Friedrich* (The Hague, 1971).
Seliger, M. 'Locke and Marcuse—Intermittent and Millenial Revolutionism', *Festschrift für Karl Löwenstein* (Tübingen, 1971).
Seliger, M. *The Marxist Conception of Ideology—A Critical Essay*, International Studies Series (Cambridge, forthcoming).
Senghor, L. *Nation et voie africaine du socialisme* (Paris, 1961).
Shils, E. A. 'End of Ideology', *Encounter*, Vol. V (November 1955).
Shils, E. A. 'Ideology and Civility: On the Politics of the Intellectual', *The Sewanee Review*, Vol. LXVI, 3 (1958).
Shils, E. A. 'The Intellectuals and the Powers: Some Perspectives for Comparative Analysis', *Comparative Studies in Society and History*, Vol. I, 1 (1958).
Shils, E. A. 'Charisma, Order and Status', *American Sociological Review*, Vol. XXX, 2 (1965).
Shils, E. A. 'The Concept and Function of Ideology', in *The International Encyclopedia of the Social Sciences*, Vol. VII (1968).
Shklar, J. N. *After Utopia, The Decline of Political Faith* (Princeton, 1957).
Sigmund, P. E., (ed.). *The Ideologies of the Developing Nations* (rev. edn, New York, 1967).
Sontheimer, K. 'Student Opposition in Western Germany', *Government Opposition*, Vol. III, 1 (1968).
Spranger, E. 'Wesen und Wert politischer Ideologie', *Vierteljahresschrift für Zeitgeschichte*, II (1954).
Stadler, P. *Karl Marx, Ideologie und Politik.* (Göttingen, Frankfurt and Zürich, 1966).
Stark, W. *The Sociology of Knowledge* (London, 1958).
Steck, H. J. 'The Re-Emergence of Ideological Politics in Great Britain: The Campaign for Nuclear Disarmament', *The Western Political Quarterly*, Vol. XVIII, 1 (1965).
Stokes, D. E. 'Spatial Models of Party Competition', in Campbell, *et al.*, *Elections and the Political Order.*
Taft, P. *The A.F.L. in the Age of Gompers* (New York, 1957).
Taft, P. *Organized Labour in American History* (New York, 1964).
Talmon, J. L. *The Origins of Totalitarian Democracy* (London, 1952).
Talmon, J. L. *Political Messianism* (London, 1960).
Time for Decision, Manifesto of Labour Party, General Election 1965 (London, Transport House).

Tingsten, H. 'Stability and Vitality in Swedish Democracy', *Political Quarterly*, Vol. XXVI, 2 (1955).
Toch, H. *The Social Psychology of Social Movements* (Indianapolis, 1965).
Topitsch, E. *Vom Ursprung und Ende der Metaphysik. Eine Studie zur Weltanschauungskritik* (Vienna, 1958).
Topitsch, E. *Sozialphilosophie zwischen Ideologie und Wissenschaft* (2nd edn, Neuwied, 1966).
Touchard, J. (ed.). *Histoire des Idées Politiques* (Paris, 1959).
Trevor-Roper, H. R. (ed.). *Hitler's Secret Conversations, 1941–4* (New York, 1953).
Tucker, R. C. *Philosophy and Myth in Karl Marx* (Cambridge, 1961).
Tucker, R. C. 'Towards a Comparative Politics of Movements-Regimes', *The American Political Science Review*, Vol. LV, 2 (1961).
Tucker, R. C. 'The Deradicalisation of Marxist Movements', *The American Political Science Review*, Vol. LXI, 2 (1967).
Vedel, G. (ed.). *La dépolitisation, mythe ou réalité?* (Paris, 1962).
Voegelin, E. *The New Science of Politics* (Chicago, 1952).
Walsh, W. H. *An Introduction to Philosophy of History* (3rd rev. edn, London, 1967).
Walzer, M. *The Revolution of the Saints, A Study in the Origins of Radical Politics* (1965; repr. New York, 1963).
Waxman, C. I. (ed.). *The End of Ideology Debate* (New York, 1968).
Weber, M. 'Die "Objektivität" sozialwissenschaftlicher und sozialpolitischer Erkenntnis', in *Gesammelte Aufsätze zur Wissenschaftslehre* (Tübingen, 1922).
Weber, M. 'Der Sozialismus—Rede zur allgemeinen Orientierung von österreichischen Offizieren in Wien (1918)', in *Gesammelte Aufsätze zur Soziologie und Sozialpolitik* (Tübingen, 1924).
Weber, M. *Wirtschaft und Gesellschaft*, Half-volumes I and II (2nd enlarged edn, Tübingen, 1925).
Weidlé, W. 'Sur le concept d'idéologie' *Le Contrat Social* (March 1959), repr. in *Res Publica*, Vol. II, 3 (1960).
Wetter, G. *Dialectical Materialism: A Historical and Systematic Survey of Philosophy in The Soviet Union*, trans. from the German by P. Heath (London, 1958).
Wiatr, J. J. 'One Party Systems—The Concept and Issue for Comparative Studies', in Allardt and Littunen, *Cleavages, Ideologies and Party Systems*.
Wiatr, J. J. 'Sociology—Marxism—Reality', *Social Research*, Vol. XXXIV, 3 (1967).
Williams, B. 'Democracy and Ideology', *The Political Quarterly*, Vol. XXXII, 4 (1961).
Wittgenstein, L. *Philosophical Investigations* (2nd edn, Oxford, 1958).
Zeltner, H. *Ideologie und Wahrheit, Zur Kritik der politischen Vernunft* (Stuttgart and Bad Canstatt, 1966).

INDEX